JOHN HANCOCK'S LIFE AND SPEECHES

JOHN HANCOCK'S LIFE AND SPEECHES

A Personalized Vision of the American Revolution, 1763–1793

Paul D. Brandes

The Scarecrow Press, Inc.
Lanham, Md., and London

SCARECROW PRESS, INC.

Published in the United States of America
by Scarecrow Press, Inc.
4720 Boston Way
Lanham, Maryland 20706

4 Pleydell Gardens, Folkestone
Kent CT20 2DN, England

British Cataloguing-in-Publication Information Available

Library of Congress Cataloging-in-Publication Data

Brandes, Paul D. (Paul Dickerson), 1920-1990.
John Hancock's life and speeches : a personalized vision of the American
Revolution, 1763-1793 / by Paul D. Brandes.
p.   cm.
Includes bibliographical references and index.
1. Hancock, John, 1737-1793. 2. Statesmen—United States—Biography.
3. United States—Politics and government—1775-1783—Sources.
4. United States—Politics and government—1783-1789—Sources.
I. Title.
E302.6.H23B73   1996   973.3'092—dc20   95-38055   CIP

ISBN 0-8108-3076-0 (cloth : alk. paper)

♾™ The paper used in this publication meets the minimum requirements of
American National Standard for Information Sciences—Permanence of
Paper for Printed Library Materials, ANSI Z39.48-1984.
Manufactured in the United States of America.

Dedication

Paul Brandes was a lifelong scholar of rhetoric and the rhetoric of revolution. Over his long academic career, he published eight books on these subjects, and this book on John Hancock was his last work. He finished the manuscript just before he died suddenly at his home in Chapel Hill, North Carolina, in February of 1990 at the age of 69. His family, including his wife, Melba, his daughter, Sarah, and his son-in-law, Scott Madry, decided to ensure that his last work was published. The family arranged for publication, and prepared the manuscript according to the publisher's instructions. Paul wrote the manuscript on his Macintosh computer, and the book was prepared for publication by his son-in-law and his research assistants Ariane Delafosse, Bob Wiencek, and Benjamin Bowen at Rutgers University in New Brunswick, New Jersey.

The family would like to express their grateful appreciation to Scarecrow Press for their kind assistance in seeing this project through to completion. They would also like to thank the many people who assisted Paul in his research.

This book is dedicated to the memory of Dr. Paul Brandes, scholar, teacher, husband, father, mentor, and friend.

Contents

Contents

PART 2 THIRTY-ONE SPEECHES BY JOHN HANCOCK

As far as can be determined at this point, the thirty-one speeches below constitute the entire extant addresses of John Hancock

Preface

Revolutionaries in the twentieth century make big headlines. Advocating the overthrow of an existing government by force generally constitutes breaking the law. Revolutionaries in the eighteenth century also made big headlines. The difference is that the eighteenth century revolutionaries of the United States have now become our founding fathers, whereas the twentieth century North American revolutionaries are looked upon as arsonists, murderers, traitors, and outlaws who wish to overthrow the government by force.

The government of the United States applauds loudly the outlaws of the eighteenth century but forbids any activity by factions in the twentieth century who would overthrow the government by force.

John Hancock was one of those "founding father" revolutionaries. Once the plots and schemes of revolutionaries are examined, their whole status as "outlaws" and "criminals" becomes obvious. John Hancock was therefore to the British an outlaw and a criminal. What benefit can be gathered from an examination of the speeches of this outlaw that will assist us in interpreting the future?

The initial purpose of this work was to publish only Hancock's speeches. As the thirty-one addresses were located in their multiple depositories, it soon became apparent that, to the reader, they would be meaningless unless the setting in which they were delivered was understood.

Hence, we undertook to examine those parts of John Hancock's life that reflect on his speeches. Endnotes, accompanying both the life and the speeches, attempt to keep the reader oriented.

As that two-fold goal developed, an altogether new concept unfolded. We began to understand the American Revolution as we never had before, and therefore the primary objective came to be not the speeches and not Hancock's life as it pertained to the speeches, but rather a new outlook on the shaky grandeur of the American Revolution. That was the story worth examining, the revolution through Hancock's eyes.

That insight into the years of 1763 to 1793 is what makes an examination of Hancock valuable to assist in winning future goals.

There have been, since our nation was founded, assertions that the American Revolution has not been properly taught in the school systems. We now agree. However, the content of what could and should be taught about the American Revolution would hardly please many of those wishing more emphasis on American history. What would happen if the following terms were applied to John Hancock, as well as Thomas Jefferson, George Washington, James Madison, and John Adams?

> traitors to the government in power
> guilty of seeking to overthrow the government by force
> arsonists
> felonious assaulters
> conspirators
> misappropriators of funds [in disposing of loyalist properties]
> thieves

How would our children react to having their founding fathers so described? Yet they were gloriously guilty of all those crimes. Otherwise, the United States of America would not have come into existence, and we would possibly be a commonwealth-like country, much like Canada.

The revolution was not only serious business; the revolutionaries risked having their heads cut off in London by order of the king. There was so little chance of winning. The odds must have been 10-1 in favor of the British. Only the selfish intervention of France saved the cause, and put the early American politicians in the quandary of supporting Louis XVI who had helped them, while the United States left the French revolutionaries to fend for themselves.

So here is the American Revolution through the eyes of one of its most patriotic supporters. We must use Hancock's eyes to look at the events with his biases. With what perspectives did the eyes of John Hancock look out onto the world of 1763-1789?

constructive visions	destructive visions
daring	vain
determined	pompous
dedicated to freedom	glory-loving
capable of leadership	vindictive

constructive visions (ctd)	destructive visions (ctd)
diplomatic	machiavellian

No wonder the previous biographers of Hancock have presented an inconsistent image, praising John with one sentence and damning him with another. This presentation will do no better. The inconsistencies of Hancock are what make him interesting. To treat him any other way than to reveal the dichotomy of his personality would be false.

The shelves of libraries are full of numerous editions of the works of Washington, the Adamses, Benjamin Franklin, and other revolutionary heroes. Why have the Hancock papers been largely ignored? It has been said that Hancock may have been a doer, but he was not a thinker. Therefore, as he proposed no new philosophy, his papers can be passed by. [1]

We hope that this volume will show that the Hancock papers are worth adding to library collections. After this work there remain to be collected his letters and his messages to the General Court of Massachusetts and to the thirteen states when he was president of the Continental Congress.

If, as a reader, you get bored with the rhetoric of the speeches, go to the endnotes that explain why Hancock dwelt on the events of the revolution. To discount him for being proud of his and his country's achievements would be like saying, "Granted. You landed a man on the moon. But that was a number of years ago. Let us concentrate on the big events to come."

Hancock did concentrate on the big events to come in his time. He was instrumental in establishing our Bill of Rights. His gaining the approval of the Massachusetts Constitutional Convention recommending a Bill of Rights was one of his monumental achievements. The Bill of Rights, not written altogether in Philadelphia, was often based on those formulated by the adopting states and forwarded to the Convention for their consideration. How could one say that the Bill of Rights is not in our nation's future? That future was in part created by Hancock.

We hope you will enjoy this puzzling personality...half selfish pomposity; half generous patriot. If you want a consistent story, this account is not for you. The revolution was not consistent. Why should its characters be so?

We hope that you find in these pages the excitement that was felt between 1775 and 1789. Would that a portion of that excitement were always alive to carry us through the years to come.

Chapel Hill, N.C.   Paul D. Brandes
                                                       18 Nov 1989

1. The Boston *Transcript* of 11 Feb 1884 reported a statement that the
Hancock family had hired someone to write a history of Hancock's life, and
that the material was collected and read, following which the family offered
the writer $1,000 to hand over the work and make no further investigation.
The writer is supposed to have taken the money and the book was never
published. It may be that the report that Hancock had smuggled $400,000
worth of goods contributed to the reluctance of the family to have the work
published. Boston Public Library, MS 284.

Acknowledgments

The depositories of the Hancock papers are detailed in the endnotes and the bibliographies. The main papers are at the Massachusetts Archives in Boston, and at the New England Historical Genealogical Society and the Massachusetts Historical Society in Boston. Others are widely scattered in the National Archives, the Pierpont Morgan Library, the British Library, the House of Lords Records Office, the Library of Congress, and the British Public Records Office.

The author wishes to express particular thanks to William Milhomme and Richard Kaplan of the Massachusetts Archives, to Nathaniel Shipton of the New England Historic and Genealogical Society, and to Peter Drummey of the Massachusetts Historical Society. Lucretia Kinney of Chapel Hill was invaluable in checking many sources, and many of the librarians at the University of North Carolina have been most helpful.

The author wishes to thank the University Research Committee of the University of North Carolina for its support of this project, and to the Harvard Faculty Club for their repeated hospitality to the researcher. He is also indebted to Mr. and Mrs. Matthew Mahoney of Beverly, Massachusetts, for offering him respite from his long sieges in the libraries.

It seems unlikely that more than thirty-one speeches are extant, although there is always hope that another will be found. The author located the addresses to Harvard by surveying the Boston newspaper at the time of the Harvard Commencements, and so located three additional speeches to his Alma Mater that had not been found in the searches at Harvard University itself.

Foreword

One of my colleagues remarked to me that he was convinced we had moved into the "post-literate age." By that, of course, he meant that no one reads anymore. We are all victims of the "video revolution." I'm not convinced that my colleague's unkind assessment is correct, but after reading Paul Brandes's analysis of John Hancock I once again realize how important the written and spoken word (not video) was to our ancestors.

John Hancock and his fellow founding fathers were people of the word. They listened to one another and read each other's works. Could there have been a revolution without James Otis crying out "No taxation without representation" or Patrick Henry boldly asserting in the Burgesses "Caesar had his Brutus; Charles the First his Cromwell; and George the Third may profit by their example?" What enormous inspiration did the patriots find in Jefferson's mightiest accomplishment, "The Declaration of Independence?" By focusing on one of these eminent men—John Hancock of Boston—Brandes encourages us to reflect on the accomplishments of all.

As someone who thought he knew John Hancock, or at least had spent considerable time sorting through the literary remains of the man, I must confess that Brandes has forced me to reread my own work. Had I to do it all over again I would take Brandes's guidance and look at Hancock differently.

Even for those who might wish to disagree with Brandes's conclusions all must celebrate his wonderful feat in bringing together 31 of Hancock's speeches. Here we have, for perhaps the only time, a collection of speeches carefully drawn together and subjected to a penetrating analysis the like of which no American of the revolutionary epoch has enjoyed.

Paul D. Brandes deserves the praise and thanks of all of us— scholars, amateur historians, antiquarians—for providing us with this opportunity to view our revolution and a key figure in that struggle in a new light. With his help I now know a good deal more about the founding of this nation.

William M. Fowler, Jr.
14 June 1993

Symbols and Abbreviations

[xxxx]	an indipherable passage striken out of the text of a speech
[sic]	an old spelling or a misspelling retained
Xt	Hancock's abbreviation for Christ
O	Hancock's abbreviation for the universe
//	a symbol used by Hancock in his text, sometimes to signify change of paragraph and sometimes a pause in delivery
A&R	Acts and Resolves of the State of Massachusetts, including both the colonial records before the adoption of the state constitution in 1780 and the early state records from 1780 to 1793. The title of this set changed from time to time, but it is consistently referred to in this volume as Acts and Resolves.
MA	Massachusetts Archives, Boston
MHS	Massachusetts Historical Society, Boston
NEGHS	New England Historic and Genealogical Society, Boston
LC	Library of Congress
NA	National Archives in Washington, D.C.
HLRO	House of Lords Records Office
BL	British Library
SPO	State Paper Office, London
HFP	Hancock Family Papers
RRC	Report of the Record Commissioners of the City of Boston
AG	American Gazette
BU	Boston University
H	Houghton Library, Harvard University
SL	State Library, Boston State House

Part I

Historical Context of the Speeches

1

An Introduction to the Events in the Life
of John Hancock that Molded His
Development as a Revolutionary: The
Diplomatic Qualities of John Hancock

The myths surrounding the career of John Hancock have allied him
more to salesmanship than to statesmanship. But just because Hancock
was a rich businessman and a successful politician does not mean that
he lacked the qualities of a diplomat. In at least three phases of the
revolution, Hancock demonstrated not only that he was a political
diplomat, but also that he knew how to carry out the politics of
diplomacy.

This introductory essay will be divided into three parts. First,
certain aspects of Hancock's life will be proposed as qualifying him as a
diplomat. Second, selected aspects of Hancock's career will be presented
so that these qualities will not have to be discussed repeatedly in the
work that follows. Third, there will be speculations as to why a rich
businessman such as Hancock chose to become a revolutionary.

Three Phases of Hancock's Life That May Qualify Him as a Diplomat

Hancock does not qualify as a philosopher of the revolution. He had no ability to express the theories of revolution. But he had something perhaps more important. He was willing to become a revolutionist, and, in achieving that objective, he developed three aspects of diplomacy that furthered his goal as the violent overthrower of one government and the peaceable founder of its successor.

First, Hancock made a major contribution to the revolution in the successes he had in maintaining good French-American relations. It was Hancock who knew how to negotiate with the French on this side of the Atlantic, while Franklin and others were handling American affairs in Paris.

Second, it was Hancock who replaced Peyton Raldolph to become the second president of the Continental Congress. Even though as president, Hancock was largely without direct powers, he nevertheless exerted a leveling influence on the colonial representatives in Philadelphia, using his role between 24 May 1775 and 29 Oct 1777 to cajole the diverse members of Congress to reach difficult agreements and to increase the general efficiency in the revolutionary assembly in Philadelphia.

Third, it was Hancock who secured the ratification of the federal Constitution by Massachusetts and therefore materially assisted the causes of those who, in Virginia and New York, were striving to have the constitution adopted. Hancock not only secured passage in the Bay State, but also pioneered Massachusetts' policy of only recommending and not requiring amendments. The posture set by Massachusetts was followed by other states in two respects:

> All but two of the states that adopted the Constitution after Massachusetts followed the lead of the Bay state by proposing amendments. Second, those states followed the Massachusetts example of recommending but not requiring adoption. (Holcombe, 3, 401)

Each of these three aspects of Hancock's political diplomacy will be amplified below.

Diplomacy with the French

When friction arose between the French forces and the colonists, it was the vain Hancock who placated the vain French military so that Louis XVI's land and sea forces would continue to cooperate and so tip the scales of war in favor of the Americans. Stinchcombe stressed the importance of the role of the French:

> French military aid had proved to be indispensable in the struggle for independence....The mere presence of the French Army and Fleet significantly altered British military planning....The French, even when inactive, changed the military balance. (Stinchcombe, 152)

The campaign at Newport, which was to have coordinated French sea forces with American land forces, was unsuccessful. As a major general in the state militia,[1] Hancock was with the ground troops under General Sullivan during the Rhode Island campaign. On 17 Aug 1778, he wrote to Dolly from a campsite in Rhode Island: "We have a strong Report that the French Fleet is seen off, if they arrive, our Business will soon be over, & hope we shall soon enter Newport." (MHS, e) But the attempt at coordination between the American land forces and the French naval forces failed. Having lived through the frustration of the defeat, John was all the more aware of the need to restore harmony between the disgruntled colonials who wanted to blame the failure on the French fleet and the French who did not want to be held responsible for their inability to cut off the sea routes of the British garrison at Newport.

Therefore, when the French fleet returned to Boston on 22 Sept 1788, Hancock sensed that immediate action was needed to breach the gap. He greeted Admiral D'Estaing with a lavish breakfast at the Hancock mansion and "was a gracious host throughout the French stay." (Stinchcombe, 57) To the extent that Hancock acted to moderate disagreements between the allies, he materially forwarded the cause of the American Revolution. Perhaps only a man who needed repeated support for his own pride could have understood how to placate the French admirals and officers and let them see that good society and good manners were active in colonial America.

The welcoming-home breakfast was only the first of many entertainments that Hancock sponsored to insure the repeated cooperation of the French. After the mishaps in Rhode Island, Hancock also gave a sumptuous banquet and ball in his mansion for about five hundred guests. James Warren in a letter to Samuel Adams dated 30 Sept 1778 described Hancock's activities as follows:

> The disposition that at first appeared to Cast an Odium on the Count and to discredit our New Allies seems to have entirely subsided and has been succeeded by the most perfect good humour and respect shown them. General Hancock has made most Magnificent Entertainments for the Count and his officers, both at his own and the public Houses and last Week the General Court Entertained them at Dinner in Faneuil Hall with much military Parade. on [sic] this Occasion the General had an opportunity of Exhibiting a Specimen of his Military Talents, etc. (Warren-Adams, 2, 48)

Warren wrote to Sam Adams describing the ball on 25 Oct 1778:

> Genl. H gives a Magnificent Ball to the French Officers, and to the Gentlemen and Ladies of the Town next Thursday Evening. indeed [sic] all manner of Extravagance prevails hereto dress, furniture, Equipage and Living, amidst the distress of the public and Multitudes of Individuals, how long the Manners of this People will be Uncorrupted and fit to Enjoy that Liberty you have so long Contended for I know not. I fear you have lost your Labour. they [sic] will be so soon fit to receive some Ambitious Master. (Warren-Adams, 2, 59-60)

During an informal dinner conversation with William H. Sumner on 21 Nov 1822, Dorothy Quincy Hancock Scott told a number of incidents about her former life with her first husband, John. (Sumner, 187-191) Concerning Hancock's entertainment of the French, Dolly said that, in 1778, Hancock had invited the Count D'Estaing and thirty of his officers for breakfast. But one hundred and fifty arrived, so that emergency preparations had to be made. "They spread twelve pounds of butter on to bread," said Hancock's wife, "and sent to the guard on the common to *milk all the cows and bring her the milk.*" The neighbors were appealed to for cake which had to be protected from being intercepted by the midshipmen as it was being brought into the house. (Sumner, 189) It is not clear whether Dolly was reminiscing about the welcoming-home breakfast, or whether her anecdote described another breakfast event.

Dolly also recalled being entertained by D'Estaing along with five hundred of her friends. Sumner remembered Dolly as saying: "The officers afterwards frequently dined at their house....The Governor also gave the officers a grand ball at Concert Hall. Three hundred persons were present." (Sumner, 189)

Hancock's self-esteem matched that of the French, enabling him to turn their vanity to the benefit of the colonists. Washington was in need of French troops to assist him. It was Lafayette who advised Louis XVI to assemble troops at Newport under Count Rochambeau. When Cornwallis elected to move to Yorktown where he thought the British fleet could protect him from the rear and he could defend himself from attack by land, the French fleet moved into the Chesapeake Bay Area. When the British fleet from New York failed to dislodge the French and was forced to return north, the combined French and American land forces besieged Cornwallis, who surrendered.

Hancock's earlier entertainment of the French paid off three years later at Yorktown. If others were slow to recognize Hancock's diplomacy in French relations, Hancock himself was not. There are repeated references in his speeches as Governor to the debt of gratitude that the colonists owed to their French allies. That debt would have been much less had not Hancock acted as a successful intermediary. Vanity met vanity. The French and Hancock liked each others' pomp and circumstance, and the diplomatic day was saved to close brilliantly over Yorktown three years later.

One factor that contributed to Hancock's success in placating the French was the happy relationship between the French soldiers and the colonists. Evidently, in contrast to the abrasive conduct of the Americans and the English towards each other, the French troops mixed well with the populace. After the British evacuated Rhode Island in 1779 and French troops moved in, Gordon reported: "During their whole stay at Newport, they [the French] did not damage the property of the inhabitants to the amount of a hundred dollars. The towns people could walk about in the evening and at night, with as much safety as if there were no troops in the place. Officers of the first rank and quality conversed with traders, merchants and gentlemen, whenever the language of either was enough understood to admit of it, with the utmost affability." (Gordon, 4, 128) The gold and silver that the French troops had to spend in the colonies also assisted in maintaining good relationships between the two allies.

The contribution Hancock made to good relations between the colonists and the French in 1778 is underlined because it was at that point in the revolution that the British sent three commissioners to the colonies to grant concessions and to seek an end to the conflict. The concessions were considerable (Davidson, 380) and included full pardon to all of the rebels. The propagandists kept up their pressure on the people to support the war, pointing out that the British could not be trusted and that the concessions could not all be effectuated. (Davidson, 381) Fortunately for the colonists, the French alliance and the defeat of Burgoyne at Saratoga greatly strengthened many hesitant patriots. The British commissioners left in the fall of 1778 with no positive results. Had they arrived earlier, before the French joined the conflict, the outcome might have been much different. It was the victory over Burgoyne that made the French believe that the Americans could win, and it was Hancock's diplomacy that maintained the French cooperation so that the Americans did win.

President of the Continental Congress

The second of Hancock's assets as a diplomat is more difficult to substantiate. However, his long tenure as president of the Continental Congress, at a most critical time during the war for independence, certainly qualifies him for limited if not extensive praise as the leader of a diverse group of colonists whose visions of what was expected of them greatly varied.

So it could be said that it was Hancock, in spite of his offensive peccadillos, who assisted in maintaining the fragile unity that allowed the Second Continental Congress to wage war against Great Britain. As his letters to his wife show, it was not easy for the rich Boston merchant to adapt to the rigors of life in boarding houses and to sit with his gout during long meetings in what must have been drafty, cold rooms. Other delegates to the Continental Congress endured the same hardships. But it was Hancock, in his position as chair, who played a major role in keeping the Congress moving. His biographer Allan (217) noted:

> He appears to have made [Congress] function more smoothly by placing in key positions men who were in sympathy with him. Lacking the independence and power of the modern Chief Executive, he had the greater justification for adopting this policy, even though it happened to serve his personal ends.

There is ample evidence that Hancock conducted much of the necessary business of the Congress. His contacts with George Washington were numerous. Those who fight the battles in the field are often remembered while those who equip the soldiers with food and equipment are forgot. There are many letters illustrating the role that Hancock played in keeping Washington and his troops supplied. For example, on 19 Sept 1775 Hancock informed Washington that he was sending by special messengers $527,480 of continental money for the paymaster and that "the Cloathing is on the way." (Smith, a) Sometimes Hancock's position as president of the Continental Congress has been compared to that of a secretary. If such a comparison is accurate, it means that "Secretary" Hancock had to make certain that General Washington and his armies were as well provided for as possible.

Why did Hancock get to be president in the first place? The Adamses decided to support him for the post because of his demonstrated ability to preside at the Boston town meetings. What evidence do we have that he performed his duties in Congress successfully?

The best evidence is negative evidence. There were few derogatory comments concerning Hancock's ability to preside. There was no serious move to replace him, until he asked for leave of absence. It is certainly true that the members of the Congress kept their editorial comments to a minimum. They all knew they had to preserve unity against a common enemy. Whatever disagreements that may have transpired within the Congress were kept from the press. But the representatives did write home. They did keep notes and diaries. There was adequate opportunity to disparage Hancock's ability to preside. But there appear to be few such comments. That there was discontent with the president was inevitable. However, what reservations the members had about Hancock's abilities did not surface into major conflicts.

There were rumblings about Hancock's maintaining the presidency when Peyton Randolph reappeared at the Congress in September of 1775. John Adams wrote to James Warren back in Massachusetts that Hancock should have stepped aside. (Warren-Adams, 1, 112; 121-123)

The historian who was a contemporary of the revolution, William Gordon, writing more in the Herodotus than Thucydides tradition, also expressed dissatisfaction with Hancock's not relinquishing the chair to Randolph. (Gordon, 3, 20) Gordon said that Hancock was reminded by his "Massachusetts brethren" that Hancock should step aside, but that "the charms of the presidency made him deaf to the private advice of his colleague, and no one could with propriety move for his removal."

These rumblings often pertained to Hancock's vanity rather than to his efficiency as a presiding officer. Gordon recognized his proficiency as president. The discontent was quickly quieted by Randolph's unexpected death soon after Randolph reappeared in Philadelphia.

Hancock himself was aware of some discontent with his policies. On 7 Mar 1776, he wrote to Cushing: "My utmost Exertions shall never be withheld for the Good of my Colony, whenever they can be useful they shall be Employ'd in that Service how ever [sic] Dangerous, and I Defy Malice itself to Contradict the sincerity and up rightness [sic] of those Assertions." (MHS, b)

As will be explained in detail in discussing Hancock's 1777 speech on taking leave of the Continental Congress, there were objections to Hancock's making an address of farewell. But again the objections related not to Hancock's abilities as a presiding officer but rather to his breaking of precedent in focusing attention on himself by taking formal leave of the Congress. If, as chair, Hancock had repeatedly shown inclinations to focus attention on himself, there would undoubtedly have been overt, expressed opposition to his remaining as president. Instead, it was only Hancock as president and Thomson as secretary of the Congress who had their names printed on the broadside of the Declaration of Independence that was released. The one comment we have about Hancock's signature on the document signed on 4 Aug is perhaps apocryphal. Legend has it that Hancock said he made his signature large enough for King George to see. [2] Hancock's rather flowery signature was his only claim to expert penmanship and undoubtedly he could easily have made it large on that specific occasion, partially because, as president of the Congress, he was probably the first to sign and therefore had plenty of room for a bold signature. Hancock knew that he was already on King George's "most wanted list" so there was no reason to be timid about his signing of such a revolutionary document. No envy was expressed by his colleagues about the role he played in signing the Constitution. No sly comments were recorded that Hancock was exceeding his proper role as president of the Congress or glorifying himself at the expense of Congressional unity.

Even though this investigation found a major contribution in Hancock's serving as president, the position taken by others, particularly Fowler, should be recognized. In 1976, in an article written before he published his biography, Fowler proposed that "Hancock's duties [as president] were minor." (Fowler, Hancock, 167) Fowler noted that Hancock "presided but did not rule," that he did not appoint chairs and committees, that the body had to adjourn into a committee of the whole before Hancock could comment on issues, and that the agenda was set by the Continental Congress itself and not by the president.

Such limitations often were and are customary in the Anglo-Saxon common law of parliamentary procedure, depending upon the customs adopted. Although in 1775-1777 the precedents of parliamentary procedure had yet to be written down in England or America, yet they were known and were followed by the Continental Congress. Congress must have made up its own rules, based upon the precedents they had noted in their various state assemblies which had had English parliamentary law antecedents.

But the long path by which royalty was slowly subjected to parliamentary rules that restrained unlicensed power on the parts of monarchs does not prevent a chair from exercising considerable and frequently controversial authority. And such power moves are not always recorded in the minutes. They are often subtle.

Two such maneuvers were involved in an incident concerning the method of debate in the Continental Congress. As John Adams pointed out, on 15 Mar 1776, when Hancock wished to partipate in debate concerning the State of New York, he relinquished the chair, not to a Whig from Rhode Island favored by Sam Adams, but appointed a person who had not served before, Harrison of Virginia. Adams (Wells, 3, 34-35) proposed that "Mr. Harrison had courted Mr. Hancock, and Mr. Hancock had courted Mr. Duane, Mr. Dickinson, and their Party, and leaned so partially in their favor, that Mr. Samuel Adams had become very bitter against Mr. Hancock and spoke of him with great asperity in private circles; and this alienation between them continued from this time till the year 1789, thirteen years, when they they were again reconciled." (Adams, 3, 35) Whereas John Adams proposed that outwardly he maintained his neutrality, Sam Adams as usual gave vent to his feelings.

Sam Adams's reaction reflects as unfavorably on Adams as it does on Hancock. The historian Gordon reported that Hancock felt comfortable with the aristocratic delegation from New York. (Gordon, 3, 20-21) Gordon went so far as to say that, in the beginning Hancock had been sympathetic with republican principles, but that "afterwards he inclined to the aristocracy of the New York delegates." Gordon stated that a member of the Rhode Island delegation lectured Hancock about showing sympathy toward the more aristocratic delegations. Hancock was never a Puritan at heart and the Massachusetts delegation could well have recognized that fact.

Since the debate for which Hancock released the chair was to concern New York, Hancock may have felt that he would be given a fairer hearing by a more aristocratic temporary chair. But there were other reasons for appointing a Virginian. Hancock may well have thought, and legitimately so, that the debate should be chaired by a non-New Englander and that a new face in the chair might show impartiality.

Many of the negative statements on Hancock are based on four sources: (a) comments by the more Puritanical members of the New England delegation; (b) the now largely discredited "Writings of Laco" by Samuel Higginison which appeared in the Boston papers of the time; (c) the comments by Mercy Warren, an avowed enemy of John; and (d) the comments of early historian Gordon who appeared to have a bias toward the Adams faction.

Naturally his Puritanical colleagues in the Continental Congress wanted a liberal appointed as temporary chair. The historian Gordon also voiced the position of the Puritan aspects of the Masssachusetts delegation. (Gordon, 3, 20-21) But it could have been very logical to do otherwise. Randolph of Virginia was unavailable to be president because he had died; Henry Middleton of South Carolina had declined to serve because of poor health. The South needed constant recognition. A Virginia delegate was in many ways a logical choice. Furthermore John Adams's comments that the Virginian had been courting Hancock's favor shows that something was to be gained by having the good will of the president.

When a Virginian and not Hancock himself was named as commander of the continental armies, it was Hancock's turn to become outraged. One of the reasons why it was logical to appoint a Southerner as the commander of the armies was to even-out the sectional representation. It was no accident that the first president of the United States was from the South, and the second from New England.

As the reports of the Continental Congress show (Item 37, Reports of the Marine Committtee and the Board of Admiralty, 1776-1781, in Papers of the Continental Congress, Microfilm Roll 440) Hancock was not only president, but he served as one of the chairs of the important Marine Committee. Others serving included Sam Adams, Henry Laurins, Richard Henry Lee, and William Whipple. (Paullin, 1, xxiv) Being chair of the Marine Committee was a responsibility that, as a shipowner, Hancock relished. His major input is recorded in the minutes of the Marine Committee, and his contribution as president is partially but not completely noted in his correspondence as president in his presidential letterbooks now at the Library of Congress and the National Archives. It is therefore difficult to conclude, as did Fowler, that in Philadelphia, Hancock was viewed as "indolent and lazy." (Fowler, Hancock, 177) There is too much of a corpus of work by Hancock performed in the several locations of the Continental Congress to so conclude. If, as has been established, he was a competent and energetic chair in Boston, it is difficult to believe that he became inactive in Philadelphia, Boston, and Yorktown. Numbers of delegates came and went during the period between 24 May 1775 and 29 Oct 1777. Hancock remained on duty during most of this time in spite of all the wearisome travel and housing, both under miserable conditions, as his personal letters document.

Sam Adams "fell out" with many people. His evaluations of Hancock were not objective. Since early in the revolution, there were always rumors of whether they were close or apart. No wonder Sam Adams biographer Wells relished quoting anti-Hancock comments. It is fortunate that, before Hancock's death, Sam Adams and John Hancock reached a reconcilation. As Fowler (Hancock, 177) noted, Hancock left the Continental Congress as an enemy of the Massachusetts delegation. His fellows from the Bay State disliked his ostentatious style of living, his willingness to tolerate the more aristocratic delegates and his impatience with a Puritanical style of living. However, Hancock left Congress with the approbation of delegates from other states. That favorable attitude persisted long enough for Hancock to be asked to return as president on 23 Nov 1785. It is difficult to believe that, as they prepared for the events of 1787 to 1789, the Congress would invite to return a leader who was "lazy and indolent."

Even Gordon (3, 21) was in general complimentary of Hancock as chair. Gordon quoted a letter from a member of Congress who, fearing that Hancock would return to Massachusetts in May of 1777, wrote as follows:

> This letter will go by president Hancock, for whose absence from Congress I am much concerned, though his great fatigue and long attendance entitled him to some relaxation. How we shall do without him I know not, for we have never put in a chairman, on a committee of the whole house, that could in any measure fill his place. He has not only dignity and impartiality...but has an alertness, attention and readiness to conceive of any motion and its tendency, and of every alteration proposed in the course of a debate, which greatly tends to facilitate and expedite business.

Curtis himself added that Hancock's forte was as chair, and that he presided "with much advantage to himself," presumably meaning much to Hancock's credit. Curtis said Hancock was better with large groups with whom he was "in his own elements, and all is animation" whereas Hancock responded less efffectively to small groups. Curtis added that he had found such a characteristic common in men of public life, "especially where there is a fondness for popularity." (Curtis, 3, 21)

In his letter to the Massachusetts General Court of 7 Feb 1777, Hancock recorded his own feelings about his role in Congress. After reminding the Court that he had been honored by being named president of the Congress, Hancock added that he had "endeavored to execute the Arduous and extensive Business so Annexed to it, in the most faithful manner, and to the best of my Abilities." Hancock, perhaps aware of some criticism against him, added: "But whether with Reputation or not," it would be up to his "American Brethren to determine the merit of his role." To them, Hancock added, "I willingly submit my Conduct." He concluded the paragraph by adding: "This much however, I may assert, that I have spared neither attention or Labour to Satisfy the wishes of Congress; and so unremitted has been my Application to the Duties of the Chair since my Appointment to it, that I have never been Absent a single hour." In typical Hancock fashion, John concluded his letter by saying that if it would develop that he would again be needed to serve his state, he would return to duty for he wished to contribute all of his energies "to save the Liberties of America, and to establish them in the firmest foundation for this purpose only I wish to Live, & for this I am willing to Die." (MA, 196. 230-231)

It is easy for anyone, let alone scholars, to disagree about Hancock. Fowler appropriately termed him "the paradoxical president." He could also be labeled as quixotic and certainly, for most people, personally unlikeable. Furthermore, sooner or later, everyone falls out with a long-standing chair. Dissentions, although often covert, are inevitable. Hancock's pomposity and his vanity were always annoying. But his patriotism was seldom questioned. It is legimate to conclude that Hancock must have played an essential role as president of the Continental Congress or (a) there would have been more comments by non-New Englanders to the contrary and (b) there would have been overt and recorded moves to replace him.

Perhaps others could have presided as well, or even better. Perhaps others besides Washington could have commanded the continental armies. Perhaps others besides Franklin and John Adams could have been as persuasive at the French and British courts. Those questions cannot be answered. We do know however that, between 1775 and 1777, Hancock successfully presided over one of the most revolutionary of assemblies ever convened. For that, he must be given credit for making a major contribution to the American cause at a time when dissention could so easily have resulted in capitulation to the British.

Massachusetts's Ratification of the Constitution

Third, it was Hancock, the consummate politician-diplomat, who swung enough votes to persuade Massachusetts to ratify the Constitution. Two questions need to be answered. First, how important was it for Massachusetts to ratify the proposed Constitution? Second, how important were Hancock's speeches of 31 Jan 1788 and 6 Feb 1788 to the Massachusetts Constitutional Convention in achieving that ratification?

The first question will be answered here. A response to the second question will be found in the headnotes to Hancock's speeches at the Boston state constitutional convention and in the special appendix dealing with that speech.

Historians have pointed out the significance of the ratification by the Bay Colony. Holcombe (3, 401) observed: "The action of the Massachusetts convention exerted a powerful, possibly a decisive, influence upon the fate of the Constitution." Virginia had been contemplating withholding adoption until the Constitution should be amended. New York was doubtful and Governor George Clinton was opposed. Once Massachusetts had adopted, the way was made possible for the federalists in New York and Virginia to prevail. (76)

Taylor (210) came to the same conclusion as Holcombe and added a specific tribute to Hancock: "No one did more, however, to remove the gravest difficulty that deterred Massachusetts, as well as many other states that were to follow her, than Hancock." Main (200) also noted how important was Massachusetts's ratification of the Constitution:

> The early victories of the Federalists...were important but not decisive. Antifederalists were strong in Rhode Island, North Carolina, New York, Virginia, and New Hampshire, and in these states the outcome was certain to be profoundly affected,and probably determined, by the action of Massachusetts. Here lay the decisive conflict; had the proposal lost in Masssachusetts, the Constitution as we know it would probably never have been ratified. (18)

William Wells remarked: "Whether, in the case of a failure, another Federal Convention would have succeeded in creating a system combining the checks and balances necessary for the cohesion of a vast republic such as ours, or whether America could ever have advanced to its subsequent glory and power under any other form, are profound questions as yet beyond mortal solution." (Wells, 3, 269)

Four letters, all written shortly after adoption by Massachusetts, illustrate how important was the decision of Massachusetts.

On 11 Feb 1788, James Manning wrote to the Rev. Dr. Smith: "I considered Massachusetts the hinge on which the whole must turn, and am happy in congratulating you on the favorable issue of their deliberations." (Main, 406) Manning attended the deliberations "more than a fortnight." (Main, 406) It was he upon whom Hancock called, on the final day of deliberations, to pray before the final vote was taken. Although Manning was supposedly taken by surprise, he is said to have dropped to his knees and prayed with a "fervid devotion, which awakened in the assembly a mingled sentiment of admiration and awe."[3] (Main, 405-406)

On 10 Feb 1788, Edward Carrington wrote to James Madison: "Your intelligence from Massachusetts is truly alarming because she is one of the Nine whose adoption can be counted upon by June. Indeed she is so important that even against Nine she & Virga. [Virginia] would be able, if not to prevent the effects of the Government altogether, to hold it in suspence [sic] longer than the State of our affairs can well admit of. I am anxcious [sic] to know the results in Massachusetts for on her every thing seems to depend." (Madison Papers, VIII)[4]

On 13 Mar 1788 Edward Carrington wrote to Henry Knox: "The decision of Massachusetts is perhaps the most important event that ever took place in America, as upon her in all probability depended the fate of the constitution. had [sic] she rejected I am certain there would not have been the most remote chance for its adoption in Virginia." (MHS, f)

On 18 Feb 1788, James Dawson wrote to James Madison: "Never perhaps was a state more divided than Virginia is on the new Constitution—its fate appears to hang in a great measure on the decision of Massachusetts bay—shoud [sic] the convention of that state adjourn without doing any thing decisive, or shoud [sic] amendments be proposed, I think, Virginia will go hand in hand with her." (Doc Hist, 4, 509-510)

These references indicate that approval by Massachusetts was critical. As will be pointed out in the material accompanying Hancock's two speeches of 1788 to the state constitutional convention, the governor played a major role in ratification. So, business man or not, Hancock's statesman-like qualities did make a difference in the adoption of the Constitution, and that difference resulted more from his skills as a diplomat than from his status as a business man.

The life and speeches of Hancock demonstrate that Hancock had definite statesman-like qualities. However, if the search is for political philosophies or expressions of new political concepts among the speeches and letters of Hancock, they are not to be found. His contributions were not manifested in written treatises, but rather in political actions. His speeches serve as a mirror to show us clearly how he assisted the revolutionary cause by his heavy political finesse.

Three Aspects of Hancock's Life that Permeated His Career

During this discussion, it will be difficult to maintain objectivity. The following three questions, limited to inquiries that reflect on many of Hancock's speeches, are raised initially in an attempt to let the reader look out at the American Revolution through the personalized viewpoint of one of its most active participants. As was the goal of his biographer Herbert Allan (x), this presentation of questions raised about Hancock's life is intended neither as an apologia nor a eulogy. When this statement does praise or apologize, hopefully the praises and apologies result only from accurate reporting or impartial speculation.

But, as one of Hancock's biographers reported, "coming to grips with John Hancock is no easy task." (Fowler, xii) Perhaps this is why John Adams prophesied in a letter to William Tudor of 1 June 1817 that "his life will...not ever be written." (Adams, 10, 261) Maintaining the objective attitude of the reporter toward this vain and capricious benefactor of the American Revolution requires eternal vigilance. A mellowed John Adams in 1817 could say of Hancock that "he was radically generous and benevolent" (Adams, 10, 259) and that Hancock's talents "were far superior to many who have been much more celebrated." (Adams, 10, 261) Charles Adams (Adams, 10, 261) concluded that, in comparison to Washington, Lincoln, or Knox, Hancock was a learned man. Adams found that Hancock "had a great deal of political sagacity and penetration into men." (Adams, 10, 261)

How does the writer hold fast to Hancock's strengths and confess to his weaknesses of "a peevishness of temper"? (Adams, 10, 261) It is so easy to over-praise or under-praise. On the eve of the revolution and during its progression, Hancock's two faces of pompous conceit and vigorous dedication confuse the writer and tend to obscure objectivity, beckoning first into periods of rejection and then into periods of adulation.

One of the factors about Hancock that annoyed even his admirers is that he almost always won and that he did not seem to be damaged by actions that would have subjected others to ridicule. The perennial winner can be a source of annoyance. Two examples of his ability to achieve glory and to weather opposition will suffice.

First, when Hancock threatened to resign his governorship of Massachusetts in 1784 and then withdrew his proferred resignation, James Warren noted that, following the episode, "his Character is neither stained with ridicule or Contempt, a privilege peculiar to himself." (Warren-Adams, 2, 236) What might have strained or defeated the character persuasion of others did not affect Hancock adversely. So, when there is a temptation to scoff at Hancock's inconstancy, there is also the reality that Hancock's peccadillos did not result in a failure of his political successes. To belittle now seems a poor form of sideline revolutionary quarterbacking.

Second, Hancock departed from the Continental Congress two weeks earlier than did John and Samuel Adams. Although Sam Adams made it a point to disapprove of pomp and circumstance, his letter of 8 Dec 1777 to James Lovell could be interpreted to show some envy of the attention given Hancock:

> Mr. [Hancock] came to this Town with great Pomp, and was receivd [sic] by the military and naval Gentlemen, I am informd [sic], with equal Ceremony. His Colleagues arrivd [sic] in the Dusk of the Evening and without Observation. He is the most happy who has the greatest Share of the Affections of his Fellow Citizens, without which, the Ears of a sincere Patriot are ever deaf to the Roaring of Cannon and the Charms of Musick. I have not seen or heard of any Dangers on the Road that should require Guards to protect one. It is pretty enough in the Eyes of some Men, to see the honest Country Folks gapeing [sic] & Staring at a Troop of Light Horse. But it is well if it is sometimes not attended with such Effects as one would not so much wish for, to excite the Contempt of the Multitude, when the Fit of gazing is over, instead of the much lond [sic] for Hosannas."

One other comment should be shared. We repeatedly came to the conclusion that, if we met Hancock today, we would not like him. He does not emerge as likeable. In his own time, he had few dedicated personal friends. We could respect him for the same qualities that earned him honor during his lifetime. Perhaps what emerges is a "likeable respect." Admiration for his courage and astuteness, yes; friendship for his endearing personal qualities, no.

Only the readers will be able to determine whether the skills of the writer were sufficient to balance successfully the ridiculous and the sublime. With Hancock, there was seldom any middle ground. Like the once-upon-a-time girl "with the curl in the middle of her forehead", when Hancock was good, he was "very very good", and when he was bad, he was horrid.

The difficulties of sustaining objectivity were faced by the four recent biographers of Hancock. Allan in 1948, Wagner in 1964, Sears in 1972, and Fowler in 1980 all struggled to maintain detachment. Their works, as does ours, reflect the numerous scattered primary sources that can be consulted in libraries and societies. With such an abundance of material, why have Hancock's letters and speeches not been previously collected and edited? Perhaps they have not been worthy of making a contribution. When this project was explained to a colleague in history, the immediate comment was: "Well, when you do get the speeches collected and edited, do they tell us anything more about history than we knew before?" A complete answer to that inquiry should be delayed until the end of this extended essay. But throughout the discussion, the focus will be on what additional perspectives we can gain, through the eyes of John Hancock, about the nature and significance of the American Revolution. The work hopes to present the events as he saw them.

The Hancock viewpoint on the revolution constantly reminds us that he became rich financially and rich historically. How should those riches best be presented? What do the eyes of Hancock tell us about his motives and his rewards? Let us begin looking at the American Revolution through Hancock's eyes by exploring what motivated him to become so dedicated to the American cause.

Was Hancock Motivated to Become a Revolutionist by Financial Reward?

A brief review of the early chronology of Hancock's life will show that financial prosperity came early to John. Hancock was born on 23 Jan 1737, the grandson of the preacher "Bishop" John Hancock and the son of preacher John Hancock. The third John Hancock left his family home at the age of seven to join the household of his Uncle Thomas. There were two reasons for being separated from his immediate family. First, Hancock's father died unexpectedly, leaving his widow with three children. Second, Uncle Thomas "was not a man to stint expense where the grandeur of his living was concerned." (Wagner, 8) Thomas and his wife Lydia were installed sumptuously but childless in Boston.

What could be more natural than that the elder son and bearer of the family name should leave the poverty of Braintree and go to live with his prosperous uncle and aunt? So John set out on his successful business career when only a child. Again, Hancock was not destined to be a loser.

John's biggest win was to be his victory in helping to found a new country. But his financial security and his political victories were inevitably frustrating to his opponents and sometimes annoying to his followers. Having acquired prosperity so early in life, Hancock appeared to consider his successes as only befitting his due. He could be, and sometimes was, a bore.

Approximately a year after moving to Boston, in order to prepare for Harvard, Hancock attended the Boston Latin School. Wagner's assertion (14) that Hancock excelled at penmanship while at the Boston Latin School is not borne out by an examination of his letters and speeches. His flourishing signature appears to have been his one major accomplishment in penmanship.[5] What his successes were in Greek and Latin and the other classical subjects is not known. That he was expected to complete his studies by reading fluently in the classical languages (Sears, 23) was in keeping with the English tradition. The colonies aspired to do no less for their scholars than was done in the mother country.

Subsequently, in 1750, at the age of 14, Hancock entered Cambridge, which was then more akin to an English public school than to the university it is today. At Harvard Hancock acquired the usual tutor; got embroiled in the usual mischief of youngsters; and studied in his freshman year the usual Greek, Latin, logic, rhetoric, and physics, followed by courses in Bible, theology, mathematics, and geometry.

On 17 July 1754, at the age of 17, Hancock was graduated from Harvard and began to assist his uncle. At that point, Thomas Hancock's business retained the original retail trade, dealing in such items as book-selling, ladies' sundries, stationery, cutlery, millinery, compasses, hour glasses, and leather, as well as the staples of tea, salt, corn, potash, and the like. The 17,000 people of Boston could purchase many of their needs from the Hancock store. Hancock's uncle had added the wholesaling of miscellaneous staples, including both the provisioning of the king's forces in Nova Scotia (Wagner, 30) and George II's armies for an attack upon Fort Beausejour. (Wagner, 32)

There was also a lively shipping business, transporting colonial goods abroad and importing goods from England and elsewhere. Uncle Thomas assisted the British in resettling the Acadians, loading the French Canadians onto his vessels and transporting them to Georgia and the West Indies. (Baxter, 133)[6] Soon the Hancock investments also included large real estate holdings, not only in Boston but in the rural areas of what is now Maine. Thomas Hancock's business was not always legitimate, but it was usually profitable. In his introduction to The House of Hancock, Baxter observed that "the smuggling of Thomas and John Hancock was at once a problem to the government and an opportunity to the individual." Baxter described the transactions poetically: "It was the black market of the day which kept open the stained door of freedom." (Baxter, xxi) Wagner asserted that Thomas Hancock "instructed his ship captains to smuggle contraband past the customs inspectors." (Wagner, 10) While, on the one hand, Thomas was cheating the British out of their customs money, on the other hand he was assisting the British in supplying their American and Canadian troops.

Uncle Thomas's interests in the book trade caused Hancock to look out at the world well acquainted with the latest literature of the day. His uncle's business in books reinforced Hancock's studies at the Boston Latin School and at Harvard and caused him to be one of the most well educated of the American revolutionaries.

Uncle Thomas was not without his political connections. He served for some time on the Governor's Council (Wagner, 28) and was appointed His Majesty's Agent for Transports. (Wagner, 28) Undoubtedly these positions helped Thomas Hancock to secure the lucrative contracts in transporting men and supplies for George II. They also contributed to John Hancock's interest in politics and facilitated his vision of the business man active in political affairs.

When John was twenty-three, Thomas and Lydia sent him to London, not only to do the "European tour" expected of fashionable young gentlemen of his time but also to make personal contacts with the Hancock business connections abroad. John therefore went from a city of less than 20,000 to a city of over 600,000. While in London, Hancock lived well, attended the theatre, and enjoyed the luxuries of London.[7] He saw the funeral of George II, observed Pitt as prime minister, and contemplated remaining for the coronation of the man who was to become his intimate enemy, George III. But his uncle and aunt longed for his company, while John, who may or may not have visited the continent, was also ready to return to Boston. He arrived back on 3 Oct 1761, at the age of twenty-four.

What sort of a vision of the world did young John have? At this point, he was undoubtedly going to be a rich and well-educated business man. Uncle Thomas had obviously aged during Hancock's absence. More and more of the business responsibilities began to fall upon John.

On 1 Jan 1763, Thomas made twenty-six-year-old John a partner in the firm. (Wagner, 47)   When Uncle Thomas died in 1764, Hancock inherited the business.[8]

It seemed likely that, after 1764, John would exert his efforts to prosper economically.   By working peacefully to remove the restrictions that the British had placed on business enterprise, Hancock could have succeeded economically in a relatively free British colony. Hancock was rich in 1770 when he seriously began his revolutionary activity. He had become rich in part by supplying the British armies, and he could have increased his fortune by continuing to support the king.   It would have been in his self-interest to minimize the disturbances.   Businessmen often find civil unrest harmful to their enterprises and tend to suppress it. Instead, Hancock encouraged civil unrest. Such encouragement was contrary to, rather than in support of, his financial interests. As Sears pointed out, "Hancock's defection from the coterie of merchant princes and their policy was unaccountable to them." (Sears, 336) His Uncle Thomas had been a loyalist. There was little precedent for his activity among his associates in business. After a period of supporting resistance to the king, most Boston merchants capitulated to the wishes of the crown and many of them ended up after the British evacuated Boston as "absentees."

Fortunately, Baxter has published an exposition of the accounts of the Hancock firm so that we can follow closely how the enterprise prospered. Although efforts to save the destruction of the Hancock mansion were unsuccessful and it was torn down in 1863, most of the records on which Baxter based his financial history of the "House of Hancock" were discovered in the garret of the old house (Baxter, 77) and have been preserved, for the most part, at the New England Historic and Genealogical Society.   Dolly Hancock had given some papers concerning financial transactions to the Massachusetts Historical Society. The records of the business transactions generally end at the beginning of the revolution, when, as Baxter pointed out, the business aspects of John Hancock's life concluded. The years they do cover are detailed in boxes of memoranda and letters stored on shelves in the stacks of the Society. We therefore have an accurate account of the prosperity of the Hancock enterprises. It has been established that, by 1774, when Hancock made his speech in honor of the Boston Massacre, he was rich. He lived in his uncle's mansion on Beacon Hill. He ate and drank too luxuriously for a man with a tendency toward the gout. His business continued until 1775, but, as Baxter concluded, it was by 1771 "already moribund and moving only on momentum." (Baxter, 279) For all practical purposes, in 1775 it ceased.

At the conclusion of his account of the Hancock business enterprises, Baxter (292-294) alleged that Hancock was not a good business man and that what had taken Uncle Thomas forty years to build up, "in the next five John brought...to a standstill; in five more, it had crumbled away." (Baxter, 293) Baxter was careful to point out that John could not be entirely blamed for the demise of the business, but nevertheless Baxter was discouraging about Hancock's mercantile abilities. "Thomas made plans that fitted in with the conditions of the times," said Baxter, "whereas John could not perceive what these conditions were, and as a result exhausted himself in swimming against the current." (Baxter, 294) Baxter noted that John Hancock's grand schemes "always seemed to go wrong." (Baxter, 294)

But it is harsh to compare the work of Uncle Thomas, whose big profits were so often derived from serving the crown and transporting its supplies and troops, with the enterprises of nephew John, whose big losses were so often derived from opposing the crown and therefore depriving himself of the possibility of making the very monies that Uncle Thomas had enjoyed. How Hancock could have carried on an expansive shipping business between 1771 and 1783 is difficult to imagine.[9] By 1774 the port of Boston was closed and carrying on a profitable trade with England was impossible.

If the conflict of interests between England and the colonies had not occurred, the Hancock business enterprises under John might have prospered, or they might have floundered. What would have happened eventually will never be known. In his letters to his agents in London, John foresaw the doom of his business when the Stamp Act was passed. Certainly, from 1766 to 1776, it was not "business as usual" as it had been during Uncle Thomas's days. What we do know is that the conflict of interests intervened to close down the Hancock enterprises and to convert what should have been a conservative businessman into a rebel.

So, a dandified, rich young man drifted until his outlook on the world became that of a revolutionist. For a revolutionist he became, in the truest sense: arsonist, smuggler, tax-evader, inciter to riots, and armed resistor. Seeing the series of oscillations between conservativism to liberalism through the eyes of Hancock presents a challenge to objectivity. We will attempt to meet the challenge by depicting those contrapuntal moves in the narrative that follows.

If Hancock did enter the revolution for economic gain, he certainly did not succeed. It is possible to say without reservation that Hancock contributed a large share of his wealth to the revolutionary cause and that his personal fortune was considerably less after the war than before.

Charles Adams concluded that "if his fortune had not been very large, he must have died as poor as Mr. S. Adams or Mr. Gerry," for, said Adams, he neglected his private affairs in order to contribute to public life. (Adams, 10, 260) As Sears remarked, "history remembers its military heroes, but forgets the men who furnish arms and ammunition." (Sears, 275) Not only did Hancock assist in assembling the arms so much needed by George Washington, but he also contributed a sizeable but unknown part of his own personal funds to assist in the revolutionary cause. Baxter concluded that "John's biggest war losses probably came from his advertised policy of letting debtors pay in paper instead of silver; this is said to have cost him 18,000 pounds sterling, but perhaps won many votes." (Baxter, 288, n.21)

It was the law of the land that colonial currency was to be accepted at its face value. Hancock felt obliged to honor that law. In a letter of 14 Nov 1783 to Captain Scott, Hancock himself acknowledged his losses: "I have lost many thousand Sterlg but thank God, my Country is Saved and by the Smiles of Heaven I am a free and Independent Man." (NEHGS, c) On 28 Mar 1786, Hancock's manager, William Hoskins, echoed Hancock's earlier comments in a letter to Captain Ebenezer Grant & Son on how much Hancock had suffered in sterling by the paper money he did take for certain debts, verifying that the Governor's fortune was much diminished by his following the rule of law. Hoskins commented:

> That there is a great Scarcity of Cash I believe is pretty Sensibly felt throughout America—and Paper Currancy [sic] tho' an happy Assistant for prosecuting the War in America yet many Individuals have felt an Irreparable Sting to their Feelings and Estates. It would be some Consolation, had Each Individual bore an Equal Part, but when we See some who Owe the whole [of] their greatness to those Wars, and those who have Impared their fortunes by it to a degree of Penury, it wounds the Mind to think of it—and makes the disproportion glaringly aggravating—you had an Invitation in the Publick prints, of paying your note in paper Currency, and at a time when it had greatly depreciated, this was at your Option but as you Neglected it, the Governor is not worst by it—thou [sic] he suffered 18000—Sterling in his fortune by what he did take for Book Debts, Bonds & Notes—but we have got our Independence. (NEGHS, d)

Hancock's letterbooks show numerous efforts, many made by William Hoskins between 1783 and 1786, to collect funds owed to Hancock since the early days of the revolution. It is likely that most of these request for Hancock's debtors to pay up were fruitless.

Not only did Hancock suffer tangible financial loses, but he expressed a willingness at a crucial point in the revolution to sacrifice even more of his assets. In December of 1775, with occupied Boston beseiged by Washington, Congress considered whether the colonial army should be authorized to destroy the city in order to rid Massachusetts of the British army and navy. In his diary, Richard Smith stated:

> The House again in Grand Comee. on the Boston Affair & after much canvassing & sundry Propositions offered, the Vote passed for directing Gen. Washn. to destroy the Army & Navy at Boston in any Way He & a Council of War shall think best, even if the Town must be burnt, 7 Colonies to 2....Mr. Hancock spoke heartily for this Measure." (Smith, b; cf. Chap. 10)

As one of the largest holders of real estate in Boston, Hancock stood to lose heavily if the town were fired. Fortunately such action was not necessarily, but it is noteworthy that Hancock offered his unqualified support for a measure that would have been very costly to him financially.[10]

Naturally, Hancock was pleased when the British evacuated Boston and his property was to some extent intact. On 25 Mar 1776, Hancock wrote to General Washington how pleased he was to receive the news that the colonials were back in control of Boston "I beg, Sir," he wrote, "you will be pleased to accept my warmest thanks for the Attention you have shewed to my Property in that Town." He requested that Captain Cazeneau be allowed to continue to look after what remained of what Hancock possessed so that Cazeneau could "take care that it be in no ways destroyed or damaged." (NA)[11]

It seems most likely that any possibility that Hancock became a revolutionist to seek economic gain can be dismissed.

Was Hancock Motivated to Become a Revolutionist for Political Rewards?

If Hancock was not motivated to become a revolutionist for financial rewards, was he inspired by political gain? In examining Hancock's political successes, it must be kept in mind that those who backed the revolution were taking an enormous gamble. On 1 Sept 1774, John Adams (Adams, 2, 361) remarked that there were "Hutchinsonian Addressers" who vacillated back and forth, many of whom ended up being overt or covert Tories. Now that the outcome of the war is known, it is not always possible to keep in mind what an enormous gamble the colonists took in opposing Britain. But many of the colonists took that risk. Others remained loyal to the king. Mayo repeated the estimate that over two thousand loyalists left Massachusetts. Only 1,100 or 1,200 loyalists, including women and children, remained in Boston during the revolution. (Mayo, 3, 253) Those who departed went to Nova Scotia or to England or to the West Indies, intending to return and claim their rewards for having been loyal to the king. Two hundred of those who were in Boston at the time of the battle of Lexington and Concord—merchants, traders, supporters of the king—volunteered to take up arms to fight the Whigs. (Mayo, 3, 254) If we add to the declared Tories the sizeable number of "Hutchinsonian Addressers," the number would probably rise to approximately half of Boston. Those who supported the revolution were on precarious ground. The letters of George Washington reflect how fragile were the chances of the colonists. The support of the French appeared to do the trick and tip the balance of the scales. But the support of the French was some time in coming. [11]

So, Hancock's political successes during the revolution could well have turned into horrendous failures, and those failures would have prevented any of the post-political successes he enjoyed as Governor of Massachusetts. When General Gage, speaking for George III, offered an amnesty to the revolting citizens of Boston if they would lay down their arms, he exempted only Samuel Adams and John Hancock. The exact statements made by Gage and King George will be presented later in discussing the events of 1775. Gage's reservation of Hancock makes it clear that Hancock's fate if the revolution had failed was to be tried for treason, probably in England where the British would be certain of a conviction.

There is evidence that overtures were made to Hancock and others to appoint them peers. A letter pushed through the iron railings of Franklin's London residence proposed that peerages be created for 200 Americans. Adams commented that Franklin affirmed that "there were in the Letter infallible Marks, by which he knew that it came from the

King, and that it could not have come from any other without the Kings [sic] Knowledge. What these Marks were he never explained to me."[12] Assuming such offers were made, overtly or covertly, they had no influence on Hancock. Whatever political rewards he was to have were to be accompanied by freedom, not by oppression.

Did Hancock Become a Revolutionist to Gain Power?

If Hancock did not seek to achieve wealth or political status by becoming a revolutionist, did he favor the colonial cause to achieve power? This question is akin to the second one raised, but has dimensions of its own.

There is no doubt that Hancock grew to like power. Once he had a taste of it, he was seldom without it until his death in 1793. There is evidence that Hancock's grasp on power irked his associates. In a letter of 8 Jan 1787, Elbridge Gerry wrote from Boston to John Adams in Philadelphia that there had been considerable debate in the Massachusetts House of Representatives about the methods that Hancock used in requesting that the House convene in the Senate chamber to hear the governor's address, that there had been a comparison between the rights of the royal governor and the prerogatives of the present governor, and that Gerry thought it his duty "as a Member of the House, to guard against our pursuing the Vestiges of Monarchy, or cloathing [sic] *Liberty* in the Rags and Tatters of the whore of Babalon." (NYP) Gerry, always a severe critic of Hancock, certainly was justified in guarding against any intrusion of monarchy, and he no doubt felt that Hancock's self-elevating of himself was more in keeping with the conduct of a royal governor than with that of a constitutional governor. So for some, Hancock showed a desire for power, even in the way he summoned the legislature to hear his addresses.

But perhaps he could have had much more power had the British won. Sears noted that "Governor Hutchinson could have pointed out a shorter road to distinction, and a much surer and safer one" (Sears, 336) than the insecure power of participation in a radical Boston club, or membership in a relatively impotent state legislature, or in the duress of trying to lead a divided Continental Congress through the difficult war years. Furthermore, just as he had wealth in 1770, he also had the power that comes with financial prestige. And he knew how to use that prestige to gain the sympathy of the people of Massachusetts. Baxter, however, concluded that Hancock turned to politics possibly because he had proved to be a failure at business. (Baxter, 284) Hancock could have sensed that his business prowess was beginning to be questioned.

Therefore, said Baxter (284), "he may rightly have guessed that a brilliant political career awaited any leader who could combine, as he did, the glitter of the *ancien regime* with unimpeachable Whig principles."[13] If Baxter's verdict again sounds harsh, it must be acknowledged that it has some plausibility. Still, the pronouncement that Hancock was inept in business during the turmoil of the years preceding the revolution must be tempered by recalling all of the difficulties that faced a shipper during those years and must be viewed with the knowledge that the lucrative trade of shipping for the crown was opposed to the interests of the American radicals who would not trade in the king's sterling.

If the desires for wealth and power could have been more certainly achieved by opposing the revolution, why did Hancock not take the path followed by so many of the "absentees" and support the crown? Or why did he not at least remain detached and attempt to profit by whoever won the contest?[14]

If the search for wealth, power, and political rewards were not the motivating forces to turn a conservative business man into a revolutionary, then the search for something else must have been the propelling factor. Before we look for that force, we need to pause to consider two aspects that influenced Hancock's vision of himself and the revolution. Then we can proceed to detail the steps that led him toward revolution.

Two Additional Elements that Must Be Kept in Mind in Examining Hancock's Revolutionary Viewpoint

1. What role did Hancock's health play in his contribution to the revolution?

Did Hancock look out at the world as something of a hypochondiac? Or was he often painfully suffering from ill health, particularly from the gout? Although these questions will be raised again in discussing Hancock's contribution to the revolution and will be considered in analyzing his speeches of 31 Jan 1788 and 6 Feb 1788, the role his health played in his contribution to the revolution needs to be introduced at this point, to consider the derogatory criticism that followed Hancock throughout his political career.

There is abundant evidence in Hancock's correspondence that he genuinely suffered from poor health. However, even with this evidence, it is still possible that Hancock put to good advantage what might have been to others nothing more than a liability. Let us review some of the considerable comment which proposes that, throughout his life, Hancock's state of health was often debilitating.

As early at 1773, when Hancock was only thirty-six years old, he was suffering from the gout. On 17 May 1773 William Palfrey wrote to Harrison and Annsley: "Coll Hancock has lately been so great indisposed that he has not been able to reply to your several last favors. He is now on a journey to Connecticut as well for the recovery of his Health as to transact some public business." (NEHGS, a)

The following year, on 10 Jan 1774, Palfrey wrote to Hagley and Hopkins that "Mr. Hancock intended to have wrote you fully by this opportunity but is prevented by indisposition, and is at present confin'd to his Bed." (NEHGS, b)

On 14 Mar 1774 Hancock was chosen moderator of the Boston Town Meeting "but by Indisposition prevented giving his Attendance." (RRC)

On 18 Aug 1774, in saluting Hancock upon his dismissal by Gage from his colonelcy, the cadets in their letter published in the *Gazette* expressed their wish that Hancock's health should be speedily restored. (cf. Chap 7)

On 7 May 1775 Hancock wrote from New York to his fiance, Dorothy Quincy: "My poor Face and Eyes are in a most Shocking Situation, burnt up & much Swell'd an [sic] a little painful. I don't know how to Manage with it." (MHS, c)

On 15 June 1775 Hancock wrote to Joseph Warren: "I have a great Duty to Do, but I will persevere even to the Destruction of my Constitution." (MHS, a)

Learning of Hancock's ailments, his prospective father-in-law, Edmund Quincy, wrote to his daughter Dolly on 22 July 1775 from Lancaster: "I am very sorry to hear of Mr. H's gout." (Quincy, 165-166) With the wedding to take place on 28 August, Hancock probably did his best to make a quick recovery. Quincy added: "I pray his health may be continued as his present station calls for such great an exertion of every mental power, as well as bodily." His prospective father-in-law also expressed concern that "his health shd [sic] not comport with the present *great business.*"

On 12 Sept 1775, Richard Smith wrote in his diary that he had attended Congress and that "Mr. Hancock having a Touch of the Gout there was no President in the Chair." (Smith, c) Hancock himself confirmed his ill health in a letter of 25 Sept 1775 from Philadelphia to William Palfrey in which he said in a postscript: "I have been sadly Afflicted with the gout, but am Abroad. Mrs. Hancock's Complimts. [sic] She is not very well." Perhaps Dolly found it more propitious to express discontent with her own health in deference to her husband. (Smith, d)

However, John and his family were able to withstand considerable hardships during his tenure as president. On 13 Jan 1777, Hancock wrote to John Treat Paine: "My Situation upon Leaving Philadelphia [to escape from the British occupation] was really distressing, you well know the State of my Family at that time, a wife but nine Days in Bed a little Infant just Breath'd in the World, a large family & considerable Effects, all to take Charge of, in the Winter Season, cold Houses to put up at, & such a Number of passengers on the Road doubtful whether I should even obtain Shelter, & among Strangers too, all these Circumstances with many others, need less to mention, plac'd me in a situation truly distressing, & indeed in what I cannot Describe, tho' I severely felt it. But by the kind hand of Providence I pursued my Journey and arrived at this place without any Accident & my wife & little one & indeed all of us bore the Journey far beyond any Expectation." (MHS, g) This letter illustrates that John did not always complain about his health, even when he had good reason to do so.

Hancock commented on his own poor health in a letter of 15 Feb 1777 from Baltimore to the Massachusetts General Court. Hancock had been in office as president since 24 May 1775. He complained of fatigue. He was in need of rest. In order to leave his post, he not only had to get permission from the national Continental Congress, but, as a representative from Massachusetts, he needed to secure the approval of the provincial Massachusetts General Court. (A&R) In requesting Massachusetts's permission for a vacation, Hancock commented: "Such close confinement both in Congress, and out of it, having at length considerably impair'd my Health, and feeling it decline every Day, I am induced to Ask your Consent to Visit my Native Country, with a view to spend a few Weeks, in hopes the Benefit of the Ride, and Relaxation from Business will Restore my Constitution and Relieve my Complaints." (MA, 196, 230, 1-2) Undoubtedly the strain of office, under what were often primitive conditions, would have fatigued a man of robust health. It is not surprising that Hancock felt the strain.

As it turned out, Congress voted to adjourn on 27 Feb 1777, to transfer from Baltimore to Philadelphia. The Congress was to reconvene on 5 March 1777. The only vacation Hancock got was from 27 Feb 1777 until 12 March 1777, when there were sufficient delegates in Philadelphia to constitute a quorum. At that point, he did not have the opportunity to return to Massachusetts. So his health must have been sufficiently robust for him to continue, even under such adversity.

On 1 Oct 1777 Hancock wrote to Dolly from Yorktown describing the hasty exit Congress had to make from Philadelphia. He assured her that he was "exceedingly well Scituated [sic] with respect to a House & Lodgings," but that "I have had since your Departure a Touch of the Cholick, which worried me much, I Rode in the Rain & was much wet, which beleive [sic] brought it on; and I have been sadly Afflicted with my old disorder, it has not yet left me, I am still unwell, but hope soon to be better." (Smith, e)

On 7 Oct 1777, John wrote to Dolly: "I have been very unwell since you left me, but Thank God, I am much better, my appetite is return'd, & I do tolerably well." (Smith, g)

In his 1777 farewell speech to Congress preceding his return to Massachusetts, Hancock complained of fatigue. In his speech to the Congress on 29 Oct 1777, Hancock stated he was ill, saying: "My health being much impaired, I find some relaxation absolutely necessary." Four days earlier, on 25 Oct 1777, in reply to a letter from General Washington of 22 Oct 1777, Hancock thanked the general for his "Expressions of Politeness & Friendship" and added: "A few Months Relaxation, will, I hope, restore my Health and Constitution." He then accepted Washington's offer of an escort to join him at Bethlehem, Pennsylvania, to protect him on his return to Boston. (Smith, f)

By March of 1788, Hancock had sufficiently recuperated to preside over Massachusetts' adoption of the Articles of Confederation. He returned to the Congress in June of 1788 after an absence of almost eight months.

Hancock felt the urge to participate in the attempt to relieve the occupation of Newport, even if his health was giving him trouble. During the Rhode Island campaign in 1778, John complained to Dolly not only about his health but about her lack of correspondence to him. "I had yesterday a bad turn of the Head Ach [sic] but am better this morning." After commenting that he rejoiced over the improvement of his son's health, Hancock wrote: "My Dear, do you not intend to give me a Line, what prevents, I beg & I am very serious that you would turn your thoughts towards me in that Way, I long to hear from you." (BPL, a)

Between 1778 and 1882, it is likely that Hancock's gout and his general tendency toward malaise did not disappear, but he was sufficiently recovered to participate in the adoption of the provincial constitution and to accept the governorship in 1780. His speeches during his early tenure as governor are not frequent, but they are encouragingly vigorous.

However, Hancock's health appeared to go into another decline, beginning in 1782. On 22 May 1782, Hancock wrote to John Wendell: "I have only Strength to Acknowledge the Receipt of your Several Letters...By Flattering myself that I had far more Recover'd my Health than I found by Experience was the Case, I exerted myself to too great a Degree & have taken such a Cold, as to give me a nervous Pain in my head, as has confin'd me to my Chamber unfit for Business for Several Days, but it seems now abating." (MHS, d)

In June of 1782, William Sullivan visited the governor and gave a somewhat unfavorable description of his state of health. "Governor Hancock had the appearance of advanced age, though only forty-five," commented Sullivan. "He had been repeatedly and severely afflicted with the gout, a disease much more common in those days than it now is, while dyspepsia, if it existed at all, was not known by that name." In a footnote, Sullivan commented: "It may be that the very general practice of drinking punch in the forenoon, and evening, by all who could afford it, was the cause of the common disease of gout." (Sullivan, 10)

On 14 Nov 1783, Hancock in Boston wrote to the heir of one of his business associates, Mary Hagley in London: "My public avocations added to my ill State of Health, have until the present moment prevented my replying to your polite letter of 19 April last." (NEHGS, e)

Evidently, because of his failing health, the governor threatened to resign in 1784. On 17 Feb 1785, he did resign. On 10 Oct 1785, one of Hancock's debtors, John Avery at Boston, wrote to John Hancock also in Boston: "I am extremely Sorry that your Indisposition of health has deprived me the satisfaction of paying my respects to you in person at this time and surely hope that a little time may restore you to perfect health." (NEHGS, f) On 25 Oct 1785, James Sullivan wrote to the secretary of the Continental Congress, Rufus King: "Our friend Hcock [sic] has been very sick at his Country Seat; he came into town last evening: I called upon him, he will soon be better." (King, 1, 111-112) Sullivan and Hancock discussed the possibility of Hancock returning as president of the Continental Congress and Sullivan thought it likely that he would. At the prospect of joining his former colleagues at the Congress, Hancock smiled and said that he "should be glad to serve his Country where he should be most useful so far as his health would admit of." But Hancock apparently remained recuperating for an extended period of time, for he did not return again after his visit of 1779 to join his old compatriots in Congress.

On October of 1789, when Washington made his first visit to Boston as president, there is considerable evidence that Hancock was badly ill with the gout. The discussions of the speech of 19 Jan 1790 detail the communication breakdowns that occurred between Hancock and Washington as to who would pay the first call upon whom. During Washington's state visit to Boston in 1789, Dolly Hancock Scott told General Sumner that Hancock had not refused to call upon the new president, "that Mr. H. had enemies as well as other folks, and although Mr. Hancock had sent out an express to the Gen. at Worcester, and invited him to dine on the day of his arrival in town, yet, as Mr. H. had the gout in his foot and hands, and could not move, they persuaded the Gen. that he was disinclined to make the first call, and the Gen. sent up a note at dinner time excusing himself." (Sumner, 190) For further details concerning the degree to which Hancock was ill in the fall of 1789, see the notes to the speech of 19 Jan 1790.

The number of speeches Hancock gave during the period of 1783 to 1785, in comparison with the greater number of addresses delivered between 1780 to 1782 and between 1787 to 1789, provides some objective measurement of the governor's state of health. Keeping in mind that Hancock was only in office for three months of 1780, he gave four major speeches between 31 Oct 1780 and 22 Jan 1782. There was just one speech in 1783, none in 1784, and only the resignation speech in 1785. When Hancock resumed the governorship, he delivered nine speeches between 1787 and 1789.

Other references to his poor health occur in his speeches of 31 Jan 1788, 6 Feb 1788, and 19 Jan 1790. Hancock's state in the fall of 1789 during President Washington's visit was seemingly very poor. Then the productivity of his speeches picked up considerably. Between 1790 and 1792, Hancock delivered eleven addresses. When, in 1793, his health again began to fail, he delivered only two speeches, one in January of 1793 and the second, his final speech, in September of 1793.

Hancock liked public appearances. They stimulated him. Undoubtedly, had he been in good health, he would have spoken more often. The number of his public appearances during his two periods as governor of Massachusetts is probably a good indicator of his state of health.

By 1790, Hancock was probably seeing Dr. Warren regularly. In an undated letter, probably written in the 1790s, Hancock wrote in the third person to Dr. Warren: "Mr. H will wish the Doc's Leave shortly [to] call on him and must many times in the Course of a Month— Actions must Determine Mr. Hancock's obligations to the Doctyor [sic] for the full he can't express in Words. Adieu." (MHS, h)

On 10 April 1791, Hancock wrote a short note to Major General Knox. The handwriting is very shaky and the brevity of the note plus the halting penmanship connote ill health. (MHS, i)

By the summer of 1793, Hancock was too ill to enjoy a visit from his nephew, Thomas Hancock. Young Thomas, who was still in school, commented: "Whilst I lament your Excellency's severe Indisposition which precludes my seeing you yet I am happy to hear that your Pain is a little mitigated—as I always rejoice in your Excellency's Health and Happiness." (NEHGS, g) The formality of this letter appears to indicate that his brother's son was hardly on intimate terms with his uncle. However, the letter included a request that Hancock pay a bill incurred in young Thomas's education, so perhaps the nephew thought it well to maintain a dignified stance with his important relative.

In the final moments of his life, Hancock wrote to Sam Adams from Concord on 31 Aug 1793: "You know me, I am weak. I refer you to Doctr Jarvis for a state of my health." (NYP, b) On 3 Sept. 1793, Sam Adams replied from Boston, saying that he had had it from Drs. Jarvis and Warren that "they are in hopes...to bring you to such a state of health as to enable you to perform the duties of State with which the people have honored you, which I pray God you may continue in many years after I am no more here." (NYP, d)

As the preceding evidence shows, it will have to be kept in mind as this personal viewpoint of the American Revolution continues that Hancock suffered from bad health, and in particular from the gout. But he also saw himself as being in bad health. Furthermore he aggravated his own illnesses by his excesses. How much his ill health used him and how much he used his ill health will continue to be debatable as this account progresses.

2. What were the major pieces of legislation that brought Hancock and others to revolt against Great Britain? (NYP, c)

Before continuing with the specific events in Hancock's career that contributed to his rhetoric, it is necessary to review briefly the parliamentary legislation, and some of the reactions to that legislation that caused such turmoil in the colonies. Such a summary will avoid reviews of the actions of Parliament during the subsequent discussion. Furthermore, this summary will show that there there were repeated acts of Parliament that were as offensive, if not more so, than the more well-known Stamp Act and Townshend Acts. Once these actions are seen in their totality, it will be easier to comprehend why Hancock and his fellow patriots were continually goaded into action against the British.

DATE*   ACT

---

*where possible, the acts are dated from the time that royal assent was given

17 May 1733 *Molasses Act. An Act for the better securing and encouraging the Trade of His Majesty's Sugar Colonies in America.* six pence per gallon duty on molasses; nine pence on rum to allow British growers to compete with the more cheaply grown molasses from the French islands. Not strictly enforced and often evaded by shippers.

1763 *An Act for the Further Improvement of His Majesty's Revenue of Customs; and for Encouragement of Officers Making Seizures; and for the Prevention of Clandestine Running of Goods into Any Part of His Majesty's Dominions.* English customs agents were to be in the colonies at their posts rather than remaining in England and letting agents do their work; colonial incoming ships were to be searched; vessels could be taken on the high seas and, if convicted of smuggling, the captain and crew of the seizing vessel would share in the profits from the sale of smuggled goods.

1763 *Proclamation Act,* limiting the territory of the colonies to what was approximately the Eastern watershed of the Appalachian mountains.

1764 *Currency Act,* making it illegal for paper money issued by the colonies to be used to pay debts.

5 Apr 1764 *Revitalization of Sugar Act. An Act for Granting Certain Duties in the British Colonies and Plantations in America...* Taxes were to be levied on all sugars, including wines and molasses, not only to regulate trade, but also to raise taxes for the crown. Also taxes on indigo, coffee, wines, silks, and other materials.

22 Mar 1765* *Stamp Act. An Act for Granting and Applying Certain Stamp Duties, and Other Duties, in the British Colonies and*

Plantations in America... Taxes on playing cards; dice; on procedures of courts of law including bails and wills; liquor licenses; university degrees; bills of lading; wine; appointments to office; articles of apprenticeship; pamphlets; newspapers; almanacs; grants of land; advertisements. Previously, only colonial assemblies had levied internal taxes, i.e., taxes on material purchased in stores on land, rather than duty collected on goods being shipped into the colonies.
*to go into effect 1 Nov 1765

8 Aug 1765 Boston learned that Hutchinson's brother-in-law Oliver was to administer the Stamp Act.

14 Aug 1765 Oliver's Stamp Act office demolished, Oliver hung in effigy from the Liberty Tree.

26 Aug 1765 Admiralty broken into, records destroyed; Hutchinson's house sacked.

8 June 1765 Massachusetts asked colonies to meet in New York in October.

3 Dec 1765 Two hunderd and fifty Boston merchants signed an agreement to import no articles from England until Stamp Act repealed; to cancel all orders not filled before 1 Jan 1766; similar moves in New York and Philadelphia. (Boston *Gazette*, 2, 9, 16 Dec 1765; Hubbard, 2, 483-4)

17 Mar 1766 Parliament repealed Stamp Act. *An Act to Repeal an Act Made in the Last Sessions of Parliament Intituled [sic], "An Act for Granting and Applying Certain Stamp Duties, and Other Duties in the British Colonies and Plantations in America..."*

1766 *Declaratory Act. An Act for the Better Securing the Dependency of his Majesty's Dominions in America upon the Crown and Parliament of Great Britain,* in which Parliament reserved the right to tax the colonies so that the intent of the repeal of the Stamp Act would not be misconstrued.

1766 *Sugar Act. An Act for Repealing Certain Duties...and for Granting other Duties Instead Thereof...* Tax reduced to 1 penny on all molasses entering the colonies, making it a revenue act and not an act to prevent trade with non-English ports. Levied a 7 shilling tax on coffee 100 weight avoir dupois. 32 pp.

28 June 1766 *Townshend Acts* on tea, paper, glass, red and white lead, painters' colors, to go into effect on 20 Nov 1766.

28 Oct 1767 Boston town meeting renewed the non importation of unnecessary and subscribed items and vowed to promote colonial enterprises.

1 Aug 1768 Merchants Standing Committee agreed not to import British goods from 1 Jan 1769 to 1 Jan, 1770.

28 Sept 1768 British troops arrived in Boston.

5 Mar 1770 Repeal of all Townshend taxes except on tea.

10 May 1773 The *Tea Act*, giving the East India Company preference.

20 May 1774 *Impartial Administration of Justice Act.*

THE COERCIVE OR INTOLERABLE ACTS

28 Mar 1774 *Port Act. An Act to Discontinue...the Landing & Discharging...of Goods, Wares, and Merchandise at the Town and within the Harbour of Boston,* closing of the port of Boston.

20 May 1774 *An Act for the Impartial Administration of Justice,* in which certain offenses in the colonies were to be tried only in England.

2 June 1774 *Quartering Act. An Act for the Better Providing Suitable Quarters for Officers and Soldiers.*

20 May 1774 *An Act for the Better Regulation of Government of the Province of Massachusetts BAY,* in which the governor would appoint the Council and magistrates, and in which the town meetings would be abolished.

22 June 1774 *An Act for Making More Effectual Provision for the Government of the Province of Quebec,* limiting expansion in the

colonies by making the Ohio River the southern boundary of Canada.
15

---

5 Sept 1774 Fifty-five delegates met in Philadelphia for the First
Continental Congress.

9 Mar 1775 Colonial trade restrained to Britain, Ireland, and West
Indies.

With these acts in mind, the steps can be traced that led eventually to
Hancock's defiance of the king, from which there was to be no retreat.
After reviewing (a) the three contributions that Hancock made to
diplomacy, (b) the three possible motivations for Hancock becoming a
revolutionist, and (c) two factors that needed clarification to avoid
needless repetition in the essay and speeches that follow, Hancock's
viewpoint on the American revolution can be more clearly presented.

NOTES

1. On 8 Feb 1776, the General Court of Massachusetts had appointed
Hancock as a major general in the state militia. He was thus mollified for
having lost his colonelcy under Gage.
2. Fowler (213) stated: "The apocryphal story of Hancock's signing has
been repeated so many times that by now it deserves to be true even if it is
not. As he sprawled that handsome signature...he remarked, 'There! John
Bull can read my name without spectacles and may now double his reward
[of] £500 on my head. That is my defiance.'" See Boyd, 1, 305-8 and 1,
433 concerning the three versions of the Declaration of Independence and
the dates on which they were given either printed signatures or were signed
by the delegates. The above statement by Hancock, if accurate, referred to
the signing in Philadelphia on 2 Aug 1776, but his printed name appeared
on the broadside issued on 4 July 1776.
3. Jackson, Turner Main, 405-406. Reuben Aldridge Guild in *The Life,
Times, and Correspondence of James Manning and the Early History of
Brown University*, (Boston, 1864) noted that Manning was president of
Brown from 1765 until his death in 1791. Manning, a well-known patriot,
was personally acquainted with many of the chief actors in the revolution.

4. Madison Papers, VIII, Library of Congress, Washington, D.C. See also Rutland, 10, 494.

5. Wagner, 14. For example, the private pocket-sized notebook that Hancock kept circa 1770 (MHS) is written in a very ordinary handwriting. In 1770, Hancock was yet young enough that his illnesses should not have affected adversely his style of writing.

6. Baxter, 133. BPL, Ch. M. 1.10, the original of a letter from General Charles Lawrence (governor of Nova Scotia) to Charles Apthorp and Thomas Hancock "for the hire of Sundry Vessels taken up by him to transport the French Inhabitants of Nova Scotia, and paid by his Order." The memorandum dates from 13 Dec 1756. This document forms part of an unusual notebook from the Chamberlain Collection that is composed of some printed text, many engravings, and some original documents. It bears the title: "John Hancock, sketch of his life with autographs and illustrations collected and arranged by Mellen Chamberlain, 1882." Although parts of the embossed leather-bound document are type-printed, there is no indication of whether other copies of the material existed. Chamberlain could have had the type set just for the portfolio now deposited in the BPL. Chamberlain's work may have been the life of Hancock referred to in the Boston *Transcript* of 11 Feb 1884 and described in the introduction to this volume on iii.

7. Hancock's Account Book in London for July of 1760 shows not only entries for his transactions with Uncle Thomas's business associates but also entries for private expenditures such as having his watch repaired, buying gloves for Aunt Lydia, and purchasing a "Jarr Wallnuts." (BPL, b)

8. The deed of the mansion from Lydia to John is dated 1764. (BPL, c)

9. "Few things stand out more clearly from the Hancocks' story than the strong rhythms that were important to trade by war, and John was unlucky enough to take over the reins during a long down-swing. At their best, the postwar years seldom offered chances so golden as those which Thomas had enjoyed; at their worst, they were times during which trade was brought to a dead stop by political troubles." (Baxter, 294) A war was being fought. The port of Boston was closed because of the conflict. Hancock's energies were spent toward the winning of that war and securing fast its victories. By the time he thought of reestablishing the firm in 1785, he was ill and his attentions were still diverted toward politics. Being governor and contributing his time toward preserving the gains of the revolution must have appeared much more attractive to Hancock in his later life than returning to the drudgery and the hazards of the shipping trade. Hancock had been a business man. Like so many contemporary men of affairs, once the attractions of politics had come his way, he had no wish to return to the life

of making money. Money he had; a country with a future was still to be secured.

10. Fortunately for Hancock, the damage to his mansion done by the occupying British forces under General Gage was minimal. "A Account of the damage done to the estate of the Hon'ble John Hancock, Esq. in the Town of Boston, by the British army since April 19, 1775, taken to December 1776." (BPL, d) The damage totaled £4,732.2.8 3/4. (Cf BPL, d)

The detailed inventories at the BPL includes such items as "a large Coach Whip," "Delph Glass Ware, broke while the House was occupied by Officers of the Army," and 1 Back Gammon Table, with its' [sic] furniture."

In a letter of 4 April 1776 to Hancock, Isaac Cazneau stated:

"The Mansion House was thought by most People a Place devoted to Destruction, has Escap'd a Scowering, in more than one Sense. The Best Furniture I put into the Chamber back of the Great Cham'r and keep't [sic] the key till about three weeks before Genl Clinton Left the House, then was sent for and the key demanded to Search for papers, I told him there was not any in the House, but that would not do, when we came to Open the Door the key would not Turne. I told him some Person had Spoil'd the Lock by Trying with some other Key, on this he seem'd much Displeas'd and said would Brake it open, he keep't the key and wishd me good morning which I took as a Signal to depart, which I did, a few days Before he Left the House he sent for me and desired I would Look about & see if any things [sic] was Wanting, told him the Great Settee was not in the House, & desired he would see returned which he did. The Back Gammon Table in the Library was wanting, but none knew any thing of it, he desired one of his Capt. to purchase one as good and send it up, but I never saw it yet." The Back Gammon table continued to be missing, for it was listed on the BPL inventory, valued at £7.

Cazneau continued: "The China and Glass ware was found out, unpack'd and put into the Great Room, I was sent for and Mr. Clinton was very angry that I did not acquaint him twas Secreted, & desired me to walk into the Hall and See the Hiden [sic] Treasure as he call'd it, said I had not used him well, if his Servants had been Dishonest it might been sold, and given Suspicion that twas done by his orders, he put it into the back Chamber with the Other things, and said twas entire as he found it, and gave me the Key. Gen'l Grant came into the House five days after G. Clinton left it but never had the Keys of Chamber or Library, The Pictures & Glasses Tables Chairs etc. are in good Order, some Kitchen Furniture, a Servants bed or two with Blankets are Missing."

Cazneau continued to describe what had happened to the out-buildings and to the gardens, saying that the damage there was considerable and that the Stable and Coach House, used as a hospital, had had many of the windows knocked out. He also described the state of Aunt Lydia's property. (NEGHS, h)

However, although the mansion house and its out-buildings might have suffered relatively minor loss, there was considerable damage to other Hancock property. During the period when Hancock was considering reviving his business, he wrote to Captain Scott: "I am rebuilding my Store upon the Dock which the Brittons burned to ashes when they were in possession of Boston, I shall Compleat early in the Spring, when I purpose to enter into the Commercial Line upon the same plan that I heretofore pursued. I have for ten years devoted myself to the Concerns of the Public. I have not the Vanity to think that I have been of very extensive Service in our late unhappy Contest but one thing I can *truly* Boast. I set out upon Honest Principles, & I strictly adhered to them to the close of the Contest, and this I defy malice itself to Controvert."

11. When Hancock left Philadelphia, he took with him his presidential papers which were later deposited in the Massachusetts Historical Society. In 1925, the Society returned the papers to Washington. (Massachusetts Historical Society, *Proceedings*, 58 (1924-1925): 250) The six volumes are now distributed as follows:

    I. Record of proceedings of the first Continental Congress. LC

    II, III, and V. Copies of letters Hancock received from such persons as George Washington, Philip Schuyler and many others. LC

    IV. 15 Sept. 1775-22 July 2776. Copies of letters written by Hancock. NA

    VI. 24 July 1776-27 Oct 1777. Copies of letters written by Hancock. NA

12. French historians sometimes overlook the second noble act that Louis XVI did. Not only did he die with dignity on the scaffold, but his support of the American Revolution created a new country.

13. John Adams to Elbridge Gerry, Passy, 9 July 1778: "We had an example here last week. A long letter, containing a project for an agreement with America, was thrown into one of our grates. There are reasons to believe that it came with the privity of the King....Full of flattery, and proposing that America should be governed by a Congress of American peers, to be created and appointed by the King; and of bribery, proposing that a number, not exceed two hundred American peers should be made, and that such as had stood foremost, and suffered most, and made most enemies in the contest, as Franklin, Washington, Adams, and Hancock, by name, should be of the number. Ask our friend [Hancock] if he should like to be a peer?" (Butterfield, 4, 149-150)

14. Baxter offered an explanation that combined the economic and political factors. There existed the possibility, proposed Baxter, that (for

whatever reasons) Hancock had not been a success as a businessman. "He can hardly have failed to contrast the poor figure that he was cutting on 'change' with the applause that he could evoke so easily at town meetings," reasoned Baxter. (284) So, if, because of the war, power did not lie or could not lie in the area of business, perhaps John concluded that power lay in the realm of politics.

15. Handlin pointed out that the most alarming provision of the Quebec Act was the agreement by the British to recognize Catholicism in Quebec. If Quebec were to be extended into Ohio, Roman Catholicism would be installed in an area that the colonists considered their rightful territory. As Handlin put it, "The people who had refused to accept Anglican bishops and who worried about any form of episcopacy were now to have Papist minions in their midst." (Handlin, 1, 211)

2

Early Revolutionary Moves

There is no doubt that on his trip to England, Hancock had been impressed with London and the monarchy. But, soon after his return, in October of 1762 Hancock joined the Masonic Lodge of which Paul Revere was a member. Conservatives join Masonic Lodges, but this particular lodge of a secret organization put Hancock in touch with men such as Dr. Joseph Warren, Colonel Josiah Quincy, and James Otis, who early favored organized opposition to the crown.

Three of Hancock's biographers (Allan, 85-86; Wagner, 47; Fowler, 55) speculated that, about this time, Hancock also joined the newly formed Long Room Club that met above the Edes & Gill print shop where was published the widely read liberal Boston *Gazette*. Paul Revere, Thomas Dawes, Dr. Benjamin Church (who later defected to the Tories), the Rev. Samuel Cooper, James Otis, and Dr. Joseph Warren were also members of this group. The society was largely secret, so there are no records of when it was formed.

Allan (86) and Fowler (55) noted that Hancock was also a member of the Merchants Club or Society, which sounds normal enough, except that among its members were Thomas Cushing, Harrison Gray, and

James Otis. Their meetings at the Bunch of Grapes, a British coffee shop, or at the Vernon's Head Tavern, no doubt included discussions of the political repercussions of the repeated acts of Parliament directed against the colonies.

1765: A Crucial Year

The year 1765 saw major moves by Boston to oppose the king. Discontent was expressed by certain power groups in Boston. In March of 1765, Hancock was elected one of the five selectmen to supervise the affairs the city. Allan (95) estimated that only 3.5 percent of the population of Boston exercised the right of suffrage. Actually a clique of Bostonians choose the nominees, whose election was virtually assured. This office of selectman placed John squarely in the middle of the political events that were to follow.

The Stamp Act

The colonies received with much disfavor the news that, on 22 Mar 1765, Parliament had passed the Stamp Act to levy duties, not on imports but on domestic sales. Heretofore, domestic taxes had been levied only by the colonists themselves. Stamps were to be affixed to the sale of playing cards, dice, legal documents, liquor licenses, university degrees, appointments to office, articles of apprenticeship, pamphlets, newspapers, almanacs, and other items noted earlier in the list of parliamentary acts. On 8 Jun 1765, Massachusetts asked that the other colonies send representatives to a meeting in New York in October to consider concerted action against the Stamp Act. Hancock was appointed to a committee to guide Boston's representatives named from the General Court as to how they were to present the attitude of the city toward the Stamp Act.[1]

The colonists, of course, considered the Stamp Act as "taxation without representation." The contrasting theory proposed by the British was called "virtual representation." The government proposed that all persons elected to Parliament were not just responsible to the small group of constituents who elected them but rather they represented not only the whole of Britain but the colonies as well. Wood put it this way:

> What made this conception of virtual representation intelligible, what gave its force in English thought, was the assumption that the English people, despite the great degrees

of rank and property, despite even the separation of some by three thousand miles of ocean, were essentially a unitary homogeneous order with a fundamental common interest. All Englishmen were linked by their heritage, their liberties, and their institutions into a common people that possessed a single transcendent concern. (Wood, 174-175)

This philosophy was expressed by Thomas Whately (Whately-Morgan) in his extended essay of 1765 in which Whately proposed that, through the doctrine of virtual representation, Birmingham, Manchester, "and the Colonies and all British subjects whatever, have an equal Share in the general Representation of the Commons of Great Britain." (Whately)

In his pamphlet, Jenyns put the British philosophy succinctly:

Copyholders, leaseholders, and all men possessed of personal property only[,] choose no representatives; Manchester, Birmingham, and many more of our richest and most flourishing trading towns send no members to Parliament, consequently cannot consent by their representatives, because they choose none to represent them; yet are they not Englishmen?...Why does not their imaginary representation extend to America as well as over the whole island of Great Britain? If it can travel three hundred miles why not three thousand? If it can jump rivers and mountains, why cannot it sail over the ocean? If the towns of Manchester and Birmingham sending no representatives to Parliament are notwithstanding there represented, why are not the cities of Albany and Boston equally represented in the assembly? (Jenyns, 6-8)

It was this philosophy that angered Hancock and the Whigs. The colonists were no more convinced by such a *noblesse oblige* argument than were the residents of newly developed industrial towns of Manchester and Birmingham. By not agreeing and by fighting a revolution, the colonists got their voting rights in 1776 whereas the residents of many of the unrepresented areas in England had to wait until 1832 and later to achieve direct and not "virtual" representation.

If the radicals in Massachusetts took a strong stand against the Stamp Act, how did a middle-of-the-roader like Hancock react?

On 6 July 1765, Hancock expressed the ambivalence of his feelings in a letter to Thomas Pownall in London. Pownall had formerly been the royal governor of Massachusetts and was a friend of the Hancock family. On the one hand, as a merchant, Hancock said he wished to remain aloof from politics; on the other hand, as a merchant, he saw how much the legislation by Parliament was adversely affecting his business. "I seldom meddle with Politicks," he wrote to Pownall, "and indeed have not Time now to say anything on that head." However, he proceeded to do just that. "I know the goodness of your Disposition towards us, and I wish we could be help'd out of our present Burdens & Difficulties, our Trade is prodigiously Embarrassed, & must shortly be Ruin'd under the present Circumstances, but we must Submit." The final phrase about submission shows either that he was still reluctant to challenge the crown, or that he thought mild sentiments might do more to encourage his uncle's old friend in London to assist in the cause of the colonists. Hancock concluded his letter by saying: "I however hope we shall in some measure be Reliev'd, & Doubt not your good influences to forward it." (MHSa) We know that some of the London merchants were active in forwarding the cause of the colonists and attended the debates in Parliament to press their petitions that relief be given.

On 14 Aug 1765, Andrew Oliver, brother-in-law of Governor Hutchinson, was hung in effigy, because Oliver was to act as a distributor of stamps for the Stamp Act. That August night, the office from which Oliver was supposed to distribute the stamps was destroyed by a mob which then proceeded to ransack Oliver's house. The next day, after receiving a delegation from Boston, Oliver resigned as distributor of the stamps.

On 22 Aug 1765, Hancock wrote to his agents that he referred them to the newspapers to realize how unfavorably the Stamp Act was being received in the colonies."...it is a Cruel hardship upon us," wrote Hancock, "and unless we are redressed we must be ruin'd." (NEHGS, a) Hancock hoped that someone would rise up and speak for the colonists, for otherwise their trade with England would halt. "Do think of us," said Hancock.

On 26 Aug 1765, a mob destroyed the home of Lieutenant Governor Thomas Hutchinson, again to express its dissatisfaction with the Stamp Act. The family had barely enough time to escape from their supper. Rioters stripped the house, carried off £900 in cash, and scattered Hutchinson's manuscripts into the streets, including volume one of his *History*. (Bailyn, Ordeal, 35)

On 30 Sept 1765, Hancock wrote to his London agents, Barnard and Harrison:

> Since my last I have receiv'd your favour by Capt. Hulme who is arriv'd with the most disagreeable commodity pay Stamps that were ever imported into this Country, & what if carry'd into Execution will entirely Stagnate Trade here, for it is universally determined here never to submit to it...& nothing but the repeal of the Act will righten the Consequences of its taking place here will be bad [sic]...& I believe may say [sic] more fatal to you than us. for [sic] Gods Sake use your Interest to relieve us. I dread the Event. (NEGHS, b)

On 14 Oct 1765, Hancock wrote again to his agents, Barnard and Harrison:

> ... it is the united Resolution & Determination of the people here not to Carry on Business under a Stamp, we shall be in the utmost Confusion, here after the 1st Nover & nothing but the Repeal of the Act can Retrieve our Trade again...it is my invariable opinion that this Act is unconstitutional...I would sooner Subject myself to the hardest Labour for a maintenance, than carry on this Business as I now do under so great a Burthen, & I am Determin'd as soon as I know that they are Resolv'd to insist on this act to Sell my Stock in Trade & Shut up my Warehouse Doors...I am very sorry for this occasion of writing so boldly, & of being obliged to come to such Resolutions, but the Safety of myself & the Country I have the honor to be a Native of require some Resolutions, I am free & Determin'd to be so & will not willingly & quietly Subject myself to Slavery.[2] (NEHGS, c)

Hancock was willing to be taxed domestically for the benefit of Masssachusetts, but he wished to be taxed by the agents of the Bay Colony for the benefit of Massachusetts and not by representatives of the crown for the benefit of Great Britain.

Later as governor, Hancock was to protest the use of profanity, but he was not above using it on occasion. In the letter of 14 Oct 1765 quoted above, Hancock wrote presumably to Barnard and Harrison that "the Ruin of this People must be the Consequence of this Act's taking place" and that "you will find it come to pass that the people of this

Country will never suffer themselves to be made slaves of by a Submission to that D——d Act." (NEHGS, d) Hancock emphatically added later in this long letter that "a thousand Guineas, nay a much Larger sum, would be no Temptation to me to be the first that should apply for a Stamp, for such is the aversion of the people to the Stamps, that I should be sure to lose my property, if not my Life." (NEGHS, d) It seems fitting to quote this letter to explain Hancock's position in regard to the Stamp Act because, as a postscript, Hancock added: "This Letter I propose to remain in my Letter Book as a Standing Monument to posterity & my Children in perticular [sic], that I by no means Consented to a Submission to this Cruel Act, & that my best Representations were not wanting in the matter."   (NEGHS, d) Therefore, by the fall of 1765, Hancock was in rebellion against the crown.

On 21 Oct 1765, he wrote to Barnard and Harrison: "... what would a Merchant in London think of paying £400 Stlg per ann. which my late Uncle paid to this Province & county[?]" (NEHGS, e) In this letter of 21 Oct 1765, he informed his London agents that the Stamp Act would cause navigation to cease. "I will not be a Slave," said Hancock. "I have a right to the Liberty & privileges of the English Constitution, and as an Englishman will enjoy them; We shall be in a most Shocking Situation after the 1st of November, & our State entire Confusion, and nothing will reinstate us but the repeal of this Act." (NEHGS, e)

On 4 Nov 1765, Hancock wrote to Devonsheir and Reeves: "I think I may Venture to say that not a man in England in proportion to Estates pays so great a Tax as I do & people in general here pay heavier Taxes in proportion than the People of England....It is such an Act as I hope in God will never be executed here; for my own part upon serious & mature consideration, I am invariably Determined not to carry on business under such a Stamp, nor ever Subject myself to be a slave without my own Consent, it seems to be the united Resolution of the whole Continent not to submit to this cruel Act, the Consequences of its taking place must be the Ruin of us, & I think we are a people worth saving." (NEHGS, f) Therefore, there was to be no "business as usual" under the Stamp Act. Hancock's business enterprises were adversely affected by the acts of Parliament as early as 1765.

Now that we have reviewed some of the early remarks by Hancock that expressed his opinions on the Stamp Act, it is necessary to review briefly why the English merchants and the colonists reacted so intensely to the imposition of what were in reality minor tax burdens.

Reasons Why the Stamp Act to Levy Domestic Taxes Was Onerous

The English reaction was slow to gain momentum. Baxter pointed out that at the outset of the imposition of the Stamp Act Barnard and Harrison were not affected by Hancock's denunciations, but that when payments from the colonies ceased and there were no more orders for shipments, "Barnard passed all his days and nights at the House of Commons listening to business connected with the colonies." (Baxter, 237) Other merchants were also involved on the side of the colonists, and "the chairman of the [English] merchants' committee...pressing for repeal" was one of Hancock's correspondents. (Baxter, 237)

The reaction of the colonists was immediate. True, in 1765, Hancock did not acquiesce to lawlessness. Although he was opposed to the Stamp Act, he did not approve of mob violence, particularly when it was aimed at the Hutchinsons who were long-standing citizens of Boston. On 25 Jan 1766, in a letter to his London agents, John stated that "the injury that has been Done the Lieut Govor [sic] was quite a different Affair & was not done by this Town, & is what I abhor & Detest as much as any man breathing & would go great lengths in Repairing his Loss, but an opposition to the Stamp Act is highly Commendable, when I say that I dont [sic] mean that every Step that has been Taken is so; but as a people, and a wide Extended Country, the general Dislike & opposition to the Act is Commendable, But I have said enough to Convince you of my Dislike to it, and I pray we may be Reliev'd." (NEHGS, g)[3] Although the events against Oliver and Hutchinson had taken place in August of 1765, it was not until January of 1766 that Hancock expressed these two-sided feelings on the incident to his agents in London.

Hancock and others expressed their concern about mob rule by calling a town meeting at Faneuil Hall, where, under the leadership of the selectmen, Hancock being one, the acts of violence were condemned. However, the leaders of the violence who were thereupon arrested were either released or mysteriously escaped. The mob evidently let it be known that, if not, there would be further destruction of government buildings.

However, lawful acts of opposition received widespread support. In October of 1765, nine states *not* including Virginia, North Carolina, Georgia, and New Hampshire had sent representatives to the Stamp Act Congress in New York. Hancock had not been directly involved, except possibly in advising the Massachusetts representatives of the attitude of the Boston merchants. The Stamp Act Congress, deferring to the Virginia resolves of Patrick Henry by approving of the Declarations, asserted the rights of the colonies to tax themselves, although the resolutions adopted were more moderate in tone than those proposed by Henry. However, the resolutions asserted the possibility of division of sovereignty. England could have certain rights, but other rights were reserved to the colonies. George III was unlikely to concur.

Bernard Bailyn (99) placed colonial opposition to the Stamp Act in a wider perspective than just its economic consequences and proposed a theory that would explain why the Stamp Act caused the colonists such concern. Bailyn reviewed the fears of Massachusetts that England would attempt to establish a Church of England episcopacy in Massachusetts. He then stated:

> Even for those who had in no way been concerned with the threat of an episcopal establishment, the passage of the Stamp Act was not merely an impolitic and unjust law that threatened the priceless right of the individual to retain possession of his property until he...voluntarily gave it up to another; it was to many, also, a danger signal indicating that a more general threat existed.

Wider Implications of the Stamp Act

The colonists began to fear a conspiracy on the part of England to deprive them of their sovereignty. Pamphleteers proposed that the English government was becoming arbitary and despotic, (Bailyn, 131) and that this despotism would extend to the colonies. In short, the Stamp Act, proposed Bailyn, was evidence that even the British Constitution was wavering from the path of representative government. The pamphleteers, proposed Bailyn, circulated the theory of corruption in the British system of government. (Bailyn, 133) The colonists, said Bailyn, saw only Switzerland, Holland, and Great Britain and her colonies as preserving democratic rights. Sweden and Denmark had lost their liberty to despotism. Poland, Spain, Russia, and France were despotic. If England began to waiver from its commitment to individual rights, said Bailyn, some proposed that it was only in the West that such liberties could be preserved.

No less a figure than the former colonial governor of Massachusetts, Thomas Pownall, proposed in his *Administration of the Colonies* that the verve of the colonists could "become in some future and perhaps not very distant age an asylum to that liberty of mankind which, as it had been driven by corruption and the consequent tyranny of government, *hath been constantly retiring westward.*" (Pownall, 44-45)

Hancock was undoubtedly influenced by such ideas to lessen his opposition to the use of force to oppose the Stamp Act. When his former idol, the British "Constitution," began to be questioned, the worshippers including John became shaken. In 1765, Hancock had not yet let the idol fall altogether, but he was fast beginning to see the flaws in the catechism. The subsequent hostile acts of Parliament, the arrival of the British troops, and above all the disclosure of the correspondence between former Governor Hutchinson and the English representatives of the crown were to have the accumulative effect of making Hancock feel that liberty needed to be preserved all the more in the colonies, if it was beginning to be dissipated in the mother country. With that background, we can resume the chronology of events that express Hancock's opposition to the Stamp Act.

Pope's Day

On 5 Nov 1765, Hancock declared himself in open opposition to the crown by an ostentatious participation in Pope's Day, the American equivalent of Guy Fawkes Day. According to the reminiscenses of Hancock's widow, Dorothy Quincy Hancock Scott, Hancock wished to convert the energies that went into the traditional battle on Pope's Day between the Northenders and Southenders into constructive purposes for the revolutionary cause. Therefore he gave a supper at the Green Dragon Tavern costing $1,000 and invited the leaders of both the North and South anti-Catholic parties to be present. It was to this group that Hancock gave the first speech of which we have any record. Dolly remembered the reaction to Hancock's remarks in this manner:

He addressed them at table in an eloquent speech, and invoked them, for their countrys [sic] sake, to lay aside their animosity, and fully impressed upon them the necessity of their united efforts to the success of the cause in which they were engaged. There is nothing more productive of domestic union than a sense of external danger. With the existence of this the whole audience now became fully impressed, and shook hands before they parted, and pledged their united exertions to break the chains with which they were manacled. The happiest results attended this meeting, and since that time the North and South End Popes have not showed their heads in the streets. (Sumner, 8, 191)

If Hancock's widow can be believed, John's first speech of record was most successful. Wagner (65) described the setting and the reaction to this speech in some detail, but his statements appear to be based on logical deductions rather than on evidence.

The Pact of the Boston Merchants

About this time, 250 of Boston's merchants, including Hancock, entered into a pact not to import British goods with a few exceptions until the Stamp Act was repealed. (Hubbard, 2, 483-484) The merchants agreed that all orders not filled by 1 Jan 1766 were to be cancelled. New York and Philadelphia made similar moves.[4] (Boston *Gazette*, 2, 9, 16 Dec 1765)

Hancock's Oscillations

On 17 Dec 1765, Hancock was evidently not present at the demonstration beneath the Liberty Tree, organized by the Sons of Liberty, to force Andrew Oliver to complete his withdrawal from the issuance of the stamps by resigning in public. Although Hancock was prepared to join other prominent members of the community in opposing the British, he was still not prepared to humiliate the crown's officers. Furthermore, he had regretted the sacking of Oliver's house in August of 1765 and, at this point, did not wish to add to Oliver's grievances against the colonists.

But Hancock's conservative trend was not to suppress his attitude of opposition to the crown. On 21 Dec 1765, Hancock dispatched three letters to two of his British agents, expressing his position on American affairs. A short note included the comment: "I think I need not add more to convince you that its [sic] [the Stamp Act] highly disagreeable to the whole continent and I have strong hopes that the Parliament will relieve us." (NEHGS, h) In a longer letter of the same date, Hancock was more emphatic. He stated that his agents could well judge how the colonies had reacted to the Stamp Act. "I have heretofore wrote you so largely & expressed my Sentiments so fully on the Subject of the Stamp Act," said Hancock, "that I think I need not add more to convince you that it is highly disagreeable to the whole continent nay further that they will never submit to it." (NEHGS, h) He asked his agents to write to him him what they knew of it from their side of the ocean. (NEHGS, h) In his letter Hancock expressed his dissatisfaction that his agents had made no mention of the matter of the Stamp Act and had not given him their opinions on it. (NEHGS, h)

As Hancock's oscillations show, appropriate moves by the British might have kept him in their camp. Eventually, however, the repetitive moves by Parliament to assert its rights over the colonies suppressed Hancock's conservative tendencies. There were repeated indications given to the colonies that they were not to be allowed to rule themselves.

Whatever their philosophies of government might be, the British were having difficulty in exerting their own authority to impose those philosophies. On 25 Nov 1765, Governor Francis Bernard wrote to England to Henry Seymour Conway, whose sympathies lay with the colonists, that he "accordingly ordered some Companies of Militia to be mustered, with unanimous advice of the Council. But the Militia refused to obey my orders; it was said that the People would have their shows....Nothing but the Expectation of an immediate attack of my person, shall drive me from *hence*." Bernard expressed the hope that "some means may be found to make it consistent with the dignity of parliament and put the Stamp Act out of the Question at least for the present." (Bernard, a) On 17 Dec 1765, Bernard wrote discouragingly to Conway: "But I think the time is come, when even a Nominal Governor, tho' without authority or pretending to any, will not be suffered to reside here." (Bernard, b) His prediction about the intolerance of a colonial governor was to prove correct ten years later. On 18 Dec 1765, Bernard wrote to Conway that Oliver had been called [but had not gone] before the Liberty Tree and had written Bernard about it. "I myself must expect to be called to the Tree of Liberty, if I stay much longer in this Town." (Bernard, c) Bernard had said that he would remain until he got the king's permission to leave, no matter how uncomfortable his situation.

By early in 1766, Bernard saw hope only in military intervention. On 19 Jan 1766, he wrote to Conway that he was "more & more assured that the People of this Town who have now got all the Power in their hands, will know no bounds, until the authority of Great Britain shall interpose with Effect." (Bernard, d) Again, Bernard was to prove a prophet. The authority of Great Britain was interposed, but without the effect that Bernard desired. Bernard added: "And even that is to be contested, if the frequent declarations of the People are to be credited; for Nothing is more familiarly asserted in common conversation than the Ability of this People to oblige Great Britain to grant them their own Terms." (Bernard, d) Bernard said that this sentiment was chiefly among "the lower kind of People; but they have learned this lesson from those who should know better."

NOTES

1. Beginning with this period, Hancock's business records are a valuable source of information on the details of his life. His political comments are rare, but, when they do occur in the course of his writing to his agents or to his staff, they are quite revealing.

The "books" below housed at the New England Historic and Genealogical Society (except for two at the Massachusetts Historical Society) were examined for this study. For the most part, the earlier books, were not used because their contents were irrelevant to this discussion.

Letterbook, 6 Mar 1735	3 Sept, 1740
Daybook, August of 1737	Nov 1739
Letterbook, 18 April 1745	16 June 1750 (MHS)
Letterbook, 21 June 1750	4 Oct 1762
Journal, 1 Jan 1755	31 Aug 1757
Wastebook, 2 July 1759	19 Aug 1762
Journal, 1 Jan 1755	31 Aug 1757
Wastebook, 1 Jan 1755	31 Aug 1757
Wastebook, 2 July 1759	Aug. 19, 1762
Letterbook, 1762-1783 (14 Oct 1767-14 Nov 1783)	
Wastebook, 8 Aug 1764	30 Apr 1767
Journal, 18 Aug 1764	9 Sept 1782
Receipt Book, 11 Sept 1764	20 Feb 1784
Letterbook, 7 Nov 1780	13 Mr 1782 (MHS)

Letterbook, 17 Jan 1783   21 Aug 1786 (kept by
                              Hoskins)

The MHS has under its Hancock Papers the original of Hancock's private notebook, measuring 3 inches by 7 1/2 inches, in which various business notations are made.

2. Hancock, on f. 136v, also commented in this letter: "... we shall have no Courts of Justice after the 1 Nover." 1 Nov was the day on which the Stamp Act was go into effect in the colonies.

3. On f. 171, Hancock had said that "it is the united Resolution of the Continent not to Submit to the Stamp Act as we look upon as unconstitutional." [sic] JH to B&H, Letterbook 14 Oct 1762-14 Nov 1783, NEHGS. (cf. Chap. Three)

4. As Thomas pointed out, the nonimportation agreements made from late 1767 were often not followed by many merchants. New York importers were more faithful to the banning of British goods than other states. (Thomas, 152) It is not possible to detail here all of the moves made by the Boston merchants to exclude English goods. There were frequent meetings and often resolutions were passed. Andrews and Thomas have summarized the dilemmas of the nonimportation agreements in detail.

The nonimportation agreements needed continual reinforcing by public meetings, and by correspondence with other ports, to coordinate efforts. On 1 Mar 1768, Hancock signed a nonimportation agreement, a copy of which is in the MHS. Andrews (43) and Rowe (154-155) reproduced articles from the agreement. Hancock was appointed chair of a committee to correspond with merchants in other colonies. (Andrews, 44, MHS, Massachusetts Papers, 1749-1768 [copy], declaration of 1 Mar 1768 signed by Hancock, John Rowe, Edward Payne, William Phillips, Thomas Boyleston, Arnold Wells, Melatiah Bourn, Henderson Inches, and John Erving Jr.) On 16 Mar 1768, the resolution was agreed to unanimously. The boycott was to last one year. No orders were to be placed except for a designated list of items. The merchants agreed to seek the cooperation of other towns in the colony. The committee met in the days that followed, and Rowe noted that Hancock was present on 11 Mar 1768. (Rowe, 155) But, by 26 July 1768, the merchants drew up another set of resolutions that was formally adopted on 1 Aug 1768. It was agreed not to import British goods from 1 January 1769 to 1 January 1770, but only sixty merchants subscribed. (MHS, O25127, no. 71; Boston *Gazette* 15 Aug 1768; Andrews 47-48) Thomas (151) noted that the agreement exempted medicines and school books. Again, on 17 Oct 1769, certain Boston merchants agreed not to import any goods from England until the acts to make revenue from taxing colonial imports were abandoned. (Thomas, 151) In order for such boycotts to be effective, it was necessary to coordinate activities with such ports in New York, Pennsylvania, and Rhode Island. Such coordination sometimes required the ports to adjust their regulations to secure conformity. (Thomas, 152) It must have been frustrating to Hancock to see the failure of his Boston colleagues and those in other colonies to support the boycott, which, if highly effective, could have resulted in the repeal of the offensive acts.

3

1766-1769: The Progression Accelerates

Keeping in mind the background of the important maneuvers of 1765, what were the next events that pushed Hancock further into the camp of Sam Adams?

As John Adams observed, (Adams, 2, 170) the year of 1766 was to bring "ruin or salvation to the British Colonies." Adams noted that "Britain and America are staring at each other; and they will probably stare more and more for some time." (2, 170) So as early as 1766, John Adams foresaw the possibility of a confrontation. Did John Adams include as a result of that confrontation separation from Britain? During this period of mutual inspection between England and the colonists, what was happening to Hancock?

On 25 Jan 1766, Hancock himself wrote to his agents in a letter previously cited that "it is the united Resolution of the Continent not to Submit to the Stamp act as we look upon it unconstitutional." [sic] (NEHGS, a) Hancock was speaking not of just Massachusetts but of the colonies as a whole, united in their opposition to the Stamp Act. What were to be the consequences of nonsubmission he did not say.

In 1765 Hancock had been nominated to fill a vacancy in the legislature but he had failed to secure the requisite votes. Between this defeat and his successful elections to the House of Representatives in 1766 and 1767,[1] the events of Pope's Day had intervened. Hancock had become more of a symbol of liberation from oppression. At his second and third attempts, Hancock was elected to the House by the small prestigious number of the Boston inhabitants who were eligible to vote. Now Hancock was not only a member of the selectmen who supervised the government of Boston, but he was also a member of the body that supervised the state. His status then required him to make decisions on issues important to the revolution. It also forced him to spend less and less time on his business affairs, a fact noted by John Adams when the second president was reflecting back on those crucial times:

> ....no man's property was ever more entirely devoted to the public....The quivering anxiety of the public, under the fearful looking for of the vengeance of king, ministry, and parliament, compelled him to a constant attendance in the House; his mind was soon engrossed by public cares, alarms, and terrors; his business was left to subalterns; his private affairs neglected, and continued to be so to the end of his life." (Adams, 10, 260)

Fifty-one years later, John Adams recalled that in 1766 he had accidentally run into Sam Adams before Hancock's mansion, and that, following Hancock's election to the House, Adam's cousin Sam had said: "This town has done a wise thing today....they have made that young man's fortune their own." (Adams, 10, 260)

The previous chapter gave evidence that Hancock began his speaking career as early as 1765. A letter in the Harvard Archives paraphrases a second speech made by John Hancock to the Boston merchants. As near as can be determined from internal evidence in the MS, the date of the speech is 25 April 1767.[2] In what spirit was Hancock able to address the merchants? By this time, a number of the merchants, satisfied with the repeal of the Stamp Act, were no longer adamant about nonimportation agreements. The letter stated that, as a number of the principal merchants were opposed, it was necessary to use "more decisive arguments than had been used before."

The narrator related that, presumably at the Merchants Club, Hancock came in shortly after nine o'clock on the morning of 26 April "and made a speech" that the letter paraphrased as follows:

> He began with expressing his sorrow at not having had it in his power to attend their meeting yesterday being necessarily detained at Cambridge by the business of the general Court, but had sent them a message offering his Vessel to carry home the goods, they paying the postage bill, and that he was still ready to fulfill his promise. He threw out many reflections against the Importers in the last vessels, said they were more criminal than the old offenders, as Lord N——h's producing a Certificate from the Custom House in London of the Goods ship'd for Boston was the sole cause why the duty on Tea was not taken off as well as those on paper, glass, etc. that there was no occasion for spending much time with these people, meaning the Importers, that it appeared to him that body might take upon themselves to send home the goods, that there was no kind of doubt if a Vessel with the plague on board was coming in here, they had an undoubted right to send her off, that he's looked upon the Cargoes of these Vessels worse than the plague, that he has talk'd upon this subject with many members of the general Court who all agreed with him on the necessity of the goods being sent back, and assured him that if they were return'd as Members next election, they would use their interests to procure instructions from their Constituents to have the expense of shipping them but repaid by the province; he also added that should any person refuse he did not doubt they would take such steps as would make them tremble. The principal argument used by him as well as by all of the other speakers, was the necessity of their saving appearances with the other provinces. Many other violent speeches were made the particulars of which I have not been able to learn. After which a vote was passed that nothing else would satisfy this body but the whole of the goods being reshipped, and Committees were sent out to demand the several Importers whether they would consent to ship home their goods.

There are several interesting references in this narrative:

a. Evidently the importers of these goods were not present at the club, for all of the references are to importers who were absent. Therefore the Merchants Club did not include all of the importers.

b. The narrative says that "other violent speeches were made," so that not only Hancock spoke out but also some of his fellow merchants, who in this instance had met two days in a row to have their morning coffee and to discuss the turmoil of the import-export trade.

c. The merchants felt sufficiently obliged to the other colonies to see that the goods were returned, seemingly by force, to maintain their obligation to their fellow sufferers in New York, Philadelphia, Charleston, and elsewhere. This indication of a unified front toward the British occuring among merchants as early as 1770 is significant. It is also significant that Hancock appeared to advocate the forceable return of the goods, as a preview of the action taken at the Boston Tea Party.

In early March of 1768, Governor Bernard became incensed by an article in the Boston *Gazette* addressed to Edes and Gill and signed "A True Patriot." (*Gazette*, 29 Feb 1768, supplement 2) The short statement, naming no names but making sweeping accusations against those in authority, concluded with this couplet:

If such men are by God appointed
The devil may be the Lord's annointed [sic].

The statement was libelous "by association." However, the House of Representatives slyly appointed Hancock, Otis, Colonel Ward, Mr. Spooner, and Captain Bradford to reply to the governor's letter of objection. The representatives informed Bernard that, since "no Particular Person, Publick or Private, is named. And as it doth not appear to the House that any thing contained in it can affect the Majesty of the King, the Dignity of the Government, the Honor of the General Court or the true Interest of the Province, they think they may be fully justified in their Determination to take no further Notice of it." (HLRO, Nov, 1768, Box 1, 1636r-1637r) The governor was advised to seek redress "in the Common Cause of the Law," hardly an avenue that the infuriated governor would stoop to follow, even if he could establish the identify the author of the article. Undoubtedly Hancock and his colleagues chuckled all the way home from the governor's mansion, congratulating themselves that the failure of the governor to ignore such newspaper stories had led him into an untenable position. Certainly Hancock's stand in this matter curried for him no favor with Bernard.

Honors Given to Hancock

Boston continued to honor Hancock. On 4 May 1768, Hancock was reelected to the assembly. This time he polled 414 votes. Sam Adams gained 432, James Otis 410, and Thomas Cushing 433. (RRC,1758-1769, 245) Furthermore, the legislators of the new General Court nominated Hancock to serve on the General Council that offered its advice to the king's representatives and mediated between the House of Representatives and the governor. Bernard refused to seat the wealthy merchant. Hancock was becoming *persona non grata* to the British, but his influence was rising with the liberal section of the populace.

As was noted in the previous chapter, on 1 Mar 1768 Hancock signed a nonimportation agreement to encourage manufacturing in Massachusetts. and served as a member of the committee to correspond with other colonies about the boycott of British goods. On 14 Mar 1768, he was reelected as selectman, named fire warden, appointed to a committee to certify the town accounts, and chosen to assist in drafting a letter of thanks to John Dickinson, who had published "Letters from a Farmer in Pennsylvania to the Inhabitants of the British Colonies." (RRC, 1758-1769, 232-242)

The Commissioners of Customs and the customs inspectors were, during this period, having their difficulties. On Friday, 18 Mar 1768, the commissioners wrote to Governor Bernard protesting that the colonists had offered "open Insult" that very morning "by affixing Effigies said to represent them upon a Tree in this Town, and as the Alarm was given this Morning at Day break by discharging of Guns. beating of Drums and hoisting of Colors." Naturally they asked the governor "to take such measures as you may judge necessary to maintain the Peace of the Town and prevent any Outrage upon ourselves or our Officers."[3] Several days later, on Monday, 21 Mar 1768, Inspector Williams wrote to the Commissioners of Customs complaining that between 200 and 300 people, "blowing Whistles and shouting along the Streets, stopped before my House, and called out for Me, upon which I raised up the Sach. A Stone was then thrown from the Mobb [sic], which broke one square of Glass." Williams was asked to declare himself a friend to his country. When he replied in the affirmative, someone cried out that "we hope we shall always find you so." The inspector, after reminding the commissioners about the incident of the effigies, concluded "that your Officers can never execute their Duty effectually, if they are liable to be unjustly treated with Public Indignities, and perhaps with Violence by the Hands of Lawless force without Remedy or Redress."

The Incident of the "Lydia"

By April and May of 1768, matters took a more serious turn. The Hancock business enterprises had been importing wine for years. As was noted above, Uncle Thomas had not always been scrupulous in paying the duties on items he imported. The nephew was to imitate the uncle. John Hancock's ship, the *Lydia*,[4] docked on 8 Apr 1768. The next day two tidesmen, Richards and Jackson, came aboard to inspect. Hancock sent them off. The following evening round 11:00 P.M., evidently Hancock was notified that a tidesman was snooping around. Accompanied by servants, John came aboard and found Richards "poking around in the hold of the vessel." (Wroth and Zobel, 2, 174) Hancock asked for Richards's papers. He found them undated. Therefore, Hancock had the tidesman physically carried on deck and would not let Richards inspect the cargo. Sometime after receiving the tidesman's report, the customs officials took action. However, as the officials had lacked the proper papers to make their search, they were challenged on that basis. (Wagner, 72) By the time the papers were available, the cargo had been unloaded. Therefore, when the commissioners requested from London a legal opinion of English Attorney General Sewall as to how to proceed, Sewall replied: "....but in the present case it is most certainly a doubtful point, whether any offence against Law has in part been committed or not; and tho' Mr. Hancock may not have conducted so prudently or courteously as might be wished, yet from what appears, it is probably his Intention was to keep within the Bounds of Law..." The attorney general therefore declined to file a complaint.[5]

The Incident of the "Liberty"[6]

However, on 9 May 1768, another of Hancock's ships, the *Liberty*, docked in Boston harbor. That very night, before the customs officials could inspect, the crew surreptitiously unloaded its cargo. The work was so strenuous that it appeared to have caused the death of the ship's captain. The next morning, when the officials boarded the *Liberty* to tax the cargo, they found presented for customs only a fraction of the ship's capacity. The commissioners claimed that, of the one hundred twenty-five pipes of Madeira wine, one hundred had been clandestinely unloaded. (Wroth and Zobel, 2, 174, 181) While the British were contemplating what action to take, the evidence was to a large extent destroyed because the *Liberty* was preparing for its next voyage. If the small number of casks of wine that the ship's captain had reported to the customs office as being on board was a false report, it was going to be difficult to establish.

It is probable that Governor Bernard attempted some private negotiations with Hancock during May of 1768. There is in the Corps of Cadet Papers a memo from Thomas Flucker to John Hancock, assigned the probable date of 22 May 1768, which states: "I saw the Governor at Roxbury Yesterday, and Intended to have seen you Last Evening—he desired me to let you know it would be agreable [sic] to him to Meet you at my house this Evening Immediately after sunset." The fact that the meeting was to be at the secretary's house after dark would indicate that Bernard hoped to have an altogether private and confidential meeting with Hancock. Whatever was hoped for from such a meeting did not materialize.[7]

However, an event occurred that encouraged the crown. A tidesman named Kirk, who on 9 May 1768 had apparently been shoved into a cabin and detained because he would not cooperate with the illegal disposal of the cargo, came forward to report that he had not been allowed to inspect the night unloading of the cargo. He reported that he had been forcibly detained below and that the other tidesman was drunk and had gone home to bed. "I heard a Noise as of many People upon deck at work hoisting out Goods," declared Kirk, stating that when the noises ceased, "Captain Marshall came down to me in the Cabin, and threatened that if I made any discovery of what had passed there that night, my Life would be in danger, and my Property destroyed."[8] It was rumored that Hancock had declared even before the ship arrived "that he would run her Cargo of Wines on Shore."[9] But rumors had not been enough to allow prosecution. Once the British had Kirk's testimony, they decided to seize the ship and to levy charges against Hancock for smuggling.

Several accounts said that Hallowell was asked to wait to seize the vessel until Mr. Hancock arrived. One John Macket is quoted as saying in his deposition: "Then I went to the Comptroller, and desired him to let the Sloop be stopped at the Wharf [Hancock's wharf], as I had sent for Mr. Hancock, and that he would be there in a few Minutes." (AG, 110) From the same source, Daniel Malcolm in his deposition said that he asked Mr. Harrison, "a superior person," to wait until "Mr. Hancock comes down, as he is sent for, and will be here in a few Minutes." (AG, 102) Caleb Hopkins and Benjamin Goodwin also were deposed as saying that Hancock had been sent for. (AG, 103; 104) However, there is no mention that Hancock ever appeared at the wharf and no record of a dock confrontation between him and the customs officials, as had taken place over the matter of the *Lydia*.

The news traveled fast that, by painting a broad arrow on its bow, the British had officially seized the *Liberty*. A crowd assembled. In his statement to the Treasury Board after his return to England, Hallowell estimated the crowd at "not above 2 or 3000."[10] The rowdies of Boston were not to let one of their emerging heroes be persecuted by an unpopular "foreign" force, particularly when the force was led by the unpopular naval officer, John Corner, the commandant of the British frigate, the *Romney*. (Allan, 108) The crowd pursued the commissioners as they left the *Liberty* and proceeded to the houses of the officials, where they did damage. As will be detailed below, eventually the customs officers had to flee to the *Romney*, and from there to the Castle, an island in Boston Harbour.

The Treasury Minutes recorded in England relative to the customs in America during this period relate in part the facts of the events in Massachusetts, but they also illustrate most clearly the detachment with which the British viewed the situation. In the opinion of the British, the colonists would simply have to shape up. Such attacks upon the customs officers could not be tolerated. Memorials were read to the Treasury from various parties and letters were exchanged with Hillsborough who informed the Treasury that adequate measures were being taken. For example, the entry of the Treasury Minutes for 21 July 1768 read:

> Read memorial from the Commr. of the Customs in America dated 16 June 1768 acquainting My lords that from the outragious [sic] behaviour of the people of Boston to their Officers, & their threats of immediate violence to themselves following the seizure of a sloop belonging to Mr. Hancock of Boston they had found it absolutely necessary in order to save his Majesty's Commission from further insult, and to preserve their own lives to take shelter on board the Romney Man of War in Boston Harbour from whence they have removed into Castle William to carry on the business of the Revenue...[11]

The picture emerges of a group of somewhat stuffy lords becoming aghast, in the Dickensian fashion, that the people might have anything to say about how they were being taxed. The king's agents were equally unaware of the serious consequences that might befall.

The details of the reactions to the seizure of the *Liberty* taken from a variety of sources were as follows. According to Bernard's correspondence with Hillsborough, there had been severe trouble on

Saturday, 10 June 1768, including batteries on Harrison and Hallowell and the smashing of the windows of their houses. A deposition by Thomas Irving, one of the customs inspectors, given to Hallowell on 11 June 1768, stated that Irving was "beaten with clubs" and seized "by the Hair, Arms, etc. whilst others were beating Me upon the Head with Clubs, calling out to murder or kill me." The deposition is undated, but undoubtedly refers to the incidents of 10 June 1768.[12] That evening, a boat belonging to the customs collector Harrison was dragged onto the Boston Common and burned. Joseph Warren's biographer, Richard Frothingham, found that "Hancock, Samuel Adams, and Warren had been in consultation; and as it is said that Hancock, and others of influence, came on to the Common while the boat was burning, the inference is a fair one, that the three came together." (Frothingham, 58) Hancock, Adams, and Warren, who seemingly emerged from Hancock's house that overlooked the Boston Common, took no action to stop the burning of the boat.

Fearing further disturbances, on Sunday, 11 June 1768, the commissioners requested asylum. On 12 June 1768, the commissioners from "on board His Majesty's Ship Romney" wrote to Governor Bernard: "...we cannot...act in any Business of the Revenue whilst under such an Influence...and therefore request your Excellency to give Directions that the Commissioners may be received into the Castle, and that they may have the Use of the Accommodations there for themselves, their families..."[13]

John Adams as Hancock's Attorney

Hancock hired John Adams as one of the attorneys to defend the accusations of smuggling. Organizing the defense was a laborious job. John Adams wrote in his diary that "there were few days through the whole winter when I was not summoned to attend the Court of Admiralty." (Adams, 2, 215-216) Adams concluded that the crown was "determined to examine the whole town as witnesses." (Adams, 2, 216) Among the arguments that Adams presented in Hancock's defense was a variation on the "taxation without representation" theme. Adams's notes show that Adams claimed the taxation of the ship was made "without our Consent." (Wroth & Zobel, 2, 198) Adams's amplification of this line of reasoning in his plea to the court is significant:

> My Clyent [sic] Mr. Hancock never consented to it. He never
> voted for it himself, and he never voted for any Man to make

such a Law for him. In this Respect therefore the greatest
Consolation of an Englishman, suffering under any Law, is
born from him, I mean the Reflection, that it is a Law of his
own Making. (Wroth and Zobel, 2, 198)

Moves by the British to Quiet the Disturbances in Boston

England felt obliged to take action. As a result of numerous appeals
to London to rescue the American customs officers, on 11 June 1768,
the very day on which the customs officials repaired to Castle Island,
Lord Hillsborough in England addressed a memorandum to the Lords of
the Admiralty requesting that "one Frigate, two Sloops, and two
Cutters" be assigned to Boston to assist in carrying out the taxing
privilege of the crown. (HLRO, a) The citizens of Boston did not
know yet of the request to send troops, but this memo precipitated the
arrival in September of 1768 of British troops. The additional buildup
of the Navy was to be a prelude to the landing of soldiers. On 8 June
1768, Hillsborough had notified General Gage that "one Regiment, or
such force as you shall think necessary" was to be quartered in Boston.
(HLRO, b) The British were coming!!!

Almost as Hillsborough was addressing his requests to Gage and the
Lords of the Admiralty, Bernard had further reason for apprehension.
When on Monday, 13 June 1768, Bernard came from Roxbury to his
town house, he wrote Hillsborough that he found several handbills
"which had been circulated around the town, and stuck up there; a copy
of which follows:"

BOSTON June 13, 1768

THE SONS OF LIBERTY

REQUEST all those who in this time of

Apprehension and Distraction wish well to

and would promote the Peace Good Order

and Security of the Town and Province;

to assemble at Liberty-Hall under Liberty

Tree, on Tuesday the 14th instance at

Ten o'clock Fore-noon precisely.

(HLRO, c)

As the Selectmen's minutes show, the town had received a report on Monday, 13 June 1768, that a seaman of Boston named David Kinney had been impressed. (RRC, 1764-1768, 296) Such a move on the part of the British was enough to provoke the calling of a rump town meeting. Bernard was more than uneasy. He had heard rumors that there was to be more trouble, and he was correct. Not only was there the impressing of seaman, but there were rumors circulating of a forthcoming British occupation to add to the bad feelings about the confiscation of Hancock's ship, *Liberty.* So there were at least three causes to stimulate unrest.

The meeting of Tuesday, 14 June 1768, announced in the above poster, began informally at the Liberty Tree, moved first to Faneuil Hall, and finally to the Old South Church where the selectmen made it an official town meeting. Governor Bernard wrote to England to Lord Hillsborough that he had been told that at least four thousand men were present at the Old South Church, (HLRO, d) so that certainly all of them did not get inside to hear the deliberations. The town meeting chose a committee of twenty-one to present a series of grievances to Bernard. In its petition, the Town of Boston said: "Menaces have been thrown out, fit only for Barbarians which already effect us in the most sensible manner, and threaten us with Famine and Desolation, as all Navigation is obstructed." (RRC, 1758-1769, 254) The town meeting adjourned until Wednesday at 4:00 P.M. at the Old South Church to hear the governor's answer.

On that same Tuesday, not finding the governor at his town house, the committee, including Hancock, proceeded in eleven carriages to the governor's mansion at Roxbury. Bernard wrote Hillsborough: "I received them with all possibile civility, and having heard their Petition, I talked very freely with them upon the subject, but postponed giving a formal answer until the next Day, as it should be in writing. I then had wine handed round, and they left me, highly pleased with their Reception; especially that Part of them which had not been used to an Interview with me." (HLRO, e) His written answer stated that he had no control over the British navy so that he could not ask the Romney to leave the harbor, but that he would exert what influence he had to prevent further impressments. He felt obliged to enforce the customs officials, and "if in so doing I shall give offence, I shall be sorry for it, but I shall never regret the doing of my duty." (RRC, 1758-1769, 256) On 14 June, Bernard did consult with Captain Corner of the *Romney* concerning the impressment of David Kinney. According to his correspondence with Hillsborough, he reported his actions to both the Council and the selectmen and afterwards, they were reported at the town meeting by one of the members of the Governor's Council. (HLRO, f) The minutes of the town meetings or the minutes of the selectmen of that period make no mention of such a report.

Although the town was probably dissatisfied with Bernard's reply, it is likely that it comprehended its logic. Bernard could not control the Navy; he had intervened to stop impressing seamen; and he was obliged to enforce customs. But the more radical of the Bostonians continued to call for action. Bernard enclosed in his letter to Hillsborough, part of which had been written on 16 June and part on 18 June, the following "incindiary [sic] paper" that he had found posted around the town of Boston.

> It is thought by the REAL FRIENDS to LIBERTY that the Fate of America depends on the steady and firm Resolution of the Town of Boston at the Adjournment of their Meeting to Morrow, it is earnestly wish'd and expected that the well disposed Inhabitants would excite each other to give their punctual Attendance at so Important a Crisis.
>
> A THOUSAND (HLRO, g)

Although undated, it can be assumed that this poster was affixed on 16 June 1766. But, in spite of what the more radical elements might have wanted done, when the town met again on Friday, 17 June 1768, the meeting only approved a strong resolution against the Stamp Act, the presence of the *Romney*, and other grievances, and then dissolved.

Although Bernard reported to Hillsborough that "just at this Time I am popular" but that "whenever my Duty obliges me to do any thing which they don't like, there's an End of my popularity, and therefore I do not expect to enjoy it a Week." (HLRO, h) And with good reason. The meeting of Tuesday, 14 June 1768, had considered but not approved the proposition "that if any person should promote or assist the bringing of troops here, he should be deemed a disturber of the peace, and a Traitor to his Country." (HLRO, i) Moreover, Bernard reported, in the part of his 16-18 June letter to Hillsborough dated 18 June 1768, that the following instruction had been given to the town representatives in their negotiations with the governor:

> Ordered. That Mr. Speaker, Mr. Otis together with such as the Honorable Board shall join, be a Committee to inquire into the grounds and reasons of the present apprehension of the people, that measures have been taken, or are now taking, for the execution of the late Revenue Acts of Parliament by naval or military force. (HLRO, j)

Bernard knew that he had already requested that troops be sent to enforce such acts, although he may not have known at that time of the orders of 8 June 1768 to Gage and 11 June to the Lords of the Admiralty. He must have sensed, however, that he was in real difficulties. Without the naval and land forces, he could not keep order; with the naval and land forces, he was likely to have considerable disorder.

Meanwhile, in another part of the forest of insurrection, an effort was being made to achieve a compromise on the issues concerning the *Liberty*. The customs was willing to release the *Liberty* to Hancock, provided he gave his word to return her when the case came to court. (HLRO, k) However, the colonists would accept no deal. Adams, Otis, and Hancock decided to defy the crown a second time, and hoped to win again, as they had won with the *Lydia*. Dr. Warren informed Hallowell at midnight on Sunday that the offer of compromise was rejected.

England Elects to Go to Trial

It had been the opinion of William DeGrey, His Majesty's Attorney General in England, in a brief issued on 23 July 1768, that, from the depositions he had received concerning the incident of the *Liberty*, there was sufficient evidence to prosecute. The crown decided to go to trial. (HLRO, l) Hancock was to pay a penalty of £9,000. Bail was set at £3,000. On 3 Nov 1768, a warrant was issued for Hancock to appear in court on 7 Nov 1768. Hancock and those charged with him were forced to make up the bail money in sterling. (Wroth and Zobel, 2, 181)

Undoubtedly this lengthy trial plus the threat of imprisonment and fines moved Hancock considerably away from moderation and, if not toward revolution, certainly toward open defiance of the king. Although Hancock gained some security in relying upon his support in Boston, the British courts were nonetheless a real threat to him. Wroth

and Zobel reported that "the trial of Hancock and the others was an
event of major political importance in the colonies." The length of the
proceedings, said Wroth and Zobel, "played into the hands of the
revolutionary propagandists." (Wroth and Zobel, 2, 184) Furthermore,
although the crown was eventually forced to withdraw its suit in the
spring of 1769 for reasons that may have been in part political and in
part the result of a change in status of the judge, (Wroth and Zobel, 2,
183-4) Hancock's ship the *Liberty* was never returned to him, because
it was decided that "the Liberty was condemned for unloading cargo
before entry." (Wroth and Zobel, II, 185) So he suffered financial loss
and personal anxiety.

The summer, fall and winter of 1768 to 1769, were uneasy ones for
Governor Bernard. He saw the trial of Hancock dragging on and on, and
sensed that the crown might lose it. He knew that the troops were
going to arrive and that their appearance would cause trouble. He could
be given no assurances that the Romney would not impress further
Massachusetts seamen. His mind was anything but easy.

The action taken by the Merchants Committee on 1 Aug 1768, to
renew the nonimportation of British goods, was an additional blow to
Hancock's business. The merchants exempted a few items from the
ban, but not many. The embargo was to go into effect from 1 Jan
1769 to 1 Jan 1770, with the prohibition of items taxed under the
Townshend Acts to continue until the acts were repealed.

Rumors of Troop Activity

In August, the Boston newspapers began to report troop movement
at Halifax. Soon it became apparent that the soldiers being assembled
in Canada were to be sent to Boston. Appeals to Governor Bernard,
some of which were led by Hancock, achieved no results. Bernard
would not convene a new General Court. Therefore, ninety-six towns
responded to the call of Boston for a rump assembly to consider the
grievances of "unfair taxation and military oppression." (Wagner, 79)
No relief was forthcoming. The subsequent arrival on 27 Sept 1768 of
British troops on twelve warships did not make the colonists passive,
but only more determined to resist.

John Adams in his diary (Adams, 2, 213-214) gave an account of the
effect that the presence of the British troops had in Boston. "A
regiment was exercised by Major Small, in Brattle Street, directly in
front of my house," noted Adams. The troops woke the Adams family
early every morning with fife and drum. Adams concluded that "their
very appearance in Boston was a strong proof to me, that the

determination in Great Britain to subjugate us was too deep and inveterate ever to be altered by us." Again, was it a part of Adams's thoughts that there might be no peaceful way to alter the British attitude, and that eventually force might have to be used?

About this time, Bernard tried to bribe Hancock with an appointment to a vacancy in the Council. Hancock refused to take the bait. (Allan, 113)

At first the colonists declined to quarter the British troops, but finally the soldiers were permitted temporary use of Faneuil Hall and the Boston Common, where their tents made a shambles right outside Hancock's front door. The Barker diary (Barker, 3) reported that on Tuesday, 15 Nov 1774, some of the troops left the Boston Common for their winter quarters, but temporarily left their tents standing so they could dry out after two days of wet weather.

Because of the history of Uncle Thomas's dealing with provisioning the British troops, it is not surprising that rumors were spread that Hancock's firm had solicited General Gage in New York for the business of furnishing supplies to the British troops in Boston. On 12 Nov 1768, Hancock wrote to the publishers of the Boston *Gazette* the following denial:

MESSRS. EDES & GILL:—

I observe in your last paper a piece signed Veritas, the writer of which says he had it from good authority, that a letter under my hand was published [shown] in a coffee-house at New York, requesting His Excellency Gen. Gage that I might supply the troops then expected, and which have arrived in this town. If such a letter has been produced there, or anywhere else, I declare it to be a forgery; for I have never made application to any for the supply of said troops, nor did I ever desire any person to do it for me. The person who produced the letter could have no other design but to injure my reputation, and abuse the gentlemen of New York.

Your humble servant,

JOHN HANCOCK

BOSTON, Nov. 12, 1768[14]

The year 1769 not only saw the dismissal of the charges against Hancock, but also continued agitation about the appearance of troops in Boston. In March, Hancock was reelected Boston selectman and a representative to the General Court. Bernard decided to reconvene the General Court, but when the court insisted on discussing the presence of troops in Boston, Bernard moved the assembly to Cambridge where the influence of Boston would be less virulent. Hancock's name was again submitted to Bernard to become a member of the Council. Again Bernard refused the appointment. By 21 June, 1769, Bernard and the General Court had had enough of each other. Bernard dissolved the assembly and announced that he was returning to England for a visit. He sailed in August of 1769, never to return. Lieutenant-Governor Thomas Hutchinson was left in charge.

On 14 Aug 1769, Hancock attended an elaborate celebration to commemorate the establishment of the Sons of Liberty and to rejoice in the recent departure of the royal governor, Bernard. Although many of the citizens of Massachusetts continued to remain loyal to the crown, they were not at all reluctant to celebrate the fall of his advisor, who, as it was said, had ill instructed the good King George III. The parade of carriages and horses proceeded to Robinson's Tavern in Dorchester for the celebration. (Wagner, 85)

Toward the end of the month of August, Hancock journeyed to New York and Philadelphia to sound out the sentiments for joint action against the moves of the British. The year ended in turmoil. British troops were still in Boston. Trade was at a standstill. The merchants were so far holding the line against imports.

The Continuing Reaction of the Merchants

On 20 Oct 1769, an unidentified Boston correspondent wrote to Joseph Harrison of the firm of Barnard and Harrison in London saying that on 18 and 19 Oct, "the Merchants had a meeting in Faneuil Hall and came to the following Resolutions, viz not to import any Merchandize themselves, or deal with any Colony or Individual Person that should presume to import until the Duties...be totally taken off."[15]

An unidentified correspondent to Joseph Harrison reported that force and threats to their lives and property had been used on merchants not at the meeting, to conform to the boycott. "Their Properties were actually unsafe, their Signs, Doors and Windows were doubed over in the Night time with every kind of filth, and one of them particularly had his person treated in the same manner." (PRO, MS 38206, 186r) On 28 Oct 1769, an unknown correspondent, perhaps the same one who sent the letter of the 20th, wrote to Joseph Harrison on the misfortunes that had befallen the editor of the *Chronicle*, Joseph Mein, and others at the hands of the Boston mob. Mein was pursued from one end of the town to the other, even into the Main Guard where he had gone for protection. A mob of 1,100 to 1,500 men stripped one man suspected of being an informer, tarred and feathered him, and led him to the Liberty Tree where he was forced to thank them for sparing his life.[16] During this incident, a person in Mein's house fired back upon the crowd from inside the house, seemingly with a gun loaded only with powder, without injuring anyone. Such incidents illustrate that things were far from quiet in Boston. Those who in their history books seemed to learn that the American Revolution began in 1775 were not told of the extent to which violence had occurred between the colonists and the British at a much earlier period.

At some point during the year 1770, the Boston merchants published a thirty-seven page pamphlet aimed at their British pro-colonial audience. They detailed how the "several acts of parliament made in the fourth, sixth, and seventh Years of his Majesty's Reign Respecting American Commerce and Revenue, and their Military and Civil Execution" were disadvantageous to both the English and the colonists. The pamphlet was careful not to name particular acts, but, by its descriptions of the hardships being caused, surveyed much of the legislation through 1766, which would include the Stamp Act, the Sugar Act, and the Townshend Acts. No names of merchants were given as authors. The pamphlet ended with the strong statement: "... any measures that have a tendency to injure, obstruct and diminish the American trade and navigation, must have the same effect upon that of Great-Britain, and, in all probality [sic], PROVE HER RUIN." (Observations)

At the end of a decade, what of the future? What were to be the policies of Bernard's replacement, Lieutenant Governor Hutchinson? Could he restore peace and harmony to a distraught colony? Would relief be given to merchants such as Hancock, or would the British continue to give offense both politically and economically to their "loyal" colonies?

NOTES

1. Boston Town Records, 1765, 141
   Otis, 388; Cushing, 538; Thatcher, 427; Gray, 570

74   *John Hancock's Life and Speeches*

Boston Town Records, 1766, 177
Otis, 642; Cushing, 676; Sam Adams, 691; Hancock, 437

Boston Town Records, 1767, p. 211:
Otis, 575; Cushing, 557; Sam Adams, 574; Hancock, 618

2. Houghton, MS Sparks 10, vol. 13, fol. 77. Since the MSS in volume thirteen come from the papers of George Chalmers, he is perhaps the author of the account. The particular MS pertaining to Hancock is entitled "Narrative of Occurrences at Boston from April 25 to May 4," and was on June 15 either entrusted to a Captain Johnson for delivery to another port or received by a Captain Johnson at another port. The MHS noted that hundreds of such letters were dispatched by ship from one port to another.

The month and day are given in the MS as 26 April, but no year is recorded on the manuscript itself. Harvard's Houghton Library dates the letter as 25 April 1770, because folio 77 of MS Sparks 10, vol. 3 has on its spine "Papers Relative to New England 1768-1770. However, internal evidence in the MS shows that the Harvard date is inaccurate. Whoever filed the letters of the Sparks collection erred.

The letter stated that "the business of the day was begun by the Clerk reading the remonstrance of the City of London, the Speech Townshend made to his Majesty to which said he his Majesty made the following ignoble reply, reading the reply." Charles Townshend served as Chancellor of the Exchequer from 26 July 1776 until his premature death on 4 Sept 1767. As the speech Hancock delivered was concerned with taxes on goods to be imported into the colonies, and since Townshend had proposed that such taxes be levied, it is reasonable to assume that the year is 1767. During a debate in the Commons on 26 Jan 1767, Townshend pledged himself "that something should be done this sessions, [sic] something should be done toward creating a revenue to bear the burden." (Simmons and Thomas, 2, 1765-1768)   On 18 Feb 1767, Townshend spoke to the Commons, which was described by Nathaniel Ryder in his diary as "superior to almost any I ever heard." (Simmons and Thomas, 2, 428) Although the Townshend duties were not officially proposed until 1 June 1767, (Thomas, 355; Simmons and Thomas, 2, 504) undoubtedly the informers of the colonists reported some of the details of the tax in letters dispatched to the colonies in February and, in more detail, as leaks made more clear what items Townshend intended to tax.

The speech referred to in the letter is probably Townshend's speech of 18 Feb 1767. Townshend's other speech of note, his so-called "champagne speech," was delivered on 8 May 1767, so it can be eliminated as the speech referred to in the letter, since Hancock delivered his remarks on 26 April.

Sparks (1789-1866) was a historian whose papers included "papers and transcripts of original documents concerning the American Revolution" and are now housed in the Houghton Library at Harvard.

3. Copy of a letter from the commissioners to Governor Bernard, 18 March 1768, PRO, Treasury Class I, 465, f.253r old number, 34r new number, 13. Inspector Williams to the Honourable Commissioners of His Majesty's Customs, 21 Mar 1768, PRO, Treasury Class I, 465

4. The logbook of the *Lydia* for Friday, 8 Apr 1768, simply noted: "At midnight Got up with Boston Lighthouse & Got a Pilot on board. at 2 A.M. made fast at the Wharfe and discharged the Pilot Passengers." [sic] NEHGS, Ship Lydia Logbook

5. "Copy of the Attorney General's Opinion on the Case of the Tidesman stationed on Board the Brigantine Lydia at Boston, Cambridge, 23 April 1768," PRO, Treasury Class I, 465, f.357v old number, 70r new number, 18. See also Wroth and Zobel, 2, 194

6. There are several accounts of the incident:

HLRO, 28-30 November 1768, "American Colonies Papers," Box 2, ff. 339r-342v, gives a copy of Customs Commissioner Benjamin Hallowell's deposition to Lord North, made when Hallowell was yet in the colonies.

Another copy is found in the PRO, Treasury Class I, 465, f.74, deposition of Hallowell on 11 June 1768 [cf.Wroth and Zobel, 2, 176, note 9.]

The HLRO, 28-30 Nov 1768, Box 2, ff.339r-342v, contains a copy of the examination of Mr. Hallowell in London at the Treasury Board on 21 July 1768 (Hallowell had left Boston on 20 June 1768 and arrived at Weymouth on 17 July 1768, appearing before Lord North, Mr. Campbell, and Mr. Jenkinson on 22 July 1768, but the document breaks off suddenly, as if pages are missing, as does the copy found in the PRO, Treasury Class I, ff.338r-340v, Copy of the Examination of Mr. Hallowell at the Treasury Board on 21 July 1768).

The American *Gazette*, 1770, #6, 448-551 (Wroth and Zobel, 2, 180, n. 25) also gives Hallowell's deposition of 21 July 1768. The *Gazette* is identical to the copies in the HLRO and the PRO, except that it states, "A true copy: in the absence of the clerk of papers, JOHN SPEED." Therefore, the former two versions may be complete.

It is also found in the The Boston *News-Letter* of 16 June 1768, 2, col 1 (cf. Wroth and Zobel, 2, 176, note 9).

7. BUA, Papers of the Massachusetts First Corps of Cadets. The date on which Flucker wrote the letter was probably Sunday, 22 May 1768.

8. "Copy of the Deposition of Thomas Kirk Tidesman in the Port of Boston dated 10 June 1768," PRO, Treasury Class I, 465, f.72 old #, 129; new # 21. For depositions favorable to Hancock, see the American *Gazette*, vol. 2, 101-112

9. HLRO, 28-30 Nov. 1768, Box 2, f. 1820r. Copy of the Examination of Mr. Hallowell at the Treasury Board on 21 July 1768. See also PRO, Treasury Class I, 468 and AG, VI, 449.

10. "Copy of the Examination of Mr. Hallowell at the Treasury Board on July 21 1768,", PRO, Treasury Class I, 468.

11. Papers of the First Earl of Liverpool, BM, Additional MSS 38340 27. "Copy of the Deposition of Thos. Irving Esqr. Inspector of Imports and Exports, PRO, Treasury Class I, 465, f. 80r old number, 137r new number.

12. PRO, Treasury Class I, 465, f. 80r, old number; 137r new number, "Copy of the Deposition of Thos. Irving Esqr. Inspector of Imports & Exports".

13. "Copy of a Letter from the Honble Commissioners of His Majesty's Customs to Govr. Bernard," PRO, Treasury Class I, 465, f.86v old number, 143v new number 31. See also Adams, 2, 215-216.

14. Boston *Gazette*, 14 Nov 1768, p. 3; Brown, 163.

15. British Museum, _____ to Joseph Harrison, enclosed in a letter dated 8 Jan 1770, from Benjamin Hallowell to Grey Cooper, Additional MSS 38206, f. 186r.

Benjamin Hallowell, comptroller of customs in Boston and his brother Joseph Hallowell, chief collector in Boston, sent the letters to Harrison in London for the purpose of their being relayed to the government. Harrison passed them on to Grey Cooper. (letter to author from British Library, 28 Aug 1987).

16. British Museum, _____to Joseph Harrison, enclosed in a letter dated 8 Jan 1770, from Benjamin Hallowell to Grey Cooper, Additional MSS 38206, ff. 188r-189r.

4

The Boston Massacre of 1770 and Its Aftermath

The year 1770 not only marked a change in the acceleration of John Hancock's adherence to the cause of revolution, but also forwarded the momentum of the whole Massachusetts Bay Colony toward rebellion. 1770 was the year of the so-called Boston Massacre. A review of what occurred in 1770 will help us to understand the migration of both Hancock and Massachusetts toward the Revolutionary War. Without examining the details of the events of 1770, it is impossible to understand (a) the personalized viewpoint Hancock took toward the revolution and (b) his commemorative speech of 1774.

Why did the events of the Boston Massacre on the night of 5 Mar 1770 loom so threateningly to the colonists? First, Boston had been forced to house British troops. The quartered troops had *not* been sent to protect the colonists from the French and Indians, but to suppress freedom of action in Massachusetts. The events surrounding the Stamp Act had convinced the British government that the citizens of Boston were seditious. The colonists, however, felt that they should have a major role in establishing their own destiny, and they resented George III trying to tell them what their obligations were and labeling them as unruly subjects. The colonists felt it was their privilege to stand up for their English rights, and that the king and his advisors should have recognized that privilege.

Second, the makeup of the troops themselves presented a problem. Some of the English officers were possibly second or third sons of the nobility, who felt that their career lay in the military, while others were of a variety of middle-class and upper-middle-class origins. Then there were the lower-ranked "men," including mercenaries who were willing to serve anywhere for pay. The higher ranks of the officers were generally encountered socially only by the upper crust of society. The lower-ranking officers and the soldiers were those who were seen daily. The appearance of foreign uniforms in a civilian population has always been a signal for trouble anywhere, and Boston was to be no exception.

Therefore it was bad enough to suffer supervision, more likely than not, by a less than acceptable class of men, but to have to relinquish the public resources in Boston in order to house those objectionable troops added an old insult to the old injury. As was stated earlier, before they were moved to their 1768 winter quarters, the troops were set up on the Boston Common, right in front of Hancock's house. What had been a peaceful stretch of green became a muddy encampment with tents and latrines. A whole series of minor disagreements had caused friction between the citizenry and the troops. Boston was waiting for a signal to show its displeasure. The events of the night of 5 Mar 1770 served as that signal.[1]

It is an easy matter so many years later to lay the blame for the massacre on either side. But the event was of more significance than *who fired first and at whom*. The people of Boston, albeit some of them were ruffians, felt Boston was their ground. Not only were there British military forces in Boston but the king's naval ships were there as well. The frigate *Romney* was in the harbour. Undoubtedly its personnel were given occasional shore leave. It is surprising that it took approximately a year and a half for a serious incident to occur. The British Army and Navy detachments were hostile troops. No matter who provoked the events of 5 Mar 1770, strong consideration has to be given to the grievances of the colonists as citizens of a town occupied by a hostile army. When the awaited-for event did arise, it was precipitated by an incident which, if properly handled, would now have been forgot.

Zobel detailed the incidents of the Boston Massacre and pointed to the evidence indicating that there were other groups of Bostonians in the streets that night. Therefore the incident in front of the Customs House may have been a part of a greater unrest. It is not appropriate here to repeat all of the details that Zobel so painstakingly related. Furthermore, there are many versions and variations on what occurred.

A general summary of the Massacre together with individualized points of view will be related below.[2]

There are a number of ways to approach the events of 5 Mar 1770. The following summary and the subsequent individualized accounts that give the facts from particular points of view should be sufficient to put Hancock's speech of 5 Mar 1774 in its proper perspective.

General Summary of the Accounts of the Massacre

There had of course been earlier scuffles between the British Army and the Boston waterfront element of longshoremen in the months before the massacre, but these had been hushed up. However, at eight o'clock at night on the snowy evening of 5 Mar 1770, Edward Garrick or Gerrish, an apprentice to a wigmaker, spotted one Captain Goldfinch and taunted him for being in debt to the urchin's master. (Wroth and Zobel, 2, 50; Zobel, 185) Soldiers of all ranks often incur debts, and it is not unusual for the street element to harrass them about "paying up." Goldfinch "had the receipt in his pocket" so he passed on by. (Zobel, 185) The incident could have ended there. But, Garrick and a companion, after escorting two girls to their home in the customs house, and after wandering around town for a while, returned to the Customs House to renew their harrassment of a sentry named White who was on guard there. When White could bear the taunts no more, he struck Garrick with his musket. The urchin undoubtedly protested as loudly as he could. A crowd collected. Snow balls were thrown. Church bells began to ring, possibly because of a confused response to the taunts of the assembling crowd daring the soldiers to "fire." Later court testimony showed that some who heard the cries of "fire" thought that the town was ablaze; others thought "fire" came from the crowd, meaning that the mob was daring the sentry to fire.

Soon the life of the lone sentry before the Customs House was endangered. Armies have a traditional manner, if circumstances warrant, of "calling for the guard." The guard was called. Captain Preston arrived with a corporal and six privates. The scuffle intensified, evidently involving physical contact between the civilians and the troops. The crowd pressed in. There was a first shot. After an interval of from six seconds to two minutes (Zobel, 198) a series of shots came from the British troops. Five Bostonians were either killed outright or died shortly thereafter. Others were wounded.

The church bells continued to ring. To maintain order, British troops were stationed at vantage points close to the disorders. Alarmed by the church bells, John Adams (Adams, 2, 229) had rushed into the street, thinking a fire had broken out. In an effort to return home, Adams walked down Boylston Alley into Brattle Square where he found soldiers drawn up with fixed bayonets in front of the Old South Church, presumably to prevent the church from being used as a meeting place by the colonists to arouse further anger against the British. Adams had to proceed along a narrow pathway left by the soldiers for passersby. Neither he nor the soldiers took any notice of each other. Lieutenant Governor Hutchinson wrote to General Gage on 6 Mar 1770 that "I went immediately abroad, and met a vast crowd of People running for their arms and prevailed on them to turn back and follow me to King street, promising them justice should be done."[3] (PRO, a) Captain Preston and the soldiers were arrested that night and confined to the jail. The next day Hancock headed a committee demanding that Hutchinson remove all troops from Boston. On 12 March 1770, Hutchinson wrote to Lord Hillsborough:

> I summoned all the Members of the Council who were near enough to meet the next morning. When I came to them I found the Select Men of the Town and [a] great part of the Justices of the Court waiting for me at the Council Chamber to represent to me their opinion of the absolute necessity, in order to prevent a further effusion of Blood, that the troops should be at such distance as that there might be no intercourse between the inhabitants and them. (PRO, b; MA, c)[4]

Hutchinson proposed that he had no right to order the troops to be removed because he was a civilian. Colonel Dalrymple, who commanded the troops, was initially against removing the soldiers, but on 10 Mar 1770 acquiesced in moving the 29th Regiment to the Castle. (Hutchinson, 3, 197; PRO, b) On 11 Mar 1770 the 14th Regiment was also removed to the castle.[5] The New York *Public Advertiser* reported that, at their first meeting with the governor, the Council advised Hutchinson to remove the troops and that "the Counsellors then separately informed the Lieutenant Governor of the absolute Necessity of the Removal of the Troops, adding that to their Knowledge there were upwards of 4000 Men ready to take Arms on a Refusal, and many of them Men of the first Property, Character and Distinction in the Province." (New York *Public Advertiser*, 28 Apr 1770, 3) The Council was certainly referring to Hancock among those "men of distinction."[6] Although it was Thomas Cushing who served as moderator of the committee that called upon the governor, Hancock was the second person listed in the minutes of that meeting (RRC) and undoubtedly played an important part in the negotiations concerning the status of the troops.

Unofficial Accounts Printed with Dispatch to Serve as Propaganda

Soon after the incident, both the Americans and the British issued pamphlets *together with depositions*, giving their points of view.

The American version (*A Short Narrative*), drafted by Bowdoin, Warren, and Samuel Pemberton and ordered printed at a town meeting on 19 Mar 1773, was largely aimed at a British audience and contained the somewhat fictitious engraving of Paul Revere, an etching that must have been produced in some hurry and may not have been the work of Revere.[7]

The British interpretation (*Fair Account*) was also issued in 1770. However, both of these versions were too hastily assembled and too much designed as propaganda to be reliable. They are valuable in that they preserved the depositions of a number of persons who were not called at the trials.

Captain Preston's Point of View

Other accounts are similarly biased. Captain Thomas Preston's version, written in the first person, a copy of which is in the House of Lords Record Office (HLRO, a) and which was published in the London *Public Advertiser* for Saturday, 28 Apr 1770, is a lengthy statement composed while Preston was in jail. Preston must have written it immediately after his confinement for it to have arrived in London and been printed between 5 Mar 1770 and 28 April 1770. It was sent not only to England but also to General Gage. (Adams, R.G., a) Gage acknowledged receiving a copy of Preston's account, stating that Preston's version was "but such a one as I can't get Printed here [in New York]; because it appears too plainly to be wrote by himself." (Michigan, a) London's *Public Advertiser* headed Preston's account as attached to "a letter from Boston" and entitled it the "CASE of Capt. Thomas Preston of the 29th Regiment."

Preston stated his version of the critical incident of the firing: "...one of the Soldiers having received a severe blow with a Stick, stept a little on one side and instantly fired, on which turning and asking him why he fired without orders, I was struck with a Club on my Arm which for some time deprived me of the use of it; which blow had it been placed on my head, most probably would have destroyed me." (HLRO, b)

Preston's statement included the observation that "the whole of this melancholy Affair was transacted in almost 20 minutes."[8]

Preston's Short Statement to the Press

Preston also released a short statement that appeared in the Boston *Gazette* of 12 Mar 1770, consisting of only one paragraph. It complimented the people of Boston, saying that Preston "shall ever have the highest sense of the Justice they have done me." Gage had his doubts about the efficacy of Preston's letter. (Michigan, a) When a committee of Boston townspeople including Hancock called upon Preston in jail, he told them that his account appearing in the London *Public Advertiser* had been edited by his friends, but he would not tell what parts were rewritten. (NYP)

Dalrymple's Account

There are several other contemporary accounts of the trial. Statements are included in the Gage correspondence, in letters between Dalyrmple and Gage, and between Hutchinson and Gage. Furthermore, Dalrymple as commander of the troops prepared a "narrative" of the events which he sent, along with Preston's account, to Hillsborough, Barrington, General Harvey, and "private friends." (Adams, R.G., 288-289; 308) Gage approved of Dalrymple sending it to England: "You undoubtedly did very right in sending Accounts home of Captain Preston's Case." (Michigan, a) On 23 April 1770, Dalyrmple sent his "narrative" to Gage. In acknowledging receipt of it on 30 April 1770 (Adams, R.G., b) Gage thanked Dalrymple for the narrative and said that he had transmitted "the Substance of it" in part back home. (Michigan, b)

That "substance" is apparently the narrative attached to Gage's letter to Lord Barrington of 24 Apr 1770. The moment of attack is described by Gage as follows:

> This Party [the soldiers & Preston] as well as the Centinel [sic] was immediately Attacked, some throwing Bricks, Stones, Pieces of Ice, and Snow Balls at them whilst others advanced up to their Bayonets, and endeavored to close with them, to use their Bludgeons and Clubs, calling out to them to fire if they dared, and provoking them to it, by the most Opprobrious Language. Captain Preston stood between the Soldiers and the Mob, parlying with the latter, and using every

conciliating Method to perswade [sic] them to retire peaceably. Some amongst them asked if he intended to order the Men to fire, he replyed [sic] by no means, and observed he stood between the Troops and them. All he could say had no Effect, and one of the Soldiers receiving a Violent blow, instantly fired. Captain Preston turned around to see who fired, and received a blow upon his Arm, which was aimed at his Head; and the Mob at first seeing no Execution done, and imagining the Soldier had only fired Powder to fright, grew more bold, and attacked with greater Violence, continually striking at the Soldiers and pelting them, and calling out to them to fire. The Soldiers at length perceiving their Lives in Danger, and hearing the Word fire all round them, three or four of them fired one after the other, and again three more in the same hurry and Confusion Four or Five Persons were unfortuntely killed, and more Wounded. Captain Preston and the Party were soon afterwards delivered into the hands of the Magistrates, who committed them to Prison.[9]

Hutchinson's Reaction

Hutchinson could not help but be profoundly disturbed by the unrest in Boston. He managed his way through the incident, but without much credit to himself. He wrote a fury of letters to a number of his correspondents. For example, in March of 1770, he wrote to Pownall: "I think I could support myself well enough at first but the spirit of Anarchy which prevails in Boston is more than I am able to cope with. I know a person of superior weight and rank will be soon appointed. He will be more regarded but he must have Powers given him beyond what his predecessors have had or it will not be politic for him to restore government in the Province." (MA, b) On 12 Mar 1770 Hutchinson wrote to Bernard an account of the events, concluding with his often pessimistic outlook:

> This Crisis might have been kept off some months if it had not been for this fatal stroke from the Inhabit.s, but the leaders of the people would never have been rest [sic] until they had effected their design unless they had found that the force was greater than they could hope to Conquer. (Ma, c)

Ramifications of the Massacre

Now that the facts of the massacre have been summarized, what effect did it have on Boston and on Hancock in particular?

Of course those who wanted Preston and the soldiers convicted wished to proceed with the trial as soon as possible, to secure a conviction while feelings were high. Adams and Hancock were among those actively petitioning the court to pursue the trial with dispatch. Governor Hutchinson, General Gage and others sought delay. (Wroth and Zobel, 3, 3-4) In his report to the Privy Council of January 1774, Bernard wrote: "Since the Event every endeavour has been excited by the People of Boston to accelerate the Trial of Captn Preston and the Soldiers who surrendered themselves up to Justice....It must however be observed that the firmness of the Lieutenant Governor, in negating.... the Election of Persons who have been most forward in opposition to the Authority of the Parliament, has in some degree checked the dangerous spirit which prevailed."[10]

Level heads prevailed. John Adams joined the attorneys for the crown. The cases began on 24 Oct 1770 with *Rex v. Preston*.

Unfortunately, the crowded courtroom and the ineptitude of the shorthand reporter made it difficult to record a transcript of Preston's trial. (Adams R.G., c) Wroth and Zobel found that no transcript of Preston's trial exists. (Wroth and Zobel, 3, 20) However, Wroth and Zobel (3, 34-35) reconstructed the proceedings based upon seven sources, the most helpful of which were John Adam's notes; the notes of Robert Treat Paine; and the version of the trial that Hutchinson sent to Hillsborough, the original of which is in the Public Record Office. (PRO, d)

In their reconstruction of *Rex v. Preston*, Wroth and Zobel included no statement by Preston in his own defense, because there was none. The law of the eighteenth century did not consider reliable the testimony of the accused. So Preston had to sit in the dock and hear others tell his story.

There was published a verbatim account of the trial of the soldiers (*Trial*). It is largely of interest to show the development of the conflict of interest between Captain Preston and the soldiers. If Preston had not given the order to fire, the soldiers were guilty; if Preston had given the order to fire, Preston was guilty and the soldiers were innocent.

In their prefacing remarks to discussing the Boston Massacre cases, Wroth and Zobel remarked that Hutchinson and even General Gage in New York concluded that Preston's only legal defense was establishing that he took action only because he was fearful of being attacked and therefore acted in self-defense. (Wroth and Zobel, 3, 2-3) But attacked by whom? The whole town of Boston? That, said Wroth and Zobel, was a difficult defense to establish. (Wroth and Zobel, 2) Hutchinson testified that he said to Preston: "How came you to fire without Orders from a Civil Magistrate?" (PRO, e) Gage wrote to Hutchinson: "...if it shall Appear that the Soldiers have fired Wantonly without legal orders...the Laws must no doubt have their due course. But if it shall appear that they were dangerously attacked, and obliged to defend themselves, and fired only in self Defence [sic] to preserve their own Lives; I trust you will do every thing in your Power, to prevent their falling a Sacrifice to the Resentment of Faction, against all principles of Justice, and by the pervertion [sic] of the Laws of their Country." (Michigan, c)

The Reaction of Boston

Boston determined to make the most of the incident to stress its displeasure with the British occupation. A glorious funeral was held for each of the dead. Although all four bodies were buried in one grave in the Granary Burying ground, each body with its relations formed a separate entry in the funeral procession. (Tudor, 33; Cunningham, 199) On 8 May 1770, Rowe estimated the crowd at the funeral as "Ten or Twelve thousand" (Cunningham, 199) and said "Such a Concourse of People I never saw before." (Cunningham, 199) It can be presumed that Hancock was conspicuous at the funerals. On 17 Mar 1770, the last funeral procession buried Patrick Carr, who had lingered on. Excitement reached a peak.

The very day of the massacre, news had been received that all of the Townshend duties except the tax on tea were lifted. That tax was to continue to show that the British had the right to levy duties if they wished. A town meeting was held. Two committees, both of which Hancock was a member, called upon Hutchinson, insisting that the troops be removed. Finally the lieutenant governor agreed to make the request. The manner in which it was carried out was discussed earlier.

The aftermath of the legal proceedings demonstrated how minor the incident could had been. John Adams, who as an attorney was almost obliged, when requested, to undertake the defense of the soldiers, agreed, with reluctance, to defend them. Adams (2, 230) suspected that the incident had been intentionally provoked by the colonists. In his diary, Adams (2, 231) spoke of the criticism he received for taking the case, but later, in 1733, he wrote that his undertaking the defense of Captain Preston and the soldiers "was...one of the most gallant, generous, manly, and disinterested actions of my whole life, and one of the best pieces of service I ever rendered my country." (Adams, 2, 317)

The trial concluded with a conviction of manslaughter for Killroy and Montgomery, with verdicts of not guilty for Preston and the other five soldiers.[11] The two guilty pleaded "benefit of clergy," an ancient plea which in its origins permitted the church to protect church personnel from secular courts and which afterward became a privilege of persons who could read to be exempt from capital punishment. At a later date, Killroy and Montgomery were released after being branded in open court.

The so-called Boston Massacre was to remain a rallying point for the colonists until the revolution began. Its yearly commemoration kept the spirit of defiance alive. In 1774, Hancock delivered the memorial address. The headnote to that speech provides further information on the massacre.

Preston wrote to Gage on 31 Oct 1770 that he was most pleased with the not-guilty verdict and asked permission to return to England. (Adams, R.G., d)[12] Preston had paid for him the expenses of his trial, amounting to £264/7, and received a pension of £200 a year. (Adams, R.G., e) Barrington found Preston very satisfied with the outcome of the events, and Gage wrote to Barrington on 6 May 1771 that Preston was "nobly recompensed for his past Sufferings, and I am exceedingly Glad that he is made so happy; for I am certain he has too much Gratitude ever to forget the Services your Lordship [Barrington] and other Friends have rendered him in his Distress." (Carter, 2, 575)

Hancock's Reaction to the Massacre

What was Hancock's attitude toward the Boston Massacre? Two incidents occurred that indicate it caused him to gain sympathy with the separatists led by Sam Adams. First, in the fall of 1770, Hancock and the two Adams were appointed to a committeee of five to develop intercolonial liaison.

Second, Hancock was named by the General Court to the Governor's Council. Hutchinson, like his predecessor Bernard refused to seat Hancock. Hutchinson, who in comparison to Bernard, was a skillful governor, arranged for a conciliatory meeting in which Hancock was to be seated on the Council in return for certain concessions on John's part. Hancock was not to be bought off with favors. Hancock was not seated. Nor would Hutchinson permit Hancock to become the speaker of the General Court.

Hancock had up to this point retained a tendency toward conservatism. He had somewhat fallen out with the separatists. But the events of 1770 appear to have cast the die. From that year on, he was seldom if ever to look back.

NOTES

1. When, in 1887, the General Court of Massachusetts voted to erect a monument to the victims of the Boston Massacre, Randolph Adams called attention to a meeting of the Massachusetts Historical Society in May of 1887 in which John H. Washburn "expressed a feeling long harbored by the informed men of Massachusetts, that those who died in the Boston massacre were the victims of their own folly," and that the legislature was obviously more influenced by "the cheaper politicians than by educated men." (Adams, R.G., 262) The result was a resolution by the society deprecating the erection of the monument.

2. For other details and contrasting points of view, see the following: Zobel; HLRO, a; Adams, *New Light*; Wroth and Zobel; Michigan, d; New York *Public Advertiser*, Saturday, 22 Apr 1770, 3-4, based upon a letter entitled "The following is a Substance of a Letter from Boston, dated the 12th March, relative to the unhappy Affair between the Townsmen and the Soldiers, on the 5th of That March."

3. See also MA, a; PRO b in which Hutchinson wrote to Hillsborough: "I went out without delay in order to go to the Council Chamber...but I was soon surrounded by a great body of men, many of them armed with clubs and some few with Cutlasses and all calling for the firearms. I discovered myself to them, and endeavoured to prevail on them to hear me but was obliged for my own safety to go into a house and from thence by a private way into King Street, the people having returned there expected me. After assuring them that a due inquiry should be made and Justice done as far as was in my power and prevailing with the Commanding Officer of the Town in the street to retire with them to their Barracks, the people dispersed." MA,

4. There is a similar earlier quotation in Hutchinson to Gage, 6 Mar 1770: "I ordered a Council to be summoned to meet today at 11 oClock. When I came to them I found the Select men and the Justices waiting for me to represent that the Inhabitants had insisted upon a Town Meeting and that it would not be in their power to keep them under Restraint, if the Troops were not removed to the Barracks at the Castle." (PRO, a; MA. a)

5. Hutchinson had to wait until 6 July 1770 to get an official reaction to his decision to intervene in military matters by sending both regiments to Castle William. The move worried him, because, although he was, as acting governor, in charge of all installations, he hesitated to take command of troops. Furthermore, the provisions on the island were the property of the

colonists, not of the king. Hutchinson feared unrest if the Bostonians felt that their property was being appropriated by the crown. What eventually resulted appears to be as follows:

a. The company on Castle William that was "in the pay of the province" was withdrawn. Their duties were to be assumed by the king's troops. Some of these colonials had been on the island for over 30 years, and their removal was grievous to Hutchinson. (PRO, f)

b. Hutchinson was to turn over all control of Castle William to an officer designed by Gage. Gage stipulated Colonel Dalrymple. The move undoubtedly was to dispose of troops financed by the colonists and replace them with troops paid for by the king.

c. The 14th King's Regiment was to remain on Castle William. Gage was to put the island into a satisfactory state of repairs, including the possibility of housing a second regiment. It was left to his discretion whether a second regiment should be dispatched permanently to the island. Gage determined that the island would be too crowded to be defended by such a concentration of troops. A shelling of the island could result in many casualties. The 29th Regiment was eventually transferred to St. Augustine.

d. Gage had sent from Halifax a small contingent of specialists to bolster the defenses of Castle William.

See the following MSS:

MHS: Massachusetts Papers, 1769-1777 [orig], #23, 10 Sept 1770, Hutchinson to Captain John Phillips, stating that Hutchinson had received a letter on 6 July 1770 from Hillsborough saying that it was the King's pleasure to withdraw one of the companies at Castle William;

PRO, b; PRO, g;

Hutchinson, *History of Massachusetts Bay*, 3, 221-224;

Carter, Gage to Hillsborough, 8 Sept 1770, 1, 267-268; Hillsborough to Gage, 6 July 1770, 2, 106-107; Hillsborough to Gage, 12 July 1770, 2, 103-105.

6. "In the present case every member of the Council [,] the Justices of Peace of Boston & divers of other Towns [,] every Select Man of Boston [,]... all the Representatives of the Town who were in Town, the Colonel of the Boston Regiment besides Other officers and principal inhabitants of the Town, and then the Town in a body, when two or three thousand were present [,] made their application to me to affect the Removal of the Troops..." (MA, a)

7. See also MHS, Massachusetts Papers, 1769-1777, [orig] 23 Mar 1770, #35. Bowdoin, Warren, and Pemberton wrote to London that they were enclosing their narrative and complained about the depositions that

were appearing in London that were taken without notifying the selectmen of the town.

MHS, Mass Papers [orig] 1768-1777, #115, 13 July 1770, letter from Sam Adams, Cushing, Hancock, Phillips, Molineux, and others to Benjamin Franklin complaining that Parliament had been willing to conceal the names of those who wrote depositions, presumably those that appeared in the English version published in London.

MHS, Mass Papers [true copy], 1769-1777, #45, 4 Mar 1770, "In Council." It was charged that Andrew Oliver had, as a member of the Council, secretly taken minutes of the Council meetings and sent them to London, where they were printed. Oliver was proclaimed "guilty of a Breach of Trust."

MHS, Mass Papers [true copy], 1768-1770, #122, 5 Oct 1770, Oliver replied to the Council that the meeting that he had reported had been quasi-public and asked leave to submit a rebuttal of the charge placed against him.

A letter of 29 Nov 1770 from Henry Pelham to Revere accused Paul Revere of plagiarism in the famous Paul Revere engraving of the Massacre. See Louise Phelps Kellogg, "The Paul Revere Print of the Boston Massacre," *Wisconsin Magazine of History*, 1, no. 1,377-387.

8. Unfortunately the original copy of this narrative is not on file in the Gage Collection at the University of Michigan. Preston's letter to Gage, dated 19 Mar 1770, in which Preston wrote, "I herewith inclose" a statement concerning what happened to him (Adams, R.G., a) forms a part of the Gage papers housed at Ann Arbor. But the University of Michigan library has no enclosure, or any indication that it ever had one. Either Gage destroyed the narrative or removed it and sent it to England, or it became otherwise separated. That Gage did not wish Preston's narrative released gives credence to the probability that he destroyed it himself. Preston probably wanted his story told, so he may have sent a copy of his statement not only to his English friends, but also to the English newspapers. Languishing in jail, Preston had little else to do except seek to try his case through the press.

9. Michigan, d; Carter, 2, 536-7. The statement below is Preston's account, which served as an addendum to Dalrymple's own version of the events. As an eyewitness, Preston is much more graphic than either Gage's account or Dalrymple's account. "The mob still increased and were more outrageous, striking their club or bludgeons one against another and calling out, Come on you rascals, you bloody backs, you lobster scoundrels, fire if you dare, G——d damn you, fire and be damn'd, we know you dare not, and much more such language as used. At this time I was between the soldiers and the mob parleying with...them to retire peaceable but to no purpose. They advanced to the point of the bayonets, struck some of them and even

the muzzles of the pieces....On which some well-behaved persons asked me if the guns were charged. I replied, Yes, they then asked me if I intended to order the men to fire. I answered, No by no means, observing to them that I was advanced before the muzzles of the mens' pieces and must fall a sacrifice if they fired... While I was thus speaking one of the soldiers having received a severe blow with a stick, stepped a little on one side and instantly fired, on which turning to and asking him why he fired without orders, I was struck with a club on my arm which for some time deprived me of the use of it....On this a general attack was made on the men by a great number of heavy clubs and snowballs being thrown at them, by which all our lives were in imminent danger, some persons at the same time from behind calling out, Damn your bloods, why don't you fire. Instantly three or four of the soldiers fired, one after another, and directly after three more in the same confusion and hurry." (PRO, c)

10. "State of the Disorders, Confusion, & Mis-government which have prevailed & do still continue to prevail in His Majesty's Province of Massachusets [sic] Bay in America," Houghton Library, Bernard Papers, 8, 226-227.

11. Wroth and Zobel (3, 50-314) reproduced a reconstruction of the cases of *Rex v. Preston* and *Rex. v. Wemms*, detailing only the Wemms trial as representative of the trials of the soldiers. The reconstructions give suffucient details of the massacre to demonstrate the skills of John Adams as an attorney.

12. Adams, R.G., d. Preston arrived in London on 1 Feb 1771, New Light, e.

5

The Developments of 1770-1773

The Repeal of the Townshend Acts and the Defection of the Merchants: 1770-1772

The repeal of most of the duties levied by the Townshend Acts in 1770 mollified the colonists, so that the years 1771 and 1772 were comparatively quiet. Normal importation of English goods was resumed. When only the tax on tea remained, the merchants could not continue the general policy of nonimportation. Newport, Rhode Island, had continued to import goods throughout the period. Georgia was also charged with continuing importation. Then New York broke the ban. Finally, when all of the colonies resumed trade, the Boston merchants acceded on 11 Oct 1770. (Barnes, 2, 504)

After 1770, when merchants saw the possibility not only of economic but also of political revolt, most of them drifted toward the Tory position. They had been shocked by the possibilities of lawlessness and were ready to sympathize with the government once that tax had been lifted. Schlesinger (308) reasoned that in the aftermath of the Coercive Acts of 1774 "the merchants found themselves instinctively siding with the home government," i.e., Great Britain. Merchants were opposed to mob rule, Schlesinger reasoned, and, although they might back measures opposed to economic restraints, they did not wish to support the "uncertain prospects that the radical plans held forth." (Schlesinger, 308) Schlesinger concluded that "from the time of the passage of the coercive acts...there became evident a strong drift on the part of the colonial mercantile class to the British viewpoint." (Schlesinger, 309) The merchants realized, said

Schlesinger, that their economic well-being rested with the protection
of the British Navy and the commerce involved in having close ties
with such a prominent mercantile power.

But Schlesinger also pointed out that "the coercive acts were equally
important in making converts to the radical position." (Schlesinger,
309) Hancock was among the converts. Baxter observed that "John
was one of the very few rich traders to move leftward into the radical
camp." (Baxter, 283) But he was not alone. There were other
businessmen in Massachusetts and in the several colonies who backed
the revolt. Main (94) noted that Massachusetts choose its first
governor not from its lawyers, but from its businessmen. Button
Gwinnett of Georgia, Jonathan Trumbull of Connecticut, Mesech
Weare of New Hampshire, Thomas Wharton of Pennsylvania, and
Nicholas Cooke of Rhode Island all derived their wealth from trade.

Yet, to many colonial businessmen, from the beginning, money was
money. Political freedoms were to be derived from England, not from
home rule. Some of those to whom tea had been consigned were rigid
Tories and had attempted to break the embargo from the beginning.
Before there was a tacit agreement to lift the self-imposed embargo, on
30 Jan 1770 there were complaints that Thomas and Elisha Hutchinson,
sons of the lieutenant governor, clandestinely removed some of their tea
where it had been stored under the stipulations of the embargo
agreement. There was a late meeting at which the charges against
Hutchinson's sons were discussed.[1]

As a merchant who would have profited financially from the removal
of the embargo, what kept Hancock allied with the radicals? Although
Hancock's finances between 1770 and 1772 undoubtedly profited from
the improvement in business, he was probably by no means convinced
that the crown contemplated permanent change. But even Sam Adams
might not have been able to keep the revolutionary spirit going if the
British had not provided Adams with more fuel. The commemorations
of the Boston Massacre, featuring in 1771 a speech by James Lovell
and in 1772 a speech by Dr. Joseph Warren, were helpful in
maintaining the revolutionary spirit. But in themselves they could not
maintained the spirit of revolt. The inept British were to provide Sam
Adams with the impetus that he so much needed.

Hutchinson's Relations with Hancock

In 1772, Governor Hutchinson, a Bostonian by birth and a graduate
of Harvard, who had served as a member of the assembly and on the

Governor's Council, had officially replaced the departed Governor Bernard. Although of local extraction, Hutchinson was a strong advocate of what was called "the Prerogative," i.e., the right of the British to tax the colonists. However, he wished to smooth matters over. Subsequent events were to prove his efforts fruitless.

In a series of moves, Hutchinson tried to win John Hancock away from the "rebels." It undoubtedly puzzled him that a man of property would side against the king.

In 1771, Hutchinson wrote: "I was much pressed by many persons well affected in general to consent to the Election [to the Council] of Mr. Hancock his connection being large, which are strongly prejudicial against me for the frequent refusal to accept him in Office. They assured me he wished to be separated from Mr. Adams...and, if I would admit him to the Council, they had no doubt there would be an end to the Influence he now has by means of his property." At this point, however, Hutchinson was waiting for Hancock to make the advances. "As there had been no advances on his part," wrote Hutchinson, "I could not think it proper for me to follow their advice." (MA, a) Hutchinson expected that, by the time another election was held, Hancock would have so altered his conduct to make it easier to appoint him to the Council.

The following year Hutchinson had higher hopes. On 24 Jan 1772, Hutchinson wrote to Hillsborough: "Mr. Hancock I have reason to think is upon such terms with his Colleagues...that they will not easily be reconciled. When divided we may hope they will be less capable of mischief." (MA, f)

On 29 Jan 1772 Hutchinson wrote to Bernard: "Hancock has not been with their club for two months past & seems to have a new set of acquaintances. By means of [illegible name], there have been some overtures. I remember what passed between him & you & therefore shall act with *greater* caution. His coming over will be a great loss to them as they support themselves with his money." (MA, b) So the following overtures were made.

First, knowing the susceptibility of Hancock to being appointed to positions of authority, Hutchinson promoted Hancock from lieutenant major which John had received in 1768 to captain colonel on 1 May 1772. (BU) The raise in rank put Hancock in charge of the First Corps of Cadets, a largely ceremonial body that appeared at state functions and could be called upon to preserve order.

Second, also in April of 1772, Hutchinson approved Hancock as speaker of the House of Representatives.

Third, at some point in this period, Hancock and Hutchinson appear to have had direct talks. In a letter of 15 June 1772, Hutchinson spoke of a meeting in which the speaker, Mr. Hancock, came to him to ask under what conditions Hutchinson would allow the General Court to return to Boston. It could have been that, at this meeting, the two discussed other matters as well, for, after hearing Hutchinson's requirements, they said they would comply with Hutchinson's stipulations "if Mr Adams did not prevent it, against whose art and insidiousness I cautioned them." (MA, c) In his *History of Massachusetts Bay*, Hutchinson stated that Hancock "expressed his dissatisfaction with the party, and with their extending their designs further than appeared to him warrantable." (Hutchinson, *History*, 3, 249) The governor responded that previous refusals to appoint Hancock to public offices did not stem from any personal animosity and that "upon a change of sentiments in Mr. Hancock, every thing past would be entirely forgotten, and it would be a pleasure to the governor to consent to his election to the counseil, where he could more easily take such share in publick affairs as he thought fit, than he could do in the house..." (Hutchinson, *History*, 3, 249) Hancock supposedly responded that his intent was rather to return to private business than to assume new public responsibilities. The British were not to conclude that Hancock's cooperation was for sale.

A fourth move was made by the British in May of 1772. Hutchinson also approved Hancock's nomination by the General Court to the Governor's Council. But, to the governor's surprise, Hancock declined to sit. (MA, d)

The government put as good a face on Hancock's refusal as it could. On 15 June 1772, Hutchinson wrote to Pownall: "You see I accepted Hancock, who has for many months gone as far with the party as has been necessary to prevent a total breach and no farther, and his refusal to accept was not from any resentment for former negatives but from an apprehension that he should show to the people he had not been seeking after it. The measure will have good consequences and end in wholly detaching him from them or lessening his importance if he should put himself into their hands again." (MA, e) On 8 May 1772, Lieutenant Governor Oliver wrote to James Gambier, resident commissioner of the navy at Portsmouth and later a Vice-Admiral: "[Adams] is no longer supported by Mr. Hancock, who appears inclined to be very civil to the Governor. He has taken a Commission from him to command the Comp'y of Cadets with the rank of Colonel." (BM, Additional MSS 39373, 63) Oliver also pointed out that Adams had not achieved as many votes in the last election for Selectman as he had before and that "the Press begins to recover its genuine freedom."

Whatever miff between Adams and Hancock may have occurred was soon smoothed over. Hancock commissioned Copely to paint portaits of Adams and himself.[2] The alliance of the radical Adams and the former conservative Hancock had not been broken.

In that same year of 1772, Hancock further endeared himself to Boston by making donations to the town—a bandstand, a fire engine, a fence and walks for the park, and money for the Brattle Street Church.

In 1772 committees of correspondence were also set up with towns in Massachusetts. The first minutes of the Masssachusetts Committee were recorded on 2 Nov 1772, with the appointment of a committee that included Adams, Warren, Church, Mollineux, and fifteen others. (NYP) Other colonies followed suit, establishing a network of communication within each colony and among the colonies.

On 9 June 1772, a British ship, the *Gaspee*, ran ashore near Providence, Rhode Island It was much hated because of its attempts to prevent the colonists from smuggling goods. A mob burned the *Gaspee*. When the British threatened to send the perpetrators to England for trial, Sam Adams gained more momentum for the revolutionary cause.

One of the disquieting moves by the British took the form of plans to pay the salaries of the governor, the lieutenant governor, and the highest colonial judges, from revenues from the Townshend Acts. In 1771 the colonists first heard of new policy toward the governors, and in 1772 of the move to pay the judges' salaries as well. The plan to change the method of paying the governor's salary was obviously aimed to allow the governor more independence. The colonies were not to get justice from their own laws, but from England. A town meeting was called for 27 Oct 1772. Pressure was put on the judges to refuse payment by the crown. Only the chief justice would not so agree. Details concerning this incident are found in the notes to Hancock's 1774 address.

1773, on the Eve of the Boston Tea Party

The year 1773 was to equal 1770 in accelerating the disaffection of Hancock with the crown.

In January of 1773, Governor Hutchinson convened the state assembly for the first time in six months to demonstrate "in as concise a manner as he could, that the colonies were settled as parts of the British dominions, and, consequently, as subject to the supreme legislative authority thereof." (Hutchinson, *History*, 3, 266; Bradford, 336-396) In his remarks, Hutchinson attributed "the cause of this disorder" to be the failure of the colonists to recognize the supremacy of the Parliament and the king. However, the answers of both the Council and the Massachusetts House of Representatives attributed the unrest in the colonies to the acts of Parliament and the House denied that the charters provided that the colonies should be within the realm of England. (Hutchinson, *History*, 3, 267-268)

On 5 Mar 1773, the third commemoration of the Boston Massacre featuring a speech by Dr. Benjamin Church went off quietly enough. On 8 May 1773, Hancock moderated the election of the town officers at Faneuil Hall. (Tudor, 42)

At this point, Hutchinson thought he saw another opportunity to divide Hancock from Adams. Again rumors were circulated that Hancock was forsaking the cause of liberty. Sam Adams said in a letter to Arthur Lee of 12 April 1773:

> "Mr. Wilkes," replied Adams, "was certainly misinformed when he was told that Mr. H. has deserted the cause of liberty. Great pains had been taken to have it thought to be so, and, by a scurvy trick of lying, the adversaries effected a coolness between that gentleman and some others who were zealous in that cause; but it was of short continuance, for their falsehood was soon detected. Lord Hillsborough, as I suppose, was soon informed of the imaginary conquest, for I have it...that he wrote to the Governor that he had it in command from the *highest authority* to enjoin him to promote Mr. H. upon every occasion." (NYP, Sam Adams Papers; Wells, 1, 470)[3]

Adams noted that Hutchinson had "promoted" Hancock by offering him a seat on the "Board," which as was pointed out earlier Hancock had refused. (Cunningham, 228; Wells, 1, 470) Adams concluded: "no one has discoursed [with] more firmness against the independency of the Go'r and the Judges than he." In May, Hutchinson saw his January maneuver of trying to separate Hancock and Adams come to naught when Hancock and Adams were again nominated for the assembly.

At the end of the month of May, Hutchinson had worse news. Benjamin Franklin had conveyed to the Sons of Liberty the correspondence that Hutchinson and Oliver had written to their English friend Whately in London between 1768 and 1769. (Hosmer, 429-438) Whoever put these letters in the hands of Franklin has never been clearly established. Hancock announced in the assembly on 31 May

1793 that in the near future an important disclosure would be made in the legislature. On 2 June 1793, Adams read the letters from the podium, and Hancock moved that those who had written such letters intended to overthrow the colonial government and replace it with arbitrary rule from England. The circulation of these letters among the colonies had the effect of showing that the British governors might be saying one thing while they were actively supporting an opposite point of view.

Nothing can illustrate better the posture of the more radical colonials than the fact that, on 4 June, in honor of the king's birthday, Hancock led his Independent Corps of Cadets on parade. Hancock's participation in the celebration of George III's anniversary may show an inconsistency on the part of Hancock. But it may also show that, after a rainy and cold spring, Boston was ready for an open air demonstration, and Hancock was not to deny himself a good parade, particularly when he could be one of the central attractions. Everyone turned out. The separatists did not wish to deny the populace the pleasures of the day, just as the parties not in power in England today do not boycott the Queen's official birthday. Furthermore, to absent themselves might make it appear that the colonists were afraid to participate. It seemed an excellent way of having your cake and eating it too. Hancock could say: "You see, I can make all these moves against the king, and he still cannot do anything but call on me to help celebrate his annniversary." The irony was perhaps too good to miss.

NOTES

1. "A few people who had agreed to store their goods untill [sic] a general importation might take place had lately violated their agreement, some by removing their goods, particularly Messrs. Thomas & Elisha Hutchinson, sons to the Lieut. Governor, who had imported a Considerable Quantity of Tea....late on Saturday night the 6th inst they found means to get into the Store where the Tea was lodged and in a Clandestine manner carried it off, with a declared intention of selling the same, & part of them...it was found were actually sold." MHS A committee composed of Cushing, Phillips, Hancock, Inches, Molineux, and six others had called upon the Hutchinsons to ask them to stop selling their tea. This report had been sent to London where it was received on 7 Mar 1770.

2. For a discussion of the disagreement between Adams and Hancock, see Wells, 1, 465-440. The portraits were painted to hang in John Hancock's drawing rooms. (Wells, 1, 475)

3. *Diary and Letters of Thomas Hutchinson,* ed. Peter O. Hutchinson (Boston, 1884), 1, 167: In a conversation between King George II, Lord Dartmouth, and Hutchinson on 1 July 1774, Hutchinson told the king: "Mr. Hancock, Sir, had a very large fortune left him by his uncle, and I believe his political engagements have taken off his attention from his private affairs. He was sensible not long ago of the damage it was to him, and told me he was determined to quit all publick business, but soon altered his mind."

6

The Boston Tea Party

Then the big event happened. Although all of the taxes levied under the Townshend Act had been repealed except the tax on tea, Dutch tea was being imported illicitly. The East India Company, whose storehouses, acccording to the Boston *Gazette* of 22 Nov 1773, were bulging with an estimated twelve million pounds of surplus rotting tea, wanted to sell their oversupply in Europe and the colonies. A simplification of the steps that led to the tea party are as follows:

a. Before the Tea Act, tea sent from China and India was warehoused in England, sold at public auction, and subject to the English "sales" tax of one shilling per pound.

b. Although the colonists were importing British tea that had its price raised by the one-shilling tax in England and by the three-penny Townshend tax assessed in the colonies,[1] much smuggled and therefore tax-free Dutch tea was making its way from colony to colony. The Townshend Act was admittedly political. The net gain to England after costs of the tea imported under the Townshend tax was only £400 per year. (Larabee, 71)

c. If both the English "sales" tax (or inland duty tax) and the Townshend tax were removed, the East India Company could more easily compete with the smuggled tea, and those who did not care to risk smuggling would go the path of least resistance and buy English tea.

d. Therefore, by the Tea Act of 10 May 1773, Parliament, Lord North, and the king were willing to allow the East India Company to ship tea directly from India to the colonies, without paying the larger English "sales" tax, but North stubbornly refused to withdraw the Townshend Tax, even though it brought in little revenue. The reason for his refusal was to show the colonists that their insolent behavior was not to be rewarded. The repeal of the Stamp Act had been enough.

e. Furthermore, the Tea Act provided that the East India Company could designate to whom the tea in the colonies would be consigned. Radical colonial merchants could be ignored, and the tea consigned to super-loyalists who would have something of a monopoly over the tea trade.

f. Such a situation subjected Boston to a series of threats:

(1) Boston had imported considerable tea under the Townshend Acts, paying the duty. Its reputation among the other colonies was suffering. If it were to accept further tea under the Tea Act, its leadership role in opposing the crown would be forfeited.

(2) If the colonies accepted the tea, they would accept the principle of taxation without representation. Once they accepted that principle officially, even though it had been accepted in single shipments after the collapse of the 1770 boycott, what other taxes would be levied? A repetition of the other Townshend Duties and the Stamp Act taxes could be the next step.

(3) If monopolies on sales of imported products could be granted under the Tea Act, what other import monopolies could be inaugurated? The giving of exclusive franchise to sell was a British custom that the colonists abhorred. It could not be allowed to make its way to America. Previously, all agents for the colonial merchants could bid at the British tea auctions. Now, only the consignees were to be allowed to sell the tea shipped directly from the East India Company.

(4) There was not much "hard money" in the colonies. Specie was short. If the tea taxes were to be paid in large proportions, it would be a drain on the colonies' specie. The Committee of Correspondence, in its circular letter released on 23 Nov 1773, estimated that the tax on tea would "drain the Colonies of one Million six hundred thousand dollars annually." (NYP)

Therefore, Boston elected to take a stand. Merchants, it is true, could continue to smuggle in tea from the Dutch East Indies, but whether Dutch tea could compete with the reduced-priced English tea was unknown. Furthermore, there were political principles involved. The time had come for the political-minded Adams, Hancock, and their colleagues to take a stand.

The hostile attitude of Massachusetts at this point is expressed in the records of the Council for 24 June 1773: "Resolved, That if his Majesty, in his great goodness, shall be pleased to remove his Excellency Thomas Hutchinson Esqr. and the honable [sic] Andrew Oliver Esqr. from the Office of Governor and Lieutenant Governor, it is the humble opinion of this Board that it will be promotive of his Majesty's service and the good of his loyal and affectionate people of this Province." (Minutes, 121) There was no effort on the part of the colonists to disguise their distaste for Governor Hutchinson and his family of subordinates.

The Moves of the East India Company to Import Tea

In August of 1773 the East India Company sought permission from the English Treasury under the Tea Act to export tea to America. Friends of the colonists alerted them of what was to come. Tea was to be sent to Charleston, Philadelphia, New York, and Boston. Consignees were designated by the East India Company.

Labaree pointed out that "unlike their counterparts elsewhere, the Boston consignees had long since become objects of local scorn." (Larabee, 105) One thing that galled the Bostonians was that Governor Hutchinson's two sons, Thomas and Elisha, were among the consignees, and son Thomas had married the daughter of another consignee, Richard Clarke. (Larabee, 104) Furthermore, Clarke's son-in-law was the painter, Copley, who had done portraits of both Adams and Hancock. As in all civil wars, families and friends had to part. Copley himself emigrated to England in 1774, where his work never achieved the significance that it had in the colonies.

It is difficult to develop a defense for Governor Hutchinson. Bailyn attempted to do so in his *The Ordeal of Thomas Hutchinson.* The fact remains that the governor persisted in allowing both of his sons to profit from what he knew would be a most unpopular issue in the colonies. As native colonists, the Hutchinsons should have used their common sense to conclude that the sons should renounce their part in the consignment. Politics and business should not have been mixed. But, to the Hutchinsons, profit was to be profit, and the king's right was to be the king's right. There is no record of any recognition on the part of the Hutchinsons that their acts, although legally supportable, were politically unwise.

The Events that Immediately Preceded the Boston Tea Party

The Boston *Gazette* provided an edited but chronological survey of the events that ended in the Boston Tea Party. Its reports, supplemented by eyewitness accounts, will serve as the structure for an account of the events of October, November, and December of 1773.

During the months prior to October of 1773 Boston had been preoccupied with the plans of the king to use royal funds to pay the salaries of the governor and the supreme court. But, on 18 Oct 1773, under the name of Praedicus, the colonials in the Boston *Gazette* reopened the issue of the tea. In a letter "To the Public," Praedicus said in part: "Nothing can be more evident than their [the East India Co's.] aim to get all the trade and property into their own power....Perhaps it is not yet too late to free ourselves from popes, devils and locusts. The fifth of November [Guy Fawkes Day] has been for two centuries celebrated in commemoration of such deliverance."[2]

By 21 Oct 1773 the Boston Committee of Correspondence had released a letter to its counterpart in other colonies alerting them to the dangers that lay ahead if the tea were to be landed. "We are far from desiring that the Connection between Britain & America should be broken: Esto perpetua is our ardent wish; but upon the Terms only of Equal Liberty....But it may be worth Consideration that the work is more likely to be well done, at a time when the Ideas of Liberty & its Importance are strong in man's mind." (NYP) The letter concluded with a warning of the prospects that awaited the colonies if the East India Company were to be permitted to ship goods directly to America. Did the committee feel that it was politically sound to profess that it sought only a redress of grievances and not independence, or was that the true sentiment of the committee? It was certainly not Adams' position and, by this point, it is unlikely that Hancock held out hope of a constructive solution. There were late overtures to the British to reach an agreement, so it is likely that many of the colonists wavered between the desire for indendence and the desire for a solution to their political and economic problems.

The circular letter of the Committee of Correspondence was followed in the 25 Oct 1773 issue of the Boston *Gazette* by a reprint of a handbill, circulated in Philadelphia, not dated and signed "Scaevola", attacking the landing of the tea.

That same day, the Boston *Evening Post* and the Boston *Newsletter* issued an anonymous defense of the tea shipment signed only "Z." Some have attributed the letter to Clarke. The writer proposed that the comments that had been appearing in the papers were "either founded on ignorance of the facts...or are intended to delude the people." (25 Oct 1773, 2) The article proposed to set the record straight.

The blunt answer to "Z" appearing under "Praedicus" in the Boston *Gazette* was addressed not to Clarke but to Governor Hutchinson and said: "You have neither cunning enough to lead nor strength to drive them; therefore at length be advised to quit dabbling in newspapers. Your speech betrayeth you, and denials but serve to draw your veracity into question." (1 Nov 1773, 2) The pointed opposition of the colonists is almost surprising. No holds were to be barred. The freedom of the press, an established tradition in England, was to be permitted in the colonies, even under these unusual circumstances.

The *Gazette* of Monday 8 Nov. 1773 reprinted the latest letter by the Pennsylvania Farmer. But more importantly, it detailed the events of 3 and 5 Nov 1773.

On Tues 2 Nov 1773, a message signed "O.C."[3] was sent to Thomas and Elisha Hutchinson demanding that they appear at the Liberty Tree on Wednesday next (3 Nov) and concluded with the words, "Fail not upon your Peril." (HLRO, b; Brown, 282) Bancroft reported that "between the first and second of November, a knock was heard at the door of each one of the persons commissioned by the East India Company, and a summons left for them to appear without fail at Liberty Tree on the following Wednesday, at noon, to resign their commission." (Bancroft, 6, 473) Hutchinson's English correspondence shows that he was aware of a printed paper posted up in Boston that read as follows:

To the Freemen of this and the Neighboring Towns.

Gentlemen.

You are desired to meet at the Liberty Tree this day
at Twelve o Clock at noon. Then and there to hear the persons
to whom the Tea shipped by the East India Company is consigned,
make a public Resignation of their Office as Consignees upon
Oath.—And also swear that they will reship any Teas that may
be consigned to them by said Company by the first Vessel sailing

for London.

Boston Nov 3, 1773   O.C. Secy

" Shew us the Man that Dare take down this."

(HLRO, c; Cunningham, 252)

According to John Rowe's diary, on Tuesday, 2 Nov 1773, this advertisement was "stuck up at almost every corner." (Proceedings, 1769-1792, 417-432; Cunningham, 252) Boyle's Journal said it was "found stuck up in all Parts of the Town" and "a large Flag was also hung out on the Pole at Liberty-Tree, and at 11 o'Clock all the Bells in Town were set a ringing." (Boyle, 367-368)

The Boston *Gazette* of 8 Nov 1773 noted that on 3 Nov an assembly of persons from Boston and other towns gathered at the Liberty Tree to wait for the arrival of the merchants. By noon, the merchants had not come. When they did not appear, the crowd of around five hundred including the selectmen and therefore Hancock, Sam Adams, and the town clerk, William Cooper, decided that further action was necessary. Sam Adams, Mollineaux, Warren, "and about five hundred more as near as I could Guess," (Rowe, 253) as the Sons of Liberty, called upon merchants Clarke, Faneuil, and Winslow to make them reject their shipments of tea. The consignees said abruptly they would pay no attention to such a rump committee.[4] The *Gazette* noted that some of the crowd, in making their way back to the Liberty Tree, got out of hand "and shewed some marks of their resentment, and then dispersed."[5] Actually violence broke out. Some damage was done to the building where the three consignees had gathered. The merchants barricaded themselves in the upstairs and avoided harm.

The Town Meetings

On Thursday, 4 Nov 1773, the selectmen agreed to call for a town meeting at Faneuil Hall for the next day. (RRC, a)

On the morning of Friday, 5 Nov 1773, at Faneuil Hall with John Hancock moderating (RRC, b), an official Boston town meeting of one thousand persons[6] followed up the actions of the rump meeting of the Sons of Liberty with considerable debate. A committee was appointed of Hancock, Inches, Austin, and Mason to call upon the consignees to resign. When the group reconvened at 3 P.M. that Friday, the committee reported that the consignees said they could give no answer because the Hutchinson sons were at Milton and needed to be consulted.

A second committee of Adams, Molineaux, and Warren (RRC, c) was delegated to inform Clarke and Faneuil that they were not "joint factors" with the Hutchinsons and could answer for themselves. The committee reported that Clarke and Faneuil would answer within a half hour.

A third committee of Hancock, Pitts, Adams, Warren, William Powell, and Nathaniel Appleton were to "wait upon Messrs. Thomas and Elisha Hutchinson Esquires at Milton, who it is reported are two of the Persons appointed by the East India Company to receive and sell their Teas, and request them, from a regard to their own Character and the Peace and good Order of the Town and Province, immediately to resign their Appointment." (HLRO, a; RRC, c)

Shortly thereafter, the answer came from Clarke, Faneuil, and Winslow addressed to John Hancock saying that they had not yet sufficient knowledge of their appointments to reply. (HLRO, b; RRC, d) Their answer was voted unsatisfactory.

On that same Friday, the second committee had some difficulty in locating the Hutchinsons. Trips to Milton met without success. It was not until the next day, Saturday, 6 Nov 1773, that the committee finally located Thomas Hutchinson. The town meeting reconvened at 11 A.M. on Saturday. Hancock, who continued moderating the meeting at Faneuil Hall, received a message from Thomas Hutchinson Jr. to the effect that Hutchinson knew nothing of such teas and could not give a satisfactory answer until the teas should arrive. (HLRO, c; RRC, e)

The assembly found both letters "daring affrontive" and adjourned. Such responses by the merchants fell on deaf ears. The colonists suspected that the consignees of the tea knew much more than they were willing to admit.

As a result, the following impasses developed:

1. The colonists ordered the merchants not to land the tea.

2. Governor Hutchinson would not give the merchants a permit for the ships to leave without unloading the tea.

3. By law, if the tea was not unloaded by 17 Dec 1773 and duty paid, the customs officers could seize the vessels and sell the tea at auction. Therefore, some action by the colonists would be necessary before 17 Dec.

4. The Boston merchants or consignees who had ordered the tea would not release their cargo, so that it could be returned to England.

5. The Sons of Liberty watched day and night to make certain that the tea was not unloaded.

The week of 8 Nov to 15 Nov 1773 was uneventful. The Boston *Gazette* of 15 Nov 1773 noted that "during this week past the town has been quiet; no person that we have heard of having attempted the smallest affront of the Tea Commissioners." However, the Committee of Correspondence continued its work.

That radical, ad hoc group could act without official approval. On 9 Nov 1773, the committee had addressed a letter to the town of Roxbury calling for another meeting on Thursday, 11 Nov 1773. (NYP, 231) Members from the Roxbury Committee of Correspondence met with the Boston group on the appointed day. Agitation continued.

On 11 Nov 1773 Governor Hutchinson had the effrontery to write to Hancock as captain of the Governor's Company of Cadets, saying: "I think it proper that you should forthwith summon each person belonging to the Company to be ready to appear in arms, at such place of parade as you think fit, whensoever there may be a tumultous assembling of the People in violation of the laws." As was to be expected, Hancock ignored the order.[7]

Matters did not remain quiet very long. When John Hancock's ship, the *Hayley*, docked in Boston on Wednesday, 17 Nov 1773, (Larabee, 113) Captain Scott brought news of the imminent arrival of the tea. Therefore, on that same day, "a considerable body of People" attacked the house of one of the consignees of the tea, Richard Clarke, breaking his windows and confronting his family, one of whom fired a shot out at the crowd without hitting anyone. (Rowe, 427)[8]

On 17 Nov, in response to a petition "from a number of Inhabitants," the selectmen convened a town meeting for Thursday, 18 Nov. (RRC, i; *Gazette* 22 Nov 1773, 2, 3)

At the meeting on 18 Nov, John Hancock was moderator. A committee was again appointed to call upon the merchants, saying that an answer must now be possible because a vessel had now arrived and asked the consignees to resign their appointments. This time, the committee did find the consignees. On that same day Clarke, Faneuil, Winslow, and the Hutchinsons sent a letter saying they were unable to comply with the town's request for as yet they had received no orders.

(RRC, f; *Gazette*, 22 Nov 1773, 2) The reply was again voted unsatisfactory. The meeting adjourned.

Finding that they could not deal with the townspeople, the consignees made a conciliatory proposal to Governor Hutchinson's Council. The tea was to be landed and turned over to the governor and his Council until it was safe for the consignees to dispose of the tea or until new directions as to its disposal had been received. (Larabee, 114-115) The *Gazette* of 22 Nov 1773 warned the Council not to interfere.

Hutchinson convened his Council on 19, 23, 27 and 29 Nov, in an effort to secure action on the proposal of the consignees, but the Council refused to act. Undoubtedly a part of the refusal was caused by two of the council members, James Otis and James Bowdoin. Of course the town was inalterably opposed to any landing of the tea. Once landed, it would be very difficult to prevent its being sold.

The forwarding of the momentum then fell to the Committees of Correspondence in several Eastern towns. Since these committees tended to be more hostile to the British than the town meetings, those who had been consigned the tea braced themselves for the worst.

The Boston committee assembled on Monday, 22 Nov 1773, at the Selectmen's Chamber and released a circular letter on 23 Nov, stating that it was necessary "to save the present & future generations from temporal and we think we may with seriousness say eternal destruction." (NYP) The committee prophesied that "you will think this tea now coming to us, more to be dreaded than plague or pestilence." The letter concluded with this forceful statement:

> Now brethren we are reduced to this dilemma, either to sit down quiet under this and every other burthen [sic] that our Enemies shall see fit to law upon us, as good natured Slaves, or rise and resist this and every plan laid for our destruction as becomes freemen.

Clarke tried another tactic. Perhaps the selectmen would still help him. He secured a meeting with them when they met on 27 Nov 1763, and proposed that "the Consignment was not of his seeking, that he was entirely clear of the matter, and that it was very disagreeable to him—that in order to restore tranquillity to the Town...he was willing to do everything that could in Justice be required of him." (RRC, g) The selectmen answered what they knew Clarke would not accept. The only way to satisfy the people of Boston was to return the tea to London.

On Sunday, 28 Nov 1773, the *Dartmouth* arrived at the Castle in Boston harbor (PRO, a) with the first shipment of 114 chests of tea (Larabee, 118)[9] since the new law had been imposed. The Boston *Gazette* of 29 Nov 1773 announced the *Dartmouth's* arrival, and said that bells would ring to organize a meeting to respond to the arrival of the tea.

On 28 Nov 1773, the minutes of the Committee of Correspondence show that the committee wrote to four towns adjacent to Boston: "we desire that you would favor us with Your Company at Faneuil Hall at 9 o'clock Forenoon [Monday, 22 Nov] then to give us your advice what steps are to be immediately taken in order effectually to prevent the impending evil; and we request you to urge your Friend [sic], in the Town to which you belong to be in readiness to exert themselves in the most resolute manner to assist this Town in their efforts for saving this ...Country. " The letter is signed by William Cooper, clerk. (NYP)

On this same Sunday, the merchant Rowe received a threatening letter. (*Proceedings in Masonry*, 28 Nov 1773, 427; Rowe, 255) Rowe had become involved because, on the ship the *Eleanor*, he had a shipment of goods other than tea. The *Eleanor* was to arrive in Boston Harbour on 2 Dec with more tea plus Rowe's consignment of other goods.

On this same Sunday, 28 Nov, the Committee of Correspondence also called upon the merchant Rotch, asking him not to bring in his ship until the 30th. (PRO, a)

On 29-30 Nov and again on 13, 14, and 16 Dec the Committee of Correspondence held unofficial mass meetings. (PRO, a) Hancock did not preside at these meetings in late November. He was present but not in the chair. The events of these meetings led to the Boston Tea Party.

On Monday, 29 Nov, signs were posted calling for a meeting at Faneuil Hall that same day. There followed the famous meetings of 29 and 30 Nov 1773, reported in the *Gazette* of 6 Dec 1773.

Significantly, the official town records are of course silent about the next two meetings. They were to be "unofficial." The selectmen of Boston met twice on that Sunday, 28 Nov 1773, violating the Sabbath, (RRC, g) but the consignees of the tea had fled to the Castle and nothing could be done. (Bancroft, 6, 477) The selectmen continued to meet in December, but their records are likewise silent about the matter of the tea. Of these moves, Hutchinson wrote: "You see they [the townspeople] print their Acct. without any attestation but tho' it is called a meeting of the people yet it is all under the Selectmen of this Town who attended the whole meeting as I am informed together with Adams & Phillips." (MA, a)

Actions of Monday, 29 Nov 1773

On Mon 29 Nov 1773, at 9 A.M. Jonathan Williams and not Hancock was apppointed moderator. Williams was a merchant and nephew of Benjamin Franklin, a native of Boston. Apparently, Hancock wished to remain a power behind the throne in these rump meetings. On 3 Dec 1773, Hutchinson wrote seemingly to Gage: "H—— who had been moderator of the Town meeting, took care to keep clear of this and they drew in a Nephew of Doctor F——s who I really pity—H—— notwithstanding has exposed himself by his unguarded speeches more than ever before." (MA, aa; Bancroft, 6, 479) Franklin himself was a native of Boston. Therefore it was natural for him to have a nephew there of some economic and political importance.

Cooper, the town clerk, served as secretary. (MA, a) Rowe said that "about One thousand People Met at Faneuill [sic] Hall where they past [sic] a Vote that they would at All Events Return this Tea." (Cunningham, 256) So many people showed up that the meeting adjourned to meet at 3 o'clock at the Old South Meeting House,[10] where Rowe estimated the crowd at 2,500. (*Proceedings in Masonry*, 427; Cunningham, 256) The Boston Committee of Correspondence in its circular letter of 1 Dec 1773 stated that up to five thousand persons had assembled, and that the meeting moved from Faneuil Hall to the Old South. (NYP) Bernard (H, d) also estimated the crowd at five thousand.

The meeting concluded that the tea had to be returned. It adjourned until 3 P.M. in order to give the consignees time to reply.

At 3 P.M., Rotch appeared in person to register his protest about the actions of the meeting. There was talk of destroying the tea. The guard would keep watch on the tea. Certainly it was to be returned. The alarmed consignees pled for time. They were given until the next day, i.e., Tuesday 30 Nov. It was John Hancock who reported to the meeting that, according to Copley, the consignees had just received their letters of appointment the previous evening and that they needed time to meet with each other before submitting a reply. (*Gazette*, 6 Dec 1773, 2, 1-2; NYP) The meeting adjourned until 9 A.M. on Tuesday.

Obviously, a watch had to be organized by the Committee of Correspondence to make certain that the tea was not landed surreptitiously during the night, and particularly on the night of 29 Nov. Bernard noted in his narrative[11] that bells were to be rung if the tea was disturbed. (H, 8, 239) Bernard recorded: "That after the Dissolution of the unlawful Assembly [of 29 Nov], Persons called the *Committee of Correspondence* met from time to time called in the Committees of other Towns to join with them, kept up a Military Watch on Guard, to prevent the Landing of the Tea, who were Armed with Muskets and Bayonets, and every half hour during the night, regularly passed the word—all is well, like Centinels in a Garrison." (H, b, 8, 241)

Hancock himself is supposed to have said that, as far as guarding the tea between 29 Nov and 30 Nov to make certain that it was not landed, "I will be one of it, rather than that there should be none." (Sworn information of Nathan Frazier, taken before Privy Council on 19 Feb 1774, concerning public meets at Boston on 29 and 30 Nov last; Davies, 7, 85; C.O.5, 763, fos 77-106d; entry of a covering letter in C.O. 5, 765, 298-307; entry of instructions, 5 Apr, in C.O. 5, 205, 427i-462) In a letter from Lieutenant Colonel Leslie, commanding the 64th Regiment at Castle William, to Lord Dartmouth dated 6 Dec 1773, Leslie reported that "Mr. Handcock [sic], 'the Governor's Captain of his Cadet Company,' was mounting guard on board them to prevent the landing of that part of the cargo, 'a most daring insult to his Excellency.'"[12] Either Lord Dartmouth had additional informants about the guard or he stretched the scope of Leslie's letter because, on 5 Feb 1774, Dartmouth wrote to the attorney- and solicitor-general: "Mr. Hancock, the Governor's captain of his cadet company, was one of the guard on board the ships."[13] By 11 Feb 1774, when Attorney- and Solicitor-General Alexander Wedderburn answered Dartmouth, the crown's attorney had concluded that the tea had been watched by "a guard headed by Proctor and Handcock [sic]." (PRO, b; Davies, 8, 47)[13] Bernard's *Narrative* said: "Mr. Hancock the Govrs Captn of his Cadet Company was one of the Guard on Board the Ships." (H, f)

However, it seems unlikely that Hancock himself actually stood guard over the tea. He may have been an honorary member of the sentinels, but probably no more than that.

30 Nov 1773

On the 30th, a letter from the Hutchinsons, Faneuil, Winslow, and Clarke dated 29 Nov and addressed, not to the assembly, but rather to Selectman Scollay, was read to the meeting. The consignees told Scollay that they had received their orders from the East India Company but that it was "utterly out of our power" to return the tea to England and suggested storing it until the impasse could be broken. (NYP, a; Bancroft, 6, 479)

Hutchinson's lack of comprehension of the seriousness of the situation is revealed in two letters. The first dated 30 Nov he addressed to Jonathan Williams, the moderator of the unofficial town meeting. Hutchinson's message which was read at the 30 Nov meeting concluded with these words: "I warn exhort and require you and each of you thus unlawfully assembled forthwith to disperse and to surcease all further unlawful Proceedings at your utmost Peril." (*Gazette*, 6 Dec 1773, 2) The Boston *Gazette* reported that, immediately after the sheriff read Hutchinson's proclamation, there came "a loud and very general Hiss." In the second, dated 2 Dec 1773, to Lord Dartmouth, Hutchinson seemed satisfied with his actions, reporting that "the next morning [30 Nov] I sent the Sheriff to the Assembly with a declaration against their proceedings." (MA, b; PRO c; Davies, 6, 249)

Copley asked if the meeting would give safe conduct to his father-in-law Clarke and others, if they would come. The assembly voted affirmatively, and gave them two hours to appear.

At 2:00 P.M., Rotch came again to protest, but said that he was willing to return the tea that was on his ship. But Rotch was only the ship owner and not a consignee. He was fearful for his ship, rather than for its cargo.

Rowe hastened to explain to a rump meeting assembled at Faneuil Hall on Tuesday, 30 Nov 1773, that he did have cargo other than tea aboard the expected ship *Eleanor* under Captain Bruce and that he "would Endeavour to prevail on him to act with Reason in this Affair and that [he] was very Sorry he [the ship's captain] had any Tea On Board—and which is very True for it hath Given [him] Great Uneasiness." (Rowe, 256; *Proceedings in Masonry*, 428) The *Gazette* reported that Rowe stated he would do his best to have the tea returned.

Copley reported back to the assembly that he had tried to get the merchants to come, and they only said that they wished to store the tea.

The meeting voted to send copies of a resolution to New York and Philadelphia, signed by John Hancock and others. The Committee of Correspondence was empowered to set up watches for any other ships that arrived in Boston bearing tea.

At the conclusion of the session, the assembly voted the town's displeasure with a number of merchants who were importing tea from Great Britain, and declared that it would prevent the landing and sale of the same. The statement was signed by Adams, Hancock, John Rowe, William Phillips, and Jonathan Williams. (*Gazette*, 6 Dec 1773, 2-3)

As noted previously, on 29 Nov 1773, the Governor's Council met but provided Hutchinson with no consolation. The Council could not accept authority over the cargo. The General Court was known to oppose the landing of the tea. Therefore, the Council consigned the tea to the guardianship of the governor. At the conclusion of the meeting, the governor again asked for advice "upon the disorders then prevailing in the town of Boston, and it was answered in general that the advise [sic] already given was intended for that purpose." (Drake, 320)[14]

On 1 Dec 1773, the Boston Committee of Correspondence issued a circular letter informing the other committees of what had transpired on 29 and 30 Nov. The atmosphere in Boston grew more tense. The two sons of Clarke, along with Thomas Hutchinson Jr. and Benjamin Faneuil, left for the safety of Castle William. Labaree concluded that Clarke Sr. was apparently at Salem. Elisha Hutchinson, and whenever he could, Governor Hutchinson, remained at their country estates. Winslow was in Marshfield. (Larabee, 122) Before leaving town, they sent word to the board of selectmen that their solution continued to be to have the tea stored until further orders could be received.

The *Gazette* of 13 Dec reported that the consignees were at Castle William. It was noted with alarm that the persons on Castle Island were arming themselves. The issue included the blunt statement to Governor Hutchinson telling him to go home.

Hutchinson's Reactions

How was the governor reacting during this period? On 3 Dec 1773, Hutchinson reported: "It is in every body's mouth that H—— said at the Core of the meeting he wou'd be willing to spend his fortune and life itself in so good a cause, but the Secretary says he can't find any body will make Oath to it." (MA, aaa) Hutchinson wrote on 3 Dec 1773: "All this time nobody suspected they would suffer the Tea be destroyed there being so many men of property active at these meetings as Hancock Phillips Rowe Dennie and others." (MA, c)

On 2 Dec 1773, the *Eleanor* docked with its tea. On 7 Dec 1773, the *Beaver* arrived with more tea. The fourth ship, the *William*, never made it to Boston, having been wrecked off Cape Cod.

The Impasse Continues

So, the three ships with tea aboard were in the harbor. The townspeople were keeping guard so that the tea could not land. Hutchinson would take no steps to break the impasse. The Boston Committee of Correspondence kept up pressure on the ship owners. Meetings were held at Faneuil Hall. On 9 Dec the Committee of Correspondence told Rotch to apply formally for clearance papers to reembark his cargo. (NYC) The authorities as usual refused.

Seeing that the stalemate remained, on Friday, 10 Dec 1773, the Boston Committee of Correspondence sent a circular letter to five towns, saying: "You are requested to meet the Committees of this and the Neighboring Towns at Faneuil Hall on Monday next [13 Dec] at 10 o'clock Forenoon, further to consult in the present exigency of the times." The letter was signed "William Cooper, Clerk." (NYC)

On Saturday, 11 Dec 1773, the owners of the ships with the tea on board, who found that they could not load outgoing cargo as long as the tea remained, petitioned the consignees of the tea that they do their duty and accept the tea shipment. (Drake, 344-348) The consignees stalled.

On 11 Dec 1773, Captain James Bruce of the *Eleanor* protested to the members of the "committee of the people" who had prevented him landing his cargo of tea that he was "nightly watched by 25 armed men on board the said ship, appointed, as he supposes and verily believes, to prevent the said teas from being landed." Bruce mentioned Sam Adams and John Hancock as among the persons present at the meeting Bruce was required to attend on 2 Dec at which he was told he might unload his other cargo but not the tea. (Drake, 355)

The Committee of Correspondence, meeting in the Selectmen's Chamber and sensing that it would be better to keep its transactions secret, merely recorded for 12, 13, and 14 Dec: "No business transacted, matter of Record."

The Boston *Gazette* made no mistake about expressing animosity toward Hutchinson. On 13 Dec 1773, at the conclusion of an article, it said: "If you do not very soon take your departure from this abused land, never to return again! I will ring you such a peal about Dutch Tea, &c. as will make your ears tingle!!!" (*Gazette*, 13 Dec 1773, 2) Obviously Boston had got wind of the letter Hutchinson had received on 14 Nov 1773, having been sent from England on 17 Aug 1773, granting him permission to return. He was to be goaded into departure, in spite of the unrest in Boston. The *Gazette* called upon Rotch to say publicly if he did not intend for the *Dartmouth* to return to London.

On Monday, 13 Dec 1773, in keeping with the circular letter issued the previous Friday, an all-day meeting of the several towns in and around Boston was held. Rotch, the owner of the *Dartmouth*, was required to attend. Rotch's deposition said that Sam Adams appeared to be in charge of the meeting and that Hancock was present. (PRO, a) The committee asked Rotch why his ship was not ready to reembark for England. Rotch replied that there were men-of-war ready to prevent the *Dartmouth* from leaving. His account stated: "he was told that the Ship must go, for that the people of Boston & the Neighboring Towns absolutely required & expected it." (PRO, a) In his December 1773 letter to Lord [Dartmouth?], Hutchinson noted: "They [the consignees who remained in Boston] were then told by the Selectmen that nothing short of sending the Teas back would be satisfactory." (MA, e)

On Tuesday, 14 Dec 1773, Rotch attended a meeting at the Old South Meeting House with Samuel Phillips Savage as moderator. (PRO, a) The merchant was told that he must have his ship at sea by Wednesday, 15 Dec. The deadline of 17 Dec 1773 was fast approaching, at which time the customs officers could seize the tea and sell it. Rotch stated it was impossible for him to put his ships to sea by 15 Dec. As a result, he was required to accompany a committee to the home of the customs officer, Mr. Harrison, to apply for a clearance. Harrison said he could not speak officially "out of Office." (PRO, a) Rotch testified that he did seek such a clearance from Harrison the next day and was refused.   Rotch, finding himself caught between the authorities and the people, entered a "protest" with a public notary. (PRO, a)

Perhaps because the representatives of the various towns had business to attend to, they did not meet on Wednesday, but adjourned their Tuesday meeting to reconvene on Thursday.

The Crucial Final Meeting

On Thursday, 16 Dec 1773, groups from Boston and nearby towns held a meeting that lasted all day. (*Proceedings*, 428; Cunningham, 257-258) As many as seven thousand men may have been present. (Wells, 2, 121; S. Adams to A. Lee, 21 Dec 1773) Deacon Tudor estimated the crowd at 5-6,000 (Tudor, 44) The *Gazette* noted that people from towns as far as twenty miles from Boston attended the final 16 Dec meeting. (*Gazette*, 20 Dec 1773) Hancock may or may not have spoken at this meeting. Francis Rotch, son of the owner of the *Dartmouth*, shuttled back and forth between the meeting and the governor, trying to persuade Hutchinson to give him a "Let Pass"

(PRO, a) to allow the ship to sail out of Boston. Rotch made two tries on that notable Thursday, 16 Dec 1773, but had to return each time to the town meeting, which remained in session, to report failure. Hutchinson had offered Rotch protection, but Rotch testified "that he dared not to accept the said offer, apprehending that if he had, his life would have been in Danger." (PRO, a) Rotch's deposition placed both Sam Adams and Hancock at the meetings. (PRO, a) Fowler placed Hancock there and observed: "Through it all, Hancock remained resolute. " (Fowler, 160) Fowler concluded that Hancock had been present throughout the meeting. "He knew," said Fowler, "that if the tea landed, then all was lost, Hutchinson would have his victory, the Whigs would be broken, and the Tories would be in the ascendancy." (Fowler, 160)

When on Thursday, 16 Dec 1773, Rotch returned for the last time at 5:45 P.M., it had grown dark in the Boston winter. The Old South had to be lit with candles. Everyone knew that tomorrow was 17 Dec, the deadline when the customs officials could seize the tea. Peter Oliver wrote that "*Adams, Hancock* & the Leaders of the Faction, assembled the Rabble in the largest Dissenting Meeting House in the Town, where they had frequently assembled to pronounce their Annual Orations upon their Massacre, & to perpetrate their most atrocious Acts of Treason & Rebellion—thus, literally 'turning the House of God into a Den of Thieves.' " Peter Oliver recorded that the crowd "whiled away the Time in Speech-making, hissing & clapping, cursing & swearing untill [sic] it grew near to Darkness; & then the signal was given, to act their Deeds of Darkness." (Oliver, 102) Of course Oliver was not present, so what information he had was hearsay. There is no doubt but that the atmosphere was set for subversion. War whoops were exchanged between the gallery and those outside. Action moved from the meeting house to the wharf. An undetermined number of "Mohawk Indians" threw 342 chests of tea overboard from the three ships. Rowe estimated the number of the whole mob being "near two thousand People." (Cunningham, 258) The captain of the *Eleanor*, James Bruce, concurred saying "that about the hours of 6 or 7 o'clock...about one thousand unknown people came down the said warf, and a number of them came on board the said ship, some of them dressed like Indians...and threw the said chests...overboard." (Drake, 357) Governor Hutchinson found himself powerless to act against the offenders. On 17 Dec 1773, he wrote to Lord Dartmouth: "I sent expresses this morning before sunrise to summon a Council to meet me at Boston but by reason of the Indisposition of three of them I could not make a Quorum." (MA, d) When he finally did get his Council together in spite of their "indispositions," they were able to give him no assistance. Indeed, he knew that, at this point, he was powerless and beyond much hope of rescuing even face from the negotiations about the tea.

On Friday, 17 Dec 1773, the Boston Committee of Correspondence wrote to the Plymouth Committee: "We inform you in great haste that every Chest of Tea was destroyed the last Evening without the least injury to the Vessels or any other property. Our enemies must acknowledge that this People have acted upon pure and upright principles." (NYP) Therefore, the ship owners like Rotch could have no basis for complaint. Their property was not injured. The consignees were the ones who lost the possibility of making profits from the sale of the tea, and, of course, the East India Company, as the owners of the tea, lost their merchandise. The ship owners were satisfied, because now they could load their cargo and sail.

The Aftermath of the Tea Party

The *Gazette* of 20 Dec 1773, made a brief summary report, saying that on Tuesday, 16 Dec, Rotch was told to get the necessary papers to send the tea back to England. On 18 Dec Rotch said that he had been refused such papers. He was told to go back to the governor and ask again. Rotch reported that the governor said there would be no pass for the tea.

"But behold what followed!" said the *Gazette*. "A number of brave and resolute men...emptied every chest of tea on board the three ships... amounting to 342 chests, into the sea!! without the last damage done to the Ships or any property." The *Gazette* was also elated by the reaction of the ship owners and the townspeople. "The masters and owners are well pleas'd that their ships are thus clear'd; and the people," reported the *Gazette*, "are almost universally congratulating each other on this happy event." The *Gazette* discreetely noted; "The particular Account of the Proceedings of the People at their Meeting on Tuesday and Thursday last are omitted this Week for want of Room." The deed had been done. There was no further need to comment.

Did Hutchinson Act Appropriately?

As was noted earlier, even in December of 1773, Hutchinson wrote that "at this point [when tea owners were applying to the Customs House for clearance] nobody suspected they would suffer the tea to be destroyed there being so many men of property active at these meetings as Hancock Phillips Rowe Dennie & others."[15] (MA, e) No wonder Hutchinson did not seek a solution acceptable to all.

Hutchinson should have sought such a compromise, but he did not. Bancroft condemned Hutchinson in the harshest terms, listing the numerous colonial institutions that Hutchinson had tried to overthrow. Bancroft remonstrated that Hutchinson had brought on the difficulty "all for the sake of places for his family and a salary and a pension for himself." (Bancroft, 6, 462) Bailyn offered apologies for Hutchinson's actions. (Bailyn, 260) But, since the tea that arrived in New York and Philadelphia was successfully shipped back to England, (Bailyn, 263) Hutchinson's decision seemed to have resulted from a stubborn effort to adhere rigidly to English law, regardless of the consequences. As a result of his recalcitrance, the separatists saw power falling into their hands. Rowe noted in his diary for Saturday, 18 Dec 1773, that he believed the confrontation could have been prevented. On 18 Dec 1773, he wrote: "The Affair of Destroying the Tea makes Great Noise in the Town—tis a Disastrous Affair and some People are much Alarm'd...I would Rather have Lost five hundred Guineas than Capt Bruce should have taken any of this Tea on board his Ship." (*Proceedings*, 428; Cunningham, 258)

What Were the Roles of Adams and Hancock?

How best can we summarize the roles played by Sam Adams and John Hancock in the Tea Party? Certainly they were present at the meetings that took place on 5 and 6 Nov which Hancock chaired. (RRC, b) They were present at the meeting on 18 Nov which Hancock chaired. (RRC, h) Rotch testified that John Hancock was one of the persons he recalled as being most active at both the meeting on 29 Nov and the meeting on 30 Nov. (PRO, a)

Hancock and Adams were also present on 29 Nov at the meeting which Hancock refused to chair. It is possible that Hancock's cadets assisted in guarding the tea ships in Boston harbor and that Hancock, as their commandant, personally supervised their surveillance. Larabee (142) so states. Larabee's source is perhaps taken from Governor Bernard's papers: "Mr. Hancock the governor's captain of the Cadet Company was one of the guards on board the ships." (Houghton, b; Fotheringham, 280, n. 2) However, the notes of the 1773 town meetings kept by William Cooper, the town clerk, make no mention of Hancock's serving as part of the guard. Cooper listed the names of the twenty-five men who were appointed on Monday, 29 Nov, to serve as the watch. Paul Revere and Benjamin Edes were among those listed, but not Hancock. (Minutes, 11)

If Hancock remained aloof from being one of the actual guard, he undoubtedly knew what was transpiring. Rotch's deposition to the Privy Council stated: "That he [Rotch] heard that a proposal had been made to Mr. Hancock to burn his Ship & Cargo two nights before the Tea was destroyed, but that Mr. Hancock opposed any such Proceedings." (PRO, a)

Hancock and Adams were also present at the meetings on 30 Nov. Hancock supposedly made a motion at that meeting. In discussing the events of 30 Nov 1773, Governor Bernard undoubtedly had Hancock and Adams in mind when he wrote: "That it is the Determination of the Body to carry their Votes and Resolutions into Execution at the risk of their Lives and Fortunes." (Houghton, e)

They were undoubtedly present on 16 Dec, which ended with the Tea Party. Governor Bernard's "Narrative" of the Tea Party events proposed that the mob, "encouraged by Mr. John Hancock, Sam Adams and others repaired to the Wharf, where three Vessels having Tea on board, lay around, and took possession of the said Vessels, and in two hours the whole of the Tea was consumed." (Houghton, c) Bernard does not attribute any words to either Adams or Hancock at the 16 Dec meeting But, during the confused sequence of events that followed Rotch's return from Milford bringing Governor Hutchinson's refusal to allow the ships containing the tea to sail, each is reported to have made a statement.

What did Adams supposedly say? Francis Rotch's testimony to the Privy Council read as follows: "That upon his going back to the Meeting, and reporting the Governor's Refusal, Mr. Adams said that he did not see what more they could do to save their country." (PRO, a) Both Bancroft (Bancroft, 6, 486) and Wells (Wells, 2, 122) repeated this statement as "This meeting can do nothing more to save the country." Wells asserted that "forty or fifty men disguised as Indians, who must have been concealed near by, appeared and passed by the church entrance, and, encouraged by Adams, Hancock, and others, hurried along to Griffin's...Warf." [sic] Wells, however, gave no source for this assertion.

What did Hancock supposedly say? Thatcher recorded George Robert Twelvetree Hewes' eyewitness account to the effect that Hancock said to the town meeting on December 16: "The matter must be settled before 12 o'clock" (Thatcher, 177-178) and "that one of the last things he heard said, in the final excitement, was Hancock's cry, 'Let every man do what is right in his own eyes.' " Hewes was ninety-three at the time he was giving his recollections of the Tea Party, so there was adequate time for distortion. Hewes told Thatcher that he had actually seen Adams and Hancock on board the ships when the tea was being destroyed. Thatcher commented: "Of the latter he [Hewes] speaks most particularly, being entirely confident that he was himself at one time engaged with him in the demolition of the same chest of tea." (Thatcher, 193) Hewes said that he recognized Hancock not only by his ruffles "making their appearance in the heat of the work, from under the disguise which pretty thoroughly covered him,—and by his figure, and gait; but by his features, which neither his paint nor his loosened club of hair behind wholly concealed from a close view;—and by his voice also, for he exchanged with him an Indian grunt, and the expression 'me know you' which was a good deal used on that occasion for a countersign." (Thatcher, 193) Thatcher added: "This is a curious reminiscence, but we believe it a mistake." (Thatcher, 193)

Perhaps neither Adams or Hancock made any inciting statements. An account, based upon the discovery of correspondence in 1859, gave a vivid description of what took place but did not mention the name of either Adams or Hancock. On 18 Dec 1773, John Andrews wrote to William Barrell of Boston: "when a general muster was assembled, from this and all ye neighbouring towns, to the number of five or six thousand, at 10 o'clock Thursday morning in the Old South Meeting house, where they pass'd a *unanimous* vote that the *Tea* should go out of the *harbour* that afternoon." (Andrews, 325) After describing Rotch's fruitless efforts to get a concession from Hutchinson, Andrews remembered that, at the evening meeting under candlelight, "the house was so crouded [sic] I could get no farther than the porch, when I found the moderator was just declaring the meeting to be *dissolv'd*, which caused another general shout, out doors and in, and three cheers." (Andrews, 326) Since Andrews did not make it inside the Meeting House, he may not have heard whatever statements Adams and Hancock made. Andrews concluded his account by describing how the Indians threw the tea overboard, speaking in a jargon that supposedly resembled what Narragansett Indians would speak, how no other cargo other than tea was touched, and how the marauders, detecting that the captain of the ship, one Conner, had secreted tea on his person, stripped him, battered him around, and left him coated with mud.

There is a somewhat enigmatic statement about Hancock made by a Major Thompson Maxwell and recorded by General James Miller of Salem. Again, as with Hewes statement, the testimony takes the form of a recollection, and Maxwell appears to have got his timing wrong as to the sequence of events on the day of the Tea Party. His statement was as follows:

In 1773 I went with my team to Boston. I had loaded at John
Hancock's warehouse and was about to leave town, when Mr.
Hancock requested me to drive my team up into his yard, and
ordered his servants to take care of it, and requested me to be
on Long Warf [sic] at two o'clock, P.M., and informed me
what was to be done. I went accordingly, joined the band
under one Captain Hewes; we mounted the Ships, and made
Tea in a trice. This done I took my team and went home, as an
honest man should. (Maxwell, 57-58)

If Maxwell's recollection of time is accurate, Hancock and perhaps
others were having people assemble down near the ships as early as two
P.M.   It seems likely that no illegal action would have been
contemplated until after dark had fallen. Of course, if Rotch had been
successful in his appeals to Hutchinson, the tea would have been
shipped back to England and no Tea Party would have been necessary.
So, if Maxwell's recollection of time is correct, the plans for illegal
activity were being set well in advance. Indeed, since the description of
the destroyers of the tea has been sufficiently well documented, advance
preparations had to be made to supply them with blankets, tomahawks,
knives, and paint for their faces.

If Hutchinson received word that Hancock had been present at the
destruction of the tea, Hutchinson would have reported it. In his letter
to Dartmouth of 17 Dec 1773, Hutchinson did not mention Hancock.
He wrote hurriedly: "a sufficient number of people for doing the work
were disguised and these were surrounded by a vast body of people who
generally, as was commonly reported, went from this meeting which it
is said was more numerous than any before and consisted of the
inhabitants of divers other towns as well as Boston but in what
proportion I have not been able to ascertain." (MA, f; Davies, 6, 256)

Naturally, some of the tea washed ashore, and there are stories that,
when patriots got word that had someone been able to hoard some of
the cargo, they would call upon the scavanger and remove the tea.
Supposedly a chest had gone ashore at South Boston. Whigs are said to
have found the person who had sequestered the chest and sold some of
its contents, recovered the funds and moved the tea to the Common, and
set it on fire. According to Hewes, Hancock came to his front door to
see the burning. (Thatcher, 187) The monies recovered, said Thatcher,
were used for "okkuppee," just then the transliteration of the Indian
word for grog. (Thatcher, 187)

The Importance of the Tea Party to the Revolution and to Hancock

Comments by contemporary witnesses to the Boston Tea Party and by subsequent historians vary concerning its import. Viola Barnes (Barnes, 2, 511) concluded that "to the disappointment of the perpetrators, the 'Tea Party' nowhere produced anything more than momentary applause." However, John Adams (Adams, 2, 323) spoke of the Tea Party as "the most magnificent movement of all." Adams continued by saying in his diary that "this destruction of the tea is so bold, so daring, so firm, intrepid and inflexible, and it must have so important consequences, and so lasting, that I cannot but consider it as an epoch in history." (Adams, 1, 323) Sam Adams wrote to James Warren on 28 Dec 1773: "The ministry could not have devised a more effectual measure to unite the colonies. Our comittee have on this occasion opened a correspondence with the other New-England colonies, besides New York and Philadelphia. Old jealousies are removed and perfect harmony subsists between them." (Warren-Adams Letters, 20-21) Governor Hutchinson himself concluded: "This was the boldest stroke which had yet been struck in America." (Hutchinson, *History*, 3, 315)[16] Peter Oliver stated: "After the Destruction of the Tea, the *Massachusetts* Faction found they had past the *Rubicon*; it was now, Neck or Nothing." (Oliver, 103)

Hancock himself was of an opinion opposite to that of Barnes. To his agents in England who were unlikely to convey his sentiments to the wrong parties, Hancock said: "...the particulars I must Refer you to Captain Scott for as indeed I am not acquainted with them myself, so as to give a Detail....No one circumstance could possibly have taken place more effectively to unite the colonies than this maneuvre of the tea. It is universally resented here." (NEHGS, a) Although by professing that he had no personal knowledge of the incident, Hancock could have been protecting himself from direct complicity even with contacts in England, and in spite of the evidence that Hancock and Adams were both among the Mohawk Indians, it is unlikely that they would have risked their leadership to participate directly. However, it must have been a temptation. And who knows? They might have been there. After sitting through all those town meetings, the physical activity of throwing the tea overboard would have given them considerable satisfaction and physical relief.

It was at this time that Hancock made another one of his ironical moves. Shortly after the Tea Party, Lieutenant Governor Andrew Oliver died. Governor Hutchinson attended the funeral. As was pointed out earlier, Peter Oliver, Andrew Oliver's brother and the Supreme Court Justice, thought it expedient not to attend. As a postscript to a letter to his brother Elisha dated at Milton on 7 Mar 1774, Hutchinson commented: "Col. Hancock has offered himself and Company to attend the Lt Govr's funeral. Unaccountable conduct." (Hutchinson, Diary & Letters, 1, 130) Hutchinson, as well as a lot of other people, did not know what to make of Hancock's bravado. In the simplest of terms, the funeral of the lieutenant governor was bound to be a big event. Hancock as usual did not wish to miss a good show.

NOTES

1. Larabee stated that the colonists had imported 600,000 pounds of dutied tea in 1771 and 1772. (71) Larabee added: "In the last three years before non-importation took effect, 1766-68, the colonies had imported 1,800,000 pounds from the mother country; in the three years following the boycott's end, the total fell off to more than half to only 787,000 pounds." (Larabee, 52) Tea continued to be drunk in the colonies, but it was not British tea. The Boston *Gazette* of 1 Nov 1773, 2, reported that "at least nine-tenths of the tea that has been consumed in this province since the non-importation agreement took place, has been imported from Holland, by way of the Southern provinces."

2. Praedicus had addressed a letter in the Boston *Gazette* of 18 Oct 1773, 2, 1-2 "To the Public."

3. O.C.= Officer in Charge.

4. Boston *Gazette*, 15 Nov 1773, 2, 1: "A great number of inhabitants also of this town and the neighboring towns met at Liberty Tree [Wed 3 Nov 1773], and there voted that the Tea Commissioners, by neglecting to appear and resign their appointment, according to the notification said to have been sent to them the Night before, had discovered themselves to be enemies of the country and would meet with their resentment." The vote of the rump meeting was taken to Richard Clarke who received it with "hauteur."

5. Whereas the *Gazette* of 8 Nov 1773 had acknowledged some disturbance on 3 Nov, the *Gazette* of 15 Nov 1773, 2, 1 reported that the unrest of that same day had resulted in "no damage."

6. Boston *Gazette*, 8 Nov 1773, 2, 1 stated that it was a "very full meeting."

7. Hutchinson to Hancock, 11 Nov 1773, First Corps of Cadet papers, Mugar Memorial Library, Boston. Boston *Gazette*, 15 Nov 1773, 2, 1 commented on the request: "...but it is very much questioned whether Mr. Hancock will think himself obliged, or even authorized by any law in this province, to pay the least regard to so very extraordinary a mandate."

8. Cf. Bernard paper, *Narrative*, 8, 233. Bernard estimated the crowd at one hundred to two hundred people.

9. Cf. Bernard, Narrative, 8, 235. It is not clear why did the British put the *Dartmouth* at the mercy of the colonists. Larabee observed that, had the *Dartmouth* remained anchored in the bay, it might have been protected by the British Navy, but that once the captain of the ship docked his ship at Rowe's Wharf, the *Dartmouth* came under the control of the townsmen guarding the tea. The answer probably lies in the determination of the British to hold fast to what they considered to be their rights. They underestimated the determination of the colonists to resist.

10. The Old South Meeting House, built in 1669 and reconstructed in 1729, and Faneuil Hall, are still only a six-minute walk apart. With narrower streets, the distance could have been either a little less or a little more. But the contemporary tourist has no difficulty in going up the hill from the market to the church in a very short period of time.

11. Bernard's *Narrative*, 8, 229-243, was based on "advice" received from Boston in letters from Hutchinson and Admiral Montague, the commandant at Castle William, and from information obtained from Captain Scott.

12. *Calendar of Home Office Papers of the Reign of George III, 1773-1775...*, ed. Richard A. Roberts, London, 1899, 175-176, entry for 28 Jan 1774, because Leslie's letters were enclosed in a letter from Viscount Barrington to the Earl of Dartmouth entered under 28 Jan 1774.

13. PRO, C.O. 5/160 folio 1; K.G. Davies, *Documents of the American Revolution: 1770-1783*, 8, 41. Two witnesses therefore associate Hancock directly with the guarding of the tea ships. Such comments are probably faulty. There were plenty of volunteers to serve as the twenty-five guards, and Hancock was needed elsewhere.

14. The role of the Governor's Council in Massachusetts differed from the council in most of the other colonies, because, instead of being chosen by the crown, it was nominated by the General Court and only subject to the governor's approval (Larabee, 115). Therefore, Hutchinson could veto those whom the General Court nominated of whom he did not approve, but he could not hand-select others to fill those places. Since the Council was elected by the legislature, it often reflected the views of the legislature. In this instance, the twenty-eight-member advisory board simply refused to offer Hutchinson any alternative to facing the issue squarely.

The records of the old Colonial Council are at the MA, but there is no entry in those records for 29 Nov 1773.

15. Davies, 6, 249: Hutchinson to Dartmouth, 2 Dec 1773: "Although this meeting or assembly consisted principally of the lower ranks of the people...yet there were divers gentlemen of good fortune among them and I can scarcely think they will prosecute their made resolves."

16. On 17 Dec 1773, Governor Hutchinson sent a brief account of the Tea Party to Lord Dartmouth in England. MA, Hutchinson Correspondence, Hutchinson to Lord Dartmouth, vol. 27, 589. (MA, d) In his letter, Hutchinson noted that the wind was "coming fair" so he had to give only a hasty account.

A second brief letter was sent on 18 Dec 1773 to Dartmouth (MA, g) 27, 594, and a third on 25 Dec 1773, 27 (MA, h) Others followed. Hutchinson was anxious to get his version of the story to his superiors before the colonists could send their version of the Tea Party.

In his letter of 24 Dec 1773, Hutchison wrote to Dartmouth: "I cannot find any persons who were at the meeting of the people willing to give an Account in writing of the persons who were most active nor of any of this action." (MA, i)

Hutchinson also referred to a second tea party in his letter of 9 Mar 1774, to Dartmouth. HLRO, 7 May 1774, "Boston Disturbances," f. 4131v: "The 6th instant a Vessel arrived from London having on board about thirty chests of Tea on account of several Traders in Tea. The next day the Vessel was hauled to the Wharf where the Vessels lay which had the East India Company's Tea; and in the evening a sufficient Number of persons disguised like Indians went on board and destroyed the Tea in a short time....The Owners of the Tea are very silent, and I think if they could find out who were the immediate Actors they would not venture at present to bring any Action in the Law against them. If they had attempted to land it, it is probable they would have shared in the fate of the Consignees of the Company's Teas, neither of which have been able to return to the Town since they were first banished." The owners were presumably Clark and Faneuil who were still at the Castle on 9 Mar 1774. It would be logical that Hutchinson would not write of the involvement of his sons as consignees. (Hutchinson, Diary and Letters, Hutchinson to Bernard, 9 Mar 1774, 1, 131) Hutchinson himself continued to stay largely at his country home in Milton, in order to avoid confronting the irate people of Boston.

7

1774: The Year Immediately Before
Open Rebellion

The Intolerable Acts

The British continued to provoke the colonists into armed
opposition. If the majority of the colonial leaders had not sought
independence in 1773, the bundle of five acts of 1774 known as the
Coercive or Intolerable Acts forwarded the colonies into revolution.
They were detailed earlier in this essay so only their names and a brief
comment will be repeated here.

The Boston Port Act of 31 Mar 1774, closing Boston to
shipping;

the Massachusetts Bay Government Act of 20 May 1774,
providing that the governor would appoint the members of his
Council;

the Administration of Justice Act of 20 May, providing for
trial of colonists in England;

the Quartering Act of 2 June 1774, providing that the crown
could seize quarters for British troops; and

the Quebec Act of 22 June 1774, extending the boundaries of
Quebec into what had previously been considered territory
belonging to the colonies.

Kelly and Harbison pointed out that "mid the indignation and determination to resist that swept America when the so-called Intolerable Acts became known, the colonists took their first steps toward extralegal or revolutionary government." (81) The committees of correspondence, already operating, received a renewed impetus from the massive public support that followed the Intolerable Acts.

Hancock lost no time in delivering his commemorative address of 1774 to present a preview of what would become the reaction of the colonists to the Coercive Acts. A detailed analysis of that speech and Hancock's speaking ability will be found later in this volume. It suffices to say here that Hancock was not an inexperienced public speaker. We have already recorded events at which he spoke to fairly large groups, although the texts of those speeches have not been preserved. Furthermore, he was an exerienced moderator and had presided at a number of the public meetings held in Boston. So he was a logical choice to give the fourth address. The committee to arrange for the commemoration was the same one charged with exchanging information with other colonial grievance committees. The committee's choice of Hancock, therefore, signalled not only that the committee could help to establish Hancock as a national figure, but also that he could help them by lending his prestige to such a revolutionary event. Undoubtedly the British considered Hancock's acceptance to speak as a point of no return in their efforts to placate him. John Adams, who had witnessed Hancock in the role of chairperson and commemorative speaker, therefore, did not hesitate to back him later for president of the Continental Congress. The commemorative address of 1774 launched Hancock on his national political career.

On 9 April 1774, General Gage was ordered by the king to sail for Boston from Plymouth Harbour in England on board the *Lively* to become both captain general and governor in chief of His Majesty's Province of Massachusetts Bay. (PRO, a; Carter, 2, 158-162) A copy of Gage's orders was sent to Hutchinson. Gage arrived on Boston of 13 May 1774.

Hutchinson, who had requested leave of absence, was relieved of his duties and departed for England on 1 June 1774. Hutchinson's feelings of rejection were mollified by a letter of 9 Apr 1774 from Dartmouth saying that the king approved of Hutchinson's conduct and that he should expect to be returned as governor if he wished, as soon as Gage had got things under control. (PRO, b; Davies, 8, 90) Hutchinson was a native colonial and would have been expected to wish to return. On

17 May 1774, Hutchinson wrote to Dartmouth: "My Lord, I don't remember ever to have received a letter which gave me greater comfort and satisfaction than your lordship's private letter of the 9th of April." With that letter, he could dispel rumors about the reasons for his departure. (PRO, c; Davies, 8, 115)

Yet, even amidst all of the friction with Hutchinson, on the surface, some cooperation continued. Hancock's Independent Cadets with their colonel in charge formed a part of the welcoming party assembled to honor the new governor on 19 May 1774. The ceremonies concluded with a banquet at Faneuil Hall. Hancock did not attend.[1]

After taking office, Gage was trying to assemble his Council, being under orders from London to reject certain previous members of the Council who had shown too much cooperation with the colonists. He rejected thirteen of those nominated. When he tried to get suitable nominees to fill the vacancies and to get those nominated agreeable to him to accept, he had difficulties. Some who had accepted were forced by mobs to sign a letter of resignation. On 27 Aug 1774 Timothy Paine informed Gage that a mob had forced him to resign his appointment to the Council. (PRO, d; Davies, 8, 166-168) Councilman Joshua Loring was threatened. Even Lieutenant Governor Oliver was forced to resign. Oliver's letter to Dartmouth of 3 Sept 1774 recounted that his home was surrounded by four thousand people, that he repeatedly refused to sign, that the people were not satisfied with his refusals, and that finally, when "the populace, growing impatient, began to press us to my windows, calling for vengeance gainst the foes of their liberty" and when he responded to "the distresses of my wife and children, which I heard in the next room," he signed, writing underneath "My house being surrounded with four thousand people, in compliance with their commands I signed my name." (PRO, e; Davies, 8, 183-184)

The Last of the Royal General Courts

An altercation occured at the conclusion of what turned out to be the last session of the Massachusetts General Court held under the command of the king's ministers. In his directions to Gage of 9 April 1774, the king had ordered that Boston "should cease to be the place of the Residence of the Governor, or of any other Officer of Government" and that the colonial affairs of Massachusetts should be administered from Salem until the king "shall have signified his Royal Will and Pleasure for the Return of His Governor to and for holding of the General Court at that Town." (PRO, f) Naturally Boston was not

pleased. The delegates who assembled at Salem on 9 June 1774 were
not in a submissive mood. It was necessary for the colonists to thwart
the king's efforts to reduce the importance of Boston as a center of the
opposition. How was that to be done? Plans had already been made for
a Continental Congress to be held in Philadelphia. Adams wanted five
delegates chosen by the Massachusetts legislature to represent that
colony in Philadelphia. On 17 June 1774, the day that the general
court opened, Adams arranged for the doors to be locked while the
legislature approved the five delegates and certain other resolutions.
When one delegate managed to get news to Gage, the governor sent
word that the general court was adjourned. However, Gage's secretary
could not secure admittance and was forced to announce the dissolution
from outside the room where the delegates were assembled. (PRO, g;
Davies, 18, 136) The governor was humiliated. The king would not
be happy with the news. Adams had suceeded in getting his delegates
appointed.

Why was Hancock not one of the five delegates chosen to go to
Philadelphia? A number of reasons can be offered. He may have been
in one of his periods of ill health. He may have been left to maintain
the momentum of the revolution in Boston. He may have wisely given
up his seat to John Adams in order to solidify the conversion of the
future second president of the United States. Furthermore, with the port
of Boston closed, Hancock had pressing business interests that required
his attention. If smuggling was going to be the only way of breaking
the British blockade, Hancock had had experience with smuggling and
undoubtedly wanted to keep his business as intact as possible.

During this period, those in England were more optimistic of
subduing the colonies than Gage could have been in Boston. On 6 July
1774 Dartmouth wrote to the governor: "The state in which you found
things at your arrival at Boston was better than I expected, and from
what has passed since I am inclined to hope that the tranquillity of the
province and the authority of government in it will speedily be
restored." (PRO, h; Davies, 8, 143) Only two months later, on 2 Sept
1774, Gage wrote to Dartmouth that he meant to avoid "any bloody
crisis" but that, if things were to be brought under control, "a very
respectable force should take the field." (PRO, i; Davies, 8, 181)

Withdrawal of Hancock's Colonelcy

On 1 Aug 1774, Gage did a spiteful act that cost the British dearly.
It is understandable why he was intensely provoked with Hancock, but
leaders need to restrain their anger. Instead Gage gave vent to his. At

Gage's instructions, his secretary Thomas Flucker wrote Hancock as follows:

Salem, August 1st 1774

Sir

I am directed by His Excellency the Captain General to acquaint you, that he has no further service for you, as Captain of the Governors [sic] Company of Cadets, and you are here dismissed from that Command.

I am
Sir your most obedient
humble servant

To the honble   Tho. Flucker Sect.
  Mr. Hancock
    Boston (BUA)

When Gage took out his vengeance on Hancock by dismissing him from his colonelcy, Hancock replied to his disbanded company: "I am ever ready to appear in a public Station, when the Honor or the Interest of the Community calls me; but shall always prefer Retirement to a private Station to being a Tool, in the hand of Power, to impress my Countrymen. " (*Gazette*, 29 Aug 1774, 1)[2]

The *Gazette* of 22 Aug 1774 reported that a committee of Colonel Hancock's Company waited upon General Gage. In its next isssue, on 29 Aug 1774, the *Gazette* noted that on 15 Aug 1774, the company delivered a letter expressing its "extreme Regret" at the removal of their first officer. The same issue of the *Gazette* printed the following letter from Gage to the company dated 16 Aug 1774:

> Gentlemen: Colonel Hancock has used me Ill, and has not treated me with that Respect that is due to the Governor of the Province; Therefore I dismissed him!—I will not be treated Ill by Colonel Hancock, nor any other Man in the Province.— Had I known your Intentions, I would have disbanded you before. Gentlemen, I accept the Standard.

On 18 Aug 1774, the company addressed a letter to Hancock which said in part:

> We will no longer detain you, Sir, than by an Assurance that it is the fervent Wish of our Hearts that your Health may be speedily and perfectly restored; that you may long live to support the superior Character you have hitherto maintain'd

and that our Country may never want so illustrious a Citizen,
to animate and conduct the Cause of VIRTUE and of
FREEDOM. (Boston *Gazette*, 29 Aug 1774, 1)

Anyone who had the slightest hope of reconciling himself with
Hancock could have predicted the reaction that would follow the
dismissal. Gage's letter clearly illustrates the arrogance that the English
took toward the colonists. Gage may well have become provoked
because Hancock did not attend Gage's welcoming banquet. But
Hancock did lead his company in the receiving ceremonies. It may have
been that Hancock's health was sufficiently fragile at that point that an
evening engagement was ill advised. Mid-May can be chilling in
Boston. Gage should have restrained his temper. He did not.

It was then plain that England was bent on challenging the colonies,
whom they thought could not begin to carry on a successful war against
Great Britain.

The Response of the Colonies to the Challenge Presented by England

On 10 Aug 1774, the Massachusetts delegates to the First
Continental Congress made a display of parting for their mission.
After having been given a farewell dinner, they assembled on the
Boston Common before Hancock's mansion to make a defiant departure,
driving off in a coach and four with livery men in front and behind. At
that point, Gage was not willing to take military steps to prevent the
assembly of the delegates. Adams and the other delegates were able to
leave Boston peaceably to begin their meetings in Philadelphia on 5
Sept 1774.

However, on 13 Aug 1774, Gage convened the Board of Selectmen.
Hancock did not attend. (RRC, a; Brown, 186) All "saving Collo.
[sic] Hancock waited" on the Governor. Gage informed the selectmen
that, according to two acts of Parliament, further meetings of the
selectmen could not be held without permission.[3] But the selectmen
had foreseen Gage's move. At their meetings, they had set the time of
the next meeting, so that the governor did not have to permit a new
session. (RRC, b) The old one would simply be continued. For
example, town meetings were held on 9 and 30 Aug and 13 Sept at
which Hancock was elected a delegate to the forthcoming General
Court. There were further meetings on 22 Sept, 25 Oct, and 1 Nov
1774, at which a committee who had waited upon the governor reported
that "he [Gage] was ready to do every thing in his Power to promote the

Peace and Good Order of the Town." (RRC, c) Therefore, the minutes
say that "we told him that at present we had no need of calling a Town
Meeting for we had two now alive, by Adjournment, one of them to be
some time this month, the other to be held in October." (RRC, d)[4]
Gage found himself again thwarted. He was forced to reply to
Dartmouth "that by thus doing we might keep the Meetings alive for
ten years." (RRC, e) In his letter of 27 Aug 1774 to Lord Dartmouth,
Gage wrote: "I laid the affair of adjournment before the new Council and
found some of opinion that the clause was thereby clearly evaded and
nearly the whole unwilling to debate upon it, terming it a point of law
which ought to be referred to the Crown lawyers." (PRO, j; Davies, 8,
166) British common law of honoring the motion as to the next time
and place of meeting had, in the eighteenth century, become recognized
as "law."

The Formation of the Rump Provincial Congress

On 1 Sept 1774, continuing under the king's instructions, Gage sent
notice for the General Court of Massachusetts to assemble, not in
Boston but again in Salem. The date appointed was Wednesday, 5 Oct
1774. On 28 Sept 1774, Gage retracted his convocation. (Lincoln, 3-4)
His reasons were that "the many tumults and disorders which have since
taken place, the extraordinary resolves which have been passed in many
of the counties, the instructions given by the town of Boston, and some
other towns, to their representatives, and the present disorder and
unhappy state of the province...made it inexpedient" to assemble a
General Court. (Lincoln, 3-4)

Nevertheless, on Wednesday, 5 Oct 1774, ninety delegates assembled
at Salem. (Lincoln, 4) Lincoln stated that on 5 Oct, "with cautious
courtesy," (4) the delegates waited the arrival of the governor to swear
them into session. On Thursday, 6 Oct 1774, still at Salem, those
delegates present organized themselves into a "convention." Hancock
was named chair and Benjamin Lincoln as secretary. In their reply to
Gage, the convention on 7 Oct asserted that "some of the causes
assigned as aforesaid for this unconstitutional and wanton prevention of
the general court, have, in all good governments, been considered
among the greatest reasons for convening a parliament or assembly."
(Lincoln, 6) The delegates notified Gage that they had resolved
themselves into a "Provincial Congress." The convention adjourned to
reconvene at Concord, a step closer to Boston.

On Tuesday, 11 Oct 1774, at Concord, the Congress confirmed the
election of John Hancock as chair and Benjamin Lincoln as clerk.

Estimates vary from 208 to 288 as to how much larger the convention at Concord was than the 90 who had assembled at Salem. (Lincoln, 4, n. 1) On 13 Oct 1774, the convention wrote Gage that his hostile preparations threatened "to involve us in all the confusion and horrors of a civil war." (Lincoln, 17) As of Friday, 14 Oct 1774, taxes were to be paid, not into the king's treasury, but into the coffers of the colony. (Lincoln, 19) On Monday, 17 Oct, the convention met at Cambridge, edging even closer to Boston.

On Wednesday, 19 Oct, a committee was appointed to explore what had to be done for the safety and defense of the province, (Lincoln, 23) and therefore the first step was taken to the establishment of a Massachusetts militia. No longer was lip service to be given to King George. The rhetoric of the Thanksgiving proclamation issued on 22 Oct 1774, omitted the words "God Save the King." (Lincoln, 28)

The Continental Congresses and the Movement for Independence

In order to determine the point at which the colonists became dedicated to independence, it is necessary to look at the actions of the Continental Congresses.

The First Continental Congress took place in Philadelphia in 1774. On 17 June 1774, Bowdoin, Cushing, Sam Adams, John Adams, and Robert Paine had been elected by the General Court during that first altercation between Gage and the rump assembly. On Wednesday, 23 Nov 1774, the First Provincial Congress of Massachusetts reappointed the same delegates, with the exception of Bowdoin. (Lincoln, 49, n. 1) Again Hancock was presumably to be left behind to keep the home front organized.

In a petition dated 26 Oct 1774, the Continental Congress offered terms to King George. The lengthy statement said that "had we been permitted to enjoy in quiet the inheritance left us by our forefathers, we should at this time have been peaceably, cheerfully and usefully employed in recommending ourselves by every testimony of devotion to your majesty, and of veneration to the state, from which we derive our origin." The statement concluded by asking that the gracious king grant them relief and stated that "all your faithful people in America" wished to remain the loyal subjects of the crown. (Journals of the Continental Congress, 1, 1774, 115-121)

It is significant that this petition was signed by Samuel Adams as one of the Massachusetts delegates. Although Adams may have sought earlier than many others to seek independence, he was still willing to accept a redress of grievances in the fall of 1774. As will be pointed out later, the king failed to give the "gracious answer" to their petition that was requested and therefore lost his chance to mollify the American colonies.

Instead, the king offered only more challenges to the freedom of the colonies. But even with all of the British acts of provocation, Davidson concluded that "secession, or independence...began to develop slowly after 1773....Only a very few of the propagandists had independence in mind and worked consciously for it before April, 1775." (Davidson, 37) If the British had acted propitiously and had not continued to threaten the colonists, the radicals who were working for independence before 1775 would not have had the support they were later given. However, the inflammatory language of the Committee of Correspondence and the enthusiastic response of the citizens of towns near Boston to that language shows undoubtedly that the spirit of revolt was alive and well in Massachusetts some time before 1773 and only the repeated mistakes of the British were needed to move dissent into armed rebellion. As early as 1766, the impasse between the British and the Americans had reached serious proportions. What would have happened to that impasse if the king had responded graciously to the petition of the Continental Congress of 1774 can only be the subject of speculation.

The British had yet a second chance. As late as 8 July 1775, from Philadelphia, the Congress wrote "to the king's most excellent Majesty" requesting that "Your Majesty be pleased to direct some mode by which the united applications of your faithful colonists to the Throne in pursuance of their common councils may be improved into a happy and permanent reconciliation." (PRO, k; Journal, "Petition to the King," 2, 1775, 158-162) The petition spoke of the king receiving "such satisfactory proofs of the disposition of the colonists towards their sovereign" that would incite their devotion as dutiful subjects. Hancock as president of the Continental Congress and forty-eight others as delegates from the states, including both Sam Adams and John Adams, signed the lengthy petition. But no reconciliation was to be forthcoming. The British were confident of winning.

As Davidson pointed out, by 1775, the mood of the colonies had shifted toward separation. In reflecting on what had been his opinions in the spring of 1775, John Adams wrote that "we ought to declare the Colonies free, sovereign, and independent States, and then to inform Great Britain we were willing to enter into negotiations with them for the redress of all grievances." (Adams, 2, 407) If the negotiations were to take place between Great Britain and independent states, had Adams contemplated that, in the redress of grievances, the states would give up their sovereignty? That seems unlikely. Hancock did not live long enough to reminisce about his attitudes in 1775. It is quite possible that he shared the views of Adams: First, independence. Then the colonists would see.

Or Hancock may have been so occupied with numerous posts that he avoided facing the eventualities of his actions. Freedom he sought. What would be the full ramifications of that freedom Hancock may not have contemplated.

It can be concluded that the British lost their chance of reconciliation by the king's failure to open negotiations in 1774.

How Were Events in Massachusetts Moving toward Independence?

Gage's responses to the messages he received from the rump convention were also not conciliatory. His reply of 17 Oct 1774 warned the colonists "of the rock you are upon, and to require you to desist from such illegal and unconstitutional proceedings." (Lincoln, 20-21)

The split between the Whigs and the Tories in Massachusetts grew wider and wider. Those who remained as Tories were soon to find it necessary (a) to convert to the separatist cause, (b) to remain under the protection of the British troops in Boston, or (c) to emigrate to such English possessions as Nova Scotia, the West Indies, or England itself. Should the rebellion be put down, they planned to return in triumph. As was said before, the odds were certainly in the favor of the Tories. Undoubtedly, even in his enthusiasm, Hancock did not fail to see the perils ahead. But, in this instance, a long shot paid off and the "absentees" lost their country and their property. The revolutionaries won a war that seemed impossible to win.

NOTES

1. In the letter of Thomas Flucker, Gage's secretary, to John Hancock, undated but probably written on 20 May 1774, (BUA, Massachusetts First Corps of Cadets Papers, A142) there is a reference to Hancock's inattentiveness to the governor, which may well be a reference to Hancock's absence from the governor's banquet. Hancock's illnesses again played a part in his political life. Was he ill on 19 May 1774, or did he use illness as an excuse to snub the new governor?

2. Boston University's collection of the First Corps of Cadets papers does not contain this letter, but includes a letter from William Palfrey to Samuel

Adams stating: "The Company had another meeting when they voted an address of thanks to their late Collo. which was presented to him by a reputable Committee and they receiv'd a very polite and friendly answer." (Letter from Mugar Memorial Library, BUA, 25 Jan 1988)

3. On 28 Mar 1774, Lord North introduced a bill to make the town meetings convened at the will of the governor, saying in debate in the Commons: "Every gentleman will naturally see the impropriety of such irregular assemblies, or town-meetings, which are now held in Boston; I would have them brought under some regulation, and would not suffer them to be held without the consent of the governor." (*Parliamentary History of England*, 17, col. 1193) As to the second of the acts to which Gage referred, he may have had in mind the "third Bill" introduced by North on 15 Apr 1774 which provided for "the suppression of the riots and tumults in the province of Massachuset's [sic] Bay." (*Parliamentary History of England*, 17, col. 1201) Lord North introduced his first bill concerning Boston on 14 Mar 1774; the second on 28 March 1774; and the third on 15 Apr 1774.

4. Gage to Dartmouth, 27 Aug 1774, *Correspondence of Thomas Gage*, 1, 366: "They replied, they had *called* no Meeting, that a former Meeting had only adjourned themselves."

8

The Revolution

By 1775, Hancock was a confirmed revolutionist, and the colony was under military control.

During 1775, Hancock held the following positions:

a. On 30 Dec 1774, at a town meeting in Faneuil Hall, Hancock had been elected a representative from Boston to the Second Provincial (Massachusetts) Congress, along with Thomas Cushing, Sam Adams, Joseph Warren, Benjamin Church, Oliver Wendell, and John Pitts (RRC, 221) He served in this capacity throughout 1775.

b. On 1 Feb 1775, Hancock was chosen president of the Second Provincial Congress of Massachusetts. (Lincoln, 83-84)

c. On 2 Dec 1774, Hancock had been named along with Thomas Cushing, Sam Adams, John Adams, and Robert Paine to represent Massachusetts at the Second Continental Congress to be held in May of 1775 in Philadelphia. (Lincoln, 55)

d. On 9 Feb 1775, Hancock was reelected by the Second Provincial Congress as a member of the Committee of Safety, along with Warren, Church, and nine others. (Lincoln, 89) This committee was to serve as a watch-dog to prevent any subversion from occuring, and presaged the famous Committees of Public Safety of the French Revolution.

e. On 13 Mar 1775, Hancock had been named selectman of the Town of Boston, along with six others. (RRC, 217)

In other words, Hancock had achieved full stature as a leader of the revolt.

Moves by the Colonists

What were the moves made by the colonists to the threats of occupation and then to actual military law? What countermoves did the British make?

In February of 1775, the Second Provincial Congress met in Cambridge. Hancock presided. Even though Hancock and other Whigs still kept their residences in Boston, the Tories had assumed control of the town. Those opposing the king began to contemplate their exodus, knowing that they could not return until the dispute was settled. While Hancock was at the Provincial Congress, his mansion was the target of physical abuse by British troops who entered his estate on the excuse that they were looking for possible barracks space. Hancock issued strenuous objections. Gage ordered the troops off the property, but not before some damage had been done.

On 14 Feb 1775, the Second Provincial Congress placed the committee of public safety in power over military supplies until such time as an army could be organized. (Lincoln, 97) This resolve set the scene for the battles at Lexington and Concord and precipitated Gage's efforts to secure for the crown the military supplies stored outside Boston.

While the colonists made their preparations, what was the posture of the British government? The king and Lord Dartmouth, the secretary of state for the American Department, augmented the steps that had been taken in early 1774.

Following the Boston Tea Party, the king had instructed Dartmouth to consult the British solicitor-general about what charges might be made against the colonists. On 5 Feb 1774, Dartmouth sent to the attorney- and solicitor-general in London a detailed narrative of the events of the Boston Tea Party. (PRO, a) In the narrative, Dartmouth noted that "Mr. Hancock, the captain of Governor's cadet company, was one of the guard on board the ships" (PRO, a) and asked if the acts described in the narrative did not constitute high treason.

On 11 Feb 1774, the attorney-and solicitor-general answered Dartmouth that specified persons, including "Handcock [sic]" were guilty of high treason. The attorney advised that those guilty of such crimes could be tried either in the colonies or in England.[1] (PRO, b)

The political conclusions that treason had been committed were made early in 1774. The result was the passage of the Intolerable Acts and the asssignment of General Gage to Boston. However, the outcome of such legislation was to arouse the colonists further toward rebellion. When the reaction of the Americans became clear, the British felt it necessary to proceed further.

In his opening address to the English House of Commons on 29 Nov 1774, the king had devoted much of his message to his continuing concerns with Massachusetts. "I have taken such measures, and given such orders, as I judged most proper and effectual for carrying into execution the laws which were passed in the last session of the late parliament, for the protection and security of the commerce of my subjects, and for the restoring and preserving peace, order, and good government, in the province of Massachuset's [sic] Bay." The king added that he would remain firm in establishing his authority over his dominions. (*Parliamentary History of England*, 18, cols.33-34) The laws were, of course, the Intolerable Acts.

The House of Commons found the posture of the colonists equally objectionable. On 2 Feb 1775, Attorney- and Solicitor-General Thurlow, during a debate on the state of affairs in America, listed for the Commons a series of acts of the colonists, and concluded: "Now, Sir, if this is not rebellion, I desire the learned gentlemen will explain what is rebellion." (*Parliamentary History of England*, 18, col. 226) As Thurlow had advised Dartmouth in 1774, open rebellion constituted high treason. The search for documentation to arrest selected colonists had so far not been fruitful. George III's correspondence with North shows how the British reacted:

(1) In a letter dated 19 Nov 1774, the king wrote to North concerning Gage's suggestion that the Port Bill be suspended. "The people are ripe for mischief," said the king, "upon which the mother country adopts suspending the measures she thought necessary: this must suggest to the colonies a fear that alone prompts them to their present violence; we must either master them totally or totally leave them to themselves and treat them as aliens. I do not mean to insinuate that I am for advice [sic] [advising] new measures; but I am for supporting those already undertaken." (Donne, 1, 216) The measures "already undertaken" included the Intolerable Acts and the instructions to Gage notifying him to act against the colonists in his best judgment. The king's alternatives, he stated, were either to subdue the rebellion or fight a war against his own subjects.

(2) Having ruled out concessions, the crown had to take further action. On 2 Feb 1775, Lord North, as a part of a plan to deal with the

unrest in the colonies, moved to declare that "a rebellion at this time actually exists within the said province [Massachusetts Bay]," with collusion from the other colonies. (*Parliamentary History of England*, 18, col. 223; Aikin, 1, 159) Open rebellion was thus proclaimed. Those who were the leaders of the rebellion knew what penalties might lie in store for them.

Implementation of the Charges of Treason

Having been given the legal support he sought, on 9 Apr 1774, as was pointed out previously, Dartmouth wrote to Gage, instructing him to return to Boston and advising the general that "the sovereignty of the King...requires a full and absolute submission, and His Majesty's dignity demands that until that submission be made the town of Boston where so much anarchy and confusion have prevailed [,] should cease to be the place of the residence of his governor." (PRO, c) Dartmouth enclosed a copy of the Attorney's report.

Although the British attorney general had ruled that the perpetrators of the Boston Tea Party could be tried in England, Dartmouth wrote Gage that it did not seem advisable to bring the instigators of the crime to England to proceed against them. Dartmouth stated:

> The object of the Enquiry made here, was to have established such a charge against the Ring leaders in those violences [during the Boston Tea Party], as might have enabled His Majesty to have proceeded against them in this Kingdom: It was found however upon the result that it would be difficult, clear and positive as the Evidence was with respect to some parts of the proceedings, to establish such a connection between the Acts of the body of the People, and the destruction of the Tea, as to leave no doubt of the propriety and effect of bringing over the persons charged to be tried here. (PRO, d)

Gage was told to employ his "utmost endeavors to obtain sufficient evidence against the principal actors therein" (PRO, d; Davies, 8, 88) and to prosecute if he saw fit. "The King," said Dartmouth, "considers the punishment of these offenders as a very necessary and essential example to others of the ill consequences that must follow from such open and arbitrary usurpations as tend to subversion of all government." (PRO, d) However, Gage was advised that, if it did not seem likely that a colonial court would convict, he should not proceed. (PRO, d) Hancock was not named in Dartmouth's letter to Gage of 9 April 1774, but he did not have to be, for Hancock had been specified in Dartmouth's letter of 5 Feb 1774 to the king's solicitor and in the reply of the king's solicitor of 11 Feb 1774.

Reactions to Gage's Arrival in Boston

Upon his arrival in Boston on 13 May 1774, Gage realized that the English authorities had passed the buck to him. Hutchinson had sailed for England on 1 June 1774. Whatever trials might result from the Boston Tea Party were to be held in the colonies and any failure to convict would be received with much disfavor in England. Gage proceeded with caution.

In the meantime, the attitudes of the king, the attorney general, and Dartmouth began to reach the colonies. There was widespread alarm. For a colonist to be tried in England was against colonial principles, but those tried would almost certainly be convicted. A letter dated London, 10 Feb 1775, parts of which were printed in the Philadelphia *Gazette* of 3 May 1775, demonstrated the extent to which Hancock risked imprisonment:

> An address to the King has past [sic] both houses, to give the
> King power to call you rebels, and to proceed against you on
> the late acts, and direct to put them in force against the
> Congress, and to support the King against the Colonies, with
> their lives and fortunes.

Later on in the same letter, the anonymous correspondent wrote that "orders have now gone out to take up Mr. Hancock, Adams, Williams, Otis, and six of the head men in Boston.—I have now a copy of the proceedings before me." The colonial sympathizer added that the British intended to seize Hancock's estate and have his fine house for General —— [Gage]. The correspondent advocated that strong measures be taken to rescue Hancock from capture:

> Tell the printers immediately to advertise for young men to go
> to Boston, and bring Hancock and his brave men away, and if
> Gage refuses, seize him...A bill of attainder is to be passed
> against them; the King is determined to make you submit...

The letter concluded that the name of the correspondent must be kept secret, because of the "great pains taken to find out who writes to America, and informs them of the proceedings of the Court."

What the anonymous letter referred to, of course, was North's proposal of 2 Feb 1775 that the colonists be considered as rebels and also to the action taken earlier than 27 Jan 1775, by the king's Cabinet. Coupled with an earlier bill introduced by Lord North on 15 Apr 1774, which provided that the governor had the power to send an accused "to Great Britain to be tried before the court of King's Bench," (*Parliamentary History of England*, 17, col. 1200) the king could arrest the leaders of the rebellion for treason and bring them to England for trial. The action to remove selected trials to England had caused much consternation among the colonists when it was passed back in 1774. North's personal vindictiveness toward Hancock and others had been plainly stated in his speech before the Commons on 15 April 1774, in which North had said: "There is one thing I much wish which is, the punishment of those individuals who have been the ringleaders and forerunners of these mischiefs. Our attention will be continually active in that point. A prosecution has been already ordered against them by his Majesty's servants, but I cannot promise myself any very good effect until this law shall have reached the province." (*Parliamentary History of England*, 17, col. 1201) Obviously, when North said that "a prosecution has been already ordered against them," he was referring to the attorney- and solicitor-general's opinion and the instructions given to Gage. The "law" that was to reach the province was Dartmouth's instructions to Gage to proceed as he saw fit.

How Could Arrests Be Made, If Gage Elected to Do So?

As Parliament had given its blessing to the apprehension of the rebels, how were the arrests to be done? By the King's Bench? That procedure could not be kept secret. So it was not to be the King's Bench that would issue warrants for the arrests, but rather General Gage acting with permission of the king's Cabinet with the king's approval. On 27 Jan 1775, Lord Dartmouth had written to Gage:

> ... it is the Opinion of The King's Servants [the Cabinet] in which His Majesty concurs, that the first & essential step to be taken towards re-establishing Government, would be to arrest and imprison the principal actors & abettors in the Provincial Congress (whose proceedings appear in every light to be acts of treason & rebellion)...and if the steps taken upon this occasion be accompanied with due precaution, and every means be devised to keep the Measure Secret until the moment

of Execution, it can hardly fail of Success, and will perhaps be accomplished without bloodshed... (PRO, e)

Therefore Hancock, Adams, and others were to be secretly arrested and imprisoned, via bills of attainder. With the courts closed and no bill of rights to protect them, the Boston leaders could be imprisoned indefinitely. If matters came to trial, the actions would probably proceed in colonial courts. It is no wonder that Gage did not so act. Even he could sense what would be the immediate reaction of the colonies.

Dartmouth, from his viewpoint in England, was not so guarded as was Gage. In his letter of 27 Jan 1775, Dartmouth again stated that all was left to the discretion of Gage to proceed or not, as he saw fit. Dartmouth, in underestimating the colonists as usual, said that, even if hostilities should occur, the colonists "were unprepared to encounter with a regular force" and so not much trouble was to be expected. (PRO, e) Dartmouth found the colonists' resistance to be composed of a "rude Rabble without plan, without concert, & without conduct" (PRO, e) and therefore should be easily put down. Dartmouth suggested that, since the temper of the colonies would make a conviction of those arrested unlikely, "their imprisonment however will prevent their doing any further mischief; and as the Courts of justice are at present not permitted to be opened, the continuance of that imprisonment will be no slight punishment." (PRO, e) So, after he received Lord Dartmouth's letter on 14 April 1775, it was still up to Gage to make the move. Undoubtedly pressure was on him to take some action. What action would he take?

Dartmouth sent Gage another letter on 15 April 1775, again saying "that the King entirely relies on your discretion." However, Dartmouth reminded Gage that "if you shall continue to be of opinion that an offer of pardon will be advisable, you do in virtue of the power already given to you by His Majesty's special commission under the Great Seal for pardoning treasons and other offences issue a proclamation within your government at such time as you shall judge proper, offering a reasonable reward for apprehending the president, secretary and any other of the members of the Provincial Congress whom you shall find to have been the most forward and active in that seditious meeting." (PRO, f) Hancock and Sam Adams would have been high among the list of those whom Dartmounth exempted from any offer of pardon. Their actions at the tea party and at the Continental Congress had put them beyond redemption. Obviously this letter suggesting the arrest of the leaders was not received by Gage until after 18 April and the battles at Lexington and Concord during which the British lost a fortuitious opportunity to capture both Hancock and Adams. Nevertheless, Gage knew whom to capture when and if he could. John was high on the list.

The Counter-Moves of the Colonists

In the meanwhile, what was happening to the Provincial Congress? Again, it is necessary to review briefly the events of 1774. As was stated previously, on 5 Oct 1774, General Gage had convened the General Assembly to meet at Salem. But he thought the better of it and attempted to prorogue the session. However, it continued to meet as a rump assembly, transferring to Concord on 11 Oct 1774, and later to Cambridge to be as close to Boston as possible. In December, when the Provincial Congress recessed, Hancock was able to spend Christmas at his home in Boston. By February the Provincial Congress was again meeting in Cambridge. Hancock and Adams were able to come into Boston to attend the annual commemoration of the massacre at the Old South Church in Boston on 6 Mar 1775. There were rumors of a plot to assasinate them at the cememony, but only an alarming disturbance occurred. A riot almost ensued when the heckling of the British officers crying "Fie, fie," was mistaken for "Fire, fire." The Barker account reported that the commotion occurred after the main speech, when Hancock briefly took the rostrum and addressed the crowd. (25-26) According to a recently published diary, the false alarm caused people to leave the Old South Church hastily by doors and windows.

By late March, 1775, the Provincial Congress was meeting again in Concord. Hancock wrote to Dolly from Concord protesting that he could say little because the room was full of people. However, he did write enough of a love letter to say that "no person on earth can be possessed of greater affection & Regard for anyone, than I have for the Lady to whom I address this, & be fully Convinc'd that no Distance of time or place can ever Erase the Impressions made & the Determinations I have form'd of being forever yours." (BPL) This is the closest to a love letter by Hancock that has been preserved. In the eighteenth century, Hancock would have been perhaps conservative in expressing his love, but his letter to Dolly from Concord shows the restraint of his particular personality.

While Dartmouth's letter of 27 Jan 1775 was on the way, Gage was still hesitant to act. Woodbury in her biography of Dorothy Quincy quoted the following as presented in a Tory ballad:

As for their King, that John Hancock,
And Adams, if they're taken;
Their heads for signs shall hang up high
Upon the hill called Beacon! (Woodbury, 69)

When the Provincial Congress adjourned to meet in May of 1775, Hancock and Adams decided not to return to Boston but rather to join Dolly and Aunt Lydia at Hancock's grandfather's house a few yards from the center of Lexington. Dolly & Lydia had felt it propitious to leave Boston, but, in joining them, Hancock and Adams were merely seeking a quiet rest from the business of state. They had no intention of entering into the immediate turmoil of the battle of Lexington and Concord. But the stage was set for the shot that made such a difference, not only to the American colonies, but also to the future of world politics.

Lord North had got two acts through Parliament in the spring of 1775 that further aggravated the colonists. The first was to restrain the trade of the New England colonies to Britain, Ireland, and the British West Indies, cutting off the colonies' thriving business with the French West Indies, the Canary Islands, Northern Africa, and the Mediterranean. (*Parliamentary History of England*, 18, cols. 285-399) The second act extended the prohibitions to the "southern colonies" except New York, Delaware, North Carolina, and Georgia. (*Parliamentary History of England*, 18, cols. 593-606) It was thought that the four colonies excluded were more loyal, an opinion which they were unlikely to have thought a compliment.

On 14 Apr 1775, the ship *Nautilus* arrived in Boston and on 16 Apr 1775, the ship *Faulcon*. (PRO, g) In his letter to Dartmouth of [22] Apr 1775, Gage acknowledged receiving the acts taken by England up to 11 Feb 1775. (PRO, g) Once he had Dartmouth's letters of 27 Jan 1775, confirming that he should proceed against the colonists as he saw fit, and once he knew from Dartmouth's letter of 22 Feb 1775 (PRO, h; Gage, 2, 185; Davies, 9, 54) that troop reinforcements as well as Generals William Howe, John Burgoyne, and Henry Clinton were to join him, Gage was ready to act. He elected to attack Lexington and Concord. Gage speculated that the same ships that brought him news of troop reinforcements and authorization to arrest the leaders had contained letters notifying the colonists of the same matters. On [22] April 1775 Gage wrote to Dartmouth: "I can't learn whether she [the ship] brought Letters to any of the Faction here, but the News threw them into a Consternation, and the most active left the Town before Night." (PRO, g) Although this essay cannot include the details of the conflict at Lexington and Concord, it should relate those events that reflect directly on Hancock.

Hancock at Lexington and Concord

Gage should not have been at all surprised by the vigor of the resistance at Lexington and Concord. His correspondence demonstrates that he was aware of how hostile the entire colony was and that the revolt was not limited to Boston. The fact that he dispatched what were obvious targets—red-coated troops, men marching down a predictable route—again shows the conceit of the British in their "regulars" and their failure to comprehend the strength of colonial opposition. Gage had advised the king that four regiments would be enough to subdue the colonists, who were being lions only as long as the British were being lambs. (Donne, 1, 164) The attempt to turn the British lambs into lions was to prove inadequate at Concord.

The spy, Dr. Benjamin Church, who delivered the third Boston Massacre address, had tipped off the British that there were supplies in Concord. The revolutionaries had spies as well, including Paul Revere, who remained in Boston to keep watch on the British. Revere noted activity that prompted the Committee of Public Safety to remove the arms from Concord. One if by land; two if by sea. At midnight on Tuesday, 18 Apr 1775, four days after Gage had received the letters from Dartmouth, Revere woke the household at the old Bishop's house. The attack was on the way. Dawes arrived a few minutes later, he and Revere having taken alternate routes, so that if one were captured, the other could still get the message through. Hancock did not wish to miss the inevitable clash of arms. It could have been more than vanity as a former colonel that caused him to want to fight himself. After all he had contributed to the cause, here he was, by luck, "on the spot," for the first major military action. He wanted to be in on it. But Sam Adams prevailed on him to leave Lexington in haste, where he was joined the next day in Woburn by Lydia and Dolly.

Gage's failure was threefold: he failed to capture Adams and Hancock; he failed to capture the arms in Concord; and he lost far more men than the colonists. The American casualties were 93; the British 273. (French, 2, 584)

Lexington and Concord Reflected in the Hancock Speeches

The reader of Hancock's speeches may find it difficult to be sympathetic with how thankful Hancock continued to be for the success of the revolution. Readers of his speeches may not understand the numerous references he made to the good fortune of the colonies. But it must be remembered that Hancock was in on the action from the beginning. Hancock's insight into the remainder of the revolution was highly influenced by being wakened at Lexington in the middle of the night, by being forced to decide between joining the fight or fleeing to safety, and by the misgivings he must have had in riding away from, instead of into, the scene of the action. He and Adams had no illusions about the effectiveness of the hastily recruited minutemen. They knew the reputation of the British soldiers. When they did get news of the battle at Concord, it must have seemed to them a miracle that the opening victory was as conclusive as it was, particularly after what could be considered the loss of the first skirmish at Lexington. The opening shots at Lexington had undoubtedly alerted the fiercely independent farmers that a fight was to happen right down the road and that they also had a chance to "get in on it." Such excitement attracts some and repels others. It attracted enough backwoodsmen with accurate rifles to rout the British and perform what was to some a miracle. It attracted Hancock, and he probably continued to feel some guilt for accepting Adams' advice and fleeing from the armed conflict.

The success of the revolution continued to be a miracle, for the remainder of the lives of the people so closely involved in it. Those who survive a war, and particularly those who win a war, are likely to want to talk about its better features. The hours that Hancock lived during the conflict at Lexington and Concord made a permanent difference in him. Even Aunt Lydia, it is said, had a bullet whiz above her head, although the present custodians of the bishop's house appear to have little knowledge of how close and how involved were the occupants of the house in the battle. Hancock's subsequent speeches as governor can only be understood if the events in his life that touched closely on the war are kept in mind.

Further Moves of the Colonists

The opening of hostilities made it imperative that Massachusetts itself raise an army and that the colonists join forces more concertedly than they had in the past. Some moves had already been made. On 8 Apr 1775, the Second Provincial Congress had authorized one of its committees to report on the raising and establishing of an army. (Lincoln, 135) On 10 Apr 1775, a letter had been sent to Connecticut, Rhode Island, and New Hampshire advising them of certain actions being taken by Massachusetts and announcing that Massachusetts would soon be sending delegates to them for advice and consultation. (Lincoln, 137) Other moves were still necessary. On 20 and 26 April 1775, the Massachusetts Provincial Congress wrote to Rhode Island, Connecticut, and New Hampshire, (Lincoln, 518-519, n.1 & 523-524) asking that they join in resisting the British. By 23 April, Massachusetts resolved to raise 13,600 men to form part of an army of 30,000 colonists. (Lincoln, 148)

The Moves of the National Continental Congress

On 22 Apr 1775, Hancock and Adams, fugitives from Boston, set out for Worcester, to proceed to Philadelphia for the national Congress. They were joined by other delegates on the way, and a military escort insured their safety. On 6 May 1775, the Massachusetts and Connecticut delegations entered New York to receive a warm welcome from the populace. On 7 May 1775, Hancock wrote to "my dear Dolly:"

> I...Set out in Procession for New York, the Carriage of your humble Servant of course being first in the Procession, when we arriv'd within three miles of the City we were met by the Grenadier Company & Regiment of the City Militia under arms Gentlemen in Carriages & on horseback and many Thousands of Persons on Foot, the Roads fill'd with people, and the greatest Cloud of Dust I ever saw, in this Situation we entered the City and passing thro' the Principal Streets of New York amidst the declamation of Thousands we were Set Down at Mr. Francis's, after entering the House three Huzzas were Given, & the People by Degrees Dispers'd. When I got within a Mile of the City my Carriage was Stop'd & Persons appearing with proper Harnesses insisted upon taking out my Horses, & Dragging me into and thro' the City, a Circumstances I would not have had taken place upon any Consideration, not being fond of such Parade, I Beg'd & Intreated that [sic] suspend the design... (MHS, a)

Much of the rest of the three-page letter is devoted to the reception John received in New York. Another attempt to withdraw the horses and let the people drag the carriage into the city was resisted. Hancock estimated the crowd at seven thousand. With Hancock's vanity, in spite of his denials, the reception must have been very gratifying to him. On 10 May 1775, the delegates reached Philadelphia. Just as Hancock's carriage had received the most honors in New York, so it did in Philadelphia. (Fowler, 188)

The expectations of the Second Continental Congress must have been most speculative. The newcomers, Benjamin Franklin, Thomas Jefferson, and John Hancock, no doubt added much stability to the group. But it appeared that there was so much to be done and so little with which to accomplish it.

Peyton Randolph of Virginia was elected president of both the First and Second Continental Congresses. When, because of ill health, he retired from the position at the First Continental Congress after less than a month, Henry Middleton of South Carolina became the presiding officer for the remainder of the first Congress. When Randolph was called back to the House of Burgesses after the Second Continental Congress began, Middleton declined to serve again as presiding officer because of poor health. Hancock was then elected unanimously. Here was one time, at least, when Hancock did not plead his ailments to avoid responsibility. The delegates wanted the Southern colonies to feel a definite part of the Congress. After two tries to pay them their prosper respect, the second Congress did not hesitate to choose a man who had already demonstrated his strengths as a revolutionary and his success as a presiding officer. At this point in his career at the Continental Congress, Hancock still had the support of his own Massachusetts delegation.

No wonder that Fowler termed Hancock's job "a Herculean task." (Fowler, 191) The delegates still owed their primary allegiance to their states; it was not certain whether Randolph was simply on leave or had been replaced; the British garrison at Boston had greatly increased in numbers and other states knew that it would not be long before the British arrived there as well. Sears observed that "the chairman of this heterogeneous and non-commissioned assemblage had to deal fairly and courteously with men from all along the coast, whatever his own predilections were." (Sears, 181) Undoubtedly the most difficult for Hancock to manage were those who retained degrees of Tory sympathy. However, in Boston, Hancock had dealt with many Tory sympathizers. It would be much easier to manage those with only some misgivings about making a complete break with England than it would with zealous Tories. John's experiences as a moderator at the tumultous meetings in Boston were now paying dividends.

At this point an action by Hancock must be noted that is difficult to comprehend, to wit, he wished to be commander in chief of the continental armies. When John Adams advanced the name of George Washington, Hancock was visibly hurt. Hancock had a very sudden change of countenance. Adams wrote in his diary that "mortification and resentment were expressed as forcibly as his face could exhibit them." (Adams, 2, 417) Although no one had suffered more at the expense of the revolution than Hancock, he was ill fitted to command an army. The most sympathetic explanation of his mistaken notion is that he wanted to keep the momentum of rebellion rolling and that he wanted to continue to be an active and not a passive part of that momentum. The most unsympathetic explanation is that he was exhibiting the vanity that he sometimes could not suppress. Whatever the case, on 18 June 1775, Hancock wrote to Joseph Warren: "The Congress have Appointed George Washington, Esqr., General & Commander in Chief of the Continental Army. His Commission is made out and I shall Sign it to morrow,[sic] he is a Gent'm you will all like. I Submit to you the propriety of providing a suitable place for his Residence, and the mode of his Reception." (MHS, b) Although Hancock was often an enthusiastic supporter of the general, the memory of the selection of Washington never entirely disappeared from the consciousness of either man, as was demonstrated when Washington made his first visit to Boston as president of the United States. On the other hand, Hancock gave his only, ill-fated son the name of John George Washington Hancock. One does not name his only son after someone with whom there is a lasting antagonism.

Again, what influence did the rivalry between Washington and Hancock have upon Hancock's outlook upon the revolution? It explains in part the lofty tone that Hancock so often took during the years between 1780 and 1788. After all, he was the governor of the state in which the armed conflict had begun. But, to Hancock's credit, even though he knew that a ratification of the federal Constitution would reduce his own powers, he insured its passage in Massachusetts, as his speeches in January and February of 1788 show. Hancock was not going to let his own vanity, no matter how great, stand in the way of achieving the goal of establishing a new nation. In the eighteenth century, Hancock was looking for a country, just as was Gandhi in the twentieth century. Although John Adams and Thomas Jefferson were to live to be old men and to die simultaneously on the same July 4th, Hancock was to live only five years after the federal Constitution was adopted. The race had been run; the battle won. Hancock's rhetoric so often shows his pride in that accomplishment. If there had been more rivers to cross, perhaps Hancock would have willed his wasted body to hold on until they were conquered as well. But he did not need to do so. His rhetoric tells us again and again that the miracle of which they had all so often despaired had been achieved. Even though Hancock was not always satisfied with the way in which his national government was progressing, it seems certain that he died contented in having added materially to the foundation of a new state. The same cannot be said of Gandhi. He had to face from the beginning a division of his country, that was only faced by Americans some seventy years after initial unity had been insured.

Meanwhile, Back in Boston

The same day that Hancock left Boston for Philadelphia, the people of Boston were trying to make a workable arrangement with Gage to keep the town viable. At a town meeting moderated by Bowdoin, the people were notified that Gage and the selectmen had met in an effort to come to a working agreement about the relationships between the inhabitants and Gage. The selectmen had worked out certain agreements with Gage and sought the approval of the town for their actions. Certain resolutions were passed at the town meeting. It was agreed that, if a battle took place between the red-coats and the colonials on the neck, the peaceful inhabitants of Boston would not be harmed. The citizens, fearing a shortage of supplies, were informed that Gage intended to encourage commerce between town and country to provision the inhabitants. Furthermore, Gage had agreed to order that those who deposited their arms with the selectmen would be given permission to leave with their effects. On 23 April 1775, Gage confirmed his agreement to allow the inhabitants who deposited their arms with the selectmen to leave, only it was specified that they should mark their arms with their names. It was also agreed that those who remained in Boston were to have Gage's protection. The town voted to accept these negotiations. (Houghton) Of course, many colonial sympathizers, including Hancock and Adams, had already left.

The Offer of Amnesty

On 12 June 1775, Gage had posted a broadside offering pardon to all who would lay down their arms, "except" only Samuel Adams and John Hancock, "whose Offenses are too flagitious a Nature to admit of any other Consideration than that of condign Punishment." (MH, c) The poster concluded with "God Save the King." George III needed saving if he was to retain his North American colonies. His cause among the thirteen states was fast being lost. The Sam Adams faction released its own copy of Gage's proclamation with the following preface:

Cambridge, June 14, 1775

The following is a Copy of an *infamous Thing* handed about here Yesterday, and now reprinted to satisfy the Curiosity of the Public. As it is replete with consummate Impudence, abominable Lies, and stuffed with daring Expressions of Tyranny, as well as Rebellion against the established, constituted Authority of the AMERICAN STATES, no one will hesitate in pronouncing it be the *genuine* Production of that perfidious, petty Tyrant, *Thomas Gage*.[3]

Gage had also decided that military occupation of Boston was not enough. Following his offer of amnesty, in the same broadside, Gage declared Boston under martial law. He had finally decided to act under the authority he had been given earlier. But, as the newspaper addendum illustrated, the colonists were not to be intimidated. Gage acted with too little too late.

On 1 August 1775, Congress adjourned until 5 Sept. Hancock was free to return to Massachusetts to assist the General Court meeting in Watertown and to marry Dolly. There was no question of returning to Boston. Undoubtedly he would have been arrested had he returned home. In his diary entry for 10 Aug 1775, Boyle noted that, in a census of the town conducted by General Gage, there were 13,600 inhabitants, including troops, women and children. Boyle concluded that about 14,000 inhabitants had fled to the country. (Boyle, 23) Many others would probably have gone, had they a place of refuge. As with many wars, the more influential have the resources to establish a second place of residence, outside the sphere of the fighting, whereas the poor have to run their chances in the only dwelling they have.

After visiting with Dolly briefly at Fairfield, where she was staying with the Burrs during the British occupation of Boston, Hancock joined the Massachusetts General Court at Watertown. He was torn between three interests: first, his recent experiences in Philadelphia; second, his allegiance to the state legislature of Massachusetts; and third, his forthcoming marriage on 28 Aug 1775, to Dolly. From Watertown on 14 Aug 1775 he wrote to Dolly, "You must Excuse me in not writing a long letter, as I am greatly Engag'd, & can only plead as an Excuse, that the more time I take in writing the longer will it be before I finish my other business," and therefore before he could join her at Fairfield. (MHS, d) Immediately after the wedding, the Hancocks set off for Philadelphia to arrive in time for the reconvening of Congress on 5 Sept.

Hancock still considered himself President of the Congress. But Peyton Randolph had returned to Philadelphia from Virginia. On 19 Sept 1775, John Adams wrote to James Warren: "Mr. Randolph our former President is here and Sits very humbly in his Seat, while our new one continues in the Chair, without Seeming to feel the Impropriety." (Warren-Adams Letters, I, 112) Hancock chose to ignore the implication that Randolph had only taken leave from his post rather than resigning it. And it was a good thing he did, for Randolph died very suddenly on 22 Oct 1775, after dining with friends.

The Treachery of Dr. Benjamin Church

The colonists had suspected for some time that the British were receiving intelligence from someone high in their ranks. Birnbaum related succinctly how the traitor was identified. (Birnbaum, 309-312) A letter intercepted on a prostitute led to the trial on 27 Oct 1775 of Dr. Benjamin Church. (Warren-Adams Letters, 1, 121-123) Church had not only been one of the orators commemorating the Boston Massacre but he had also been a founding member of the Committee of Safety and had been appointed director general of the colonial hospitals. The Continental Congress voted to have Church tried before the General Court of Massachusetts. It undoubtedly was a difficult time for Hancock, who had to accept the duplicity of one in whom he had had implicit faith. It was pitiable for so many of Church's former friends to attend his Boston trial and to see him imprisoned. There is apparently no record of Hancock's reaction to the treason of Church. However, it must have both shaken him that a person so highly placed was a traitor and relieved him that such a source of information to the British had been detected. Fate took a hand in his eventual demise. Having been granted the right to emigrate to the West Indies, Church left the colonies in 1776, only to die at sea when his ship sank with all hands lost.

The events of 1775 had caused George III to modify his position but slightly. His message to the opening session of his Fourteenth Parliament (*Parliamentary History of England*, 18, cols. 695-698; LC:

Evans, #14788) concerned mainly North America. The king remained adamant about total submission of the "rebellious war," saying:

> The authors and promoters of this desperate conspiracy have, in the conduct of it, derived great advantage from the difference of our intensions and theirs. They meant only to amuse by vague expressions of attachment to the Parent State, and the strongest loyalty to me, whilst they were preparing for a general revolt. On our part, though it was declared in your last session that a rebellion existed within the province of the Massachusett's [sic] Bay, yet even that province we wished rather to reclaim than to subdue.

King George announced that he had increased his naval and land forces. After the colonies had been subdued, he stated he "should be sensible of their error" and "ready to receive the misled with tenderness and mercy." Although no names were mentioned, George referred to "the traitorous views" of the leaders of the revolt. The king knew what instructions had been sent to Gage. His rancor toward Hancock was unexpressed but inevitably present.

After the speech, a petition from the City of London was presented which included the statement that the City feared "the loss of the most valuable branch of our commerce, on which the existence of an infinite number of industrious manufacturers and mechanics entirely depends." Hancock's requests for assistance from his London contacts had not been altogether in vain. However, the king remained deaf to both the colonists and the British merchants.

The Follow-Through of the Revolutionist

So often in the history of revolutions, those who are responsible for the opening moves are not around to celebrate the victory. Mirabeau never saw the French constitutional monarchy firmly established. Gandhi was not permitted to live to see India develop, even with the crippling division from the Muslims. Martin Luther King Jr. did not survive to see the continued momentum of the movement he so carefully nourished. But the outstanding men of the American Revolution were more fortunate. For the most part, the leaders lived to see success, but not without paying the price of hard work to achieve that success.

One part of living through the events of a revolution may be to see yourself eclipsed by others. Hancock had that experience when, by spending his time in Philadelphia, he was replaced by others at his posts in Massachusetts. On 12 June 1776 he wrote to his friend Cushing: "I find I am left out of both House and Council, I can't help it, they have a right to do as they please, I think I do not merit such treatmt [sic] but my Exertions & my Life are & shall be at their Service." (MHS, e)[4]

On 2 July 1776, the Congress adopted the resolution of Richard Henry Lee of Virginia that "these United States are, and of right ought to be, free and independent States." When the Committee of the Whole of the Continental Congress finished debating the draft of the Declaration of Independence as prepared by John Adams, Benjamin Franklin, Thomas Jefferson, Robert Livingston, and Roger Sherman, and the Congress had approved the version adopted by the Committee of the Whole, it was Hancock, along with the secretary of the congress, Charles Thomson, whose printed signatures appeared on the document issued in a broadside on 5 July 1776, dated "In Congress, July 4, 1776." Hancock's name stood with Thomson's on the preliminary broadside copy. Some fifty of the remaining delegates signed the parchment copy on 2 Aug 1776, and the rest in the days and weeks that followed. The king undoubtedly received copies of the document hurriedly printed up during the night of 4-5 July. Such open rebellion certainly made the name of Hancock even more infamous in London than before.[5]

After the signing in Philadelphia in August, the story goes that Hancock called upon all of the signers to hang together, provoking what is said to be Benjamin Franklin's rejoinder that if they did not all hang together, they would certainly all hang apart. (Malone, 91) When these remarks are studied in history books, the emphasis seemed to be placed on the skill of Franklin's repartee. Now we can equally appreciate Hancock's comment on the serious possibility that, if the war were lost, the signers and particularly Hancock faced the possibility of death.

Hancock's signature appears in the center of the parchment copy, almost certainly because he was president of the Congress. The document as exhibited in the Archives shows the large John Hancock signature. Hancock is supposed to have said, as he signed, that he wrote his name large enough so that John Bull could read it without spectacles "and could double the reward on his head." (Malone, 92) If these remarks were made, they were certainly an example of "whistling in the dark." All of the signatories knew that placing their names on such a declaration placed their lives in jeopardy. So the act of signing was an auspicious one.

Resignation as President

Hancock remained president of the Continental Congress until 1777. On 15 Oct 1777, he requested leave of absence and thereby, in a precedent set by himself, a relinquishment of his presidency. Why did Hancock decide to leave the Continental Congress? Wagner (155) reasoned that, by the end of October, Hancock saw that both the British troops in Philadelphia as well as the Continental Army at Valley Forge, some twenty miles away, would be inactive until the winter was over. With the troops at a stalemate, it would be a good time to be absent. A second and third factor probably played a part. It is possible that Hancock wished to mend his political fences in Boston and to enjoy some respite from the two and one-half years he had spent as president of the Continental Congress. Whatever the reason, Hancock decided to depart and wished to make a brief parting speech. Such a request now seems normal.[6] But the Continental Congress had not welcomed speechmaking. Its sessions had been perforcedly executive sessions. The secretary kept accounts of proceedings, but there were to be no stars.[7]

Certainly Hancock knew of the custom of frowning on formal speechmaking, no matter how short. It was like him to challenge it. On 29 Oct, Hancock did make a brief speech, announcing his departure. On 30 Oct 1777, Sam Adams wrote to Warren:

> Yesterday Morning Mr. H[ancock]...made a formal Speech to Congress in which he reminded them of his having served them as President more than two years....But it is not improbable that you may have a Copy of it; for a Motion was made in the Afternoon by Mr. D—— of N.Y. that a Copy should be requested, and Thanks returned for his great Services and a Request that he would return and take the Chair. This Motion was opposed by several Members, but it obtained so far as to request the Copy, and this Day the latter Part of the Motion will be considerd [sic]....We have had two Presidents before, Neither of whom made a parting Speech or receivd [sic] the Thanks of Congress.[8]

It is easy to conclude that the Congress was ungracious in offering resistance to Hancock's saying a few words to them, and it is hard to believe that the New England delegates voted to defeat the motion to offer Hancock their thanks for his services. Hancock must have gone home disgruntled having received no vote of thanks from his colleagues, taking his presidential papers with him. If Sam Adams was behind the maneuver, he paid for it dearly when Hancock became governor of Massachusetts and Hancock exerted his influence to unseat Adams's adherents. The two men did join forces in 1788, with Hancock as governor and Adams as lieutenant governor, to secure the ratification of the federal Constitution. But there appears to be, at that point, no indication of a personal reconciliation.

There is nothing in the Hancock speech to the Second Continental Congress as reproduced in this volume from the copy in the National Archives that could offer the least offense. Certainly the pressure he was under in breaking precedent influenced Hancock's rhetoric on that occasion. It would be interesting to speculate on what the speech might have been like, had there been no undercurrents of opposition to its delivery. It is possible to conclude, after reading some of Hancock's more tumid speeches, that the pressure resulted in a simplicity that is more complimentary to Hancock than what he might have delivered had he felt no constraints. But Hancock had an uncanny knack of analyzing his audience. He had not served as president for over two years without that sense of audience feedback dictating to him how he should phrase his remarks.

John left Philadelpha and was met on the road by Dolly. Although their reunion was a happy one, they were no doubt saddened by the memories of the death of their first child, baby Lydia, who had died while Dorothy was staying the summer in Massachusetts. Allan (241) found evidence that the child was apparently born in November of 1776 and died in August of 1777. If these dates are correct, Dorothy Hancock had to journey the one hundred miles from Philadelphia to Baltimore with a one-month-old child at a time when Philadelphia was threatened by the British and the Congress had to move to Maryland on 12 Dec 1776. By 5 Mar 1777, she journeyed with the child back to Philadelphia, and eventually back to Massachusetts to spend the summer of 1777.

So in November of 1777 it was with heavy hearts and exectations of producing another child that the president and his wife met in Connecticut and undertook the painful stage coach ride back to Boston. Hancock had received the requested escort from Philadelphia to Boston, and was accorded the privileges he thought he merited at his homecoming. On 10 Mar 1778 he presided over the adoption by Massachusetts of the Articles of Confederation. The Boston Massacre continued to be celebrated until it was replaced by the 4th of July celebration, (Sears, 234) and Hancock presided over the eighth

anniversary of the massacre at Faneuil Hall. He continued to chair the
town meetings and served as a member of the Massachusetts legislature.

A Return to the Continental Congress

On 3 June 1778, after the birth of a son, Hancock set out on the
two-week journey for Yorktown, where the deputies were meeting,
Philadelphia having been occupied by the British. He had been absent
from Congress for six months, and was no longer its president. Henry
Laurens of South Carolina was presiding over two important items of
business: first, the adoption of the treaty with France and second, Lord
North's offer to grant the colonies all they had originally requested, in
return for a cessation of hostilities. But the colonies were not to be
diverted. The crown had waited too long. The delegates were much
encouraged that a treaty with France was soon to be signed. The answer
sent to Lord North stated that negotiations would be possible after
England recognized the colonies as an independent state.[9]
On 18 June 1788 the British abruptly left Philadelphia for New
York. The Americans reentered on the same day. Five days later, on
23 June 1778, John wrote to Dolly from Yorktown about his concern
for her health following the birth of their son. He expressed his
impatience in not hearing from her. (Walsh, 537) Only six days later,
he wrote to her again, this time from Philadelphia, to which the
Congress had returned. The letter, dated 29 June 1778, was largely
concerned with domestic concerns and gossip. However, Hancock did
say that he had "the pleasure to Tell you that my Health is really
better'd by the Journey, pray God it may continue to Advance." (MHS,
f; MHSP, 148) Hancock presumably was referring to the long journey
that he made from Boston to Yorktown early in the month rather than
the shorter journey from Yorktown to Philadelphia that took place in
late June.
When the British army left Philadelphia for New York and Congress
returned to its old quarters, Hancock returned to Boston to preside at the
town meeting over what was to be done about the status of "absentees,"
a subject that comes up repeatedly in Hancock's speeches and which
served as the subject of his last address in 1793. There was not much
sympathy among the revolutionaries for the Loyalists or Tories. On 1
May 1776, the Massachusetts legislature had passed the "test law" to
regulate loyalty to the revolution. Those who failed to qualify were
required to surrender their arms, for which they were paid. (A&R, 5,
479-484, 1 May 1776; Mayo, III, 262) There was particular hostility
toward any Tory who had taken refuge with the British or assisted the

enemy. On 16 Oct 1778, the General Court published a long list of those were were permanently exiled.[10] To a request of the absentees that they be permitted to return, the answer was almost always a blunt refusal. Those who had left the colonists to fend for themselves against a superior British Army and Navy were not to be welcomed back home when the rebels had won. The absentees had made their choice, which had seemed a safer bet to them at the time than siding with the rebels. The Tories were to lie in the beds that they had made. This inflexible ban on absentee return was to be Hancock's position repeatedly in both his speeches and his messages to the General Court after he became governor.

The Rhode Island Campaign

The summer of 1778 saw the last incident in John Hancock's military career during the efforts to combine the forces of the colonists and the French to secure the liberation of Rhode Island. As long ago as 8 Feb 1771, Hancock had been named a major general of the state militia by the Massachusetts legislature. In August of 1778 the "general" went with 5,000 militiamen from Massachusetts to Rhode Island, but plans to coordinate a sea and land attack on Newport failed. As it turned out, Hancock's chief contribution was not a military one but a diplomatic maneuver. When the failure of the expedition threatened to divide the French and the colonists, it was Hancock who stepped in to placate d'Estaing and the French. A frequent theme in Hancock's speeches was the contribution of the French to the American cause. It was stated earlier that Hancock was partially responsible for maintaining good relations with the important ally. If his conduct as a commander in the expedition left much to be desired, (Sears, 254-257) he made up his deficiencies in the area of diplomacy.

Hancock returned only once more to Philadelphia, in May 1779, as a delegate. But he remained only a short time before returning to Boston. These few weeks marked the end of his career with the Continental Congress. (Wagner, 157) Six years later, knowing that Hancock had resigned his post as governor of Massachusetts and hoping to attract the most qualified people to the Continental Congress, Hancock was again elected president of that body on 23 Nov 1785. Sanders (29) established that Hancock wrote that he hoped to come shortly, but John did not ever go. If his health was so poor that he could not remain as governor, it was certainly so poor that he could not become president of the Continental Congress. It may be, as Sanders speculated, that he accepted the appointment to antagonize Governor Bowdoin, who had defeated Hancock's preferred choice of Cushing to succeed Hancock as governor of Massachusetts. Or it may be that he remembered his dedication to his country and hoped to make a further contribution. But Hancock's career in the Continental Congress was over.

NOTES

1. PRO, C.O. 5/160, fo. 40; Davies, VIII, 46-48. The attorney general, after giving his opinion that "the acts and proceedings stated...do amount to the crime of high treason," commented specifically on the actions of Hancock as follows: "The Proceeding on the twenty-ninth of November and the following days, which ended in the destruction of the Dartmouth's cargo, consist, [sic] of the transactions of the unlawful Assembly holden by Williams as Moderator; a guard headed by Proctor and Handcock [sic] in pursuance of the resolutions there taken; the unlawful Meeting holden on the thirtieth, with the very violent resolutions taken there; the proceeding of Their Committee; and the attack on the Vessel, apparently, made under the influence of the same Committee."

2. Gage's account of the battle to Dartmouth on 22 April 1775 made it appear that Smith, Pitcairn, and Percy, the commanders of the British troops, were heroes and that "the loss sustained by those who attacked is said to be great." (PRO, g) Gage faulted the colonials not making "one gallant attempt" during the eighteen miles that the British troops marched back to Boston, but rather fired "from behind the walls, ditches, trees, etc." In an official report from Gage to Dartmouth, the figures given by the British were 65 dead, 180 wounded, and 27 missing, or a total of 272. The report read: "We lost a good many though nothing like the number of rebels killed." (PRO, i)

3. Among the Adams papers at NYP [KVB 1775, June 14] is a copy of Gage's proclamation that had been reprinted in a Cambridge newspaper on 14 June with the royal insignia at the head of the document replaced by the introduction given it by the colonists.

4. The Boston town records show the following:

10 May 1774—Hancock named to the General Court
30 Dec 1774—Hancock chosen as one of the "new delegates" in keeping with a request of the late Provincial Congress. The new delegates were to assemble on or before 1 Feb 1775 in Cambridge

13 Mar 1775—Hancock moderated the meeting at which he was
   chosen one of the seven selectmen
(Hancock left for Philadelphia on 22 Apr 1775)
5 Mar 1776—Hancock chosen one of seven selectmen
1 May 1776—Hancock chosen for the Committee of
   Correspondence
23 May 1776—Hancock not named one of the twelve
   representatives to the General Court
22 May 1777—Hancock again named to the General Court
13 May 1778—Hancock again named to the General Court

Therefore, Hancock was omitted from the legislature only one year, 1776, when he was obviously going to be at the Continental Congress. It must have been nothing more than his vanity that caused him to wish to remain a delegate to a body he could not attend. Evidently his displeasure was made sufficiently known that he was named in 1777, even though he was in no position to attend.

5. There is much debate about the manner in which the Declaration of Independence was signed. At one point, Jefferson stated that the Declaration was signed on 4 July by every member except Mr. Dickinson. However, no such copy is known to exist. No copy is known to exist "signed" on 4 July 1776 by Hancock and Thomson. In his letterbook for 5 July 1776, Hancock has copies of the letter he wrote to New Jersey and Pennsylvania, sending them what must have been the printed broadside of the Declaration of Independence. (MA) The copy was undoubtedly rushed off to the printer and possibly lost there. For details on the interesting antecedents of the signing of the Constitution, see Boyd, ed., I, 305-308, and Malone, 89-92.

6. Efforts to locate the written request to the Congress that Hancock may have made have proved fruitless. No such request was located among the papers of Charles Thomson, the secretary of the congress. The National Archives could find no copy. It also does not exist at the MA. The National Archives reasoned that "it is quite possible that Hancock's note, if one was written, was lost during one of the transfers of the Papers of the Continental Congress." (cf. Smith, 8, 124.)

7. Secretary Thomson kept three sets of notes: the Rough Journal, the Corrected Journal, and the Secret Journal of the Congress. Madison, of course, kept notes on the Constitutional Convention of 1787, at which time there was some speechmaking. (Scott, James Brown, *James Madison's Notes of Debates in the Federal Convention of 1787...*, New York, 1918)

8. Warren-Adams Letters, I, 378. Sam Adams is ungracious, but accurate. As was pointed out earlier, Peyton Randolph had served briefly as president

of the First Continental Congress from 5 Sept 1774 to 22 Oct 1774, but relinquished the chair because of indisposition. He was succeeded by Henry Middleton of South Carolina, who presided for the remainder of the First Continental Congress, from 22 Oct 1774 until 26 Oct 1774.

Peyton Randolph again presided as president of the Second Continental Congress from 10 May 1775 to 24 May 1775 before leaving to attend to affairs in Virginia. Middleton, pleading ill health, declined to replace Randolph. Hancock was elected president on 24 May 1775. (J.B.Sanders, *The Presidency of the Continental Congress*, 1774-89, Chicago, 1930, 11) But neither Randolph or Middleton had contributed the energies to the office that Hancock had offered.

9. The *Journals of the Continental Congress* for 9 Nov 1775 (3, 343, footnote 1) stated that the original petition of 1774 was presented to the king on 1 Sept 1775. When the Americans in London pressed for the king's answer, they were told "that as his majesty did not receive it on the throne, no answer would be given."

The journals also show that on 18 July 1778, the Continental Congress ordered that the correspondence from the British envoys to President Henry Laurens be published. Congress then made official its letter of 17 June 1778 to the British commissioners that "they would be ready to enter upon the consideration of a treaty of peace and commerce, not inconsistent with treaties already subsisting, when the king of Great Britain should demonstrate a sincere disposition for that purpose; and that the only solid proof of this disposition, would be an explicit acknowledgement of the independence of these States, or the withdrawing his fleets and armies." Congress concluded that, since neither of these stipulations had been met, no answer to the envoys' letter would be made. It ordered that its resolution declaring that no response would be given be published.

Innes, a British historian, wrote in 1895 that after the French-American treaty, the reaction to Lord North's bills of 17 Feb 1778 recognizing the claims of the colonists was refused by the Continental Congress. Innes stated: "The first condition of treating must be the recognition of independence." (Innes, 301-302) Innes noted that the treaty with France converted the war as much into a naval action as a land action.

The letters to Thomas Jefferson during this period reveal clearly the attitudes of the colonists. On 2 May 1778, Richard Henry Lee wrote to Jefferson that "Genl. Amhers[t] and Adml. Keppel are arrived in Philadelphia as commissioners from the King and Parliament of G.B. to carry into execution the very curious plan that one of the inclosed papers contains. Tis happy for America that her enemies have not sufficient ability to give even a specious appearance to their wicked designs." (Boyd, II, 175) On 23 June 1778, Lee wrote to Jefferson: "Governor Johnstone tries every art to gain admission among us. He abuses his Masters, flatters America, and is willing to yield us every thing if we will be perfidious to our Ally and again submit to the domination of his King and Parliament...But it is too late in the day. The Sunshine of liberty and independence prevails over the dark arts of Tyranny and its Tools." (Boyd, II, 201) On 20 July 1778, Lee wrote to Jefferson: "The B. Commissioners have sent us a second letter, very silly, and equally insolent. The preleminaries [sic] insisted on by Congress (an acknowledgement of Independence or a withdrawing of their fleets and Armies) have not been either of them complied with, this letter is to receive no answer." (Boyd, II, 205)

10. Cf. Hancock's speech of 1793.

9

1779: The Prelude to Becoming Governor

To understand Hancock's activities during 1779, it is necessary to provide additional background material. Once the states had signed the Declaration of Independence, they needed to adopt state constitutions. British law and procedures no longer applied. Surprisingly, Massachusetts was the last of the thirteen states to complete such an action. (Bacon, 3, 182) As was pointed out previously, the last General Court under the British had been held in 1774. The rump provincial assembly succeeded to the royal General Court, but an official election of a provincial assembly was needed. On 19 July 1775, a newly elected provincial assembly met in Watertown, chose a new council which was to have both legislative and executive powers, and named James Bowdoin as president of the council. (Bacon, 3, 182) How was the assembly and its council to evolve into an assembly to draft a state constitution? There was squabbling of course, but eventually, the assembly of 17 June 1777 resolved itself into a Constitutional Convention. In January of 1788, the resulting constitution was submitted for popular vote and overwhelmingly rejected. On 19 Feb 1778, the assembly requested a popular vote on whether the people wished to have a new constitution, and, if so, would they empower their representatives to the next assembly to draft such a constitution. The voting was fragmented, but sufficiently favorably so that on 17 June 1779, the assembly requested that the people choose delegates to a constitutional convention. (Journal, 2-3)

The Massachusetts Constitutional Convention

On 1 Sept 1779 the convention met at the old meeting house in Cambridge. Present were, of course, John Hancock, as well as Samuel Adams, James Sullivan, Theophilus Parsons, Henry Higginson, John Lowell, John Adams, and others noted elsewhere in this volume. There is little doubt but that Hancock aimed at being named the first executive under the newly formed constitution, and he achieved that goal. What was the prelude that led to his being elected governor?

On 2 Mar 1780, the convention adjourned, recommending a procedure by which the towns could vote on the constitution proposed by the convention. On 7 June 1780, the Constitutional Convention met at the Brattle Street Church in Boston to receive the data from the towns. The returns were naturally confusing. But five years had gone by, during which other states had resolved their difficulties. Those in charge thought that any doubts should be resolved in favor of adoption. On 16 June 1780, James Bowdoin announced that the new constitution would go into effect following the fall election. On 25 Oct, John was chosen the first governor of Massachusetts.

Hancock did not play a leading role in drafting the constitution. He served on committees, particularly those concerning the militia which, as Fowler (226) pointed out, pleased his inclination to consider himself a military man. Perhaps Hancock did not wish to become embroiled in yet another squabble between the Eastern and Western counties. He had had enough bickering in Philadelphia to last him a lifetime. Perhaps he thought it best to remain aloof from internal squabbles so that he could be elected governor without having to take sides. Or perhaps it was his almost perennial bouts with the gout. Or perhaps he realized that, in contrast with the political philosopher John Adams, Hancock did not have as much to contribute to the philosophy of government as he did to its diplomatic execution. For whatever reason or combination of reasons, the fact that Hancock remained largely aloof from the drafting of the constitution helped him to win yet one more victory. His ambition to be governor was fulfilled.

Hancock was sufficiently proud of the Constitution adopted by Massachusetts to quote from it during his time as governor and to use its "Declaration of the Rights of the Inhabitants of the Commonwealth of Massachusetts" in some respects as a model for the compromise resolution that he and others proposed to secure the adoption of the federal Constititution.

It is interesting to observe the degrees by which the several colonies began to become a nation. Cooperation had existed before the outbreak of the war through the committees of correspondence, and then, after 1774, in the Continental Congresses. Some indication of the sense of unity can be determined by the description the colonists gave to their "country." The terms "United States of America" and "United States" were frequently used in the early period. Unity is exhibited in the degree to which the misfortunes of one colony were felt by others. Much sympathy was given to Boston and to Massachusetts for their courage, as is evinced by the welcomes given Hancock on his journey to Philadelphia. Massachusetts was also aware of the needs of others. On 29 Oct 1781, when Cornwallis was proceeding northward from Georgia, the General Court passed a "Resolve Appointing a Committee to Open a Subscription for the sufferers of South Carolina and Georgia and Requesting the Governor to Issue a Brief for Voluntary and Free Donations for Said Sufferers." (A&R, a) It was during this period that Cornwallis was capturing Savannah and South Carolina, causing many patriots to be deprived of their homes and offering much consolation to the Tories. Cornwallis was to proceed through the Carolinas to Virginia. The Battle of Kings Mountain had not yet come. Boston remembered its period of dispossession. It felt obligated to share with its fellow colonists.

The Revolutionist as Governor: The Transition from Rocking the Boat to Anchoring It Safely in the Harbor

Because the speeches made by Hancock during the years from 1780 to his death in 1793 detail much of what concern his rhetorical history, this portion of the introductory essay can be brief.

Hancock had been generally absent from Boston from 1775 to 1777. The posts in Massachusetts to which he was and was not elected have been reviewed earlier. His political fences in his home state needed mending.

Once he returned from Philadelphia to Boston, he reconstructed his regional status quickly. Undoubtedly one of the reasons for his asking for a leave of absence was the knowledge that his political base at home was deteriorating. When vain men do good deeds, they are often suspected of ulterior motives. Hancock did good deeds. There were reasons why his deeds could be considered selfless; there were other reasons why his deeds could be considered selfish. Hancock came from a religious background, where contributing to charity and church were duties, not options. As a child, he had lived in moderate circumstances, and for much of his life, he was responsible for shoring up his brother Ebenezer (Allan, 122) and for contributing to the welfare of his mother and sister. On the other hand, he knew that being generous to the public would increase his popularity at the polls.

So it is up to each student of Hancock to decide what were his motives. But whatever they were, he was generous with his funds. He looked after those widows and orphans that he so often mentions in his speeches. He helped to support the children of Joseph Warren, the hero of Bunker Hill. (Fowler, 225) On 22 May 1772, Hancock donated "a new & finely constructed Engine for the extinguishing of Fires" to the Town of Boston, provided that it be stationed near Hancock's wharf and that he have preference in its use. (RRC, a) This latter example shows the mixture of selflessness and selfishness that often appears in Hancock's actions.

In return, by throwing his bread upon the waters, he received that tenfold recompense. Shipowners gave him a beautiful carriage, captured as booty in the war. Boston has had many heroes. Hancock was among their first. John Fitzgerald Kennedy was among their most recent. Hancock came to the office of governor as a public benefactor. That theme shows up in his speeches and explains much of his rhetorical posture.

After he had shored up his Boston fences, he returned briefly to Philadelphia. Fowler speculated that part of the reason for his return was that the state Constitutional Convention was bogged down and that he could not expect to be governor in the immediate future. Fowler (229) also noted that there was talk of Hancock's being an absentee delegate.

When he returned to Boston after less than a month in Philadelphia, he could pride himself on several events. There had been a commemoration of the signing of the Declaration of Independence, and since Hancock and Thomson had "sponsored" the document in advance of the other delegates, he felt the celebration was in part in honor of him. Furthermore, the Comte d'Estaing brought on his ship the first French ambassador to the newly declared country. Last, he could sense that what had begun under his leadership in 1775 as a gamble was now an acting, viable body. He had helped to lay those foundations firmly by his leadership. He could return to Boston, knowing that matters in the Continental Congress were proceeding satisfactorily.

The forthcoming election for governor under the new Massachusetts Constitution became a contest between Bowdoin and Hancock. As early as 11 July 1780, Warren wrote to John Adams that Bowdoin had reentered public life to compete for the governorship with Hancock.

Warren noted that the loser was going to suffer personally. "The Vanity of one of them will sting like an Adder if it is disappointed," noted Warren, "and the Advancements made by the other if they dont [sic] succeed will hurt his Modest pride." (Warren-Adams Letters, 2, 135)

However, by the time September arrived, Hancock had little difficulty in being elected the first governor of Massachusetts. He received 858 of the 923 votes cast, with Bowdoin receiving 64 votes and Samuel Adams 1 vote. (RRC, b) Again, assuming that the estimates of the population of Boston in 1780 are correct, out of a population of 20,000, the governor was elected with only 858 eligible and voting. The general population in Boston did not vote. Gordon (3, 498) noted that, after being sworn in, "a grand feu de joie was given by the militia companies. Thirteen cannons were fired by the artillery, and three vollies by the independent company. The cannon at the Castle and Fort Hill, and on board the shipping in the Harbour were fired upon the occasion. The governor, senate and house of representatives, then attended divine service...at the Old Brick Meeting-house...When the service was finished, they proceeded to Faneuil-hall, amidst a great concourse of people, where an elegant entertainment was provided." The newspapers of the day reported the festivities in some detail.

After all, there being no Articles of Confederation then in place, Massachusetts was an independent sovereign state. A new era was to evolve. His ally, Cushing, was Hancock's lieutenant governor. What were the major events of John's career between 1780 and 1793?

The Perennial Governor: 1780-1785; 1787-1793

Hancock remained in office from 1780 until he resigned on 29 Jan 1785. The details of the more important actions he took during his first sequence as governor are reflected in his annotated speeches. In general the addresses reflect his satisfaction at being in a position of leadership in a new country. On 14 Nov 1783, he wrote to Captain Scott:

> I have for ten years past devoted myself to the Concerns of the Public. I have not the Vanity to think that I have been of very extensive Service in our late unhappy Contest but one thing I

can *truly* Boast. I sat [sic] out upon Honest Principles & I strictly adhered to them to the Close of the Contest. Of this I defy malice itself to Controvert. I have lost many thousands Sterlg. but thank God, my Country is Saved, and by the Smiles of Heaven I am a Free and Independent Man, and now my Friend I can pleasurably Congratulate you on the return of Peace which gives me a Contenance to retire from Public Life & enjoy the Sweets of Calm Domestick Retirement & Pursue Business merely for my own Amusement. (NEGHS, a)

It is in this same letter that Hancock spoke of reopening his business, a goal that he was not to achieve. Although John was most reasonably wealthy, he began to think again of making money. On 6 May 1782, he wrote that he had not yet been paid for the two years and eight months he had served as the chair of the Congress, even though he had been asked to send a bill twelve months before. (BPL)

In contemplating his retirement, Hancock gave Captain Scott no indication that the cause might be his failing health. For whatever reasons, resignation was on his mind. According to the famous letter from Warren to John Adams of 26 Feb 1784, Hancock had threatened to resign in 1784, but, after making his wishes known, changed his mind. (Warren-Hancock, 2, 236) However, a year later, the decision was irrevocable. In his speech of resignation, he pled ill health. However, others have proposed that the gout was again his old excuse for avoiding responsibility. Because of the war, the finances of the state were in a deplorable condition. Some historians reason that Hancock thought it best to let someone else take the heat of the financial depression so that he could return later unscathed. But, as Hancock's speeches show, he repeatedly encouraged the legislature to act on the financial problems of Massachusetts. There was no immediate crisis in January of 1785. Again each observer must decide for what reasons Hancock left office. One thing is certain. In contrast to previous years, Hancock made no speeches to the General Court in 1784. As much as he loved an audience, it seems reasonable to assume that he resorted only to sending messages to the General Court during 1784 because his health demanded it.

Bowdoin, and not Cushing whom Hancock favored, became governor. (Warren-Adams Letters, 2, 262) Warren made his usual stinging evaluation of Hancock's motives:

Mr. Hancock's Influence, which was great, was in favour of Cushing, more probably to keep a Door open Himself at another Election, and by that means retrieve the Mistake he made in his Resignation, than from any other Principle. All other Parties were obliged to unite to defeat his Purposes, and he at last in Despair of his main Design, gave out that he did not care who was chose [sic] if it was not the Man on Milton Hill. If Ambition was my ruling Principle, and I was a Politician, I should have shaken Hands with this *mighty* man; but as it is I will still be honest and continue to despise his Caprice, Incapacity, and Indolence, and do every Thing I can to prevent his again having it in his Power to disgrace this Government by an Administration of Imbecility and weakness. (Warren-Adams Letters, 2, 262-3)

In Philadelphia and elsewhere, now that the war was over and the treaty signed, there was general unrest with the Articles of Confederation. The articles were not adequate to permit the development of a new nation. Therefore, on 1 July 1785, the General Court passed a "Resolve Recommending a Convention of Delegates from All the States, for the Purpose Mentioned." (A&R, b) The purpose was to revise the confederation and report to Congress what was necessary in order to effectuate the changes. What began, therefore, as a movement to modify the Articles of Confederation ended in presenting an entirely new Constitution.

Of course, many of the delegates to the convention were also the delegates to the Congress. But technically, the two bodies remained separate. Leadership in both groups was needed. Therefore, when on 4 Nov 1785 the term of the representative from Virginia, R.H. Lee, expired as president of the Continental Congress, the national assembly on 23 Nov 1785 again elected John Hancock as its president. As was noted earlier, the Congress knew that Hancock was no longer serving as governor. It would have been prestigious to have had Hancock as their presiding officer. However, although on 30 Nov, Hancock expressed the hope that he might be able to travel to Congress in "ten or twelve Days," he never arrived. (Sanders, 29) Hancock's attention was focused on his own health and on his home state. He was to make no further contribution to the deliberations in Philadelphia. Furthermore, during the period that he was out of office in Massachusetts, his son John slipped and fell on the ice and died on 27 Jan 1787.[1] Therefore 1787 was received with sadness for John and Dolly. Hancock's reassumption of the chair of governor later in the spring could hardly have consoled the family for its loss.[2]

Hancock Reelected Governor

After becoming governor, in noting that the governor's salary had been discussed in the last General Court when Bowdoin was governor, Hancock sent a message to the General Court on 21 June 1787:

> To prevent a Decision on a subject the Constitutionality of which must in its nature be attended with some uncertainty [sic] You will permit me, Gentlemen, to make a voluntary offer of three hundred pounds to the community to be deducted from my Salary for the present year. (MA, a)

This was an amount equal to what Bowdoin had objected being deducted from his salary earlier. (A&R, May session, 1787, Chap. 42, 991) Undoubtedly Hancock made the gesture to spite his political enemy. Hancock added, however, that, if matters improved, he hoped that his gesture would not serve as a precedent.[3]

On 28 June 1787, the General Court accepted his offer, saying: "The embarrassed situation of this State, pleads in behalf of our Constituents to accept your generous & unsolicited favour, tho at the Same time, we would not wish to have it operate as a precedent to influence any successor in office, to relinquish any part of his yearly salary." (A&R, c) It has been proposed that Hancock was not altogether prepared for the alert manner in which the General Court accepted his proposal. However, his beneficience to the state had long been demonstrated. There is no reason to believe that he made the offer expecting it to be declined. If ulterior reasons can be assigned to his gesture, it could be said that he wished to demonstrate the contrast between his governorship and that of Bowdoin. Such a demonstration of generosity might have been helpful in letting the public know that Hancock was back and that "happy days are here again."

Shays's Rebellion occurred during the interregnum of Governor Bowdoin. However, its residue remained when Hancock reassumed office in 1787. In retrospect, Shays's efforts may seem feeble. But, to a state government that had adopted its constitution only five years before and to a national government that had not yet established its Constitution, rebellion loomed large. It was to be seventy-five years after Shays that Massachusetts and the federal government were faced with a major rebellion. But the minor one of 1785-1788 was a real threat to new governments. The details of Hancock's role in Shays's Rebellion are given in discussing his speech of 17 Oct 1787.

A second matter of major importance had to be settled during Hancock's second years as governor. Massachusetts had to accept or reject the federal constitution. The A&R for the 1787 October session show a "Resolve Recommending to the People to Choose Delegates for the Convention, to Meet at the Statehouse in 'Boston,' the Second Wednesday in 'January' Next, Agreeably to a Resolution of Congress, etc." (A&R, d) A detailed summary of the part played by Hancock will be presented in connection with an attempt to reestablish his speech of 31 Jan 1788. But it should be emphasized here that the adoption of a federal constitution involved two aspects that are not always remembered. First, each state that adopted the federal constitution relinquished its own sovereignty. The contemplation of such a loss is undoubtedly what delayed adoption by three of the larger states: Massachusetts, Virginia, and New York. Second, in spite of their mutual interests and common heritage, it was no sure thing that the states would adopt the constitution. It had taken strong-arm tactics to unite France; Germany and Italy were still fragmented; Britain had expended much of its strength in putting down rebellions in Scotland, Wales, and Ireland. Only eternal military vigilance kept the four components of Great Britain united. Although the colonies had not the extended European periods to build the fragments of nationalism, still Virginia was close to two hundred years old, and Massachusetts and New York not far behind. In light of what it has taken to unite other fragmented groups, the gamble that the states were taking in joining together seems all the more threatening. No wonder Hancock and Adams hesitated before they endorsed the new Constitution. But endorse it they did, and thereby took a major step in forming that "more perfect union."

Hancock made one final bid for national office. He let it be known that he would accept the vice presidency under George Washington. However, his ill health prevented him from making extensive contacts. When the ballots were counted, Hancock came in fifth. John Adams was to be the first vice president of the new nation.

The Fourth of July

The Fourth of July remained an important day in the lives of the founders. It is possible that both John Adams and Thomas Jefferson willed themselves to die on 4 July, for on 1826 the two constant correspondents did just that. The date was particularly important to Hancock, for, as has been pointed out before, it was under the printed signatures of President Hancock amd Secretary Thomson that the

printed version of the Constitution was issued on 5 July 1776.
Therefore, in a message to the General Court dated 10 June 1790,
Hancock suggested an addition to the firing of cannon on 4 July as had
been provided by the General Court in 1786. (A&R, e) Hancock
proposed that he was aware of the heavy financial burden the people
were now under, but that a limited exception should be made to
celebrate 4 July: "I therefore think it to be my duty to suggest the idea
of your appointing some person or persons to provide a frugal collation
in the Senate Chamber at twelve o'clock upon that day to which the
Foreign Consuls & other Foreigners of distinction may be invited."
(MA, c; A&R, f) So could have begun the many meals and picnics on
4 July as well as the receptions given by the foreign ambassadors and
consuls of the United States.   However, on 23 June 1790, the General
Court declined to recommend the "collation," saying that the great debt
under which the people were laboring did not make it advisable.[4]

For Hancock in 1790, 4 July was "the birthday of a nation; it was a
day pregnant with greater events in a political view of freedom than the
world had ever seen; not only the nation of which we are a part, but all
the Nations of the World will probably derive great & lasting blessings
from it, a free discussion of the rights of Men was then proclaimed &
has since been supported by a great and increasing people." (MA, c;
A&R, f)

Hancock's final years as governor are best told by the speeches he
delivered during that period. However, the familial ties of the Hancock
family are not addressed there. Hancock's mother, Mary, had first been
married to a man named Thaxter. After Hancock's father's death, she
had married the Reverend Daniel Perkins. Mary, Hancock's sister, had
not only taken the name of her step-father, but also married his son,
Richard Perkins. Hancock's brother, Ebenezer had been looked after by
John in a number of ways. There is, among the letters in volume 17 of
the New England Historic and Genealogical Society papers, an
affectionate letter of 2 April 1793 from grandson Thomas Hancock, son
of Ebenezer, to his grandmother, Madame Mary Perkins, in which
grandson Thomas said: "In your Company I always felt myself
extremely happy, & you, my amiable grandmother, tho' in your
advanced age, have been call'd to part with the best of sons, yet this
must always console you that he often wiped the tear of sorrow from
the Cheek of Affliction, & is now for ever happy in the realms above
—Wishing you every happiness & that your sun when it sets in this
world, may rise more glorious in the Celestial hemisphere." The letter
illustrates, in the few months before Hancock's death, the warmth that
could be felt in his family.

Hancock's last speech on 18 Sept 1793, concerned the issue of states' rights. Hancock had become alarmed that the powers of the federal government exceeded those that he had contemplated. An exchange of letters between Hancock and Adams shows clearly that, although he was soon to die, his fighting spirit was not yet extinguished. On 31 Aug 1793, Hancock wrote Adams from Concord:

> I never more devoutedly wished for *Mens sana in corpore sano* than at the present moment. I am alarmed. Watchman. What of the night. Where is the chronicle to be erected that is to be inadmissible to your eye and mine and its possessor so elevated above the tower of Babel in height as not to be look'd on by such mortals as you and I. My friend what are we coming to, it is full time for serious consideration and resolute exertions. It is time to step forth and oppose the [paper damaged here] of opinions & pursuits that are attempting to establish a System foreign to your ideas & mine to which neither you nor I will bear let the consequence be what it may....I feel for my Country & will not give up the liberties of the people to the last drop of my blood. You know me, I am weak....I refer you to Doctr Jarvis for a state of my health.
>
> I am   Your friend.
>
> J.H. (NYP)[5]

Adams answered from Boston on 3 Sept 1793, saying he had it from Drs. Jarvis and Warren that "they are in hopes...to bring you to such a state of health as to enable you to perform the duties of the State with which the people have honored you, which I pray God you may continue in many years after I am no more hence." (NYP) The final exchange of comments between the two such dissimilar men who had joined forces for a cause greater than either of them cannot be other than touching.

Hancock died at 5 a.m. on 7 Oct 1793 and was buried on 14 Oct 1793 (Tudor, 107) His passing cannot be considered a tragedy.[6] He had lived well. For his physical well being, he had lived too well. He had seen a people threatened with a loss of the liberties they considered their rightful heritage. The ancestors of the colonists had left home to enter a threatening world. After meeting the challenge of establishing their initial settlements, British imperialism offered them a new threat. He had seen that threat withstood and conquered, when the odds of victory were most tenuous. He had seen the basis laid for the prevention of new threats. Not many have lived through and participated in such a self-satisfying period. In comparison, John Kennedy's Camelot seems no more than a pause. Hancock, the vanity-ridden pragmatic diplomat, died fulfilled. Amen.

Wagner (149-150) summed up Hancock's complex simplicity well when he said: "If, as his enemies charged, he tried too hard to be well liked, it was a trait that would find its counterpart in the American character for generations to come. In signing the Declaration of Independence he had taken a bold stand, but he knew that the ties to England...could not be severed without pain as well as joy." Hancock overcame the pain and lived to rejoice in his speeches over the satisfaction of a successful revolution.

NOTES

1. In the depository of the NEHGS in a small envelope embossed with the letter "G" protected only by a covering manila envelope is what purports to be a lock of the hair of John George Washington Hancock. The item was presented to the society by Mrs. Sarah Greenough of Boston and bears some authenticity because the name "Greenough" is associated with other Hancock primary source material. On the envelope is written: "Govern'r Hancock's son came to his death, by a fall on the ice while at Hingham at School."

2. Some unrecorded events caused Hancock to quarrel with his Brattle Street Church. On 7 Jan 1787 Hancock wrote in the third person to the Brattle Street Society: "...so many circumstances have Taken place which are exceedingly disagreeable to him, and others which he has not ever had the least notice, are soon likely to take place, that he begs leave to Detach himself from the Committee, and to be considered as having no kind of connection with the Concerns of the Society, other than as a common holder of a Pew, which he meant to retain." (MHS [orig]) On 18 Jan 1787 Isaac Smith wrote back that he could recollect no meeting of which Hancock had not been notified. (MHS [orig]) Hancock did retain his membership. His obituary notices listed him as a member of the Brattle Street Church.

3. When on 8 Mar 1787 the general court proposed to lower the salary permanently from £1,100 to £800, Bowdoin wrote to the court on 9 Feb 1787 (document misdated, should be March) that he objected to the governor being dependent on the General Court for support. He was motivated by no pecuniary motive, for he might not be reelected. "My inclination would lead me to retirement: but if it should be thought, I can be further serviceable to the Commonwealth, I will not desert it." Bowdoin added that it would be acceptable to him, if he was reelected and if the

legislature requested, to reduce his salary, "although my annual expenditures do much exceed the whole amount of the Salary." He thought the legislation unwise because it would prejudice his successors. (MA, b)

4. MA c, House Unenacted #A3376B, 23 July 1790. The message and the answer to it are contained in the same envelope. The Court wrote: "...considering the great burden of debt under which the Citizens of this Commonwealth now labour, it is the duty of the Legislature in general, to act as much upon the principles of economy, as the nature of our situation & particular circumstances will admit, consistently with the honor & dignity of Government, & that in the present instance, it will not be expedient for Government to burden their Constituents with any expense on account of a collation."

5. Only the final initials are in Hancock's hand. A copy of this letter is among the papers in the NEGHS collection, Box 17.

6. In the BPL there is a scrapbook catalogued as MSH. 5.10 that contains miscellany concerning Hancock's burial. Included are a large swatch of his hair, which may or may have not been taken at his death because it bears no gray hair whatsoever; the order of the procession for his funeral (included in the march were the professors from Harvard and a committee from the Brattle Street Church); and several transections of Hancock's tomb at the Granary Burying Ground.

Dorothy Quincy Hancock's marriage to Hancock's former close associate, Captain James Scott, on 28 July 1796, could well have pleased even the vain Hancock. After all, she was only 46 when Hancock died. Scott was a widower and Dorothy waited three respectable years before remarrying. Sentimentally she chose for her second marriage 28 July, the date of her first marriage. Hancock's relationships with Scott were among the best he had. On 3 June 1789 he wrote to Scott: "I wish you happy in every view and am Your Real Friend, J.H." (NEHGS, Letterbook 1783-1786 [copy], John Hancock to James Scott, 3 June 1785) Hancock customarily addressed his letters to the sea captain as "Dear Scott."

10

The Rhetorical Style of an Entrepreneur Turned Revolutionist

Three important factors in Hancock's background contributed to preparing him as a public speaker:

a. His father and grandfather had both been preachers. Since "the Bishop" lived until Hancock was fifteen, John saw both his father and his grandfather compose their sermons. To the extent that they served as a model of speech composition, they appear to have contributed two of Hancock's principles of speech composition:

1. Write out speeches, much as one would write out a sermon. This factor will be discussed in more detail under "arrangement."

2. Deliver speeches with vigor. "The Bishop" and his son had to be effective preachers to get and retain pulpits. Third-generation John saw that audiences could be controlled by effective delivery.

b. The traditional New England town meeting placed prestige on oral communication. John undoubtedly had models to follow in assuming his role as town moderator.

c. John had had the equivalent of the contemporary English "public school" education. He had studied rhetoric and, in his classes, he had been trained to deliver discourses. Furthermore, he had been given sufficient exposure to what we would now term classical literature so that he could draw quotations from well-known literary figures as he wished.

So we have a religious man, knowledgeable of the Bible, with role models to show him how to make a speech or to preside over a meeting, and with the equivalent of a first class prep-school education. What sort of speaker did this background produce?

Invention

When Hancock spoke during the latter part of the eighteenth century, the age of the baroque had not ended. Wordsworth's preface to the *Lyrical Ballads* was still a number of years away. Therefore it is not surprising to find that Hancock's general approach was more tumid than would be used today. What lay beneath this tumidity?

Emotional proof: Hancock used basically four emotions: love of country; pride in achievement, particularly the self-established Puritan ethic; abhorence of vice; and fear of and thanks to the Divine Being.

Other emotions were used from time to time. William Livingston of New York and New Jersey established the first New Jersey newspaper during the revolution. (Davidson, 12) Davidson concluded that Livingston's "essays, broadsides, and speeches all show a real knowledge of crowd psychology." Davidson reasoned that "the most important motive in warpsychosis is not reason or justice, or even self-interest, but hate" (Davidson, 12) and that Livingston knew it. In his 1774 Boston Massacre address, Hancock knew the power of hate as well. Note the following passages that were designed to increase the hatred that the colonists had for the British and their occupation:

> Ye dark designing knaves, ye murderers, parricides! how dare you tread upon the earth, which has drank in the blood of slaughtered innocents.

> And you, however you may have screened yourselves from human eyes, must be arraigned, must lift your hands, red with the blood of those whose death you have procured, at the tremendous bar of GOD.

Davidson commented as follows:

> The most important theme of the war propaganda was the depravity and cruelty of the English; in the prerevolutionary period other themes had been relatively more important, but during the war no other suggestion received so much

emphasis. By arousing hatred and disgust for the British, the propagandists hoped not only to spur the people on to greater efforts in support of the army but also to prevent a possible settlement short of independence. (365)

Hancock's speeches as governor during the years 1780 to 1783 do not demonstrate the sort of venom that was shown in the Boston Massacre address. But the former were deliberative oratory while the latter was epideictic oratory. The only other epideictic speeches we have by Hancock are the Harvard commencement addresses and the Thanksgiving Day address of 1789. By that time, hatred toward the British was not needed. However, there are emotional passages in the gubernatorial addresses that provoke the same negative attitude toward the British.

Did the British deserve such vilification? Davidson would answer that question affirmatively. "The British waged a cruel and predatory war," stated Davidson, "fought with bitterness and malice; from their lust and rapacity no one, nothing was safe." (365) Everywhere the troops went, said Davidson, burning and pillaging took place.

Ethical proof: There is no difficulty in finding detrimental estimates of Hancock's character. Among the most unfavorable is that of his inveterate opponent, Thomas Hutchinson. Perhaps they disliked and distrusted each other all the more because they were both native colonists of several generations. Hutchinson had chosen to remain loyal to George III; Hancock had taken the road less traveled. The following description depicts Hancock at his worst:

The uncle [Uncle Thomas] was always on the side of government. The nephew's ruling passion was a fondness for popular applause....he found work for a number of tradesmen, made himself popular, was chosen select man, representative, moderator of town meetings, etc....His natural powers were moderate, and had been very little improved by study, or application to any kind of science. His ruling passion kept him from ever losing sight of its object; but he was fickle, and inconstant in the means of pursuing it; and though, for the most part, he was closely attached to Mr. Samuel Adams, yet he has repeatedly broken off from all connexion with him for several months altogether. Partly by inattention to his private affairs, and partly from want of judgment, he became greatly involved and distressed, and the estate was lost with much greater rapidity than it had been acquired. (Hutchinson,3, 214-215)

Yet Hancock could form, if not close friendships, at least firm loyalties. From Philadelphia on 17 Jan 1776, Hancock wrote to Cushing that he sympathized with Cushing's not returning to Congress. Hancock volunteered: "I never Flatter, but shall ever in future unbosom myself to you, and write freely, in Confidence that I can Rely on your Friendship, & form a Conviction that you are deserving of the Esteem I have for you...." (MHS, a)

Baxter found that the defects in Hancock's character, i,e, "tardiness, spleen, and unreliability" might have been overcome by his "energy and boldness of design" so that Hancock, with more foresight and perhaps luck, could have been a success as a businessman. (294)

Dolly Hancock in her reminiscences said plainly that he gave orders and expected them to be carried out. She recounted two anecdotes that demonstrate his obstinacy. First, because the cook was exhausted from entertaining the French, the cook failed to properly pluck the feathers from the turkeys served at table. Hancock ordered a turkey to be roasted with its feathers on, and pretended not to smell the stench. (Sumner, 189)

The second incident reveals the extent to which the gout affected Hancock's nerves. Although the record says nothing as to why Hancock gave orders that only pewter be used and not china, it seems obvious that the noise from the china plates grated unmercifully on his nerves frayed to the breaking point by the gout. Hearing the noise of china, he had his servant Cato bring the plate upstairs and throw it out the window. Cato tried to fool Hancock by throwing it on a stand of grass where it would not break. When Hancock did not hear the breaking of the china, he ordered Cato to go down and smash it against the wall. (Sumner, 189) This second incident illustrates the extent to which Hancock's illnesses with the gout made his temper irascible. It also helps us to understand that what others considered to be a convenient illness may have been, at least at times, more of a real impediment to his leading a life of even tenor. It could account in part for his capriciousness and inconstancy in his political life.

As Carl Hovland pointed out in *Communication and Persuasion* (21 ff), the speaker's intent has much to do with his persuasiveness. Repeatedly, Hancock's intent has been evaluated as selfish. What evidence is there to the contrary?

In the fall of 1775, when the British were occupying Boston, George Washington faced the possibility of attacking Boston and therefore risking the destruction of the city. As a new commander-in-chief, he wished to get the approval of Congress if such a move had to be made. Congress resolved itself into a committee of the whole to consider the report of a Committee of Conference that had conferred with George Washington at Cambridge, Massachusetts, between 18 and 24 Oct. Certain matters discussed at that conference had been acted upon by Congress, but the status of Boston had not been decided. On 12 Dec, members could not reach agreement. There exist notes by John Dickinson on a speech he made opposing the move. (Smith, 502-503) As Congress was in a committee of the whole, Hancock was no longer in the chair and was therefore free to speak on the matter. Although his exact remarks are not recorded, it was noted by Richard Smith in his diary that "Mr. Hancock spoke heartily for this Measure." (Burnett, 1, 284) On 22 Dec 1775, Congress resolved "that if General Washington and his council of war should be of opinion, that a successful attack may be made on the troops in Boston, he do it in any manner he may think expedient, notwithstanding the town and the property in it may thereby by destroyed." (Journals, 22 Dec, 1775, 444-445)[1] That same day, Hancock wrote George Washington of the actions of the Congress. He enclosed the resolution about Boston. "You will Notice," said Hancock, "the last Resolution Relative to an Attack upon Boston, this pass'd after a most serious Debate in a committee of the whole house, and the Execution Referr'd to you, and may God Crown your Attempt with Success, I most heartily wish it, tho' individually I may be the greatest sufferer." (Abbot, 2, 589-590)

The duality of Hancock's selfishness and selflessness are demonstrated in consecutive paragraphs of his letter of 7 Mar 1776 to Thomas Cushing. (MHS, b) At the end of his letter, Hancock wrote Cushing:

> I hope you will send me my commission as Major General that I may appear in Character, I assure you this Appointment pleases me, I think I know a little of the duty, and on any Return I will Endeavour under the Direction of your Board to put the Militia upon a Respectable footing, I will not be wanting.

In the very next paragraph, Hancock wrote:

> My utmost Exertions shall never be witheld for the Good of my Colony, whenever they can be useful they shall be Employ'd in that Service however Dangerous, and I Defy

Malice itself to Contradict the sincerity and uprightness of those Exertions.

Hancock relied greatly upon maintaining a nonpartisan approach to character persuasion. He avoided the turmoil of colonial politics, so that, particularly in the case of the ratification of the federal Constitution, he could step in, unscathed by the bickerings and by the genuinely deep-seated disagreements that had preceded his appearance, and use his detachment to propose that he could approach the matter impartially. For such tactics, Hancock has received much unfavorable criticism. His failure to play politics caused him to be termed a consummate politician. Fowler (246 ff.) characterized his administration as *laissez-faire* and found Hancock's inactivity on bills concerning federal and state excise taxes "shenanigans." (Fowler, 248) Allan stated that John Quincy Adams "underestimated the ability of the master politician [Hancock] to steer a safe course between the treacherous shoals toward which popularity and ambition beckoned him." (319) Hancock can certainly be faulted by those of us who "pitch in and do the dirty work" for so often winning his political battles by remaining aloof. It must have been a most annoying factor of character persuasion to his contemporaries.

But it cannot be forgot that, in matters of major importance, Hancock did not hesitate to put his character on the line. First, Hancock departed from the posture of many of his fellow businessmen in aligning himself firmly with the revolution. It is true that he assumed this position after some hesitation, but such hesitation can only be considered prudent. As a result of his declaration, Hancock lost much of his fortune, risked being imprisoned in the king's gaol in London, and caused himself much personal inconvenience in traveling around the colonies and absenting himself from the comfort of his mansion on Beacon Hill. Second, Hancock departed from his neutral posture unreservedly to support the national Constitution. Again, he took this position after surveying the ground carefully. But his speeches of 31 Jan 1788 and 5 Feb 1788 make his position clear. If the Constitution had not been adopted, Hancock would have suffered a major political defeat. Third, Hancock's name as president of the Second Continental Congress appeared on the Declaration of Independence almost a month before the others signed. If the British had won the war, what would have been Hancock's alternatives? Exile in France? Gaol in England? Loss of all his wealth?

There is certainly evidence to show that, in his political maneuverings, Hancock can be convicted of opportunism. But, on at least three major issues, he put his career on the line. Without those declarations, the history of the United States might be quite different.

Hancock's love of pomp and circumstance and his lavish manner of living drew criticism when he was governor and has continued to draw criticism by historians. After pointing out that the Americans, having dismissed George III, broke precedent and did not seek out another monarch to replace him, the Handlins observed that the independence of the colonists "revealed a commitment to republicanism, always there, long silent, now openly trumpeted." (O & L Handlin, 228) The Handlins observed that any attempt to imitate aristocracy, including "John Hancock's every effort at display while governor of Massachusetts," only brought censure. The earlier lavish entertainment of the French brought disapproval in the letter of 25 Oct 1788 from Warren to Adam cited above. Artemas Ward had favored Bowdoin as first governor and was unhappy with Hancock because he had delayed so long in settling the money that Harvard had entrusted to Hancock during 1773-1777. (Martyn, 257) Ward also felt, said Martyn, that Hancock "devoted too much time to social functions and too little to affairs of state." (258) George Billias (103) reported that Elbridge Gerry found that "Hancock was a self-interested political manipulator, a dangerous demagogue, and a man unworthy of the principles of the Revolution." Gerry wrote to Sam Adams on 8 Jan 1781 that Hancock's first term as governor showed "Vestiges of Monarchy." (NYP) Hancock dressed in the style used by the more prominent citizens of Boston. Sullivan commented that, in Hancock's time, "dress was adapted quite as much to be ornamental as useful. Gentlemen wore wigs when abroad, and commonly, caps, when at home." When Sullivan visited Hancock at the governor's home about noon in 1782, he described the governor as wearing "a red velvet cap, within which was one of fine linen. The latter was turned up over the velvet one two or three inches. He wore a blue damask gown, lined with silk; a white plaited stock, a white silk embroidered waistcoat, black satin small-clothes, white silk stockings, and red morocco slippers." (Wells, 2, 210-211; Sullivan, 10) However, there is also evidence of favorable reaction to Hancock's lavish display and the import of his mansion on Beacon Hill. To begin with, Hancock's style of living did not prevent his being repeatedly elected as governor. Since the electorate in Boston was limited to the more wealthy in society, that electorate did not voice its disapproval of Hancock's standard of living by voting him out of office. Furthermore Hancock, as has already been observed, was astute enough as well as compassionate enough to make extensive gifts to Boston and its poor. "For whatever reason," concluded Fowler (225-226), "John Hancock

was a generous man and the people loved him for it. He was,"
continued Fowler, "their idol." The ornate carriage in which he drove
through the streets of Boston, "hardly in keeping with Revolutionary
austerity," (226) had been a gift from the owners of a Newburyport
privateer who had captured it as war booty. Concerning the carriage,
The Pennsylvania *Ledger* for 11 Mar 1778 noted:

> John Hancock of Boston appears in public with all the
> pageantry and state of an Oriental prince; he rides in an elegant
> chariot, which was taken in a prize to the "Civil Usage" pirate
> vessel, and by the owners presented to him. He is attended by
> four servants dressed in superb livery, mounted on fine horses
> richly caparisoned; and escorted by fifty horsemen with drawn
> sabres, the one-half of whom precede and the other follow his
> carriage.

It would be interesting to know how Hancock reacted to what may
be an exaggerated account of his vanity.

The populace of Boston, however, loved Hancock's display just as
the British citizenry today likes to see its royalty parade through the
streets of London. So, for his love of ostentation, the poor country
nephew who inherited his rich uncle's fortune received both praise and
blame.

Hancock's reputation as a benefactor plus his position as governor
made him subject to many appeals for funds. In the files of the New
England Historic & Genealogical Society is one particular poignant
appeal dated 15 Dec 1791. In addressing the governor, Elisha Sylvester
of Greene in Lincoln Company stated that, although he was reluctant to
beg for assistance and that he knew that the governor had many such
requests, he also knew that the governor held himself "under an
obligation to assist, and relieve mankind, in every land" and "to
condescend to the infirmities, & misfortunes, of your fellow citizens."
Sylvester, after describing the pitiful state of his family and his
inability find work, begged the governor to help him find employment
among the affluent neighbors of the area "or, to contribute a small sum
to my relief." Sylvester described himself as at his wit's end. The
plight of such a pioneer sings out through the ages. The reader of the
letter sent with such fervor cannot help sense what Hancock himself felt
in receiving it. Although there is no record of a reply, the fact that it is
found with so many of Hancock's personal correspondence indicates that
it came to Hancock's personal attention. It is hoped that the relief of

Elisha Sylvester was among the many good deeds that Hancock did for his fellow colonists. (NEHGS, a)

Hancock was not always free with his funds. In a message to the General Court of 28 Jan 1785, Hancock noted that the expenses for the celebration of the Day of Return of Peace had exceeded the £20/10 appropriated. Hancock noted that, for the balance, "which sum I stand chargeable with, and am call'd upon for, but I persuade myself, that as the Expense was incurred by the Public, the General Court will be pleased to order payment from Public Funds." (MA, a)

There is also the unexplainable failure of Hancock to restore to Harvard all of the funds that had been entrusted to him during the Revolutionary War. All of the monies seemingly were never recovered. The matter became heated:

> At a meeting of the Overseers of Harvard College on 6 May 1783, the Lieut [sic] Governor, chairman of a Committee appointed to settle accounts with the late College Treasurer, reported verbally that they had not accomplished that business: Thereupon Voted unanimously, that upon the day to which this meeting shall be adjourned, this Board will come to a final resolution respecting the measures necessary to effect a Settlement of the late Treasurer's account in case they shall not then be settled, and that the Secretary be, and he is hereby directed to furnish him with a copy of this vote.

> Attest Simeon Howard Secret'y
> (NEHGS, b)

Hard feelings continued between Hancock and Harvard. In 1788 A new treasurer was appointed. Although Hancock had had his personal fortune decidedly reduced, it would appear that Hancock had sufficient funds to restore the Harvard endowment. Baxter said: "John handed over most of the securities, but he could not be persuaded to finish off his accounts and pay a balance of some £800 that lay in his hands." (291) Why he hesitated for the remaining years of his life to settle his accounts with Harvard is not clear. To look upon it in a light favorable to Hancock, it could have been that, in the confusion of the war, the funds were so commingled with his own that he no longer knew what was owed to Harvard and he was unwilling to accept their estimate. To look upon it in a light unfavorable to Hancock, it could have been that he looked upon Harvard with such a patronizing air that he felt he could settle his accounts with them when he got good and ready. After all, he may have said to himself, he gave his great effort to win the war and he had lost considerable funds, so why should Harvard not also suffer? Such a possibility conflicts decidedly with Hancock's repeated requests in his addresses to the General Court to support Harvard. (Quincy, 182-209)

Logical proof: Hancock's speeches are not noted for syllogistic reasoning or chains of enthymemes. The premises are simple and the approach simplistic. Below are some of the major premises for his syllogisms:

All who hear this message should be persons grateful for God's grace.

Americans should be grateful for freedom and prosperity.

The state should support widows and orphans.

The legislators should support Harvard University.

The colonists should be proud of their developing domestic industries.

Either we will raise the necessary militia or we will be defeated.

If we wish our children to be educated, we must establish schools.

Such major premises can only be defended on the basis that Hancock never forgot the miracle of the American victory and he wished to bask in the glory of that victory and share it with the deserving and the less fortunate. Although some propose that Hancock's premises concerning the absentees were lenient, his speeches do not bear that out. The major premise that comes through most clearly is:

All absentees are persons who have forfeited their colonial rights.

Hancock was to make exceptions to this "all absentees" as well he should have. But the strength of the main posture was not seriously affected by making exceptions.

In respect to Shays's Rebellion, Hancock proposed a major premise that avoided the application of capital punishment:

Capital punishment is a punishment that should be avoided for
the public good.

Again Hancock's premises were not profound. He was not a
complex political scientist. His inaptitude in political thought is well
illustrated by the minor role that he played in drafting the state
constitutions.

II. Evidence

Hancock's legislative speeches would have featured much more
evidence if he had not attached to his speeches the letters that he had
received for consideration by the General Court. There was no need to
quote from these letters. The legislature could have them in their
entirety. Furthermore, there were repeated "messages" sent from the
governor's office to the legislature, and they could contain the evidence
that the legislature needed.

Hancock quoted from the state constitution, from the Bible, and not
infrequently from literature. What few statistics he gave were loosely
documented. The use of evidence was not one of Hancock's strong
points in delivering his addresses.

III. Arrangement

If Hancock followed the model of his family preachers in composing
his speeches, he also followed what is often the vague or nonexistent
structuring of ideas that often is featured in sermons. An examination
of the several manuscripts in Hancock's handwriting show that he
started writing at the beginning and stopped at the end. There was no
outline, no careful arrangement of points. Readers of Hancock's
speeches often hunger for organization. They thirst for transitions.
Occasionally, Hancock signals that he is going to a new point by
inserting, "Gentlemen of the Senate and Gentlemen of the House," but
the signal does not appear to relieve to any major extent the desire of
the listeners for structure.

IV. Style

Hancock featured two styles, the less tumid approach used in his speeches to the General Court, and the more tumid figurative style that he exercised in the six occasional addresses that have been preserved for us.

Hancock's figurative style featured a sizeable number of the classical figures of composition. Many of these he had undoubtedly learned in school and at Harvard. Others he may have assimilated from his reading and his stay in England. Rather than discussing stylistic features in general, there will be presented below examples of his usages, designating the speech from which the example was taken. In this manner, the striking quality of Hancock's florid epideictic speeches can be clearly revealed. Some of the usages are trite and some novel and some with finesse. Since Hancock's figurative style is most evident in his six occasional speeches, the following abbreviations will be used:

    5 Mar 1774......BM (Boston Massacre)
    19 Dec 1781.....1781H (Harvard, from the English translation)
    19 July 1788....1788H (Harvard)
    26 Nov 1789.....Sermon
    20 July 1791....1791H (Harvard)
    19 July 1792....1792H (Harvard)

Other speeches from which examples will be taken are noted by date.

1. Figurative Style

Naturally the examples below do not form an exhaustive list of the figurative language in the thirty speeches of Hancock, but only serve to demonstrate that he was capable of a variety of usage.

Alliteration

BM...felicity of my fellow men persons and properties

    traitors and trampling

    the people soon were aware of the poison which, with
    so much craft and subtilty, had been concealed: loss
    and disgrace ensued; and perhaps, this long-concerted
    masterpiece of policy

1791H...they form the minds and manners of its future members

1792H...the love of liberty

1781H...to that most recent revolution which is
renowned throughout the entire world

1781H...we will offer all aid, motivation, and consolation
(*also assonance*)

1791H...rather than to partake of careless ease and splendid
pleasures in a state of Slavery

1792H...cannot fail to present the felicity of our country

1792H... lead them in the path of peace

1792H... and the great and good men of our own state

1792H...afford us the fullest assurance of the advantages

Syncopated alliteration

BM...assist the sun

easy to foresee

unfeeling Russian

we then expect

Anaphora

1791H...When we contemplate. . .
when we see the sons of Harvard
when we see them respected in palaces abroad...
when we see, by the learning here acquired...

1791H...It is with you, young Gentlemen...to add lustre to
the brightness of your Country, or
to check her
progress in glory with an interval of darkness.

> We wish to inspire your ambition with this idea, and
>   to excite you by a sense of your importance in
>   the community

> From the publick then,
> from the civil fathers of their country,
> from the patriots

1792H...They who love their country's happiness...
     they who delight in national liberty...
                    and
     they who feel a zeal for true national glory

     May they be a blessing to their country.
     may they continue to reflect honour upon...
     may you, Sir, continue to receive...
                    and
     may your labours and the labours of all...

Sermon...Can we ascend...
     Can these sentiments...
     Can there be a more natural...
     Ought we not...
     Can any thing be...

Andiplosis

1781H...How much and how bright a hope all men have
     grasped from your learning...the
     vote of all the Fellows announces...

1788H...From your learning and known ability, respectable Sir,
     your fellow citizens have formed the most sanguine
     expectations

BM...For us he bled, and now languishes

Antithesis

BM...not only that ye pray but that ye act

Apophasis

BM...I mean not to boast, I would not excite envy
    but more emulation

Assonance

1781H...upon whose grave the togate race

BM...miserable Monk

Asyndeton

BM...The attentive gravity,
    the venerable appearance...,
    the solemnity of the occasion
            [all] join to a consideration

BM...Yet Monk, thou livest not in vain;
    thou livest a warning to thy country...
    thou livest in affecting an alarm...

BM...A well disciplined militia is a safe, an honorable guard

Consonance

BM...and leave you to improve

BM...does not the sight plant daggers in your souls

BM...the glory of a George

Epistrophe

Sermon...the Niggard shrinks; and he that was unjust, may be still
    more unjust

Isocolon

BM...by all that is dear

by all that is sacred
by all that is honorable

Oxymoron

BM... drowsy justice

sceptered robbers

1791H...careless ease

Parallel structure

1788H...you will annually send forth men
                        formed to guide the cabinet
                        direct the arms, and
                        extend the commerce

BM...the one sex into extravagance ...
      the other into infamy and ruin

1791H...it embellishes the path of Science
      cherishes Literature and
      promotes the Interest of our Republic.

Parenthesis or the aside

1781H...The native skills, here so faithfully taught, oh, may they
      forbid it that morals fail! May they forbid it that
      faults bring shame upon things well born!

BM...(and would to Heaven there could be an answer)

BM...but if I was possessed of the gift of prophesy

Sermon...and I believe justly

Polysyndeton

Sermon...and when we love, & Move, & have our Being

Rhetorical question

BM...Did not a reverence for religion sensibly decay?
Did not our infants almost learn to lisp our curses...
Did our youth forget they were Americans...

Sermon...Can we feel ourselves entertained and delight'd...
Can we ascend in our Minds to the true Author...
Can these Sentiments be warm and lively...
Can there be a more natural or proper Manner...
Ought we not to meet in solemn Assemblies...
Can any Thing be more reasonable and more...

2. Stylistic Devices using Exaggeration

Apostrophe

BM...Tell me, ye bloody butchers, ye villains high and low!

Personification

BM...meek-eyed charity

drowsy justice nodding upon her rotten seat

1781H...Our Alma Mater gave birth...nourishes...taught.
1781H...the Sons of Harvard

1792H...the sons of Harvard

BM...the affrighted stars that hurried through the sky

BM...drowsy justice... still nods upon her rotten seat

Metonomy and synecdoche and their variations

1781H...having embraced such a constitution to your breast

1792H....inherent to the breast of man

1792H...men, who shall take the people by the hand

BM...let us by no means pull off the harness

BM...But if the unappeared manes of the dead

BM...honest father clothed with shame

1792H....the walls of Harvard

BM...when virtue has one erected her throne within the female
breast

3. Stylistic Devices to Form Comparisons

Analogy

1788H...When we see, by the learning here acquired, Religion
stripped of that delusive and dangerous garb, which
ignorance and supersitition have wrapped her in and
exhibited, in that simple and unaffected dress, in which
alone she can honour the Deity, and bless mankind—we
cannot but deeply revere our ancestors and rejoice in
the fair inheritance they have transmitted us.

BM....meek-eyed justice

BM...when Heaven in anger, for a dreadful moment, suffered
hell to take the reins, and sacrilegiously polluted our
land with dead bodies of guiltless sons

Historical/literary allusions

Letter to Adams, 31 Aug 1793: Watchman. What of the night?

1781H...for the purpose of installing you in the Curile Chair

1781H...(possibility of the Horace quotation, Odes)

1781H...(possibility of a reference to Virgil)

1781H...(possibility of a reference to Aeneid)

1788H...seat of the muses

Sermon...(reference to Columbus)

BM...(Virgil's Aeneid, 6, 621-2; 625)

Metaphor

1777...heart felt pleasure
  unanimity may go hand in hand
  the business annexed to it

1781H...we who are here blossoming and
      pleasantly flourishing
  Our Alma Mater...gave birth...and nourished
      that which has been born.

1788H...to be carried on the wings of imagination
  youths thirsty for science

Simile

BM...like burning tapers at noonday, to assist the sun in
  enlightening the world

4. Literal Style

Hancock wrote a good sentence. The spelling of words was more in flux than it is now, so he used often used variants from modern spelling. One characteristic of his literal style is that he never split an infinitive. For example, in his very first address to the General Court on 25 Oct 1780, Hancock said: "I shall endeavor strictly to adhere to the Laws of the Constitution." In his following address on 31 Oct 1780, Hancock noted: "I cannot therefore omit warmly to commend them to your care and patronage." Other examples are:

>   BM...strenuously to oppose
>   Sermon...rightly to enjoy
>   Sermon...and properly to enjoy them

As will be observed below, Hancock used an extended vocabulary and was able to vary his style of sentences, using the loose and periodic sentences along with the very short sentence.

Unusual vocabulary

> allured; viciate; poltroon; manes; assuage,
> salubrious; jeopard; tutelar; besom; emulation;
> diffusings; miscreant, public weal, augurs

The short sentence

31 Oct 1777: You are the best judges.

BM...But that plot was soon discovered.

We have all our common cause.

Periodic sentence

BM...Though some of you may think yourselves exalted to a
> height that bids defiance to human justice, and others
> shroud youselves beneath the mask of hypocricy, and build
> your hopes of safety on the low arts of cunning,
> chicanery, and falsehood, yet do you not...

The degree to which Hancock was faithful to his manuscripts is not known. If there had been major variations, the newspapers of the day could (but not necessarily would) have noted them. The best evidence that Hancock stayed pretty close to his manuscripts lies in the personality of the man himself. He did not like to be taken by surprise. He preferred certainty, when he could get it. It seems likely that he "interpreted" his speeches verbatim from the manuscripts.

Delivery

It is not altogether clear the technique Hancock used to deliver his speeches to the General Court. Because there exist identical copies of some of his addresses in the files of both the House and the Senate, he must have furnished two copies to the General Court. But what did he have with him when he spoke? And how did the speeches get to the secretaries of the two houses?

There are a few clues. The *Journal of the House* said of his 31 Oct 1780 speech, that the governor spoke, "after which his Excellency presented a copy thereof to the Speaker of the House & retired." (MA, b) This may have been a customary practice. Hancock seemingly took two copies of his address down to the chamber in which he was speaking (usually the House Chamber because it was larger), delivered the speech from one of them, and then presented each house with a copy. Such a supposition is somewhat supported by the comment in the *Journal of the Senate* concerning Hancock's speech of 22 Jan 1782: "And the Honorable Speaker laid on the Table, the Speech of His Excellency to both Houses, with a file of Papers." (MA, c) The comment does not specifically say that Hancock furnished the General Court with two copies of his speech, so the question is not resolved by the comment on the 22 Jan 1782 speech.

However, a comment in the House journal concerning the 24 Sept 1783 speech makes it more likely that Hancock brought two copies with him when he spoke. The *Journal of the House* for 25 Sept 1783 (MA, d) stated: "A copy of this speech being delivered to the Speaker, the House retired into their own chamber where the same was read and 3 o clk P.M. [sic] assigned for considering thereof." As Hancock had spoken on this occasion in the Senate Chamber, it seems very unlikely that the Senate would have permitted the House to "be delivered" a copy of the speech without retaining a copy for itself.

There is so little comment about the success of Hancock's speeches to the General Court that it is difficult not to exaggerate the one comment found. In his letter of 1787 to Sam Adams, Elbridge Gerry wrote that he had not attended Hancock's speech to the General Court to hear "his Excellency's Speechification" and that a debate had ensued "respecting the Impropriety of the Governor's Speechifying to the Legislature, and of his calling the Members from their Seats to attend him, on *any* Occasion, during their Debates." (NYP, b) It is not difficult to envision how an outspoken critic of Hancock would have found his addresses "speechy" and referred to them as "speechification."

Effective delivery can be enhanced by height. There is disagreement about Hancock's height. Was it unusually commanding for the height of people in the eighteenth century, or was he of average height for his period?

Wagner (64) found him a tall person: "At twenty-eight, Hancock was so striking in appearance that strangers in town turned to stare when he strode by. Nearly six feet tall, he looked every inch an aristocrat, from his dressed and powdered wig to his smart pumps of grained leather. Wagner acknowledged that he had stooping shoulders, but attributed those to the gout and Hancock's other bouts with illness. In another section of his biography, Wagner (31) asserted that Hancock was "nearly six feet tall and sturdily built" with "dashing good looks as well." Wagner asserted that "his dark eyes were penetrating, his mouth was firm, his chin determined."

Wagner seemingly got his information about Hancock's height from William Sullivan's reminiscences: "As recollected at this time Gov. Hancock [in 1782] was nearly six feet in stature, and of thin person, stooping a little, and apparently enfeebled by disease. His manners were very gracious, of the old style of dignified complaisance. His face had been very handsome." (Sullivan, 10)

Fowler (50) described Hancock as "handsome." Fowler asserted that "though not tall, he was slender and well-proportioned." After receiving permission to open the glass case in the Old State House that contains the clothes that Hancock wore in 1780 when he was first inaugurated governor, Fowler (245) measured the garments and concluded that "John Hancock was approximately five feet, four inches tall: neck, fourteen and a half inches; sleeve, thirty-three inches; waist, thirty-one and a half inches; and chest, thirty-eight inches." This evidence is more objective perhaps than the Sumner description. If we allow for shrinkage of the garments caused by cleaning, we can arrive at an approximate height of Hancock as five feet, six inches tall. In his day, this was an encouraging height.

Most of the primary sources on Hancock's delivery are terse. For example, concerning his speech of 5 Mar 1775, the Boston *Gazette* noted that the oration was received with "universal applause." Other accounts in the Boston *Post-Boy*, the Boston *Journal*, the Massachusettts *Gazette,* and the Boston *Weekly News Letter* followed suit. The *Royal American Magazine* of March 1774, in reprinting the speech, noted only that Hancock "very affectionately addressed the audience" in Monk's behalf. The only eyewitness account is found in John Adams' diary for 5 Mar, 1774:

> Heard the oration, pronounced by Colonel Hancock in commemoration of the massacre. An elegant, a pathetic, a spirited performance. A vast crowd, rainy eyes, etc. The composition, the pronunciation, the action—all exceeded the expectation of everybody. They exceeded even mine, which were very considerable. Many of the sentiments came with great propriety from him. His invective, particularly against a preference of riches to virtue, came from him with a singular dignity and grace. (Adams, 2, 332)

Thomas, who spoke from personal experience about Hancock's later speeches, noted that a man who had heard Hancock's Boston Massacre speech told Thomas "that the multitude who listened to it, were wrought up to such a pitch of phrenzy, that a single sentence from the oration, calling upon them to take arms, and drive the murderers from their town, would have been at once carried into effect. Such was his control over them, many could not keep their seats, from indignation." (Thomas, 1, 245)

In speaking of his later speeches, Thomas recalled Hancock's form as "elegant" and his facial expression as "beautiful, manly, and expressive." Hancock was capable of exciting his audience to "the highest pitch of phrenzy" or he could "sooth them into tears" as he wished. Thomas' description of the final speech of 1793 is particularly vivid:

> A town meeting was called, upon a question of great excitement. Old Faneuil Hall[2] could not contain the people, and an adjournment took place to the Old South Meeting-house. Hancock was brought in, and carried up to the front gallery, where the Hon. Benjamin Austin supported him on the right, and the celebrated Dr. Charles Jarvis upon the left, while he addressed the multitude. The governor commenced, by stating to his fellow citizens, that "he felt" it was the last time he should ever address them—that "the seeds of mortality were growing fast within him." The fall of a pin might have been heard such a death-like silence pervaded the listening crowd, during the whole of his animated and soul stirring speech, while tears ran down the cheeks of thousands. The meeting ended, he was conveyed to his carriage, and taken home, but never again appeared in public." (Thomas, 1, 244)

This account is somewhat puzzling, because state documents show that Hancock, in addressing the status of the absentees, was speaking on a question of interest to many, but that the speech was read for Hancock in the State House and not at the Old South Meeting House. Hancock himself did make the final remarks, so what Thomas may have remembered was the act of the governor being assisted by Austin and Jarvis in delivering his few concluding sentences of adieu.

NOTES

1. Abbot may be the source of the quotation in Mabel M. Carlton's brief essay on Hancock published in 1922 for the Hancock Mutual Life Insurance Company. In her essay, Carlton quoted Hancock as saying: "Although I am probably the largest property-owner in the city, I am anxious that the thing should be done if it will benefit the cause." (Carlton, 10) What Hancock wrote to Washington on 22 Dec 1775 was: "You will Notice the Last Revolution Relative to an Attack upon Boston....I most heartily wish it, tho' individually I may be the greatest suffered." (Abbott, 2, 589-590)

2. Faneuil Hall was not only a meeting house, but also an active market. Acts & Resolves 1783, 18 Feb 1784, Chap. 29, 564-566: "Be it enacted... That the lower floor of Faneuil Hall, and the land around the same, bounded and described as follows...is now improved for market use, reserving for public use the streets leading through the said market square for public passing as usual; be, and they hereby are, set apart as markets for meats, vegetables and grain."

Part II

Thirty-One Speeches by John Hancock

HEADNOTE

Date: 5 Mar, 1774

Occasion: On the past three anniversaries of the Boston Massacre, a public ceremony had been held, featuring a speech by an outstanding Bostonian. The news that Hancock, who was not only one of the town's richest citizens, but also a respectable businessman, was to deliver the commemorative address on 5 Mar 1774 was greeted with considerable interest. Hancock's biographer Wagner (102) observed that "it was not the words that spellbound John's audience so much as the man who delivered them."

The British interpreted the act as widening the gap between Hancock and the king, while the radicals celebrated the breach. What details are known about the celebration of the fourth anniversary of the Boston Massacre?

The committee appointed by the Massachusetts House to exchange information with other colonial grievance committees was in charge of the celebration. This committee, dominated by Whigs with Sam Adams as one of its members, felt it highly politic to enlist the service of an outstanding Bostonian merchant whose fellow shippers were suffering from the opposition of the radicals to the laws of England. This particular 5 Mar fell on a Saturday. Although a certain amount of business must have gone on as usual, much of the town's activity centered on the anniversary. The British stayed home, making themselves inconspicuous. The colonials and their dignitaries assembled at Faneuil Hall for preliminaries, but had to adjourn to the Old South Church since the crowd was so great. How many did Hancock address? The present seating capacity of Faneuil Hall is around 950, but prior to 1806 the building was only half as wide as it is now and the existing balconies were not present.[1] Old Faneuil Hall did not have permanent seats, so that, during Hancock's time, it could have accommodated around one thousand persons standing. Because it was necessary to move the ceremony, there must have been an audience in excess of one thousand persons. How many more? Assuming those seated plus maximum standees, close to two thousands may have been accommodated in the Old South Church to hear Hancock. Many others gathered outside, not able to gain admittance.

After Sam Adams made some introductory remarks, John Hancock, who had just recovered from the gout, delivered his attack. The moment when Hancock took his position at the sacred desk must have been tense. As the audience heard the vigorous way in which he denounced the British, there must have been an increase in the number who thought revolution inevitable. It was one thing for Sam Adams and his crowd to agitate against the king; it was quite another for one of the town's most wealthy and respected citizens to take an uncompromising position. Allan (144) in his biography reconstructed the scene as follows:

> It was a spell-binding tirade of inflammatory rhetorical questions, extravagant accusations, gore-dropping passages, and passion-rousing apostrophes that was received, even by intellectuals, with reverberating plaudits and with tears.

The newspapers of the day were terse in comment and discouragingly in agreement. The Boston *Gazette* of 7 Mar 1774 noted the three items reported by all newspapers:

1) the celebration began at 10:00 A.M. at Faneuil Hall where Adams was chosen moderator;

(2) the assembly moved to the Old South Meeting House or Church where "a prodigious crowd of people" heard the speech; and

(3) the oration was received with "universal applause."

The *Gazette* noted that, since the anniversary of the massacre fell on a Saturday evening, i.e., the Sabbath eve, the customary exhibition of the portraits of the soldier "murderers" and the citizens "slaughtered" by the troops would be put off until Monday evening when they would be displayed at Mrs. Clapham's in King Street. As the meeting broke up, a generous collection was taken for Christopher Monk. (Wells, 2, 140) The Massachusetts *Spy* of Thursday, 10 Mar, reported that "a vast concourse of people attended the oration, which lasted about three quarters of an hour, and was received with...approbation." The *Spy's* comments were evidently copied from the Boston *Evening Post* of 7 Mar 1774, or else the newspapers shared the same reporter, for the accounts are identical. The Boston *Post-Boy and Advertiser* reported largely what had been noted in the Boston *Journal*, and the Massachusetts *Gazette* and Boston *Weekly News Letter* followed suit. The *Royal American Magazine* of March 1774, reprinted the speech but added nothing of importance, saying only that Hancock "very affectionately addressed the audience" in Monk's behalf.

The Boston Town Records for 1774 are terse in their comments. They do note that the speech was scheduled for delivery at 12 o'clock. Perhaps it took two hours for the 10 A.M. preliminaries so that the speech was designed to begin at noon. Apparently a formality was kept of having a committee notify the speaker that the oration was expected to be delivered at noon in the Old South Meeting House. Hancock having expressed his willingness to so oblige, he delivered his oration "to a large and crowded Audience and was received by them with great Applause." (RRC, 18th report, 149)

The only eyewitness who appears to have recorded his contemporary observations of the speech in any detail was John Adams, who made the following entry in his diary for 5 Mar 1774:

Heard the oration....an elegant, a pathetic, a spirited performance. A vast crowd, rainy eyes, etc. The composition, the pronunciation, the action--all exceeded the expectations of everybody. They exceeded even mine, which were very considerable. Many of the sentiments came with great propriety from him. His invective, particularly against a preference of riches to virtue, came from him with singular dignity and grace. Diner at neighbor Quincy's with my wife... The happiness of the family where I dined, upon account of the Colonel's justly applauded oration, was complete. The justice and his daughters were all joyous. (Wells, 2, 332)

Thomas, who spoke from personal experience about Hancock's later speeches, noted that a man who had heard Hancock's Boston Massacre speech told Thomas "that the multitude who listened to it, were wrought up to such a pitch of phrenzy, that a single sentence from the oration, calling upon them to take arms, and drive the murderers from the town, would have been at once carried into effect. Such was his control over them, many could not keep their seats from indignation." (1, 245) Thomas himself recalled Hancock's form as "elegant" and his facial expression as "beautiful, manly, and expressive." Hancock, said Thomas, was capable of exciting his audience to "the highest pitch of phrenzy" or he could "sooth them into tears," as he wished.

In a letter from John Andrews to William Barrell dated 14 Apr 1775, Andrews stated: "Have inclosed [sic] you the anniversary Oration delivered by John Hancock Esq, it's generally afforded to be a good composition, / and asserted to be his *own* production / both spirited and nervous, I can't myself judge of its merit, as I did not hear it delivered nor have I allowed myself time to peruse it since its publication." (MHS)

Unfortunately for posterity, John Rowe, the Boston merchant who kept a diary during the prerevolutionary period, wrote for his entry of 5 Mar 1774: "Mr. Hancock delivered An Oration this day at Dr. Sewalls [sic] Meeting house to the Greatest Number of People that ever met on the Occasion. I tryd to get in but could not. Some Gentlemen speak of the Oration with Great Applause." (Rowe, 264)

Although there is smoke indicating that Hancock did not write all of his Boston Massacre speech, there is sufficient fire to indicate that he could have done so had he wished. The sources that question Hancock's authorship are based on hearsay or just rumor. On 29 July 1840, Noah Webster wrote to Ebenezer Thomas:

> In the year 1774, Mr. Trumbull was a student of law in the office of John Adams. Mr. Hancock was, at that time, a wavering character; at least he was so considered by the leading Whigs of that day. It was a matter of no small importance to bring him to a decision, as to the part he was to take in the crisis then approaching. To effect this object, the more staunch leading Whigs contrived to procure Mr. Hancock to be appointed to deliver an oration on the anniversary of the Massacre; and some of them wrote his oration for him, or a considerable part of it.....Judge Trumbull related to me these facts, as from his personal knowledge. (Thomas, 2, 169)

The second piece of evidence from William Wells who was inclined to favor his subject, Sam Adams, is even more questionable:

> It is known among a few that Samuel Adams composed nearly the whole of this oration for his friend. A letter asserting this as a fact, written in 1787, by one who personally knew both Adams and Hancock, was in existence a few years since, but has been lost. Mrs. Hannah Wells has repeatedly stated that she knew the time and place where her father used to meet Hancock while preparing the speech, but, as a girl, she had been cautioned not to mention it. Mr. Joseph Allen, a nephew and special favorite of Adams and a frequent visitor at his house, used to say that Hancock was long closeted with Adams

on several occasions, a week or two before delivering the oration. (Wells, 2, 138)

Third, Alice M. Baldwin (156) reported that it was said that yet a third person, this time Samuel Cooper, pastor of the Brattle Square Church of which Hancock was a member, wrote the oration. Baldwin may have rested her assertion on a reference in the diary of William Bentley, who noted on 7 Feb 1787: "[Cooper] was much in favor with Hancock, and the political papers of that Gentleman were in common opinion ascribed to him." (Bentley, 1, 52) It may well be that Hancock discussed the ideas for his speech with Dr. Cooper, who in turn gave his opinions as to what should be said. When Cooper, a prominent liberal, heard the sermon, he could well have recalled his conversations with Hancock and reasoned that portions if not all of the speech were his.

There are alway those who claim authorship of the speeches of the deceased. John F. Kennedy and Mirabeau have had others claim to have written their speeches. Of course Hancock consulted with Adams. The two were intimate, and Adams may have done all he could to influence what Hancock had to say. But both men would have appeared ridiculous had the speech resembled too much the sort of propaganda for which Adams was already famous. A proud Hancock would have avoided the charge of borrowing too liberally from his interesting but seedy friend.

Furthermore, the speech bears resemblances to the orations of 1771, 1772, and 1773. For example, Lovell, who delivered the first oration in 1771, began with short excerpts from Caesar and Cicero, while Joseph Warren, who followed in 1772, took his text from Virgil, as did the later-convicted traitor Dr. Church in 1773. It was therefore natural for Hancock to open with a passage from the *Aeneid*. All of these gentlemen recited their introductory quotations in Latin. Communication can be effectively achieved, even if the words themselves are not understood. Hancock could say by quoting Virgil that the sentiments of the colonists were not new but in keeping with Roman tradition. Much of Hancock's Boston Massacre oration was formulated in the classical mold in keeping with his education at Harvard, so it is questionable to propose that a Harvard graduate could not have composed as vigorous a speech as Hancock delivered in 1774.

SOURCES

Early Bound Accounts

The first edition was published in Boston by Edes & Gill in 1774: *An Oration: Delivered March 5, 1774, at the Request of the Inhabitants of the Town of Boston to Commemorate the Bloody Tragedy of the Fifth of March, 1770.* A second edition appeared in 1807, and the first edition had appeared in an edition of the Boston Massacre speeches published by Edes in 1785.

Early Newspaper Accounts

Boston *Gazette*, 7 Mar 1774, 3, 1; Massachusetts *Spy*, 10 Mar 1774, 2, 3; the Massachusetts *Gazette & Boston Post-Boy & Advertiser*, 28 Feb 7 Mar 1774, 3, 2; *Royal American Magazine*, March, 1774, 125-136; Massachusetts *Gazette and Boston Weekly Newsletter*, 10 Mar 1774, 3, 2; Boston *Evening Post*, 7 Mar 1774, 2, 3.

Some Later Republications

Among the publications that have reprinted the oration are the *Magazine of History*, XXIV, #3, extra no. 95 (1923), 31-42; *Modern Eloquence*, XIII, 1125-1136 (1903 edition); and Niles Hezekiah, ed, *Principles & Acts of the Revolution*, Baltimore, 1882, 38-42.

TEXT OF THE ADDRESS

Vendidit hic auro, patriam, dominumque potentem
Imposuit: fixit leges pretio atque refixit.
Non, mihi si linguae centum sint, oraque centum,
Ferrea vox, omnes, scelerum: comprehendere
formas, ...possim (Virgil, Aeneid, 6, 621-2; 625-7)

Men, brethren, fathers and fellow-countrymen: The attentive gravity, the venerable appearance of this crowded audience; the dignity which I behold in the countenances of so many in this great assembly; the solemnity of the occasion upon which we have met together, joined to a consideration of the part I am to take in the important business of this day, fill me with an awe hitherto unknown; and heighten the sense which I have ever had, of my unworthiness to fill this sacred desk; but allured by the call of some of my respected fellow-citizens, with whose request it is always my greatest pleasure to comply, I almost forgot my want of ability to perform what they required. In this situation I find my only support, in assuring myself that a generous people will not severely censure what they know was well intended, though its want of merit, should prevent their being able to applaud it. And I pray, that my sincere attachment to the interest of my country, and hearty detestation of every design formed against her liberties, may be admitted as some apology for my appearance in this place.

I have always, from my earliest youth, rejoiced in the felicity of my fellow-men; and have ever considered it as the indispensable duty of every member of society to promote, as far as in him lies, the prosperity of every individual, but more especially of the community to which he belongs; and also, as a faithful subject of the state, to use his utmost endeavors to detect, and having detected, strenuously to oppose every traitorous plot which its enemies may devise for its destruction. Security to the persons and properties of the governed, is so obviously the design and end of civil government, that to attempt a logical proof of it, would be like burning tapers at noonday, to assist the sun in enlightening the world; and it cannot be either virtuous or honorable, to attempt to support a government, of which this is not the great and principal basis; and it is the last degree vicious and infamous to attempt to support a government, which manifestly tends to render the persons and properties of the governed insecure. Some boast of being *friends* to *government*; I am a friend to righteous government founded upon the principles of reason and justice; but I glory in publicly avowing my eternal enmity to tyranny. Is the present system, which the British administration have adopted for the government of the colonies, a righteous government? or is it tyranny?—Here suffer me to ask (and would to Heaven there could be an answer) what tenderness, what regard, respect or consideration has Great Britain shewn, in their late transactions for the security of the persons or properties of the inhabitants of the colonies? or rather, what have they omitted doing to destroy that security? they have declared that they have, ever had, and of right ought ever to have, full power to make laws of sufficient validity to bind the colonies in all cases whatever: they have exercised this pretended right by imposing a tax upon us without our consent;[2] and lest we should shew some reluctance at parting with our property, her fleets and armies are sent to enforce their mad pretentions. The town of Boston, ever faithful to the British crown, has been invested by a British fleet; the troops of George the III have crossed the wide Atlantic,[3] not to engage an enemy, but to assist a band of traitors in trampling on the right and liberties of his most loyal subjects in America—those rights and liberties which, as a father, he ought ever to regard, and as a king, he is bound, in honor, to defend from violations, even at the risk of his own life.

Let not the history of the illustrious house of Brunswick inform posterity, that a king descended from that glorious monarch, George the II, once sent his British subjects to conquer and enslave his subjects in America, but be perpetual infamy entailed upon that villain who dared to advise his master to such execrable measures; for it was easy to foresee the consequences which so naturally followed upon sending troops into America, to enforce obedience to acts of the British parliament, which neither God nor man ever empowered them to make. It was reasonable to expect that troops, who knew the errand they were sent upon, would treat the people whom they were to subjugate, with a cruelty and haughtiness, which too often buries the honorable character of a *soldier* in the disgraceful name of an *unfeeling ruffian*. The troops, upon their first arrival, took possession of our senate-house,[4] and pointed their cannon against the judgment hall,[5] and even continued them there whilst the supreme court of judicature for this province was actually sitting to decide upon the lives and fortunes of the king's subjects.[6]

Our streets nightly resounded with the noise of riot and debauchery; our peaceful citizens were hourly exposed to shameful insults, and often felt the effects of their violence and outrage.—But this was not all; as though they thought it was not enough to violate our civil rights, they endeavored to deprive us of the enjoyment of our religious privileges;[7] to vitiate our morals, and thereby render us deserving of destruction. Hence the rude din of arms which broke in upon your solemn devotions in your temples, on that day hallowed by heaven, and set apart by God himself for his peculiar worship. Hence, impious oaths and blasphemies so often tortured your unaccustomed ear. Hence, all the arts which idleness and luxury could invent, were used to betray our youth of one sex into extravagance and effeminacy, and of the other into infamy and ruin; and did they need succeed but too well? Did not a reverence for religion sensibly decay? Did not our infants almost learn to lisp out curses before they knew their horrid import? did not our youth forget they were Americans, and regardless of the admonitions of the wise and aged, servilely copy from their tyrants those vices which finally must overthrow the empire of Great Britain? And must I be compelled to acknowledge, that even the noblest, fairest part of all the lower creation did not entirely escape the cursed snare? when virtue has once erected her throne within the female breast, it is upon so solid a basis that nothing is able to expel the heavenly inhabitant. But have there not been some, few indeed, I hope, whose youth and inexperience have rendered them a prey to wretches, whom, upon the least reflection, they would have despised and hated as foes to God and their country? I fear there have been some such unhappy instances; or why have I seen an honest father clothed with shame; or why a virtuous mother drowned in tears?

But I forbear, and come reluctantly to the transactions of that dismal night, when in such quick succession we felt the extremes of grief, astonishment and rage; when Heaven in anger, for a dreadful moment suffered hell to take the reins; when Satan with his chosen band opened the sluices of New England's blood, and sacriligiously polluted our land with the dead bodies of her guiltless sons. Let this sad tale of death never be told without a tear; let not the heaving bosom cease to burn with a manly indignation at the barbarous story, through the long tracts of future time: let every parent tell the shameful story to his listening children 'til tears of pity glisten in their eyes, and boiling passions shake their tender frames; and whilst the anniversary of that ill-fated night is kept a jubilee in the grim court of pandaemonium, let all America join in one common prayer to heaven, that the inhuman, unprovoked murders of the fifth of March, 1770, planned by Hillsborough,[8] and a knot of treacherous knaves in Boston, and executed by the cruel hand of Preston[9] and his sanguinary coadjutors, may ever stand on history without a parallel. But what, my countrymen, withheld the ready arm of vengeance from executing instant justice on the file assassins? perhaps you feared promiscuous carnage might ensue, and that the innocent might share the fate of those who had performed the infernal deed. But were not all guilty? were you not too tender of the lives of those who came to fix a yoke on your necks? but I must not too severely blame a fault, which great souls only can commit. May that magnificence of spirit which scorns the low pursuits of malice, may that generous compassion which often preserves from ruin, even a guilty villain, forever actuate the noble bosoms of Americans! But let us not the miscreant host vainly imagine that we feared their arms. No; them we despised; we dread nothing but slavery. Death is the creature of a poltroon's brains;[10] 'tis immortality to sacrifice ourselves for the salvation of our country. We fear not death. That gloomy night, the pale faced moon, and the affrighted stars that hurried through the sky, can witness that we fear not death. Our hearts which, at the recollection, glow with rage that four revolving years have scarcely taught us to restrain, can witness that we fear not death; and happy it is for those who dared to insult us, that their naked bones are now piled up an everlasting monument of Massachusett's bravery. But they retired, they fled, and in that flight they found their only safety. We then expected that the hand of public justice would soon inflict that punishment upon the murderers, which, by the laws of God and man, they had incurred. But let the unbiased pen of a Robertson,[11] or perhaps of some equally famed American, conduct this trial before the great tribunal of succeeding generations. And though the murderers may escape the just resentment of an enraged people; though drowsy justice, intoxicated by the poisonous draught prepared for her cup, still nods upon her rotten seat, yet be assured, such complicated crimes will meet their due reward.[12] Tell me, ye bloody butchers! ye villains high and low! ye wretches who contrived, as well as you who executed the inhuman deed! do you not feel the goads and stings of conscious guilt pierce through your savage bosoms? Though some of you may think yourselves exalted to a height that bids defiance to human justice, and others shroud yourselves beneath the mask of hypocrisy, and build your hopes of safety on the low arts of cunning, chicanery and falsehood, yet do you not sometimes feel the knawings of that worm which never dies: Do not the injured shades of Maverick, Gray, Caldwell, Attucks and Carr,[13] attend you in your solitary walks, arrest you even in the midst of your debaucheries, and fill even your dreams with terror? But if the unappeased manes of the dead should not disturb their murderers, yet surely even your obdurate hearts must shrink, and your guilty blood must chill within your rigid veins, when you behold the miserable Monk, the wretched victim of your savage cruelty. Observe his tottering knees, which scarce sustain his wasted body; look on his haggard eyes; mark well the death-like paleness of his fallen cheek, and tell me, does not the sight plant daggers in your souls? unhappy Monk! cut off in the gay morn of manhood, from all the joys which sweeten life, doomed to drag on a pitiful existence, without even a hope to taste the pleasures of returning health! yet Monk, thou livest not in vain; thou livest a warning to thy country, which sympathizes with thee in thy sufferings; thou livest in affecting, an alarming instance of the unbounded violence which lust of power, assisted by a standing army, can lead a traitor to commit. For us he bled, and now languishes. The wounds by which he is tortured to a lingering death, were aimed at our country! Surely the [sic] meek-eyed charity can never behold such sufferings with indifference. Nor can her lenient hand forbear to pour oil and wine into those wounds, and to assuage at least, what it cannot heal.[14]

Patriotism is ever united with humanity and compassion. This noble affection which impels us to sacrifice every thing dear, even life itself, to our country, involves it in a common sympathy and tenderness for every citizen, and must ever have a particular feeling for one who suffers in a public cause. Thoroughly persuaded of this, I need not add a word to engage your compassion and bounty towards a fellow citizen, who, with long protracted anguish, falls a victim to the relentless rage of our common enemies.

Ye dark designing knaves, ye murderers, parricides![15] how dare you tread upon the earth, which has drank in the blood of slaughtered innocents, shed by your wicked hands? How dare you breathe that air which wafted to the ear of heaven, the groans of those who feel a sacrifice to your accursed ambition? but if the laboring earth doth not expand her jaws; if the air you breathe is not commissioned to be the minister of death yet hear it, and tremble! the eye of heaven penetrates the darkest chambers of the soul, traces the leading clue through all the labryinths which your industrious folly has devised; and you, however you may have screened yourselves from human eyes, must be arraigned, must lift your hands, red with the blood of those whose death you have procured, at the tremendous bar of GOD.

But I gladly quit the gloomy theme of death, and leave you to improve the thought of that important day, when our naked souls must stand before that being, from whom nothing can be hid. I would not dwell too long upon the horrid effects which have already followed from quartering regular troops in this town; let our misfortunes teach posterity to guard against such evils for the future. Standing armies[16] are sometimes (I would by no means say generally, much less universally) composed of persons who have rendered themselves unfit to live in civil society; who have no property in any country; men who have given up their own liberties, and envy those who enjoy liberty; who are equally indifferent to the glory of a George or a Louis;[17] who for the addition of one penny a day to their wages, would desert from the Christian cross, and fight under the crescent of the Turkish sultan, from such men as those, usurping Caesar passed the Rubicon; with such as these he humbled mighty Rome, and forced the mistress of the world to own a master in a traitor. There are the men whom sceptered robbers now employ to frustrate the designs of God and render vain the bounties which his gracious hand pour indiscriminately upon his creatures. By these the miserable slaves in Turkey, Persia, and many other extensive countries, are rendered truly wretched, though their air is salubrious, and their soil luxuriously fertile. By these, France and Spain, though blessed by nature with all that administers to the convenience of life, have been reduced to that contemptible state in which they now appear; and by these Britain—but if I was possessed of the gift of prophecy, I dare not, except by divine command, unfold the leaves on which the destiny of that once powerful kingdom is inscribed. But since standing armies are so hurtful to a state,[18] perhaps my countrymen may demand some substitute, some other means of rendering us secure against the incursions of foreign enemy. But can you be one moment at a loss? will not a *well disciplined militia* [19] afford you ample security against foreign foes? We want not courage; it is discipline alone in which we are exceeded by the most formidable troops that ever trod the earth. Surely our hearts flutter no more at the sound of war, than did those of the immortal hand of Persia, the Macedonian phalanx, the invincible Roman legions, the Turkish Janissaries,[20] the Gens des Arms of France,[21] or the *well known grenadiers of Britain.*[22] A well disciplined militia is a safe, an honorable guard to a community like this, whose inhabitants are by nature brave, and are laudably tenacious of that freedom in which they were born. From a well regulated militia we have nothing to fear; their interest is the same with that of the state. When a country is invaded, the militia are ready to appear in its defence; they march into the field with that fortitude which a consciousness of the justice of their cause inspires; they do not jeopard their lives for a master who considers them only as the instruments of his ambition, and whom they regard only as the daily dispenser of the scanty pittance of bread and water. No, they fight for their houses, their lands, for their wives, their children, they fight pro aris et focis,[23] for their liberty, and for themselves, and for their God. And let it not offend, if I say that no militia ever appeared in more flourishing condition, than that of this province now doth;[24] and pardon me if I say—of this town in particular—I mean not to boast; I would not excite envy but manly emulation. We have all our common cause; let it therefore be our only context, who shall most contribute to the security of the liberties of America. And may the same kind Providence which has watched over this country from her infant state, still enable us to defeat our enemies. I cannot here forbear noticing the signal manner in which the designs of those who wish not well to us have been discovered. The dark deeds of a treacherous Cabal, have been brought to public view. You now know the serpents who, while cherished in your bosoms, were darting their envenomed stings into the vitals of the constitution.[25] But the representatives of the people have fixed a mark on these ungrateful monsters, which, though it may not make them so secure as Cain of old, yet renders them at least as infamous. Indeed it would be affrontive to the tutelar deity of this country even to despair of saving it from all the snares which human policy can lay.

True it is, that the British ministry have annexed a salary to the office of the governor of this province, to be paid out of a revenue, raised in America without our consent. They have attempted to render our courts of justice the instruments of extending the authority of acts of the British parliament over this colony, by making the judges dependent on the British administration for their support.[26] But this people will never be enslaved with their eyes open. The moment they knew that the governor was not such a governor as the charter of the province points out, he lost his power of hurting them. They were alarmed; they suspected him, have guarded against him, and he has found that a wise and a brave people, when they knew their danger, are fruitful in expedients to escape it.[27]

The courts of judicature also so far lost their dignity, by being supposed to be under an undue influence, that our representatives thought it absolutely necessary to resolve that they were bound to declare that they would not receive any other salary besides that which the general court should grant them; and if they did not make this declaration, that it would be the duty of the house to impeach them.

Great expectations were also formed from the artful scheme of allowing the East India company to export tea to America, upon their own account.[28] This certainly, had it succeeded, would have effected the purpose of the contrivers, and gratified the most sanguine wishes of our adversaries. We soon should have found our trade in the hands of foreigners, and taxes imposed on every thing which we consumed; nor would it have been strange, if, in a few years, a company in London should have purchased an exclusive right of trading to America.—But their plot was soon discovered.—The people soon were aware of the poison which, with so much craft and subtilty, had been concealed; loss and disgrace ensued: and, perhaps, this long-concerted masterpiece of policy, may issue in the total disuse of tea in this country, which will eventually be the saving of the lives and the estates of thousands—yet while we rejoice that the adversary has not hitherto prevailed against us, let us by no means put off the harness. Restless malice, and disappointed ambition, will still suggest new measures to our inveterate *enemies.*— Therefore let us also be ready to take the field whenever dangers calls: let us be united and strengthen the hands of each other, by promoting a general union among us.—Much has been done by the committee of correspondence for this and the other towns of this province, towards uniting the inhabitants;[29] let them still go on and prosper. Much has been done by the committees of correspondence, for the houses of assembly, in this and our sister colonies, for uniting the inhabitants of the whole continent, for the security of their common interest. May success ever attend their generous endeavors. But permit me here to suggest a general congress of deputies, from the several houses of assembly, on the continent, as the most effectual method of establishing such a union, as the present posture of our affairs requires.[30] At such a congress a firm foundation may be laid for the security of our rights and liberties, a system may be formed for our common safety, by a strict adherence to which, we shall be able to frustrate any attempts to overthrow our constitution; restore peace and harmony to America, and secure honor and wealth to Great Britain even against the inclinations of her ministers, whose duty it is to study her welfare; and we shall also free ourselves from those unmannerly pillagers who impudently tell us, that they are licensed by an act of the British parliament to thrust their dirty hands into the pockets of every American.[31] But I trust, the happy time will come, when with the besom of destruction, those noxious vermin will be swept forever from the streets of Boston. Surely you never will tamely suffer this country to be a den of thieves. Remember, my friends, from whom you sprang.—Let not a meanness of spirit, unknown to those whom you boast of as your fathers, excite a thought to the dishonor of your mothers. I conjure you by all that is dear, by all that is honorable, by all that is sacred, not only that ye pray, but that you act; that, if necessary, ye fight, and even die, for the prosperity of our Jerusalem. Break in sunder, with noble disdain, the bonds with which the Philistines have bound you. Suffer not yourselves to be betrayed by the soft arts of luxury and effeminacy, into the pit digged for your destruction. Despise the glare of wealth. That people who pay greater respect to a wealthy villain, than to an honest upright man in poverty, almost deserve to be enslaved; they plainly shew that wealth, however it may be acquired, is in their esteem, to be preferred to virtue.

But I thank God, that America abounds in men who are superior to all temptation, whom nothing can divert from a steady pursuit of the interest of their country; who are at once its ornament and safe-guard. And sure I am, I should not incur your displeasure, if I paid a respect so justly due to their much honored characters in this place; but when I name an *Adams*, such a numerous host of fellow patriots rush upon my mind, that I feel it would take up too much of your time, should I attempt to call the illustrious roll; but your grateful hearts will point you to the men; and their revered names, in all succeeding times, shall grace the annals of America. From them, let us, my friends, take example; from them, let us catch the divine enthusiasm; and feel, each for himself, the God-like pleasure of diffusing happiness on all around us; of delivering the oppressed from the iron grasp of tyranny; of changing the hoarse complaints and bitter moans of wretched slaves, into those cheerful sons, which freedom and contentment must inspire. There is a heart-felt satisfaction in reflecting on our exertions for the public weal, which all the sufferings an enraged tyrant can inflict, will never take away; which the ingratitude and reproaches of those whom we have saved from ruin, cannot rob us of. The virtuous asserter of the rights of mankind, merits a reward, which even a want of success in his endeavors to save his country, the heaviest misfortune which can befall a genuine patriot, cannot entirely prevent him from receiving.

I have the most animating confidence that the present noble struggle for liberty, will terminate gloriously for America. And let us play the man for our God, and for the cities of our God; while we are using the means in our power, let us humbly commit our righteous cause to the great Lord of the universe, who loveth righteousness and hateth iniquity. And having secured the approbation of our hearts, by a faithful and unwearied discharge of our duty to our country, let us joyfully leave our concerns in the hands of Him who raiseth up and putteth down the empires and kingdoms of the world as He pleases; and with cheerful submission to His sovereign will, devoutly say,

> Although the fig shall not blossom, neither shall fruit
> be in the vines; the labor of the olive shall fall, and
> the field shall yield no meat; the flock shall be cut
> off from the fold, and there shall be no herd in the
> stalls; yet we [I] will rejoice in the Lord, we [I]
> will joy in the GOD of our [my] salvation.[32]

NOTES

1. In 1742, the Huguenot Peter Fanueil built on public land a market house two stories in height, 100 foot by 40 foot. However, not all of Boston favored a central market. Petitions succeeded in closing the market

in 1747 and 1748 It was subsequently reopened, only to be closed again in 1752. In 1753, Faneuil Market was again opened with stalls leased to merchants. In 1761, the market burned, leaving only the walls. A lottery was held to restore the building, but provision was made that the town of Boston had to again approve the new building being used as a market. It is not possible here to detail all of the subsequent history of Faneuil Hall, but a few additional facts can be noted. On 18 Feb 1784, the General Court passed legislation that not only permitted the lower floor of Faneuil Hall to be used as a market, but reserved the land around the building for similar use, stipulating that anyone selling produce except in the restricted area be fined. (A&R, 1784, 18 Feb 1784, Chap. 29, 654-566; this act of 1784 was repealed on 11 Feb 1785, A&R, 1784, 11 Feb 1785, Chap. 37, 114) In 1805, the building was enlarged to its present status, adding a third story and widening the width to 80 feet. (Quincy, 11-13) The names Faneuil, Bowdoin, and Revere are only a few of those that comprise the contribution that the French Huguenots made to Boston.

2. The several acts of Parliament to which the colonists took objection were reviewed in the introductory essay to this volume. A brief summary is in order here. The Sugar Act of 1764, although the revival of an earlier act of 1733, marked the beginning of a new policy by the British Parliament in its attitude toward the American colonies. Taxes were to be aimed not at regulating trade, but at raising monies for the crown. Taxes were to be collected on all sugars, including wines and molasses. Since the balance of trade was always against the colonial shippers, the new taxes threatened to bankrupt many merchants.

The Stamp Act of 1765 added insult to injury by requiring revenue-raising stamps on playing cards, dice, legal documents, liquor licenses, university degrees, appointments to office, articles of apprenticeship, pamphlets, newspapers, and even almanacs. Taxes were not to be levied just on imported goods, but on the domestic sale of merchandise. This departure irritated the colonists greatly, because, until then, domestic taxes had been levied only by the colonial legislature themselves. The Admiralty Courts, an archaic survival in the law of England, were to have jurisdiction, and there was no provision for trial by jury in the Admiralty.

The Tea Act of 1773 was aimed to bring the East India Company out of bankrupty by conferring on it a monopoly of the colonial tea market. Its actual financial impact upon the average colonist was negligible, because it did not raise the 3 penny tax on tea and, by permitting the East India Co. to ship from its warehouses to the retailer, it eliminated the middleman and made the price of tea either the same or cheaper. But it injured the Boston merchants, because they could not compete with a state-sponsored monopoly. The dread of state monopolies was something the colonists had brought with them from England, and they did not wish to see the custom begin in America.

3. The first troops arrived on 28 Sept 1768.

4. What is now known as the Old State House.

5. From 1747 to 1769, the colonial courts of law were customarily held in the Council (or Senate Chamber) in the Old State House. In a 1817 letter to William Tudor, John Adams described the sittings as follows: "In this chamber, round a great fire, were seated five Judges, with Lieutenant-Governor Hutchinson at their head, as Chief Justice, all arrayed in their robes of scarlet English broadcloth; in their large cambric bands, and immense judicial wigs." (Adams, 2, 245) However, in 1769, the courts moved into a three-story building, said Wroth and Zobel (Wroth and Zobel, 1, xlviii) and the courtroom was located on the second floor "with a chimney and fireplace behind the judges' seat." Since Hancock distinguishes two places troubled by the British occupation, i.e., the Senate House and the building where the supreme court of Massachusetts was sitting, it can be assumed that the "judgment hall" was the newer structure close by the State House in what was then Queen Street and is now Court Street.

6. England sought to transfer the judiciary more and more to England or to institutions controlled by England. The colonial courts were considered too lenient toward the colonists. The specific reference of Hancock's remarks is not clear.

7. Boston was a town of less than 20,000 inhabitants. Therefore, when the House of Commons in 1774 passed as a part of the Intolerable Acts an act providing for quartering of British soldiers with the citizenry of Boston, rather than on Castle Island and in government buildings, the burden on the colonists became more severe. The churches of Boston served not only as places of religious worship, but also as meeting houses for a variety of activities, some of them political.

A note from the Old South Association in Boston in response to a letter of 13 Jan 1987, noted that the church was turned into a riding school by the British. "Pews were torn out and burned as fuel along with Thomas Prince's priceless library," noted Cynthia Stone in her reply for the association. Evidently the subsequent histories of the Old South Church defer to Sermon II of four sermons preached by the Reverend Benjamin B. Wisner on 9 May 1830, on the history of the Old South Church, in which Wisner as pastor of the Old South gave the following account of the British occupation:

> During the occupancy of Boston by the British troops [i.e., spring, 1775 March, 1776], the congregation was broken up,

most of its members having sought an asylum in different country towns. Their parsonage-house on Marlboro Street—formerly the mansion of Winthrop the first governor,—was demolished, and the materials used for fuel. Their Meeting House was turned into a riding-school for Burgoyne's regiment of cavalry; the pulpit and pews, and all the inside structures, being taken out and burnt for fuel, except the sounding-board and east galleries, the latter of which were left for the accommodation of spectators; and in the first gallery a place was fitted up where liquor and refreshment were furnished to those who came to witness the feats of horsemanship here exhibited. Many hundred loads of dirt and gravel were carted in and spread upon the floor. The south door was closed; and a bar was fixed over which the cavalry were taught to leap their horses at full speed. In the winter a stove was put up, in which were burnt for kindling many of the books and manuscripts from Mr. Prince's library. (Wisner, 33-34; Bynner, 2, 516-517)

It was not until 1782 that the society returned to its traditional location. After the depature of the British, the congregation had received permission from the Anglicans to occupy nearby King's Chapel, which, as the edifice for the Church of England congregation, had few parishioners, the congregation having been dispersed as Tories. One possible reason why Hancock had a copy of the Protestant Episcopal prayerbook in his library (MHS) is that, when he did not attend the Brattle Street Church, he attended the Old South services held in King's Chapel where he renewed his acquaintance with the Church of England prayerbook that he had undoubtedly used during his visit to England.

When in 1782 the Anglicans desired to resume services, the congregation began a restoration of the Old South which was completed in the spring of 1783 "in the same general style in which it now appears, except the pulpit, the form as well as the substance of which have since been changed." (Wisner, 35) Therefore, the present Old South Church, although it occupies the same spot as when Hancock delivered his commemorative address and presumably the same superstructure, had to be renovated.

Some confusion results from the fact that colonial Boston had four churches in the North End, all of which at one time or another were known as the "North Church."

First, there was the "Second Church on North Square" (1677) made of wood and used as a Congregational Church. This "Old North Church" was torn down by the British for firewood in 1775-6.

The second and third North Churches were built in 1714 and 1721, but do not figure in this narrative. (Wheildon, 21-23)

The North End also had what we now call the "North Church" (1723) constructed of brick and known in Revolutionary Boston also as Christ's Church, a place of worship for Anglicans. This "Christ's Church" or the "North Church" became famous as the source of the signal for Paul Revere's ride because it was built on high ground and, with its steeple, could serve as a warning beacon from afar. Paul Revere's old school friend, the sexton of Christ's Church, Robert Newman, allowed Captain John Pulling to display the lanterns that Revere provided. (Wheildon, 51) This church, on Salem Street, exists today, and bears a tablet briefly stating that from its steeple the lanterns were "displayed" on 18 Apr 1775, and is visited by tourists every year.

Hancock was not exaggerating, then, when he accused the British of interfering with worship. But most of the worst of the interference occurred after the 1774 oration was delivered.

Frothingham stated that, at the time of the Boston occupation, the Old North Church (Congregational) "was in good repair, and might have stood many years." (Frothingham, 328) On 23 Oct 1786, the General Court passed "An Act for the Confirming of the Second Church in Boston, So Called" (A&R, 1786, Chap. 36, 3 Oct 1786, 76-77) recognizing that the congregation of the "Old North Meeting House" had been worshipping in the absence of their church at the New Brick Church, and that the two had united under the name, "the second Church in Boston." Permission was given for the Old North Church to sell its former location, even though the deed to the property could not be found.

Frothingham (328) also noted that the Brattle Street Church, of which Hancock was a member, was also occupied by the British troops as a barracks. Many of the Bostonians who could and did leave town were in favor of the revolutionary cause. Since most of those who left would have been Congregationalists and since many of those who stayed plus the British troops that arrived would be Anglicans, the Congregational churches were not being used and therefore could be appropriated by the British army. The fact that some of the pastors of the Congregational churches were ardent patriots and that a number of the revolutionary meetings had been held in the Old South Church encouraged the British to occupy the churches.

Not only were troops quartered in public buildings, but in private homes as well. The quartering of troops had long been objected to in England. Therefore, Amendment III was added to our Bill of Rights: "No soldier shall, in time of peace, be quartered in any house, without the consent of the owners, nor in time of war, but in a manner to be prescribed by law."

8. On 20 Jan 1768, Wills Hill, first Marquis of Downshire and second Viscount Hillsborough, was appointed secretary of state for the colonies. It was he who on 6 June 1768 ordered a regiment to Boston to intimidate the colonists.

9. Captain Thomas Preston, officer of the day, had ordered his men to load and then placed himself before them to prevent unnecessary violence.

10. A poltroon is a common soldier, cowardly and weak.

11. Apparently William Robertson (1721-1793), an eloquent pulpit orator who was equally renowed as an historian. In 1759 he published a *History of Scotland during the Reigns of Mary and of James VI...* and a *History of the Emperor Charles V...* Three years after Hancock delivered his speech, Robertson published a *History of America* in two volumes. He was a Whig with liberal political philosophies. Hancock may well have studied his works at Harvard.

12. The trials of the soldiers were held in October of 1770. By then, the troops had been removed and passions quieted. Only two soldiers were found guilty of manslaughter, and their sentences were limited to branding. In this passage Hancock appears to refer to a heavenly sentence to be passed upon the British, including their soldiers.

13. Crispus Attucks, a mulatto and one of the leaders of the street gangs, may have attacked the soldiers outside of Murray's Barracks where the 14th Regiment was quartered, shortly before the massacre. Other casualties were Samuel Gray, a ropemaker, who had been involved in a similar incident with the 29th regiment three days earlier, as well as Patrick Carr and James Caldwell, bystanders who had left their houses when the alarm bell sounded and were shot in the street. Samuel Maverick, a seventeen-year-old boy, also ran out of his house when he heard the alarm and was killed as he crossed the street.

14. Christopher Monk, a young man who was shot in the lungs and never regained his health. According to the Selectmen's Minutes, (23rd RRC, 1769-1775, 212), the collection taken up for Monk amounted to £42/12/4. Eventually the monies contributed amounted to £319/13/3 "old tenor," and the fund was supervised by the Boston selectmen in Monk's behalf. (Brown, 183)

15. *Parricides* can have a variety of meanings, including murderers of their fathers, murderers of close relatives, and those who commit treason, presumably who therefore "murder" their country.

16. Martin (15, 120) described the nature of the British standing army whose ranks were composed of "the ne'er-do-wells, the luckless, and the 'poorer sort.' " If there was no other way to make a living, the poor could enter the "standing army" and at least have subsistence and a minimal allowance. The Americans also detested the thiry thousand "Hessians," the

German soldiers, many of whom were from Hesse-Kassel, hired by the British to fight against the Americans. While the German princes who hired off their armies received large bonuses, the Hessians themselves received about 25 cents a day. Because they were fighting for money and not out of patriotism, some of them deserted and joined the ranks of the colonials. On the other hand, the Americans received much help from Friedrich von Steuben, a captain in the Prussian army, who volunteered his services as an officer in the revolutionary ranks, and who did much to discipline the American army.

Very early in the conflict, Massachusetts faced the dilemma of fighting the war with militia or with a standing army. Shortly after the incidents at Lexington and Concord, on 16 May 1775, the rump Massachusetts provincial congress wrote to the Continental Congress in Philadelphia, saying: "We are now compelled to raise an Army, which with the assistance of the other colonies, we hope under the smiles of heaven, will be able to defend us and all America from the further butcheries and devastations of our implacable enemies." (*Journals of the Continental Congress*, 2, 77) Perhaps it was the continual fear of a "standing army" that contributed to what Curtis (1, 58) called the unfortunate move upon the part of the Congress early in the war to enlist soldiers for only a short period. Washington (*Writings of George Washington*, 3, 278) pointed out this mistake in a letter to Congress as early as 9 Feb 1776. After a long debate, the Continental Congress on 16 Sept 1776 did approve a general plan to create a sizeable standing army, with a land bounty promised to those who enlisted for three years. (*Journals of the Continental Congress*, 2, 357)

17. George III and Louis XVI.

18. Bailyn (*Ideological Origins*, 1967, 63 ff.) provided the basis for the colonial fear of standing armies: "This fear of standing armies followed directly from the colonists' understanding of power and of human nature: on purely logical grounds it was a reasonable fear." That fear, continued Bailyn, was based upon the examples of Turkey, France, Poland, Spain, Russia, Sweden, and Denmark, all of whom were then experiencing despotic governments.

19. The Second Constitutional Amendment reads: "A well regulated militia, being necessary to the security of a free state, the right of the people to keep and bear arms, shall not be infringed."

20. Until 1826 the name given to the standing army of the Ottoman Empire. Bailyn (*Ideological Origins*, 1967, 63) observed that the Turks were to the colonists the "legendary, ideal types of despots who reigned unchecked by right or law or in any sense the consent of the people; their

power rested on the swords of their vicious janissaries, the worst of standing armies."

21. The regular French army was supplemented by the *gens d'armes*, a sort of national guard from which came the word *gendarme*.

22. A member of a regiment which, in the beginning, was armed with grenades.

23. In defense of our altars and our fires.

24. This is something of an exaggeration on Hancock's part. The militia that fought at Lexington and Concord were far from exemplary troops, and the members of the militia dispatched to aid George Washington were fine men but largely untrained.

25. A reference in some manner to Cleopatra.

26. These financial changes, long rumored but finally effectuated in December of 1770, occured with the promotion of Lieutenant Governor Hutchinson to governor in an effort to make the new governor more independent of the colonists. As the dates of this note show, the battle had been raging several years, and Hancock's speech was given in the midst of a most intensive interchange. We have included here both what preceded and what followed his speech, since the timeliness of his remarks is best understood by a realization of the significance of the incident.

It is somewhat complicated to establish the chronology by which the governor and the judges were to be paid directly by the crown out of the proceeds of the Townshend Acts, rather than being paid (and therefore responsible) to the General Court. To clarify the sequence of events, there is an effort in this note to discuss separately the salary of the governor from the salaries of the judges, but the two were sufficiently intertwined that the dichotomy is only moderately successful.

The Salary of the Governor

As the colonies were under the crown, the king and his ministers could take unilateral action in many matters concerning their possessions in America. Governor Hutchinson had long been unhappy with his salary. Hutchinson's correspondence shows that, in July and September of 1767, he had hopes of being given a substantial increment from the crown. (Bailyn, *Ordeal*, 146-147) In December of 1767, Lord North, then chancellor of the exchequer, was quoted directly as saying that Hutchinson's salary would be paid out of the Townshend duties, and Hutchinson was notified in June of 1768 that the amount would be £200, seemingly to supplement his existing salary.

North's official position solidified the rumors that had been circulating in the colonies, causing Hutchinson much unfavorable publicity. Hutchinson was disgruntled. After all, since Bernard had left, Hutchinson had only been Lieutenant Governor, and no move had been made to promote him. Then, on 7 Dec 1770, Hillsborough sent off to Hutchinson the official appointment as governor, with an order that he was to be paid £1500 out of the income from the tax on tea.

The news of the change in method of payment had to filter through to the colonists. When the change of the governor's status appeared to be official, the Massachusetts House met to condemn the royal salary and proposed to Hutchinson in July of 1772 in a report of an assembly committee (Hutchinson, *History*, 3, 404-405) that he must refuse the emolument and take his salary from the assembly. A logical reply by Hutchinson dated 14 July 1772, concerning the relationship between the crown and the colony, made little impression on the colonists. (Hutchinson, *History*, 3, 406-410)

The Judges

No sooner had Hutchinson issued his reply than further rumors were circulated in Boston that the high court judges would receive their salaries from the crown as well. Andrew Oliver, the lieutenant governor, had knowledge of the matter by 31 Aug 1772, for he wrote to England on that date to the former governor Francis Bernard, saying that, once such news was circulated, "the newspapers will presently sound a fresh alarm." (Hutchinson a, 136)

On 28 Oct 1772, the town of Boston notified the governor that a rumor was being circulated that the superior court judges were to be paid by the crown. "It is...the humble and earnest request of the Town that your Excellency would be pleased to inform them, whether you have received any such advice relating to a matter so deeply interesting to the Inhabitants of this Province." (18th Report RRC, 89) Hutchinson replied that it was not proper for him to reveal the contents of his correspondence. Therefore, on 20 Nov 1772, the Boston Town Meeting issued a pamphlet based upon the votes and proceedings of the meeting and distributed the pamphlet to each town in Massachusetts. (18th Report RRC, 94-108) Bailyn noted that, although there had been other confrontations between assemblies and governors, there had never been one "so deliberately aimed at probing the most sensitive issues of Anglo-American relations." (Bailyn, Ordeal, 208) The somewhat lengthy petition was divided into three parts:

  a. A statement of the rights of the colonists, which began with a proposal of the "natural Rights of the Colonists" to life, liberty and property, an interesting phrase foreshadowing the language of the Declaration of Independence.

    b. A list of infringements on those rights.

    c. A letter of correspondence to the other towns in the colony.

John Adams in his diary noted that "in the year 1773 arose a controversy concerning the independence of the Judges. The King had granted a salary to the Judges of our Superior Court, and forbidden them to receive their salaries, as usual, from the grants of the House of Representatives, and the Council and Governor, as had been practiced till this time. This, as the Judges' commissions were during pleasure, made them entirely dependent on the Crown for bread as well as office." (Adams, 2, 316)

On the other side, Peter Oliver (107) argued that having to be dependent upon the colonies for their salaries made the judges altogether dependent on Massachusetts.

On 22 Feb 1773, Hutchinson wrote to Lord Dartmouth that a committee of the House of Representatives questioned the Supreme Court judges about the source of their salaries. The judges, said Hutchinson, tried to avoid giving a direct answer, pleading "that they had not sufficient knowledge of the tenor of the Grants made by his Majesty nor had they received any Warrant and one or more added that it was possible the Governor might not have it in his power to consent to any Salaries from the Assembly." Hutchinson took the position that the judges should accept payment from Massachusetts only up to the date when the king's grants began. (MA, Hutchinson Correspondence, 27, 22 Feb 1773, 452)

To counteract that move, the General Court, said Oliver, made increased colonial grants for one year to begin at the point where the king's grants were to go into effect. (Oliver, 108) Oliver would not agree to accept the money from Massachusetts, even though the chief justice's salary was increased from £150 to £300 and that of the other judges from £120 to £200, to match the grants offered by the crown.

The assembly of 26 Jan 1774 resolved to force Hutchinson's hand. The judges were either to relinquish their offices or to refuse to accept salaries from the crown. Although Oliver had served as a member of the court for eighteen years, as chief justice for two years (Bailyn, Ordeal, 265) and was a native-born colonist, he was resented not only because he was accepting his salary from the king, but also because he had no training in law (HLPO a, f. 4140v) and was part of the "family cartel" of Olivers all profiting from a distribution of offices within the family.

On 1 Feb 1774, the General Court sent the four judges what amounted to an ultimatum, requiring them on or before 8 Feb 1774, to accept the grant of salary from the General Assembly and to refuse to accept the king's salary. The resolution acknowledged that Judge Edmund Trowbridge had already agreed to accept his salary from the colonists, but protested that they had received no such assurances from the other four justices.   (HLPO b) Hutchinson found himself in an untenable position, not only in regard to his own salary but in regard to the salary of his family member, Peter Oliver, and the other three judges.

The Chief Justice

On 14 Feb 1774, Hutchinson wrote to the Earl of Dartmouth: "The House of Representatives have...demanded an explicit answer from the Judges of the Superior Court, whether they would take such salaries as should be granted by the General Assembly, without receiving any salary from the King for the same services: concluding with a menace if they did not comply. The Chief Justice gave his answer that he not only had taken his salary from the King for the last year and a half, but thought it his duty to do the like for the time to come, and set forth at large his reasons for doing so." (Hutchinson, Diary & Letters, c, 1, 137)

The Boston *Gazette* of 21 Feb 1774, reported that Oliver had received the king's salary from 5 July 1772 to 5 July 1774. (HLPO c)

The Remaining Justices

Hutchinson noted in his correspondence that "one of the judges [Trowbridge], upon returning home, sickened and died" and that the messenger from the assembly lay the order on the breast of the dying man who renounced the royal salary shortly before he died. (Hutchinson, Diary & Letters, b, 1, 144; Oliver, 109) Hutchinson and Oliver may have been indulging in rumors about Trowbridge, because the assemblies' resolution of 1 Feb 1774 had recognized Trowbridge's acceptance of its terms. Therefore, there would have been no need to put a confirmation of his agreement on "the dying man's breast."

When Judges Nathaniel Ropes, Foster Hutchinson, and William Cushing finally agreed to reject the king's salary as long as they received compensation from the General Court, (Hutchinson, Diary & Letters, c, I, 137) Peter Oliver's refusal left him isolated. (Hutchinson, Diary & Letters, b, 1, 144) Oliver himself noted that his residing at his country estate thirty miles from Boston probably saved him from giving up the king's grant. (Oliver, 109)

The Impeachment of Oliver

The last recourse of the assembly was to prevent the court from sitting, by force, if necessary. (Hutchinson, Diary & Letters, b, 1, 145) The House of Representatives sent Oliver a message asking which grant he would accept, the king's or the General Court's. Oliver replied he would accept the king's grant. (Oliver, 110)

A select group was determined not to let Oliver sit. Court was to open on 15 Feb. Before Peter Oliver could make the journey to Boston, on 11 Feb, the General Court commanded Governor Hutchinson to remove his brother-in-law from office and ordered Oliver not to open court. A violent snow storm kept Oliver from getting to Boston on 15 Feb. He set out but had to turn back. Before 17 Feb, when court was to resume, Oliver had received the ultimatum from the House of Representatives not to appear. Hutchinson refused to remove Oliver, but Oliver thought it more expedient to remain in the country.

The representatives then took a symbolic but important step. On 24 Feb 1774, the assembly formally impeached Oliver. However, it was the royal governor's prerogative to appoint the judges so the act of the legislature could only show public sentiment. No prosecution of Oliver was held, because the governor would not authorize a special trial of the chief justice.

On 8 Mar 1774, Peter Oliver was obliged to miss the funeral of his brother Andrew Oliver, the lieutenant governor, for fear of being attacked. (Oliver, 112)

On 9 Mar 1774, Hutchinson wrote to the Earl of Dartmouth that "the Articles of Impeachment [against Peter Oliver] will have a lasting stain upon the Character of the Government." (HLPO d) Without more help from the crown, and that help was not forthcoming, the governor could not set forth what was plainly in his mind, i.e., colonial sedition, As Bailyn noted, "everything, Hutchinson wrote to his contacts in England, now depended on the willingness of the British government to intervene." (Bailyn, *Ordeal*, 267) The quartering of troops had not proved to be enough. Boston would have to be occupied. Hutchinson had written King George of his weariness and despair. The governor booked passage for England, a passage that he was prevented from taking because of continued unrest in Massachusetts.

The arrival of General Gage in Boston on 13 May 1774 relieved Hutchinson of command and therefore of having to make further decisions concerning the judges. He and his family left for England on 1 June 1774. Peter Oliver remained. There was no reason for him to go to England to report to the king. On 19 Apr 1774, a grand jury at Worcester refused to serve under Peter Oliver until the salary question was settled. The matter remained a major point of disagreement between the General Court and the governor. Finally the events of Lexington and Concord left Oliver isolated in Boston under British protection. When the British forces evacuated Boston in 1776, Oliver emigrated with them, going first to Halifax and then to Birmingham, where he died in 1791. Thus the salary question as to the chief justice was never altogether settled.

27. A reference to the exposure of Governor Hutchinson's attitudes toward the colonies by the reading of the letters that Benjamin Franklin sent to the colonies.

28. A reference to the Tea Act.

29. When the English Parliament announced (a) in 1771 that the salary of the Massachusetts governor and (b) in 1772 that the judges were to be paid by the crown as well, a town meeting was held on 28 Oct 1772, which voted that a commiteee of Sam Adams, Joseph Warren, and Benjamin Church be formed to formulate the rights of the colonies and present them to Governor Hutchinson. (RRC, 89) The Boston Town Records of this period showed extended negotiations between the town and Hutchinson. On 2 Nov 1772, the first Committee of Correspondence of twenty-one persons was appointed. Although Hancock moderated the meeting, he was not appointed to the committee. On 20 Nov 1772 the Committee presented its long statement of grievances, a copy of which was sent to each town in the province. So the dispute over the judge's salaries precipitated the appointment of the famous Committee of Correspondence.

30. This pet objective of Sam Adams shows his influence upon the speech. Also, Hancock's willingness to adopt the concept of "a general congress of deputies" demonstrates how far he had come to concluding that the wishes of the colonists could not be reconciled with the crown.

31. A reference to the Stamp Act.

32. Habakkuk (King James version) 3:17-18.

HEADNOTE

Date: 29 Oct, 1777[1]

Occasion: After having served as presiding officer of the Second and succeeding Continental Congresses, Hancock decided to ask for two month's leave to return to Massachusetts. On 15 Oct 1777, Hancock announced his desire for leave.[2] Before departing, Hancock desired to address the Congress. It was not the custom for representatives of the Congress to give speeches, perhaps because the Congress did not wish to aggravate the already existing rivalry among the colonies and because the Congress did not wish to emulate the English Parliament. Republicanism was the order of the day. However, Hancock still wanted to speak. There was opposition. Fowler noted: Some delegates viewed it as more posturing by a man who was nearly as good an actor as he was a politician. (219)

The *Rough Journal Proceedings of the Continental Congress*, 31 Oct 1777, 143, noted that, at four o'clock, it was ordered that Hancock's speech be entered in the journal. The following discussion then occurred:

> It was then moved [by either James Duane or William Duer of New York (Smith 8, 124, n. 5)] that the thanks of Congress be presented to John Hancock, Esq for the unremitted attention and steady impartiality which he has manifested in discharge of the various duties of his office, as president, since his election to the chair on the 24th day of May, 1775.

> After debate, it was moved that the consideration of this motion be postponed, till the sense of Congress be taken on a general proposition, and on the question put,

> Resolved in the affirmative. [i.e., Congress should decide, before considering Hancock's motion, on the suitability of offering thanks to any of its members.]

> It was then moved to resolve, as the opinion of this Congress, that it is improper to thank any president for the discharge of the duties of that office:

> And the yeas and nays being required:[3]

A tie vote resulted in the failure of the motion that no president should be thanked. Once that motion has been defeated, it was possible to take up the original motion that had been postponed. Connecticut, New York, New Jersey, Virginia, North Carolina, and South Carolina voted to thank Hancock, whereas the northern states, New Hampshire, Massachusetts, Rhode Island, and Pennsylvania, voted against.

It may be that the Congress was disturbed by the split vote because the journal shows that following these votes, other matters were postponed and the session was adjourned until ten o'clock the next day.

As Sanders (13) noted, "This first Presidential 'farewell address' was a subject of unfavorable comment among the republican group in Congress." Samuel Adams, in a letter to James Warren of 30 Oct 1777, after paraphrasing the address, commented as follows: "I have given you this merely as a Peice [sic] of News, leaving you to judge of the Tendency and probable Effect of the Speech and Motion. We have had two Presidents before, Neither of whom made a parting Speech or receivd [sic] the Thanks of Congress." (Burnett, 2, 537; Warren-Adams Letters, 1, 377-378)

A few days later, on 4 Nov, Adams again wrote to Warren reporting the controversial votes on the propriety of giving thanks to a retiring president. Congress, said Adams, "labord [sic] a whole Afternoon" on 31 Oct 1777. (Burnett, 2, 541; Warren-Adams, 1, 378-379; Smith, 8, 226) Adams noted that, in the discussion, "the Principle was objected to--it was urgd [sic] to be unprecedented, impolitick, dangerous." As it turned out, Adams gave Hancock the letter of 30 Oct 1777 addressed to James Warren with the unfavorable comments about Hancock, for Hancock to take back to Massachusetts, demonstrating the ruthlessness that Sam Adams could manifest.

The speech was delivered in the chamber of the Continental Congress in Philadelphia, a room with sufficiently good acoustics so that a speaker such as Hancock who had been used to presiding in the chamber could make the most of his speaking abilities. Paul H. Smith referred to the address as "a florid farewell speech." (Smith, 8, 124, n 5) It would be difficult to term the brief address "florid." Smith may have allowed the unfavorable comments of Samuel Adams to draw him into an unwarranted conclusion.

There was no great audience of delegates assembled. In his letters of 16 Oct 1777, Laurens complained to Gervais that, as others besides Hancock were going to leave, the house would be reduced to twenty or twenty-one members.

SOURCES

Rough Journal Proceedings of the Papers of the Continental Congress, 31 Oct 1777,[4] Papers of the Continental Congress, Item 1, 11, 143-4, National Archives, Washington, D.C; *Journals of the Continental Congress*, 9, 852-3 Washington, D.C.: Library of Congress, 1907.

Although Sears (225) footnoted the copy of the address he printed in his 1913 biography of Hancock as "Mass. State Archives, Ms. vol. 196, 23," a letter from the archives dated 2 June 1981 stated that the Sears citation referred to a letter from the Council to Washington of 7 Dec 1776, and that the archives could locate no copy of a "taking leave" address in their papers. Personal searches of their papers by the author assisted by the archivists at the MA were also unproductive. Undoubtedly Sears found the address at the MA but his reference appears to be faulty.

A copy of the address appears in Frank Moore, ed., *Diary of the American Revolution*, 1, 516-7, along with a satirical version of the adddress in dialect. Moore's source of the satire is not known. The preface to the diary stated: "The materials of these volumes are taken from Whig and Tory newspapers published during the American Revolution, private diaries, and other contemporaneous writings."

There is no reference to the "notice" given by Hancock in the *Journals* nor is there any recording of Laurens's motion. As was noted elsewhere, efforts to obtain a copy of any written request by Hancock have been unsuccessful.

TEXT

Gentlemen: Friday last compleated [sic] two years and five months since you did me the honor of electing me to fill this chair. As I could never flatter myself your choice proceeded from any idea of my abilities, but rather from a patrial opinion of my attachment to the liberties of America, I felt myself under the strongest obligation to discharge the duties of the office, and I accepted the appointment with the firmest resolution to go through the business annexed to it in the best manner I was able. Every argument conspired to make me exert myself and I endeavoured by industry and attention to make up for every other deficiency.

As to my conduct both in and out of Congress, in the execution of your business, it is improper for me to say any thing. You are the best judges. But I think I shall be forgiven, if I say, I have spared no pains, expence [sic], or labour to gratify your wishes and to accomplish the views of Congress.

My health being much impaired, I find some relaxation absolutely necessary, after such constant application, I must therefore request your indulgence for leave of absence for two months.

But I cannot take my departure, Gentlemen, without expressing my thanks for the civility and politeness I have experienced from you. It is impossible to mention this, without a heart felt pleasure.

If the course of so long a period, as I have had the honour to fill this chair, any expressions may have dropped from me, that may have given the least offence to any member, as it was not intentional, so I hope his candor will pass it over.

May every happiness, Gentlemen, attend you, both as members of this house & as individuals and I pray heaven, that unanimity & perseverance may go hand in hand in this house, and that everything, which may tend to distract or divide your councils be forever banished.

NOTES

1. The *Journals of the Continental Congress*, 9, 1777, showed that Hancock took leave of Congress on 29 Oct 1777. (cf. Frank Moore, *Diary of the American Revolution*, 1, 516, NY, 1860) The short address itself appears in the *Rough Journal* of 31 Oct 1777, so there was a textual copy of the address from which it would be entered. In fact, on 29 Oct 1777 the secretary, who had been made chair until a new president was chosen, was instructed to ask Hancock for a copy of his speech. That copy has not survived. (cf. endnotes 6 and 7 of Chapter Eight)

2. On 16 Oct 1777, Henry Laurens wrote to John L. Gervais: "Our President gave notice yesterday of his purpose to quit the Chair and

Congress next Week. I moved the House to intreat and solicit his continuance, to my surprise, I was seconded and *no more.*" (Burnett, 2, 522) It is of course possible that Hancock's giving notice was only oral and could have been made somewhat informally, perhaps at the close of the business on 15 Oct 1777 so that no written request was ever made and Thomson did not enter it in the *Rough Journal*, thinking it would be covered when Hancock actually departed.

3. On this vote, New Hampshire, Massachusetts, Rhode Island, and Pennsylvania voted yea with South Carolina divided. The states were pronounced equally divided, resulting in a defeat of the general proposition that no president should be thanked. When the original motion to thank Hancock was put, a 6-4 vote on the motion was recorded. There was one nay vote from Virginia, but the other three delegates from Virginia voted yea. Therefore, Connecticut, New York, North Carolina, South Carolina, and New Jersey, along with Virginia, were counted as voting in favor of thanking Hancock, whereas Massachusetts along with Rhode Island, New Hampshire, and Pennsylvania voted in the negative. Maryland was considered "unrepresented," as only one of its delegation was present. Presumably Georgia and Delaware were not represented. As a result of the favorable vote, Hancock's replacement, Henry Laurens of South Carolina, wrote to Hancock on 3 Nov 1777, "It is with great pleasure I obey the Order of Congress by transmitting the inclosed Testimony of the Love & Esteem of your Country in a Vote of thanks for your long & faithful Services in the Chair. I likewise enclose a certified minute Shewing the authority under which I have the honour of addressing you." (Smith, 8, 224)

4. The originals of the *Rough Journals*, with the exception of volume 15, which has been missing since 1835, are located in the National Archives. There are reproduced on National Archive Microfilm Publications: *Papers of the Continental Congress, 1774-1789*, rolls 8 & 9, Item #1, *Rough Journals*, volumes 9-14, 16-17 are on the second reel covering the dates, except for the missing volume, of 14 Apr 1777, and including the notes concerning Hancock's resignation.

HEADNOTE

Date: 25 Oct, 1780

Occasion: After a committee of the two houses had counted the ballots for governor, a committee of both houses was appointed to call upon Hancock and request his attendance at the council chambers to be sworn into office. Where Hancock had to be "waited upon" is not known, but it was outside the State House. Even if the committee had had to go to the mansion on Beacon Hill, the distance was not great. Before being administered the oath, Hancock made the speech below. The council chambers provided an excellent speaking situation and Hancock undoubtedly made the best use of it. According to the newspapers of the day, Hancock spoke in the council chamber where both houses were assembled.

SOURCES

Independent Chronicle, 2 Nov 1780, 2; Boston *Gazette*, 30 Oct 1780, 2; Massachusetts *Spy*, 9 Nov 1780, 1; *Independent Ledger,* 23 Oct 1780, 2; Brown, 226.

TEXT

It would have ill become me at so early a Moment after being notified of my appointment by the respectable Committee of this Honorable Assembly, to appear here to comply with the qualifiying Requisitions of the Constitution, had not the Circumstances of the Returns made the Choice a matter of Publick Notoriety some Weeks past, and receiving it from such Authority as confirmed its reality, led me to contemplate the subject; and, although fully sensible of my inability to the important Purposes of the Appointment, yet having in the early Stage of this Contest, determined to devote my whole Time and Services to be employed in my Country's Cause to the utter Exclusion of all private Benefits, even to the end of the War, and being ever ready to obey the Call of My Country, I venture to offer myself; ready to comply with the Requisitions of the Constitution, as to external Qualifications, assuring you and my Country, that I shall endeavor strictly to adhere to the Laws of the Constitution, and regularly and punctually attend to the Duties of the Department in which my Country has been pleased to place me.[1]

NOTES

1. In a letter from James Warren to John Adams, Warren wrote about the forthcoming election:

> The Election of Gov'r, Lieut. Gov'r and Senate to be made on the beginning of September. Mr. B[owdoin] has again come into public Life that he may with greater Advantage stand as a candidate, in competition with H[ancock] for the highest honor and rank in this State. who [sic] will carry the Election is very uncertain. I dont envy either of them their feelings. the Vanity of one of them will Sting like an Adder if it is disappointed, and the Advancements made by the other if they dont succeed will hurt his *Modest* pride. the [sic] upper counties will be for H., the Interest of the other will lay in the lower ones." (Warren-Adams Letters, 2, 135)

HEADNOTE

Date: Tuesday, 31 Oct 1780

Occasion: Initial address to the General Court after having been named governor of the commonwealth of Massachusetts. The General Court consisted of both houses of the legislature, but there is no record of whether the address was given in the house or senate chamber.

SOURCES

Journal of the House, SL, 1, part 2, 39-46*; *Journal of the House*, MA, 1, part 2, 39-46*; The Boston *Gazette* 6 Nov 1780, 1-2; *Independent Chronicle* 2 Nov 1780, 4; *Independent Ledger* 6 Nov 1780, 2; Massachusetts *Spy* 9 Nov 1780, 2.

The speech has been reprinted in the following: Abraham E. Brown, *John Hancock: His Book*, 267-270; *Poole's Annual Register of the Executive & Legislative Departments of the Government of Massachusetts*, 1854, 17-19; and *The Bostonian Society Publications*, 1, 2nd series, 70-5.

*No copy in either Senate journal. The *Journals* of the Senate in both the Archives and the State Library say "vide speech," meaning "see the speech on file." But there is no manuscript copy in place in the Massachusetts Archives.

TEXT

Gentlemen of the Senate and Gentlemen of the House of Representatives.

With a sincere and warm heart I congratulate you and my Country on the singular favor of Heaven in the peaceable & auspicious settlement of our Government upon a Constitution framed[1] by the Wisdom & sanctified by the solemn choice of the people who are to live under it. May the Supreme Ruler of the World be pleased to establish and perpetuate the new foundations of Liberty and Glory!

Finding myself placed at the head of this Commonwealth by the free suffrages of its citizens,[2] while I most sensibly feel the distinction they have conferred upon me in this Election, I am at a loss to express the sentiments of Gratitude with which it has impressed me: in addition to my natural affection for them, and the obligations they have laid upon me, I have now a new and irresistible motive ever to consider their happiness as my greatest interest and their freedom my highest honor.

Deeply impressed with a sense of the important Duties to which my Country now calls me, while I obey the call, I most ardently wish myself adequate to those duties, but can only promise in concurrence with you Gentlemen, a faithful & unremitting attention to them, supported as I am by the advice & assistance of the Council, happily provided by the Constitution, to whose judgment I shall always pay the greatest respect, and on whose wisdom and integrity I shall ever rely. May unanimity among the several branches of this new Government consolidate its force, and establish such measures as shall most effectually advance the Interest and Reputation of the Commonwealth. This can never be done, but by a strict adherence in every point to the principles of our excellent Constitution, which on my own part I engage most sacredly to preserve.[3]

Gentlemen, Of all the weighty business that lies before you, a point of the first importance and most presssing necessity is the establishment of the Army in such consistency and force, & with such seasonable and competent supplies,[4] as may render it, in conjunction with the respectable Forces sent to our assistance by our powerful & generous Ally, an effectual defense to the free Constitutions and Independence of the United States. You cannot give too early or too serious an attention to the proportion of this business that falls to the share of this Commonwealth.[5] The mode we have too long practised in reinforcing the Army by inlistments [sic] for a short time, has been found to be at once greatly ineffectual & extremely burdensome. The Commander in Chief, in whose abilities and integrity we justly repose the highest Confidence, has repeatedly stated to us the great disadvantages arising[6] from it; and the necessity of an Army engaged for the whole war and well provided is now universally felt and acknowledged.[7] Nor should a moment of time be lost in prosecuting every measure for establishing an object so essential to the preservation of our Liberties, and all that is dear to us. Care at the same time ought to be taken that the necessary supplies be committed to men on whose principles and affection to our great cause, as well as capacity for such a series we may safely depend.[8]

The support of the public faith stands in close connection with this measure of defence, and indeed is absolutely necessary to it, and to the whole interest and honor of the state. No expedient should be unexplored, no necessary measure unattempted, no nerve in Government or the Community unexerted, to maintain our Credit, and remove all just ground of complaint from the Army that protects us, or from those who have in any instance relied on the public engagements. What Friend to his Country would not cheerfully bear his full proportion of the expense necessary for this purpose?[9] And I doubt not [,] you will take all possible care that no more than such a proportion be laid upon any man or any class of men. This is not only a clear point of Justice from which no Government can in any instance recede without injuring and dishonoring itself, but is of particular importance to the internal peace and good temper, and consequently the safety of the Commonwealth. Doth not this safety also require a stricter attention than I fear has been paid, to the methods and purposes of an intercourse with Great Britain, and that more effectual measures may be taken to prevent Flags of Truce from conveying intelligence, or improper persons to those who are waging a war from being at large among us without prudent checks, especially in our Sea Ports? In all such cases[10] your vigilance will discern and your fidelity provide where it may be needed, a proper guard to the public safety.

The present situation of the Eastern part of this state,[11] and the protection of our Sea Coasts, Navigation and Commerce,[12] in all which not only the interest of this and the United States, but that of our Allies is deeply concerned, are important objects that require particular attention. If we look to the Westward,[13] we see recent incursions and savages of the Enemy; so that from every quarter, we are loudly called upon to employ the most speedy and strenuous efforts for providing funds that may be depended on; and,[14] establishing an Army sufficient, by the blessing of Heaven, for the complete deliverance of our Country: [sic] Its resources improved with judgment and spirit are adequate to such a purpose. Nor can I forbear[15] to observe that we may enter upon this business immediately, with less expense, and greater advantages than in future time.

You are fully sensible, Gentlemen, that the separation which the Constitution has made between the Legislative and Judicial powers, and that just degree of Independence it has given to the latter, is one of the surest guards to the PERSONS, PROPERTY, and LIBERTIES of the subjects of this Commonwealth, and accordingly you are, I am thoroughly persuaded, heartily disposed to support this INDEPENDENCE, the honor and vigor of the SUPREME JUDICIAL DEPARTMENT in its whole constitutional extent.[16]

Sensible of the importance of christian [sic] piety and virtue to the order and happiness of a State, I cannot but earnestly recommend[17] to you every measure for their support and encouragement that shall not infringe the rights of CONSCIENCE, which I rejoice to see established by the Constitution on so broad a basis.[18] And if any thing [sic][19] can be further done on the same basis for the relief of the public teachers of RELIGION and MORALITY, an ORDER of men greatly useful to their COUNTRY, and who have particularly suffered in the defence of its rights, by the depreciation of our currency,[20] as also for the relief of WIDOWS and ORPHANS, many of whom have been distressed in the same, and who are particularly committed by Heaven to the protection of civil RULERS, I shall most readily concur with you in every such measure.[21]

A due observation of the Lord's Day[22] is not only important to internal RELIGION, but greatly conductive to the order and benefit of civil society. It speaks to the senses of mankind, and by a solemn cessation from their common affairs, reminds them of a Deity, and their accountableness to the great Lord of all. Whatever may be necessary to the support of such an institution, in consistence with a reasonable personal liberty, deserves the attention of civil Government. Manners, by which not only the FREEDOM, but the very existence of REPUBLICS are greatly affected, depend much upon the public institutions of RELIGION, and the good education of youth. In both these instances our fathers laid wise foundations, for which their posterity have had reason to bless their memory. The public schools[23] and our University at Cambridge,[24] very early founded by them, have been no small support to the cause of LIBERTY, and given no dishonorable distinction to our Country.

The advantages they are still capable of affording to the present and future generations are unspeakable. I cannot therefore omit warmly to commend them to your care and patronage.[25] The laws will now require to be accurately revised, and particularly that which regulates the MILITIA, on which the safety of a Commonwealth naturally rests. This revision you cannot fail to attend to as early as circumstances will allow, which will lead you not only to adapt[26] the LAWS in the most perfect manner possible to the defence of the State, but also for the suppression of idleness, dissipation, extravagance and all those vices that are peculiarly inimical to Free Republics, and for the encouragement of those opposite virtues that are particularly friendly to such a form of Government.[27]

In such measures as I have now mentioned and in every other tending to promote the public welfare, you may always depend on my cheerful concurrence with you, and giving every dispatch in my power to the public business. And I shall from time to time seasonably communicate to you such information & proposals of business as may be proper to lay before you.

May this new Government diffuse a new animation through the whole political body. The PEOPLE expect much from it, perhaps more[28] in some points than circumstances will allow it to perform; but standing as we do upon their choice and affections, and strenuously exerting ourselves as we ought for their interest, they may find it happily advanced.

May Heaven assist us to set out well, to brighten the auspices of our Constitution, to render it still more loved[29] & admired by the CITIZENS of the Commonwealth & to recommend it to the whole world, by a wise and impartial, a firm & vigorous administration of it.

John Hancock[30]

NOTES

1. Poole's Annual Register

2. As was pointed out in the introductory essay, not many of Boston's citizens met the franchise requirements. Therefore, when in 1766 Hancock was elected one of Boston's four representatives to the General Court, he polled only 437 votes.

3. The minor role that Hancock played in the development of the Massachusetts Constitution of 1780 was presented in the introductory essay. For the text of this constitution, see Taylor, 127-146.

4. Lotteries were used to raise money for supplying the Continental Army. A&R 1780, Chap. 15, 19 Feb 1781, 28-29, provided for "An Act for Instituting a Lottery for the Sole Purpose of Cloathing the Massachusetts Part of the Continental Army." Chapter 205 of the April 1780 session, 19 May 1781, 475, resolved that the managers of the lottery be granted five percent of the proceeds.

There were more direct methods for securing funds for supplies for the soldiers. Chapter 61 of the A&R, May 1781 session, resolved "that the selectmen of each town be, and hereby are empowered, to draw money out of the treasuries of their respective towns, to enable them to procure the cloathing [sic] required of such towns....And in case there is not money sufficient in such town treasuries for that purpose, the assessors of such town or towns are required....to assess the freeholders...for so much money in specie as said selectmen shall certify to be necessary for such purpose."

5. The General Court in Boston was prompt in taking up the governor's request. The *Journal of the House* for Thursday, 2 Nov 1780, 54, stated:

"Ordered that 3 o'clock this afternoon the House will take into consideration His Excellency's Message and the letter from His Excellency Genl. Washington which were sent down from the Hon. Senate by the Secretary."

What actions were taken? *The Acts and Resolves of the Commonwealth* shows repeated attention given to the raising of supplies and to the conscription of men. For example, Chapter 54 of 16 Nov 1780, October Session, 161-163, contains an act to borrow money to fill up the quotas for the Continental Army for three years. Chapter 104 of 2 Dec 1780, October session, 190-201, allotted to each township or plantation the number of men requested to supply the Massachusetts quota of 4,240 men. Chapter 143 of 6 July 1781, May Session, 703, included a "Resolve Requesting the Governor to Loan His Excellency General Washington, during the Recess, such Military Stores as he shall want, and can be spared." Chapter 362 of the January, 1781 session, 825, dealt specifically with the town of Tewskbury in meeting its quota of conscripts. Chapter 363, A&R 1781, January Session, 825-826, asked for a more "effectual method for recruiting the army, than by a resolve of December 2, 1780." Chapter 198 of the April, 1780 session, 472, approved on 18 May 1781, appropriated £20,000 to the committee of supplies. Chapter 200 of the April, 1780 session, 472-474, was a lengthy resolve concerned with supplying the Massachusetts quota for the Continental Army, and Chapter 38 of the May 1781 session, 621-624, dealt a length with "compleating [sic] this Commonwealth's quota of the Continental Army, Agreeable to a Resolve of the 2d December, 1780."

Washington's request for troops was detailed in his letter to John Hancock of 15 June 1781. At that point Washington asked for 2,700 men plus 500 for the campaign in Rhode Island. (Fitzpatrick, 22, 221)

6. Poole omits "arising."

7. As early as 9 Feb 1776, Washington had written to Hancock as president of the Continental Congress, saying that "the disadvantages attending the limited enlistment of troops are too apparent to show, who are eyewitnesses to them, to render any animadversions necessary; but to gentlemen at a distance, whose attention is engrossed by a thousand important objects, the case may be otherwise." (Jared Sparks, 3, 278)

When Washington arrived in Cambridge to take charge of "the continental army," it consisted only of troops enlisted for short periods of time by Massachusetts, New Hampshire, Rhode Island, and Connecticut. The troops were supervised by their own officers and acting under their own military law. The terms of most of these men would expire in the fall of 1776. (Curtis, 1854, 1, 58-59) Washington faced chaos. Only longer enlistments of men committed to a national army and not to state militia could serve to establish a continental army.

The original enlistment form (Journals, 1775, 2, 90) read as follows:

> I _____ have, this day, voluntarily enlisted
> myself as a soldier in the American Continental Army, for one year,
> unless sooner discharged: And I do bind myself to conform, in all
> instances, to such rules and regulations, as are, or shall be
> established for the government of the said Army.

On 29 Nov 1780, in order to encourage longer enlistments and to insure that the recruits understood that they would have to serve under officers from outside the Bay Colony, the Massachusetts General Court approved the following form:

> We the subscribers do hereby several inlist [sic] ourselves
> into the service of the United States of *America* [note
> the early use of this phrase], to continue in that service
> for the term of three years, unless sooner regularly dis-
> charged: We engage to be under the command of the General
> Officers of the United States of *America*, which are or
> may be appointed and faithfully to observe and obey all such orders
> as we from time to time shall receive from our officers; and
> to be under such regulations, in every respect, as are or may
> be provided for the army of the aforesaid States.

> Dated this   Day of   A.D. 1780

However, enlistments were sometimes made on nothing more than scraps of paper, as is illustrated by the following note scribbled on a fragment. This particular enlistment was captured by the British in the northern campaign and forms a part of the papers transported from Quebec to England and is now in the British Library:

> I Do Acknowledge, that I have this Day Inlisted [sic] myself
> a Soldier in the Continental Army in Colo Seth Warners' [sic]
> Regiment in Capt. Wolcotts [sic] Company to Serve During the
> Present War Between Great Britain and America Binding myself
> Closely to adhere to the Rules and Regulations of the Army.

> Bimington [sic] 31st of March 1780 Joseph Pearson(?), Sec of David
> Tracy

(British Museum, additional MSS 21, 845, f. 115r)

Nor was there consistency in all enlistments. Some men were promised one thing to enlist, others were promised something else. And the promises were not always kept, as is illustrated by the notes below:

The United States of America in Acct. with Moses Crosby (Fifer?)
Major of Col. Seth Warner Regimt in the Service of Said States
for a Part of three years Pay & Clothing. Jany 13 1780

Do* **2 Hats & Coat 1 pr Breeches 2 pr Shoes**
Cv** by 1 Hat 2 Coats 4 Jacket
Dito by 2 Breeches, 6 Shirts

dito **2 Frocks & 1 pr overhalls & stock**
Dito by 6 pr Stockings & 1 Pr Shoes

dito **1 Blanket**
Dito by 1 Frock & 1 pr overhalls
Dito by 2 Stocks & Two Blankets

*"Due"
**perhaps "collected" or "received"

Having at my inlisting received but twenty Dollars which was but one half my Bounty money the above charged articles are due

Bennington 13th June 1780

Personally appeared before me Moses Crosby
and made solemn oath to the truth of the
above amount

Jonas Tray Justice of Peace

Therefore I request Thomas Colman Esqr Paymaster to the above mentioned Regiment to draw in my behalf the above mentioned two hats, one Coat, one pair Breeches, one Pair overhalls Two pair Shoes, Two Frocks, one Stock & one Blanket together with all the monies yet remaining due to me for my service for the Term of three year Last past in the above Regiment whose compliance with must oblige his humble servant—

Thomas Colman Esqr   Moses Crosby
Paymaster to Col Warner's Regiment

(British Library, additional MSS 21, 845, f. 117r)

The enlistment forms for officers appointed by Congress could be much more ceremonial. One of the captured American documents in the British Library is a certificate of appointment of one "Benjamin Hopkins Gentleman" to be adjutant to the regiment of foot where Seth Warner, Esquire is colonel. The commission, signed with an unusually flourished Hancock signature, was evidently among the papers of the American forces when they were captured. (British Library, additional MSS 21, 845, f. 108r)

Good officers were also needed. On 20 Jan 1777, Benjamin Franklin wrote a letter carried by Captain [La] Balme, whom he recommended to the Congress for its officer corps. (British Library, additional MSS 21,844, f. 265r) The letter, countersigned by Ch.W. Thompson, Esquire, formed #13, Secret Service, of documents captured from then Colonel La Balme when he was taken prisoner by the English.

After the Battle of Lexington, on 16 May 1775, the Provincial Congress of Massachusetts asked the Continental Congress for assistance. Massachusetts informed the national Congress that it was raising a force of men and had asked other states to do the same. Furthermore, Massachusetts suggested the establishment of an American army. (Curtis, 1, 20; *Journals of the Continental Congress*, 2, 81)

The *Journals of the Continental Congress*, 1776, 4, 344-345 reported that Congress sent a recommendation to Massachusetts to persuade new enlistees and those reenlisting to serve for three years, with the inducement that such three-year enlistees be given "1 Felt hat, 1 pr. yarn Stockings, 1 pr Shoes."

8. Washington was continually short of supplies and men. On 17 April 1781, the general wrote a circular to the New England states requesting that each state supply the equipment for the troops as requested. (Washington, 21, 469)

On 25 May 1781, Washington wrote to Hancock, asking for "as great a loan of Powder of the State of Massachusetts as can possibly be spared." (Fitzpatrick, 22, 113)

On 15 June 1781, Washington wrote to Governor Hancock that "I must particularly intreat your Excellency's attention to my requests...for Powder and Cannon. If, as I have been informed, the State is possessed of large quantities of materials for making powder, which can with facility be worked up at the Mills of Stoughton and Andover, they can with more safety and convenience afford to make a loan to the continent, at this important moment, as they may replenish their Magazines by working up the materials." (Fitzpatrick, 22, 221)

9. In January of 1780, the General Court addressed the inhabitants of Massachusetts as to how to raise £939,075 for the army. "We do not think that you have lost or can lose sight of the GRAND OBJECT for which you were compelled, reluctantly, to draw the sword." Yet, in Chapter 249 of the 1780 session, Massachusetts sent a letter to the president of the Congress asking if they were not being asked to give more than their share. (A&R, 1780, 10 March 1781, 373-375)

10. *Gazette* reads "successes."

11. A letter from Machias in the Eastern Territory of 27 Sept 1779 announced that "Major (???) Forster who commands this Eastern Regiment of Militia, has at the request of Colonel Allen without any resolve of Court, or order of Council, taken upon him to draught a number of men out of the different Companies in his Regiment to march to Machias, to do Garrison duty under Colonel Allen one month." The correspondent, Stephen Jones, reported that some of the men would not follow the orders at all and that some of them at first complied, and later wished to return home to their families. Charges of desertion resulted. The letter was entrusted to a French officer, a Captain DaBarie (a search by the National Archives failed to identify Captain DaBarie) who was evidently captured en route because the letter forms a part of the captured correspondence taken first to Quebec and later to London. (British Library, additional MSS 21, 844, ff. 167r-168r) It was therefore not always easy to secure militia to defend what is now Maine.

Matters continued to be difficult in Maine well into 1781. On 22 Dec 1780, Hancock wrote to the president of the Continental Congress in Philadelphia that Colonel John Allan had been sanctioned by Congress as superintendent of the Eastern Indian Department, that Massachusetts had repeatedly furnished him with the necessary supplies and had applied to Congress for assistance with the expense, but had received no answer. (Hancock Family Papers, Massachusetts Historical Society) On 3 Mar 1781, Hancock wrote a letter to the commander of the French forces at Newport, complaining that the British, with two or three armed vessels, "are daily committing the most horrid depredations, and cruelties on the Inhabitants who Reside on or near the Sea Coast in those parts." Hancock explained that the naval forces of the commonwealth of Massachusetts were not sufficient to oppose these raids and asked that French ships then anchored in the port of Boston together with perhaps one frigate from the French fleet at Newport "Cruise for a few Days on the Eastern Coast of this Commonwealth for the purpose of Capturing or Destroying any of the Enemy's Vessels that may be found infesting the same." Hancock said that

Massachusetts had equipped its ship, the *Mars*, with guns to accompany the French ships to Maine. (Hancock Family Papers, Massachusetts Historical Society)

12. Rhode Island, and in particular Newport, to the south of Boston, had been in British hands between December of 1776 and October of 1779. The facilities at Newport, which were then rivaling those in Boston and New York, provided a point from which Massachusetts shipping could be endangered. The British also raided other Rhode Island communities. As Newport had been evacuated by the time Hancock made this speech, his reference was probably to subsequent British raids into Massachusetts territory, along the coast and from the British base at New York.

13. The colonists were always fearful of an invasion from Canada. That fear persisted until the end of the war. As early as 20 Mar 1776, as president of the Continental Congress, Hancock instructed Benjamin Franklin, Samuel Chase, and Charles Carroll to go to Canada to explain to the Canadians that the invasions of their territory by the colonists were defensive in nature and "that we shall put it in the Power of our Canadian Brethren to pursue such Measures for securing their own Freedom and Happiness, as a generous Love of liberty and sound Policy shall dictate to them." (National Archives of the United States, Record Group 360, Item 12A, Volume 1, 78 cf. Peter Force in 1844, 5, col. 411) In a letter to Hancock dated 25 June 1781, Washington reported that "there is very great reason to apprehend an incursion of the enemy from Canada." (Fitzpatrick, 22, 265) Militia from Massachusetts and New York were stationed near Albany to discourage a British invasion.

14. The "and" appears in the *Gazette*.

15. Poole reads "bear."

16. The Massachusetts Constitution of 1780 provided in Article 30 of the "Bill of Rights" that "in the government of this Commonwealth the legislative department shall never exercise the executive and judicial powers, or either of them: The executive shall never exercise the legislative and judicial powers, or either of them: The judicial shall never exercise the legislative and executive powers, or either of them; To the end it may be a government of laws and not of men." (Taylor, 131)

17. *Bostonian Society* reads "commend." Benjamin Franklin had a like concern for the effects of inflation on the less affluent: "The Depreciation of our Money must, as you observe, greatly affect Salary Men, Widows, and Orphans. Methinks this Evil deserves the attention of the several legislatures, and ought, if possible, to be remedied by some equitable law, particularly adapted to their Circumstances." (Franklin, 7, 293, Franklin to Samuel Cooper, Passy, 22 Apr 1779)

18. Article 3 of the constitution of 1780 provided for the state support of religion. The provisions were broad and invested much power in the state to finance and to control religion.

19. The *Gazette* and *Independent Ledger* follow Hancock's custom of separating these two words.

20. Ferguson, 1961, 32 gave the following table:

DEPRECIATION OF OLD CONTINENTAL CURRENCY
Currently Required to Purchase $1.00 Specie

	1777	1778	1779	1780	1781
January	1.25	4.00	8.00	42.50	100.00
April	2.00	6.00	16.00	60.00	167.50
July	3.00	4.00	19.00	62.50	
October	3.00	5.00	30.00	77.50	

In the 1780 session, in Chapter 3, there was passed an act to regulate the payment of interest on government securities. Also in 1780, Chapter 148 attempted to compensate for the depreciation of pay ordered for the army but not yet paid.

21. Sometimes the legislature passed acts to relieve the suffering of specific persons. In the May 1781 session, in Chapter 5, the legislature provided for the support of Daphne, an infirm slave of an absentee, delegating to the town of Marlborough the obligation of maintaining her livelihood.

22. Chapter 58, 351-355, of the January 1791 session passed "An Act Providing for the Due Observation of the Lord's Day and Repealing the Several Laws Heretofore Made for that Purpose." Among other provisions, the act provided that anyone who failed to attend church for three months would be fined 10 shillings.

A&R, Chapter 53, 20 June 1781, 634-635 shows the repeated attention of the legislature to the Sabbath. Chapter 53 was entitled "Resolve Directing the Committee to Revise the Laws to Take into Consideration the Laws for the Due Observation of the Lord's Day, and to Prepare a Bill for Preventing Drunkenness and Other Atrocious Vices." Legislation continued into 1782 with Chapter 23, 22 Oct 1782, 63-70, again providing for an observation of the Lord's Day. Evidently there were elements in the Massachusetts population that were less reverent than some would have them be. Hancock himself might have noted the advice of the resolve that stated that "spirituous liquors" enfeeble the body and shorten the life of men.

There was continued legislation about the Lord's Day. On 8 May 1792, Chap. 58, 351-355, it was again provided that anyone not attending church for three months be fined ten shillings. This time the tithing men were instructed to enforce the act.

23. Not only did the local towns keep up the elementary schools, but the legislature was continually encouraging the establishment of academies. For example, Chap 23, September session, 419-421, of the 1793 legislature endorsed the establishment of Groton Academy, and named its overseers. On 17 June 1793, 349-351, Chapter 5, the General Court approved the establishment of Westerfield Academy in Hampshire. On A&R, 1788, 21 Jan 1789, Chapter 34, 51-56, the General Court approved a grammar school to be established in the eastern part of Roxbury. These are only two of the many acts passed by the General Court to support education. The purpose of the legislation was in part to make certain that the academies were properly financed.

24. Even in the early confused days of the war, Massachusetts provided for the support of Harvard. For example, on 3 Oct 1775, the provincial legislature provided for £100 payments to Professors Wigglesworth and Winthrop, both Hollisian Professors at Harvard University. (A&R, Chaps 217 and 218, 92, 20 Sept 1775 session) Chap. 5 of the 1780 Constitution provided specifically for the support of Harvard University. The legislature made frequent provisions for supporting the institution.

For example, the May 1781 session, 6 July 1781, Chapt. 145, 703, provided for £47/19/4 to Stephen Sewall for his services as Hancock Professor of Oriental Languages to the 1st of the previous June; Chapter 150, p. 706 provided £175 to Samuel Williams, Hollisian Professor of Mathematics; Chap. 152, 707, provided £150 to the Reverend Edward Wigglesworth, Professor of Divinity at Harvard. The 1784, May Session, Chap. 75, 3 July 1786, 306-307, made grants to Willard, Wigglesworth, and Pearson, the Hancock Professor of Hebrew and other Oriental languages.

On 19 Oct 1781, Chapter 240, 754-755, the General Court provided that, if Joseph Willard would accept the presidency of Harvard, he was to be paid £300 for his first year in office, plus moving expenses.

Chapter 65, the 1782 session, 22 March 1783, 172, exempted faculty and students from poll taxes.

The May 1783 sessions, 11 July 1783, Chap. 96, 727-728, entitled "Grants to the President and Fellows of Harvard Colleges," made specific grants to President Joseph Willard; Professor of Divinity Edward Wigglesworth; and Hollisian Professor of Mathematics Samuel Williams.

25. At his death in 1764, Thomas Hancock, John's uncle, had given £1,000 to Harvard to establish a chair of Oriental languages. (Fowler, 48) The *Acts & Resolves* of the House shows repeated attention to Harvard. For example, 1781, May session, Chapter 145, 703, of 6 July 1781, appropriated £47/19/4 to the Hancock Professor of Oriental Languages. Evidently the bequest of Thomas Hancock did not prove sufficient to bear all of the costs of teaching Hebrew to the Harvard scholars. The 1781, May session, Chapter 149, dated 6 July 1781 appropriated £175 to the Hollisian Professor of Mathematics at Harvard.

26. Poole and the *Gazette* read "adopt."

27. Evidently the vices inimical to a free republic did not include the enjoyment of imported luxury items. Indeed such an inclusion would have seriously injured Hancock's shipping business. On the same day that it printed the text of Hancock's speech, the Boston *Gazette* published an advertisement that the firm of William and John Molineux had ready for sale such imported goods from England as superfine broadcloth, "cassimeers," Dutch lace, wines, silk handkerchiefs, and the like.

28. The *Journal of the House* reads "perhaps in some points more than."

29. The *Independent Ledger*, the *Independent Chronicle*, and the *Bostonian Society* read "beloved."

30. Athough the record of the speech in the *Journal of the House* is in the hand of a professional scribe, the signature could be Hancock's. It highly resembles his customary signature, and it has two characteristics that make it differ from the record of the speech: first, it is less steady and more shakily done, and second, the quill of the pen at least three times in the two short words shows that the pressure put on it by the writer caused it to spread and thus widen the trace of ink. Such pressure on the quill seldom exists in the remainder of the transcription.

HEADNOTE

Date: Friday, 5 Jan 1781

Occasion: The *Journal of the House* for Friday, 5 Jan 1781 stated:
"The Secretary came down from the Hon. Senate & informed the House
His Excellency was in the Senate chamber & requested their attendance
there, and the Speaker being absent, Genl Warren was desired to be at
their Head. Accordingly the House went up where His Excellency was
pleased to make the following speech to the Houses."

SOURCES

Journal of the House, vol. 1, part 2, 189-191, MA; *Journal of the
House*, vol. 1, part 2, 189-191, SL*
     This speech does not appear in the Boston *Gazette*, the *Independent
Ledger*, the Massachusetts *Spy*, the *Independent Chronicle*, or the
Continental and Weekly Advertiser.

*No copy in either Senate Journal.

TEXT

     Gentlemen of the Senate & Gentlemen of the House of
Representatives: Nothing new or important respecting the internal State
of the Commonwealth has occurred since your recess, but so many &
weighty are the matters relating to the ensuing Campaign, which
remain yet to be accomplished as rendered your meeting at this time
absolutely necessary.
     I shall direct the Secretary to lay before you some letters I have
lately received, by which you will see the present state of the Army,[1] &
be able to judge of the adequateness of the measures already taken for
the supplies of it[2] & in what manner those measures have been
executed.[3]
     When I first met you, Gentlemen, in General Court I urged in the
most pressing manner the establishment of the Army according to the
late Plan & Requisitions of Congress, & the warm recommendation of
the Commander in Chief.[4] The necessity of the most speedy &
vigorous measures for fully accomplishing this purpose is far from

being abated. It must fall with the greatest weight upon my mind; and as it deserves, I doubt not you are disposed to give it your first & Most Serious attention. The circumstances of these Free States, the just expectations of our great and Generous Ally,[5] who has already sent such a Force to our assistance, and is still ready to afford us further Aid,[6] our own Honor and Safety—all call upon us to employ every means for forwarding & compleating [sic] our Military preparations, the efficacy of which must, in a great measure, depend upon their being early made.[7] The present situation of our Country is critical. It demands the instant, the generous, the united and animated exertions of all that wish well to it and particularly of those in Government. Such exertions would soon place it by the blessing of Heaven into a secure & happy Condition,[8] by establishing and providing for an Army, that may efficaciously cooperate with our Allies for its defence. Nor need I remind you that we cannot fail in this point without leaving the field to our enemies, & opening the Door for such miseries to overspread[9] the face of our country as cannot be thought of without Horror.[10]

Gentlemen—

I shall seasonably lay before you in separate messages[11] such branches of public business as shall appear to me to deserve your attention, and most readily concur with you for the despatch of all.

John Hancock

NOTES

1. On 4 Dec 1780 (A&R, October session, Chap. 114, 205-210), the state legislature had proportioned the manner in which the towns and plantations should meet the quotas for the Continental Army. Chapter 38 of the May 1781 session (A&R, 16 June 1781, 621-624) infers that the requests had not been complied with when Hancock spoke on 5 Jan 1781, because the legislature felt required to issue further orders as to the manner in which the quotas were to be filled.

2. As is evidenced by Hancock's letter to Washington of 15 Aug 1781, there was considerable correspondence between George Washington and Hancock on the matter of supplies. In his 15 Aug letter, Hancock assured George Washington that he had laid the general's letters speedily before the assembly, and that powder, mortars and cannon had been dispatched by transportation furnished by Massachusetts. He also said he had been

informed by Mr. Phelps, of whom we shall hear more later in connection with the western lands of New York, that Massassachusetts had furnished more than its supply of beef for July, and that Phelps had found the supply of beef plentiful so that the quota for Massachusetts could be met in the future. Rum had been gathered at Springfield and was being sent to "camp" as soon as possible. (MHS, Hancock Family Papers, letter of Hancock to GW, 15 Aug 1781)

3. "Mr. Secretary came into the House with the Papers referred to in his Excellency's Speech and laid the same on the Table." (MA, *Journal of the House*, vol. 1, part 2, p. 191)

4. The reference in this speech is probably to a request by Washington in his letter of 15 Dec 1780, "which points out the pressing necessity of effectual measures for recruiting the army to its full complement, be immediately communicated to the respective legislature or executives." (*Journals*, 18, 1780, 1182) Hancock was responding to the copy he had received via the Continental Congress.

In the April session of A&R 1780, Chap. 12, 17 Apr 1781, 382, Massachusetts had placed the soldiers recruited on 2 Dec 1780 and on 9 Feb 1781 under the command of General Washington and the supervision of Major General Lincoln. The problem being resolved in this legislation concerned whether state soldiers served under a national commander or were only obliged to follow the orders of state officers. Obviously Washington could not have formed an army of troops not rigidly under his command.

Washington was to write Hancock and to the states in general several times concerning recruits for the Continental Army. On 30 June 1780, Washington sent a circular letter to the states (of New England) in which he pointed out that the recruits had not yet joined up in the prescribed manner. "The present crisis," said Washington, "is by far the most important and delicate that this Country has ever experienced, and it pains me in the extreme that we are so backward in all our measures." (Fitzpatrick, 19, 104- 5)

On 21 Feb 1781, Washington congratulated Hancock on the shipment of provisions from Massachusetts for the Bay State recruits. (Fitzpatrick, 21, 268)

On 17 Mar 1781, Washington wrote that he had had to send troops to Virginia to cooperate with the French and "I must therefore intreat [sic] the interference of your Excellency's countenance and Authority with the persons in the different Townships, whose business it may be to procure the Levies, not only to send forward those to the places of rendezvous, which have been raised, but to attend to completing the deficiencies where any may have happened." (Fitzpatrick, 21, 339-340)

On 4 June 1781, Washington wrote for five hundred recruits from the "State of Massachusetts to repair to Rhode Island." (Fitzpatrick, 22, 160)

On 30 July 1781, Washington wrote Hancock for six hundred men who were to be sent to Albany for the protection of the northern frontier. (Fitzpatrick, 22, 436-437)

On 31 Jan 1782, Washington sent a circular to the several New England states saying that he realized that he had already had much to say concerning the need for recruits, but that, "at this advanced stage of the War," he did not wish to insult anyone by continuing to ask for support but that he felt that "unless we strenuously exert ourselves to profit by these successes [in Virginia], we shall not only lose all the solid advantages that might be derived from them, but we shall become contemptible in our own eyes." (Fitzpatrick, 23, 477-478)

5. As early as 1776 and 1777, French assistance to the colonies offered material aid to the American cause. Stinchcombe estimated that, in its victory over the British at Saratoga on 17 Oct 1777, the American army "received 90 per cent of its arms and ammunition from French merchants." (9)

Another way that the French assisted the colonists was in bringing "hard money" into the colonies. When the French army and navy used American facilities, they paid not in the highly inflated paper currency, but in currency that had maintained its international value. (Gordon, 4, 129)

The victory at Saratoga encouraged the French to make official their support of the American rebels. Two treaties were signed on 6 Feb 1778. The first, the Treaty of Conditional and Defensive Alliance, provided that France would recognize American independence and renounce all claims in the North American continent in exchange for the opportunity to unseat the British from the West Indies. The second, the Treaty of Amity and Commerce, was confined to providing trading benefits to both parties. The alliance with the French was highly important to the Americans, both in material and in morale, and had to be continually bolstered. The letters and circulars issued by Washington during this period exhibit considerable concern for the relations with the French. On 24 May 1781, Washington issued a circular to all the New England states announcing that he and the Count de Rochambeau had arranged for the colonial and French armies to converge. On 3 Aug 1781, Washington wrote to Hancock that the contingent of the Massachusetts militia, according to de Rochambeau, had not arrived in Rhode Island and would Hancock take what steps he could to rectify the deficiency? On 16 Sept 1782, Washington wrote to Hancock that the admiral of the French fleet, the Marquis de Vaudrueil, was fearful of being bottled up in Boston Harbour by the superior British fleet and that the militia of that area around Boston needed to be prepared to assist the French, should such an attack come. (Fitzpatrick, 25, 167)

6. According to Stinchcombe (145), France had originally intended to embark two divisions from Brest. However, when the forces arrived in Brittany, there were only ships enough to accommodate five thousand. Rochambeau and his army arrived off Newport, on 11 July 1780. Although there was still talk of the arrival of a second division, the blockading of Brest by the British and a scarcity of French ships combined to limit the French expeditionary force to the original five thousand. According to Smith (13) D'Estaing sailed from Toulon and reached "his destination" on 18 July 1780.

7. The General Court was repeatedly in attention to the needs of the militia. For example, in the January session of 1780 in Chapter 75, 259-260, one Joseph Baker was directed to lay his accounts before the General Court for the cost of salted beef and pork.

Chapter 175, 323, of the January 1780 session provided for, £200 to be paid to General Lincoln.

Chapter 182, 327-328, of the same session provided for an additional, £100 to General Lincoln.

In the October session of 1780 in Chapter 62, 166-167, $100,000 was appropriated for transporting stores to the army. In the January 1781 session in Chapter 421, 854-855, funds were made available to pay the Dutch firm of John de Neufville and Sons.

On 17 Nov 1780, Chapter 62, 166-7, Charles Miller was awarded £10,000 for purchasing supplies for the army, and Nathaniel Appleton 100,000 new dollars for transporting stores for the army. It is interesting that, in the same piece of legislation, both dollars and pounds were used, probably because that is the way in which the two debtees issued their bills.

In the May 1781 session in Chapter 40, 625-628, it was resolved to raise five hundred men for the defense of Rhode Island. The monthly salaries of surgeons was set at eighteen pounds, and for drummers and fifers, at two pounds four shillings per month.

In the September 1781 session in Chapter 219, 744, Oliver Phelps was authorized to salt, or cause to be salted, beef for the militia and to sell the tallow and hides to purchase salt and barrels. A&R, 1781, September session, Chapter 190, 729, of the September 1781 session provided for the payment of £616/0/6 to pay for 46,000 weight of bread and flour.

8. The scribe in the *Journal of the House* crossed out "position" and wrote in "condition" on the line, so that the correction was made at the time the scribe was preparing the speech for the official record. From what the scribe was copying is not clear, but he probably had Hancock's copy before him, which has since been lost.

9. The scribe in the *Journal of the House* had written "oberspread" so it was necessary for him to convert the "b" into a "v."

10. Hancock himself would certainly have suffered considerably at the hands of the British if the colonists had lost the war. Unless he had escaped, it was likely that he would have been imprisoned in England.

11. We have not attempted to reproduce the many written messages that Hancock sent to the General Court. Some of them exist in manuscript form, and others are reproduced in the A&R during Hancock's second term as governor.

HEADNOTE

Date: 19 Dec 1781

Occasion: Speech of Governor Hancock delivered in Latin at the inauguration of President Willard of Harvard

Chapter 240 of the September 1781 session of the General Court provided for the payment of £300 to the Reverend Joseph Willard for his services in said office.

SOURCES

Harvard Archives MS UAI 50.27.73*; Massachusetts *Spy*, 3 Jan 1782, 1; Boston *Gazette*, 31 Dec 1781, 1.

Quod faelix[1] faustumque sit Universitati nostrae, Ecclesiae Christi, totique Reipublicae Massachusettensi, convenimus hodierno die ad te, Reverende Domine, in sellam curulem[2] inaugurandam. Quantam spem et quam praeclaram conceperunt omnes de tua Eruditione, Sapientia, Fide, et Auctoritate, atque ac de omnibus aliis Dotibus quibus ad hoc onus[3] instructus es et ornatus, annunciant omnium Sociorum suffragia, Concensus Curatorum pariter unanimis praedicat, et Gaudia[4] per omnium vultus iam nunc diffusa testantur. Quod tua rerum literarum administratio, haec guadia non solum salva sed etiam in dies aucta, reddet nos persuasos habemusmum. Sub tua cura et moderamine videre Pietatem, Virtutem et Literaturam hic vigentes at amoene efflorescentes vovemus simul et speramus. Artes ingenuae hic fideliter doctae, oh vetent mores deficere! Vetent dedecorare bene Nata Culpas![5] In his rebus Tibi, Domine, Adjutores erunt Professores literati et Tutores. Vestris laboribus consociatis, videbimus, si quid veri mens augurat, vivos etiam plures quam antea, egregie ornatos ad omne officium et civile et Ecclesiasticum, ornamenta hujusce Reipublicae et defensores futuros. Videbimus eos qui causas optime orabunt, qui caeli[6] Meatus accurate describent et Surgentia sydera dicent. Quanquam enim occuli nostri quocumque inciderint, augurs amicum mihi carissimum Winthrop requirunt. Quamquam ille Scientia Mathematica, l'tteris variis, et omnibus Rebus ornatus, hue! Mortuus sit in cuius Sepulcrum Gens Togata[7] Flores eximios sparsere; vivit attamwn, et Adest Eius Alumnus, Successor, ejusdemque Laudis Aemulus—Williams.

Alma mater nostra, Revolutionem istam nuperrimam et per totum orbem celebratam quodam modo peperit, partamque aluit. Ipsa docuit

Filios suos Naturam Liberatis et Pretium; docuit quibus modis eam
defendere, et Constituionem civilem formare Principiis integris et
liberrimis innixam. Te talem Constitutionem sinu amplexam[8] tenere,
et illis qui ad eam administratandam a Populo designati suntesse
fidelem; te quoque operam daturum ut Juvenes Fidei tuae commissi,
eadem sentiant, et magno Amore Libertatis sint perculsi, minime
Dubitamus.

Iam vero ad me olim Alumnum et semper huiusce Universitastis
amantissimum attinet officium quod lubentissime sum praestaturus.
Ex Perscripto igitur, et nomine totius Universitatis Senatus,
Consentientibus simul honorandis Curatoribus ac reverendis, trado tibi
hoc Sigillum, hos Libros, Chartas ac Claves, Insignia et Testimonia
quod una cum istis tibi Traduntur et Concreduntur omnes auctoritates
tum in eos qui Litteris dediti sunt, quam in omnes alios aut intra muros
digentes, aut ullo modo ad Communitatem attinentes, ut et omnes
Jurisdictiones, Potestates, Proprietates ac Privilegia quibus
Antecessores tui fructi sunt in modo tam amplo quam illi fruebantur,
aut frui debuerunt.

Domine Reverende, te Praesidem Universitatis Harvardinae, rite
electum, constitutum et inauguratum, toti huic conventui celeberrimo
pro more indigitio, ac palam annuncio.

His Solemnibus ad Ritum peractis ultro spondemus, Preses
Reverende, tibi probere, ut possumus, omnia Auxilia Incitamenta et
Solamina quae reddant Auctoritatem tuam jam ratam et sanctitam
maxime quoque utilem et inclutam, ac litteris cum Divinis tum
humanis praecipue auspicatam.

Translation:

Because this is an auspicious and favorable occasion for our
university, the church and the entire commonwealth of Massachusetts,
we have gathered together today, reverend sir, for the purpose of
installing you in the Curule Chair. How much and how bright a hope
all men have grasped from your learning, wisdom, faithfulness,
leadership, and all other endowments by which you have been prepared
and equipped for this duty, the vote of all the fellows announces, in a
like manner the unanimous agreement of the curators proclaims it, and
the joy which is now spread abroad throughout the countenance of all
bears witness to it. We are persuaded that your direction of the affairs
of learning will return this joy not only in making it safe, but also in
having it grow day by day. Under your care and management, we who
are here blossoming and pleasantly flourishing pledge and at the same

time hope to see piety, virtue, and learning. The native skills, here so faithfully taught, oh, may they forbid that morals fail! May they forbid that faults bring shame upon things well born! In these affairs, sir, the learned professors and tutors will be your helpers. When your labors have been united we will see, if the mind anything of truth, to a greater number than before, those surpassingly trained for every duty, both civil and ecclesiastical, adornments of this republic and its future defenders; we will see those who excellently plead causes, who accurately describe the paths of the heavens and who speak of the rising of the stars. Although indeed whichever ways our eyes should fall, they are searching for my dear friend Winthrop. Although that man, who was distinguished in mathematical wisdom, in various kinds of learning, indeed in all things, although he is dead, upon whose grave the togate race has spread splendid flowers, nonetheless he lives, and his pupil, successor, and one who is worthy of the same praise is present— Williams.

Our alma mater in some degree gave birth to that most recent revolution which is renowed throughout the entire world and she nourished that which has been born. She has taught her sons the nature of liberty and its price, she has taught them by what means to defend liberty and how to form a civil constitution relying upon principles that are pure and more free. We have little doubt that you, having embraced such a constitution to your breast, are holding on to it, that you are faithful to those who have been chosen by the people to administer it, that you are about to exert yourself so that the young men who have been entrusted to your faithfulness might feel the same things and be moved by a great love of liberty.

Now, in truth, that duty has fallen to me, an alumnus of this university and one who loves her most dearly, a duty which I am about to fulfill most pleasantly. Therefore, according to the ritual, and by the authority of the Senate of the entire university, together with the consent of the honorable and reverend curators, I hand over to you this seal, these books, the charter and keys, the insignia and testimonia, because together with these are handed over and entrusted to you all authority over both those who are given to learning and all others who either dwell within the walls or who are in any way concerned with the community, just as are handed over all authority, power, rights, and privileges that your predecessors enjoyed in a measure as full as they enjoyed them or as they ought to have enjoyed them.

Reverend Sir, according to custom I declare and openly proclaim to this most notable assembly, that having been duly chosen, appointed, and installed, you are the president of Harvard University.

With these ceremonies having been properly conducted, we freely pledge, reverend President, that as much as we are able we will offer all aid, motivation, and consolations which should render your authority, now ratified and greatly solemnized, useful and renowned and eminently favorable both for human and divine letters.

NOTES

1. "Faelix" is a misspelling which could have arisen from the loss of the distinction between the pronunciation of the vowel and the diphthong.

2. The Curule Chair was the chair used by the highest magistrates of the Roman Republic.

3. The manuscript reading of "onunus" could have occurred by dittography.

4. The MS reading of "gaudia" is a misspelling.

5. The MS reads "cuplae." The accusative is required in order to serve as the subject of the infinitive. The nominative seems to be derived from an allusion to Horace's *Odes*, IV.4.32-36:

> Doctinae sed vim promovet insitam
> Rectique cultus pectora roborunt
> Uticumque defecere mores
> Indecorant bene nata culpae.

There is a variant reading of "dedecorant" for the largely synonymous *indecorant*. In C.E. Bennet's translation of the Loeb Classical Library edition, the lines read: "Yet training increases inborn worth and righteous ways make strong the heart; whenever righteousness has failed, faults mar even what nature has made noble."

6. The MS reading of "cali" is a misspelling. Compare with Virgil's Aeneid 6.847-851:

> excudent alli spirantia mollius aera
> (credo equidem), uiuos ducent de marmore uultus.
> orabunt causas melius, caelique meatus
> describent radio et surgentia sidera dicent:
> regere imperio populos, Romane, memento...

> For other peoples will, I do not doubt,
> still cast their bronze to breathe with softer features

or draw out of the marble living lines,
plead causes better, trace the ways of heaven
with wands and tell the rising constellations;
but yours will be the rulership of nations,
Remember, Roman...

7. *Gens togata*, meaning the Romans (cf. Aeneid 1.282):

> Quin aspera Juno,
> quae mare nunc terrasque metu caelumque fatigat,
> consilia in melius referet, mecumque fovebit
> Romanos, rerum dominos gentemque togatam.

8. The MS. appears to read "amplextam." "Amplector" is deponent, i.e., passive in form, but active in meaning. The perfect participle thus needs to be masculine, not feminine, to agree with *te*. The deviation from standard Latin may be common in later Latin. It is possible that the verb was no longer deponent in this late period.

HEADNOTE

Date: January 24, 1782

Occasion: The *Journal of the House*, 2, 22 Jan 1782, 469-470, commented: "Mr. Secretary Avery came in & said his Excellency the Governor is in the Chair in the Senate Chamber, and requested the attendance of the House—and the House attended accordingly. [Struck out is "The House returned and adjourned to three o'clock P.M."] The House returned, and the Hon. Speaker laid on the table the Speech of his Excellency to both Houses with a file of papers. The Speech is as follows, viz."

The *Journal of the Senate*, 2, Wednesday, 23 Jan 1782, 211 commented: "The Secretary came in with a Message from his Excellency the Governor to acquaint the Senate that he had just receiv'd the Vote of both Houses... but that his bodily Indisposition and the Stormy Weather prevents it and he begs the Indulgence of the two Houses till tomorrow morning eleven oClock [sic],"

Evidently, Hancock did not appear at eleven o'clock as he had informed the Senate, causing both chambers to adjourn to three o'clock.

In the Senate chamber, there was some dispute as to whether the president of the Senate should give up his arm chair to the governor. It was resolved that the president should retain his seat and that an arm chair should be set for the governor. (*Journal of the Senate*, 2, 210-211, MA)

SOURCES

Journal of the House, 2, 470-472, MA; *Journal of the House*, 2, 470-472, SL.*

Independent Chronicle, 31 Jan 1782, 1; Massachusetts *Spy*, 7 Feb 1782, 1; *Independent Ledger*, 28 Jan 1782, 3; Boston *Gazette*, 28 Jan 1782, 3.

*No copy in either Senate Journal.

TEXT

Gentlemen of the Senate & Gentlemen of the House of Representatives—With particular pleasure I embrace this first opportunity to congratulate you on the important & glorious success with which it has pleased heaven to crown the arms of these United States, & those of our illustrious Ally in the reduction of York, & the surrender of Lord Cornwallis & his whole Army: an event that reflects signal honor upon the Council & Plans of France & America, & upon the skill & bravery of the leaders & forces who have so happily executed them; An event that gives new lustre to the name [sic] of Gen. Washington, the Count De Grasse[1] & the Count de Rochambeau,[2] & forms an additional ground of friendship & mutual confidence between the allied nations.[3]

The pleasing prospect now opening to our view is in no small degree brightened by the memorable advancement of our Arms through many difficulties in South Carolina & Georgia; a fruit under the divine smiles of the ability, firmness and perseverance of Gen. Green, and the gallant officers & men under his orders.[4]

These events, together with the general face of the War in other quarters of the globe must have their effect in humbling the power with which they are contending, & at the same time cannot but raise our own expectations of speedily seeing the Independence, Peace & Happiness of these states established upon a solid basis. But you are sensible, gentlemen, as I can be, of the fatal consequences that might still ensue, should we in this moment of victory & joy abate our vigilance, & relax our efforts: & thus give a new spring to the hopes & exertions of the enemy. Our claims, righteous as they are, have hitherto been supported only by force, not by any impression which their own manifest justice have [sic] ever made upon the minds of our enemies; & by force thru' the favor of Heaven, must these claims be finally established. The success of our negotiations in Europe, those negotiations by which our Freedom, our rights of commerce & fishing, our honor & Happiness, & even our own being as a nation will be determined, depends not altogether upon reasoning & address, but greatly upon the strength & good condition of our Armies in the field. The sword must give energy to Justice and firmness & Equity to peace. Our present situation does, therefore, at once indispensibly oblige & highly encourage us to add fresh vigor in our Military operations, immediately to complete our quota of the Continental Army with effective men, & to make every provision that it may be well supplied.[5] Accordingly, I shall lay before you, gentlemen [sic], every paper I have received during your recess respecting this most essential object, as well as others that concern the order & welfare of the State, fully persuaded that you will give every attention and dispatch to the public business which circumstances will allow, & our constituents have a right to expect, towards which you may be assured, nothing on my part shall be wanting.

Gentlemen, at the close of the last session when you had finished on your part the matters that were before you, a number of Bills & Resolves were brought to me, with a pressing desire that I might immediately decide upon them, & give you a Recess: upon this occasion I found myself embarrassed between a desire not to detain you, & the duty which I owe to the Commonwealth, by giving a deliberate consideration to matters of such length & importance. Your candid attention, Gentlemen, to this circumstance in public business, will I am persuaded relieve me as much as may be from any such future embarrassment.

(signed) John Hancock

NOTES

1. Francois Joseph Paul de Grasse (1722-1788) was put in command of a flotilla of troops from France to join Lafayette on the Chesapeake Bay. His ships participated in the defeat of Admiral Hood's fleet and thus assisted in the eventual withdrawal of the British from the Revolutionary War.

2. In 1780 Jean Baptiste Donatien de Vimeur, Comte de Rochambeau (1725-1807) sailed for America with approximately six thousand men to join General Washington. The combined forces of French and colonists met up with the fleet of Admiral de Grasse and all were present at the Battle of Yorktown. The Americans honored Rochambeau by giving him two cannons captured from the British. Upon his return to France, the comte was decorated and made Marechal de France. For an account of his experiences in America, see *Memoires*, 1, 237 ff. Rochambeau clarified that it was from the port of Brest that the flotilla sailed. (Memoires, 1, 237-243) He verified that he was forced to divide his forces into two. While he was negotiating to get both corps on ships, and was meeting with resistance from the French naval commander, he was forced to accept sailing with only one-half of his men, because the British were arming a flotilla to follow them and the Americans were in need of immediate help.

3. As was noted in the introductory essay, Hancock did much to keep the fences mended between the Americans and the French officers. In a letter dated 30 Sept 1778, James Warren wrote to Samuel Adams that "General Hancock has made most Magnificent Entertainments for the Count and his officers, both at his own and and the public Houses and last Week the General Court Entertained them at Dinner in Faneuil Hall with much military Parade." (Warren-Adams Letters, 2, 48) On 25 Oct 1778, Warren wrote to

Sam Adams, in some disgust: "Most People are Engaged in getting and some in spending Money as fast as they can. superb [sic] Entertainments are very Common. Genl. H[ancock] gives a Magnificant Ball to the French Officers, and to the Gentlemen and Ladies of the Town next Thursday Evening. indeed [six] all manner of Extravagance prevails." (Warren-Adams Letters, 2, 59-60) Woodbury stated in her account of Dorothy Quincy Hancock (160): "...it is chronicled that General Hancock gave a superb ball, before the departure of the fleet, at Concord Hall, at which were present His Excellency Count D'Estaing and a number of officers belonging to the French fleet." Woodbury reported that about a hundred of the fashionable women of Boston were present to impress the French with the pulchritude of American females. Woodbury (156-158) recounted a story that, when Dorothy Hancock had been told that thirty French officers were coming to breakfast, John had to change the number to one hundred and fifty so that orders had to be given to go out and milk all the cows on the common. When the young officers arrived, they not only ate all the food that had been prepared but also went into the garden and helped themselves to the fresh fruit from the trees "for which Count D'Estaing afterwards apologized."

4. In 1778, Cornwallis had been pretty much having it his own way in the South. After landing in Georgia and quickly conquering it, he proceeded to Charleston, where the colonists' General Lincoln was unable to defend the city with his 5,500 troops in comparison to Cornwallis's 8,000. However, not all was to go well with the British. General Green's position was to annoy Cornwallis without being forced into total confrontation of the armies. Skirmishes favorable to the Americans were fought at Guilford Courthouse in North Carolina and Cowpens in Georgia.

Cornwallis had placed his southern troops under the command of Major Ferguson and marched his major forces to Yorktown. Ferguson and his loyalists decided to take a stand on King's Mountain, an elongated elevation just south of what is now the North Carolina-South Carolina border. He felt that the position was impregnable. But he reckoned not with the "mountain men" and the Piedmont troops who joined together to besiege the Tories and the British. The result was disaster for the British. The colonists fought from behind the heavy undergrowth coming up the sides of the "mountain," and pinned the British more and more on the high elevations where they were easier targets. The reports of casualties vary. The best estimate is that the colonials lost 28 killed and 62 wounded, totalling 90, whereas the British has 206 killed, 128 wounded, and 648 taken prisoner, with 122 otherwise classified as casualties, totaling 1,104 in all. (*Historical*, 31) Ferguson himself was killed. It was the end of British supremacy in the deep Southern states. The rebels took out their revenge on the captured loyalists, to make up for the crimes that the loyalists had committed on the revolutionaries. Tories were hung and imprisoned. The incentive of Tories to aid the King's cause in the South was definitely stifled.

5. There were numerous efforts to raise recruits. The January 1781 session, Chapter 539, 933, provided that there should be no more enlistments for drummers and fifers. Evidently the enrollments in that area were in excess, perhaps because such persons might be less likely to be in combat. In the May 1781 session, three chapters dealt with recruitment. Chapter 38 provided for the completion of the quota for the Continental Army; Chapter 69 raised the question of what to do with some men who had been rejected for service; Chapter 96 concerned the recruitment of 2,700 more men, as had been urged by George Washington.

HEADNOTE

Date: 25 Sept 1783

Occasion: The *Journal of the House*, 4, 178, read as follows: "The Secretary came down & said that his Excelly [sic] the Governor was in the chair at the Senate Chamber & requested the attendance of the House Whereupon the House went up to his Excellency who addressed the two Branches of the Legislature as follows viz."

The *Journal of the House*, 4, 182 read: "A copy of the speech being delivered to the Speaker, the House retired into their own chamber where the same was read and 3 o clk assigned for considering the speech."

The speech was evidently prepared on 24 Sept 1783, for the copies transcribed into the *Journal of the House* are so dated. But the minutes of the House show that the speech was delivered on 25 Sept 1783.

SOURCES

Sources: *Journal of the House*, 4, 178-181, MA; *Journal of the House*, vol. 4, 178-181, SL.*

Boston *Gazette* 29 Sept 1783, 2; *Independent Chronicle*, 2 Oct 1783, 1-2; Massachusetts *Spy* 9 Oct 1783, 4; *Independent Ledger*, 29 Sept 1783, 3.

*No copies in either Senate Journal.

TEXT

Gentlemen of the Senate, and Gentlemen of the House of Representatives.

I am happy to meet you at an era when our Country after a long and arduous Contest for her Rights & Independence is at length blest with peace,[1]—A peace that gives us the quiet possession of the dear objects for which we have contended; that closes such scenes of devastation and blood as we have beheld; that secures to us very ample territorial advantages,[2] and opens to our view the most flattering prospect of future prosperity in an extended Agriculture, Fishing and Commerce; a Peace that comes to us attended with remarkable plenty, & a variety of other important blessings.[3] I cannot appear Gentlemen, so insensible to the publick [sic] felicity, as not warmly to congratulate you upon so extraordinary and pleasing a combination of events.

Looking back upon the memorable scene through which we have passed, contrasting it with our present ease and security, and looking forward to the bright objects of our hopes, what acknowledgements are due from us to the Supreme Ruler of the world for the uncommon favour he has been pleased to express towards the United States? Those, who under His Providence, have been distinguished instruments of procuring for us these blessings, can never be forgotten by us. We cannot take a retrospect of our late severe Conflict, and not recollect with every return of respect and friendship how easily our August Ally acknowledged, and how much he contributed to the support of our National Sovereignty, and Independence. We cannot trace the course of the War and not be sensible of the part which his brave forces bore in those successes that prepared the way for our present happy settlement, an alliance so honorable, and that has already proved so fruitful & advantageous to these States cannot fail to be carefully cultivated by us in all time to come.

While we value & enjoy the blessings of liberty & peace, it is impossible we should forget our own patriotic Army, to whose gallant and persevering services, amidst peculiar hardships and discouragements, we are so greatly indebted for these blessings. Such services are sure to engage our attention, and the recommendation of them must come with particular might from a Commander in Chief, dear to a Country which he has gloriously defended, and who, throughout all the various & trying scenes of the War, has uniformly possessed, in an uncommon degree, the confidence of the States as well as of the Army. I am persuaded, Gentlemen, that this Commonwealth will be ever ready to comply with the reasonable requisitions of Congress for a final settlement with so meritorious an Army in a manner dictated by justice & honour.

Divine Providence has most kindly put into the hands of these States the means of our political happiness, and nothing seems wanting to complete it, but a proper improvement of these means. Our all depends upon our union. This is our Palladium.[4] By this we have hitherto been saved, & the preservation of it can alone continue our liberty & safety, our peace at home and our respectability abroad. But this depends on the temperament & energy of that general government which was instituted on purpose to combine the Sovereign States into one political body, for their common security, and to draft forth in just proportions the united strength of all for effecting the important purposes of their confederation. How to strengthen & improve this union, so as to render it more completely adequate to such purposes is a question of no small importance, & demands the immediate & serious attention of these states. That it may be done greatly to the advantage of all, & without real injury to the internal government of any, and that our welfare, if not our very existence, as a free nation is suspended upon it, I am fully persuaded.

In the meantime I hope that ardent affection for liberty & independence which has already carried us successfully through so many difficulties, will still animate us to act up to the grand intention & the true spirit of the confederation. In this hope I feel myself indispensably obliged in the most earnest manner to call upon you, Gentlemen, & upon all the good citizens of the Comm'th to strengthen the hands of Congress, particularly by making every exertion for a speedy payment of our proportion of the National expense,[5] a measure now become absolutely necessary to the support of public credit, to the most essential purposes of our sacred league, and to appeasing the loud complaints of those whose just demands upon the public have already remained too long unsatisfied.[6] When measures of such extreme importance to the publick are not seasonably accomplished, through unreasonable jealousies, or a diversity of sentiment respecting the mode, it is easy to foresee the dreadful consequences.

The internal interest of this Commonwealth at the same time demands our particular attention. Much is necessary to be done, that many worthy citizens may have a satisfying prospect of realizing that large portion of their property which they have entrusted to the hands of Government. They justly expect to see that every exertion is at least for its firm security, & for the punctual payment of the interest of every publick obligation. When once an adequate provision is made to satisfy so moderate and reasonable an expectation, publick credit will be revived, the Honor of the Commonwealth will be supported, its real interests will be greatly advanced, & government will possess, as it ought ever to do, the firm confidence of the community.

I have directed the Secretary to lay before you several letters I have received during the recess, which I recommend to your consideration.

The restoration of Peace will, it is highly probable, open an extensive trade and intercourse with all parts of the world, which may make some further regulations necessary with respect to vessels visited by contagious distempers. I submit to your consideration the propriety of revising those laws, and if on examination they should be found deficient, I doubt not but you will immediately take effectual measures to remedy such defect.

The preservation of trees suitable for masts in the Eastern parts of this Commonwealth is an object of great moment, & demands the attention of the legislature.[7]

I have called upon the Treasurer for the state of the Treasury, in consequence of which he has made me a representation, which you will receive with the other papers.

The Secretary will also lay before you a Letter from Col. Allen[8] relative to the encroachments there is reason to think the British are making on the territories at the Eastern boundary of this state.[9] This is a matter that ought to be attended to immediately to prevent disputes hereafter. I submit it therefore, together with the other matters mentioned in his Letter to your consideration.

I shall lay before you in separate Messages what further may occur to me worthy of your notice. I shall be ready to concur with you in every measure tending to promote the public weal.

Signed

John Hancock
(by the scribe)

Sept. 24, 1783
(so dated in both SL and MA copies)

NOTES

1. As is pointed out elsewhere, the colonists were not supposed to reach a settlement with Great Britain without the consent of Spain and France. But the colonists ignored that provision of their alliance with France. The treaty of peace was signed on 3 Sept 1783, and officially ratified by Congress on 14 Jan 1784.

2. The charters and grants given by the crown to the several colonies were not always clear as to their western extremities. Oftentimes more than one colony laid claim to the same western land. Massachusetts proposed that its charter of 1629 extended its borders, not only in conflict with territory that New York claimed under Indian treaties, but also in rivalry to the claims that Congress had to territory extending to the Mississippi River.

To create an expanse of land that could be sold by Congress to help pay for the war, it was necessary for all of the original states to cede to the federal government the lands they claimed west of the Allegheny Mountains. However, that took some time and some persuasion. Finally, in April of 1785, Rufus King and Samuel Holton as the delegates from

Massachusetts were instructed to cede to the federal government all of the claims of Massachusetts west of New York.

This left unresolved the conflicting claims of Massachusetts and New York to lands east of Lake Erie and south of Lake Ontario, in what might be called the panhandle of New York State. On 14 Mar 1786 (A&R Feb Session, Chap. 107, 1787, 895-897) the General Court moved to inform the members of Congress from Massachusetts that a committee was negotiating with New York to settle the claims. On 5 July 1786 (A&R 1786, Chap. 18, 53) the General Court gave their agents power to settle the territorial claims with New York out of court. Eventually Massachusetts ceded to New York the title to two sets of disputed lands: the so-called "Boston Ten Townships" and the land lying west of the "pre-emption line" and east of the claims renounced by the states to the federal government. The latter tract of land was by far the more extensive.

Massachusetts also had extensive land holdings in Maine, the sale of which promised to contribute much-needed funds to pay off the balance of the Revolutionary War debt not assumed by the federal government. Sales of these lands were arranged to help pay for Massachusetts's war debt. For example, a lottery of certain of the Maine lands was arranged. After the lottery, those who won petitioned the General Court for permission to swap the lands they won in the lottery for property contiguous to some of the land they had won. They could therefore consolidate their holdings in one large tract. (A&R January, 1783, Chap. 149, Mar 18, 1784, 882-883)

Finding that prospective settlers were having difficulty in raising comparatively large sums to purchase big tracts, the General Court instructed its agents to sell the Eastern lands in small tracts, each six miles square. (A&R January, 1791, Chap. 130, 5 Mar 1792, 508)

The sale of the western lands, where there were more disputes as to title, posed more difficulties. There was not only an internal impediment to establishing rights to the lands between the Mississippi and the Appalachians, but the British continued to occupy a number of their outposts in the territory that had been ceded to the United States in the peace treaty. As Curtis noted (1854, 1, 256), "After a lapse of three years from the signature of the preliminary articles, and of more than two years from that of the definitive Treaty, the military posts in the Western country were still held by British garrisons, avowedly on account of infractions of the Treaty on our part." Those American infractions were based upon allegations that the Americans owed property and debts to the Tories, but the motive of the British was more likely to have been a continuance of the lucrative fur trade with the Indians rather than a desire to enforce the treaty rights of the Tories.

Not only were the western lands occupied by the British, but areas of Maine and the northern border with Canada were also affected. The British had long threatened the holdings of Massachusetts in Maine. As early as 7 Aug 1775, the Provincial Assembly concerned itself with the manner in which the British were supplying Boston by making inroads on the cattle, sheep and wood in Lincoln County and dispatched whale boats to Deer Island to protect that area. (A&R Chap 62, 1st session, 7 Aug 1775, 33) On 13 June 1784, Major General Henry Knox, who had fought with Washington at Yorktown and was Washington's particular friend, wrote from New York to General Frederick Haldimand in Quebec that Congress had instructed him to request "the precise time when each of the posts within the United States, now occupied by the troops of His Britanick [sic] Majesty shall be delivered up agreeably to the definitive treaty of peace." (British Library, additional MSS 21, 835, ff. 236r-237v) General Frederick Haldmand, a Swiss-German and rigid disciplinarian, was governor and commander-in-chief of Canada from 1778-1784.

It was important for more than one reason to establish firm boundaries with British Canada. Colonial debtors who wished to escape payment were making their way to Tory country. Without anything like extradition treaties, only persuasion could help. Therefore, on 12 May 1783, Hancock wrote to Governor Haldimand saying that he had received news that two debtors had not fled to New York as had first been thought, but had made their way to Quebec. Having no hope of obtaining custody over the men, Hancock asked that the governor assist in recovering the funds that they had embezzled from Massachusetts. (British Library, additional MSS 21, 835, ff. 156r and v) The letter is signed with Hancock's characteristic signature and therefore is the original and not a copy, as is true of many of the documents in the British Library from Canada.

As a result of Hancock's speech, the General Court appointed a committee to investigate the situation in the east. On 20 Oct 1784, Hancock sent a message to the legislature saying: "Yesterday the Commissioners appointed by the General Court to Enquire what Encroachments were made by British Subjects in the Eastern Territories of this Commonwealth, delivered their report, which I take the earliest opportunity to lay before you." (NEHGS, Box 29) The message by Hancock shows how his health was causing his handwriting to further deteriorate.

3. Feer (1, 71) said of the passage that begins with "a peace" and ends with "other important blessings": "This was not simply the rhetoric of a public celebration. It represented the firmest convictions of thousands of people as reflected in their newspapers, correspondence, and diaries."

4. In this sense, a revival of the classical traditions of democracy. Andrea Palladio (1518-1580) became a popular architect of buildings based upon

classical designs, using soft colors, harmonious blends, and symmetrical proprtions. Mount Vernon is considered an outstanding example of Palladio's style of architecture in the United States.

5. Because they were, for all practical purposes, independent states, the colonies were able to enact excise taxes. Chapter 12 of the 1783 General Court provided a detailed schedule for taxing imports into Massachusetts, such as wine, coffee, tea, cocoa, raisins, snuff, tobacco, wrought silver, and clocks. So, with the war concluded, Massachusetts in spite of her debts did have funds on which it could draw. However, in spite of pleas from the Congress to consent to a proportional tax to relieve the national debt, the states were reluctant to do so, particularly states like Massachusetts which claimed that other states had failed to "call in" their share of federal paper money, i.e., to redeem on the state level, at a discounted rate, the proportional amount of "continentals" that had been assigned to them. "Calling in" their paper money by other states would drain away from Massachusetts the highly devaluated continentals that were circulating within Massachusetts, since colonists would take such currency to other states to redeem them for specie or for updated paper money. (Felt, 199) Massachusetts directed two letters to the Congress, explaining its situation. (A&R 1782, September session, Chap. 74, 304-307)

6. Since the earliest stages of the war, the several states and the Congress had used a variety of means of supporting the war by direct and indirect methods of "taxation." Now that the war was over, those who had loaned money to the governments; had in their possession devalued paper money; had had their possessions requisitioned, for which they had in turn been given notes of credit; or had in various other ways contributed to the support of the national cause, wanted "satisfaction."

How had the states and the Congress financed the war?

It would be an oversimplification to say that the colonies raised money to fight the war in four or five ways. The most accurate position to take is that the colonists raised money any way they could.

Harlow pointed out that there was not much taxable money circulating in the colonies and that additional funds that might have been taxable were largely cut off by the war, which limited trade. (Harlow, 47) In the beginning, the prospects for a victory by the colonists were sufficiently remote so that foreign loans were not possible. But gamble they must, as gamble they did.

In order to understand why their methods were so eclectic, we need to remember several things:

a. The colonists had worked hard to execute their revolt, but they had spent little or no time in deciding how to proceed once the open break with England had been made. Some of the most important men in leading the revolt were ineffectual in carrying it through, e.g., Patrick Henry.

b. The governing bodies had been English. When they were dissolved in 1774-1776, new political entities had to be established. Before funds could be raised, there had to be agencies to raise them, and those agencies were highly inexperienced in finance.

c. The colonies were relatively short on cash, and this shortage had been accentuated by British actions before 1776 and the trade blockade during the war diminished resources further. It is always surprising that the colonial governments and the national Congress could raise as much money as they did through taxes. The cause of revolution and eventual freedom was doubtful. In time of war, people tend to hoard their money rather than release it. What money was released in the early enthusiasms for the war had often been exchanged for notes that inflated rapidly.

d. The Tories, who were often the more prosperous members of the colonies, making money out of favors received from the king, emigrated, taking what valuables they could carry. A major source of income resulted from confiscation of their lands, but, again, it took funds to purchase the confiscated lands, and capital was short in the colonies during the war.

So, as Harlow noted, the colonists gambled on the one asset they had and which we will call the bunch of thirteen carrots of freedom. (Harlow, 48) The colonists themselves pointed this out to their constituents. Felt (183) noted: "The ability of the United States must depend on two things; first, the success of the present revolution, and secondly, on the sufficiency of the natural wealth, value, and resources of the country." The states had seen under the king what oppressive measures could do to prosperity. The Port Act in Boston had closed commerce altogether. The Exclusionary Acts had further limited trade. However, once victory had been won, money could be made. The gamble was enormous. In the beginning, only a minority of the colonists thought they could win. The colonists also pointed to the doubts that many had had at the beginning. John Jay observed: "That the time when honest men might, without being chargeable with timidity, have doubted the success of the present revolution, we admit; but that period is past. The independence of America is now as fixed as fate, and the petulant efforts of Britain to break it down are as vain and fruitless as the raging of waves which beat against their cliffs." (Quotation printed in a circular letter from John Jay, president, Continental Congress, 13 Sept 1779, ordered as Chap. 338, 4 Oct 1779 of A&R of the Province of Massachusetts Bay, 21, 185-189; cf. Felt, 183-4) Until France broke the deadlock in 1779, no foreign power was willing to loan money to the United States. For three years, the colonies had to make it on their own.

Below is a summary of the means used by the colonists to raise money to support the war:

(a) *Bills of credit*: Making it on your own requires ingenuity. In their raising of funds, the colonists were ingenious. Their most lucrative approach was the issuance of paper money. These bills were issued in denominations of six, nine, ten, twelve, fourteen, fifteen, sixteen, eighteen, and twenty shillings. The 1775 issuance was not to exceed £26,000 and the certificates were sometimes known as "soldiers' notes" (Felt, 163) and could be used as a medium of exchange. The process was simple. Without deference to whether there were reserves of gold and silver to back up the certificates, Massachusetts simply printed up the "bills of credit" and issued them as pay, it being understood that the soldiers would use them to buy what they wished. The notes called for interest, of course, but their depreciation was such that the interest gave no relief to the person holding the notes. It should be evident that there were limited facilities to produce such "bills of credit." Paul Revere's workshop was used. The notes of the Third Massachusetts Provincial Congress of 4 June 1775 record that a committee was appointed to report on their issuance, that a messenger was provided to rush them from Revere's to the ailing Major Fuller who had to sign them, and that two captains were assigned "to attend Mr. Revere whilst he is striking off the notes for advance pay to the soldiers, night and day... till they are all struck off." (*Journals*, 1771-1774, 297)

Harlow pointed out that, in taking this approach, the colonists made a contribution to the techniques of public finance. (Harlow, 46) The process is described below:

(1) Notes were issued without support to pay the salaries of soldiers, to buy supplies, etc., or issued by states as security for funds loaned to a colony by its citizenry.

(2) These notes became "paper money" because they were used by the soldiers to buy materials to support their families and were in turn loaned by money lenders to citizens who in turn paid their taxes back to the state with the very money it had issued.

(3) Those who ended up with the "paper money" as well as those who had negotiated such notes paid a "tax" to the state or the Congress issued the notes, because the agency had got full value for the notes whereas the negotiators and holders received or could receive much less.

(4) This "tax" occurred in spite of legislation requiring the paper money to be exchanged at par for specie, because the value of the paper money sank. If such deflated currency were called in at a ratio of ten old notes for one new note, the new notes fell in value as well.

So those states that issued the paper money for full value when it was issued extracted what amounted to a tax on those who negotiated the paper money.

The same gain to the colonial and national governments would have resulted if the governments had exacted heavy taxes from the colonists, while the money remained constant in value. Not only would such heavy taxes have been unpopular, but securing such large sums from a tax bill would not have been possible. The money was simply not there, as far as the average colonist was concerned. However, taking it from such colonists, little by little, as their currency devaluated, was an unconscious, less painful way of gaining the same tax money. As Benjamin Franklin observed in a letter written at Passy to Thomas Rustin on 9 Oct 1780:

They [the Continental Congress] issued an immense Quantity of Paper Bills, to pay, clothe, arm, and feed their Troops, and fit out Ships; and with this Paper, without Taxes for the first three Years, they fought and baffled one of the most powerful Nations of Europe. They hoped, notwithstanding its Quantity, to have kept up the Value of their Paper. In this they were mistaken. It depreciated gradually. But this Depreciation, tho' in some Circumstances inconvenient, has had the general good and great Effect of operating as a Tax, and perhaps the most equal of all Taxes, since it depreciated in the Hands of the Holders of Money, and thereby tax'd them in proportion to the Sums they held and the time they held it, which generally is in proportion to Men's Wealth. (Franklin, a)

Franklin also noted:

"Their Business [Congress's] has been done and paid for by the Paper Money, and every Man has paid his Share of the Tax according to the Time he retain'd any of the money in his Hands, and to the Depreciation within that Time. Thus it has proved a Tax on Money, a kind of Property very difficult to be taxed in any other Mode; and it has fallen more equally than many other Taxes, as those People paid most, who, being richest, had most Money passing thro' their Hands;" (Franklin, b, 234)

In a short essay, Franklin explained the financing as follows:

This Currency, as we manage it, is a wonderful Machine. It performs its Office when we issue it; it pays and clothes Troops, and provides Victuals and Ammunition; and when we are obliged to issue a Quantity excessive, it pays itself off by Depreciation. (Franklin, *Of the Paper Money of the United States of America*; Franklin c, 294)

(b) *Impressment*: Ferguson (58) pointed out that "as early as December 1776, Congress authorized Washington to impress goods and services," i.e., if a person with a team of horses would not agree to exchange his horses for "paper money" issued him by the state's agents, the person was forced to accept such "paper money." On 31 Jan 1778, the provincial legislature appointed a committee to secure blankets, stockings, and shoes, and empowered the committee to seize such items if the owners refuse to accept a reasonable price, and to pay for them in cash. (A&R, Chap. 694, 31 Jan 1788, 264) In 1781, the Massachusetts General Court provided for the impressment of teams of oxen for the quartermaster corps. Farmers owning the teams could be required to go no more than fifty miles, but had to furnish their own victualing, both for themselves and for their teams. (A&R, Chap. 44, May, 1781, 105-6)

Impressment was resorted to only when absolutely necessary. People whose goods had been impressed had to redeem by their "paper money" (provided that they still held the notes and had not used them as the equivalent of money to make purchases), receiving a discounted rate for their notes, in spite of laws requiring that "paper money" be received at par value. Impressment, except against loyalists, was to be avoided, if widespread support for the war by the colonists was to be maintained.

(c) *Confiscation of absentee assets*: The state governments did get funds from the sale of lands confiscated from the Tories, but such income was not a major source of funding for the war. Confiscation of loyalist assets is dealt with more extensively in connection with Hancock's final speech in September of 1793.

(d) *Lotteries*: In spite of the rigidity of religion in many of the colonies, lotteries were held to raise funds for civic improvements such as building bridges and for the war effort. On 19 Feb 1781, Massachusetts held a $100,000 lottery to raise money for clothing for the troops. Prizes were "treasury notes" bearing six percent per annum. (A&R, Chap. 15, 19 Feb 1781, 25-29)

(e) *Issuance of loan notes and treasury notes*: Harlow (49) noted little difference between treasury notes and bills of credit. Dewey (3, 342) stated that as early as May of 1775, Massachusetts floated a loan of £100,000, in denominations as low as £4 , bearing six percent interest. Did the public have funds to buy these notes, and if so, would they purchase them? On 14 May 1775, the Massachusetts Provincial Congress so urged their constituents, saying that the notes issued would in all likelihood be honored by the other colonies and that it was the patriotic thing to do to subscribe. "If you should furnish the money that is now needed, you will perform a meritorious service for your country, and prove yourselves sincerely attached to its interests; but, if an undue caution should prevent your doing this essential service to the colony, the total loss, both of your liberties and that very property which you, by retaining it, affect to save, may be the unhappy consequence." (Journals, 1771-1774, 256)

A second £100,000 of loan notes were floated in August of 1775 with the phrase "Issued in defence of American liberty" printed on the notes. (A&R, Chap. 2, 23 Aug 1775, "An Act for Making and Emitting of Bills of Public Credit"; Dewey, 3, 343; Felt, 167)

In all, Massachusetts issued only $4 million of paper money, in contrast to much larger sums issued by Virginia and North and South Carolina. (Dewey, 3, 343)

(f) *The famous "continentals."* A fourth manner in which "paper money" entered into circulation was via the national Continental Congress. Congress's issuances took two forms. First, Congress could issue "continentals" for its own use, to pay for the several types of expenditures it needed to make to process the war. Again, there was no collateral for these notes, and they therefore depreciated rapidly. Second, Congress could issue notes, apportioning the amount that each state was to redeem. In 1775, for example, Massachusetts was responsible for redeeming $434,244 of the "continentals," it being left up to each colony to determine the means of taxing its citizens to send payment to Philadelphia in four equal installments, in November of 1779, 1780, 1781, and 1782. (Felt, 166) Martin observed, however, that less than half of this paper money was ever received by the states. (Martin, 180) It was impossible for each colony, which did not have funds to deem its own notes, to redeem those of the national government. Therefore, Harlow (51) observed that, as of 3 Sept 1779, the continental bills in circulation amounted to $159,948,880 while the total of tax moneys raised by the states to send to Congress, "presumably for the purposes of redemption," totalled only $3,027,560.

(g) *In kind*: If Massachusetts levied a tax which it thought many colonists would find difficult to meet in paper money or in specie, it could give its citizens the option of paying for it in produce, e.g., beef, pork, grain, etc. The taxables could report to the appropriate office and have their produce credited against their account, often at a fixed rate advertised by the General Court. On 23 June 1781, Massachusetts asked for a loan of rum, salt, and beef, with certificates issued in return. No total amount of such commodities needed was named. (A&R, Chap. 59, 23 June 1781, 636-9) Such flexibility in taxation not only was useful to the citizens, but also was helpful to the government that needed such supplies badly to keep an army well supplied.

(h) *Sale of land*: Footnotes in the Hancock speeches detail some of the efforts of Massachusetts to raise money by selling both its eastern lands in Maine and its western lands in New York state. The Congress also tried to raise money to pay off the debt by selling its lands in Kentucky, Tennessee, and the Northwestern Territory. Felt (208) stated: "They hoped that their extensive lands, which were repeatedly offered for sale, would afford them funds to liquidate a large portion of their debt. But in this, and every other effort, they were painfully disappointed." For example, the *Annals of Congress* (1, 412-414) show that on 28 May 1789, under a section entitled "Western Lands," there were complaints that the western acreage was being offered for sale in too-large plots and that a land office should be set up so smaller purchases could be made. The Congress was also concerned that squatters on the land waiting to establish their rights would be preempted by an absentee who bought large acreage on which the squatters had settled.

(i) *Foreign loans*: For a detailed discussion of the foreign loans received from France, Spain, and Holland, see note two in the speech of 9 Oct 1783. Although the interest on some of these loans was deferred, that was not always the case. Even a portion of the principal could become due. For example, A&R, Chap. 421, 16 Feb 1782, January Session, 854-855, ordered that John de Neufville and Sons of Amsterdam be paid approximately £400.

So it worked like this: a government needed money to buy supplies for the war; the government had little or no specie measured by the Spanish dollar or the British pound, i.e., gold or silver; therefore, the government issued paper money generally without any financial backing; the paper money depreciated in value; therefore the debt of the state or Congress was easier to pay off, because the debt could be satisfied with devaluated currency.

By 1781, the country attempted to return to a specie basis and began calling in the paper money. In the end, "continentals" devaluated at the rate of 1,000 to one. (Harlow, 61) Each state, including Massachusetts, determined the ratio at which its notes could be redeemed for specie, the devaluation resulting in heavy losses for the holders of the notes. As was noted earlier, Hancock himself lost large sums of money by accepting the paper money at its face value as a payment for debts owed to him. As a public official and a patriot, he was not expected to do less. At the outset of the war, there were heavy penalties exacted from those who would not accept the paper money at its face value. But, before the war was over, the discounting was so widespread that the penalties could not be invoked.

Of course Congress could ask the states to furnish "specie." Between 1780 and 1781, said Martin, Congress asked the states for over $10 million in specie, but received "less than one tenth of that amount." (Martin, 180)

Devaluation made the state and federal currencies worth much less than their face value, thus the phrase, "not worth a continental." Martin (181) noted that, in 1780, Congress circulated interest-bearing notes "to replace the worthless Continental dollars at an exchange ratio of forty to one." Therefore, one who held forty of the old "continentals" could exchange them for one new "continental."

One of the ways to put the highly devalued paper money out of circulation was to levy a tax on the colonies which could be paid in paper money. When this paper money was received by Congress, it was burnt. Benjamin Franklin pointed out that, in order to dispose of the highly deflated currency, Congress levied what appeared to be high taxes, but, as they were paid in the deflated notes, the burden was not excessive. "By these Taxes," he observed, "15 Millions of dollars, of the 200 Millions extant, are to be brought in monthly and burnt. This Operation," he continued, "will destroy the whole Quantity, to wit, 200,000,000, in about 14 Months. Thirty Millions have already been so destroy'd." (Franklin, b, 233) As the letters sent by the Massachusetts General Court to the president of the Congress and to the Congress itself on 21 Oct 1782 show, the idealistic solution hoped for by Benjamin Franklin was not altogether successful, because the states did not send in their quotas per month, even as highly inflated as the currency was.

However, those with little resources suffered most from the financing of the war. These people were among those Hancock kept on his mind. Because of his early childhood, the loss of his father, and the continued state of need of his mother and siblings, Hancock had continual reminders of the needs of the poorer class. Benjamin Franklin noted that the depreciation of the currency caused the chief sufferers to be orphans, widows, and those on fixed incomes. (Franklin c; Harlow, 62) However, in many ways, there was not much that could be done for the poor who held paper money or who had been paid in paper money for the loss of their fathers and husbands. As Harlow pointed out, one of the contributions to economics made by the colonists was the issuance of paper money to finance a war, when there was little or no security to back such issuances. (Harlow, 46) Harlow (50) noted that in Delaware and Georgia, paper money was backed by mortgages on real estate and by land confiscated from the Tories, but that elsewhere there was little collateral to support the redemption of the currencies issued by the states. Franklin noted that the depreciation had a certain fairness to it, however, in that depreciation was an indirect tax upon all individuals who held the paper money. Harlow observed that the effect of the depreciation was spread out over an extended period, so that what would have been disastrous had it come all at once was often bearable when stretched over a period of years. (Harlow, 48)

7. A&R 1781, Chapter 27, 4 Mar 1782, 546-547, repealed the legislation that had prohibited the exportation of masts and spars out of the state, presumably to encourage commerce with other states and not with Great Britain. Such repeal encouraged the cutting of timber. Therefore, Chapter 22, 1783 session, 24 Oct 1783, 550-551, provided for measures to protect the cutting of white pine without a license.

8. John Allan, a native of Edinburgh, Scotland, first settled in Nova Scotia but left Canada because he was opposed to the policies of the British government. On 7 Sept 1777, he was appointed by the Massachusetts Council to command the troops to be stationed at Machias in what is now Maine, where he obtained the friendship of the Eastern Indians for the colonists.

9. The difficulties with the Eastern Territories (or Maine) stemmed in part from the failure of the colonists to enforce strictly the provisions of the treaty of peace. During the war, the Continental Congress had left to the states the authority to confiscate the lands of the absentees. When the peace treaty was signed, it permitted Congress to recommend to the states that some amelioration be made to the absentees, but it *specifically* provided that debts contracted before the war and due to citizens in the United States by British subjects, or due to British subjects by citizens of the United States, remained unextinguished. States such as New York, Pennsylvania, and Virginia had passed acts contrary to the debt provision, and South Carolina provided that the debts of colonists to Britons could be made good by grants of land.

Therefore, in reply to the complaints of John Adams, the ambassador to the Court of St. James, that the British had not evacuated colonial lands, including Maine, the British countered that the treaty would only be kept when both sides met their obligations. (*Secret Journals*, 4, 209; and Curtis, 2, 170-174) The British said in effect that the difficulties in Maine would cease when the difficulties with collecting debts owed by the colonists to English merchants had ceased.

The territories in Maine had been giving Massachusetts difficulties for some time, so the problem was not a new one for the General Court. On 24 Apr 1781 (1780 April session, Chap. 71, 408-410), while the war was still in progress, the General Court provided for the protection of the eastern counties. On 3 Mar 1781, Hancock wrote: "By an express just now arriv'd from the Eastern part of this Commonwealth, we have Rec'd advice that the Enemy with Two or Three Arm'd Vessels are daily committing the most horrid Depredation & Cruelties on the Inhabitants who Reside on or near to the Sea Coast in those parts." (MHS)

In the May 1782 session, the General Court decreed (A&R, Chap. 109, 4 July 1782, 243-4) "that every idea of deviating from the treaty of the United states with his Most Christian Majesty in the smallest article, or of listning [sic] to proposals of accommodation with the court of Great Britain in a partial and separate capacity, shall forever be rejected by us with the greatest abhorrence and detestation." No territorial claims of the United States were to be sacrificed.

The A&R October, 1784 session, Chapter 10, 265 dated 21 Oct 1784, concerned the encroachment of the British on the territory of Massachusetts. As late as 8 July 1786 (A&R May, 1786 session, Chap. 127, 341), the General Court was concerned with freedom of access to the St. Croix River, in the treaty which served as the dividing line between Maine and Nova Scotia.

When the peace treaty was signed, the Tories moved to the east side of the St. Croix River and formed the settlement of St. Andrews on Passamaquoddy Bay. However, the ill feelings that had developed between the Tories and the colonists were not dissipated by the treaty. The Tories resented the confiscation of the lands that had been theirs to the southwest of the St. Croix, and the colonists could not forget the Indian raids and the pillage of the British incursions during the war, particularly on the settlements in the Penobscot River area. The residents of the newly created province of New Brunswick were even reluctant to consider the St. Croix as the dividing line designated in the treaty.

This boundary problem continued to be called to Hancock's attention as late as 1785. Governor Carlton of Maine wrote to Hancock that he hoped the settlement of the boundary line "would be considered with temper and attention, essential to the preservation of national peace and harmony." (Williamson, 2, 511) Bowdoin remained involved during his governorship.

In discussing the pros and cons as to whether Maine should become a separate state from Massachusetts, Williamson said that one of the arguments against separating Maine from Massachusetts used in January of 1786 at the Maine state convention was that "the encroachments of the British upon our eastern borders may be resisted with more success, and the dispute settled with more ease, if the connexion be continued, than if it be dissolved." (Williamson, 2, 527)

At the heart of the problem lay an ambiguity in the Treaty of Paris itself. During the war, the Continental Congress had perforce left to the states the authority to confiscate the lands of the absentees. Many of these absentees who had removed themselves to Halifax, the West Indies, or England would naturally seek restitution. The treaty reflects that the American negotiators were well aware of this eventuality.

As the negotiations with the British progressed, Congress foresaw two problems. First, by what means were they to insure the removal of the British troops from territories then occupied by the British in the west along the Mississippi River, in the territory of Maine, and elsewhere? George Rogers Clark had waged a strenuous campaign in the west but the British remained entrenched in a number of areas. Second, Congress knew that there would be pressure by the emigres to include in the treaty provisions for the restoration of their confiscated lands.

In their secret journals, (Microfilm Publication M247, *Papers of the Continental Congress, 1776-1789*, roll 18, item 4, *Secret Foreign and Domestic Journal, 1780-1786*, 186-187), Congress stipulated phraseology in the treaty as follows: "That Congress place the utmost confidence in his Majesty's assurances that he will readily employ his good office in support of the United States in all points relative to their prosperity, and considering the territorial claims [amended to add "as stated in the instructions to their ministers on the 13 August 1779"] of these states as heretofore made, their participation in the fisheries, and of free navigation of the Mississippi not only as their indubitable rights, but as essential to their prosperity, they trust that his Majesty's efforts will be successfully employed to obtain a sufficient provision and security for those rights. Nor can they refrain from making known to his Majesty that any claim of restitution or compensation for property confiscated in the several States will meet with insuperable obstacles, not only on account of the sovereignty of the individual States by which such confiscations have been made, but of the wanted devastations which the citizens of these States have experienced from the enemy and in many instances from the very persons in whose favour such claims may be urged: That Congress trusts that the circumstances of the allies at the negotiation for peace will be so prosperous as to render their expectations consistent with the spirit of moderation recommended by his majesty."

However, when the peace treaty was signed, it permitted Congress to recommend to the states that some amelioration be made to the absentees, but, as said above, it specifically provided that debts contracted before the war, due to citizens in the United States by British subjects or due to British subjects by citizens of the United States, remained unextinguished. Therefore, if a shipping firm in Britain owed a shipping firm in Massachusetts a debt, that debt remained unextinguished. Similarly, if a shipping firm in Massachusetts owed a debt to a shipping firm in Britain, such debt remained unextinguished. This provision of the treaty met with resistance. On 10 Nov 1784, Massachusetts directed the common law courts to suspend the collection of interest on British debts until Congress should clarify to what extent such debts were due. (A&R 1784, October session, Chap. 77, 300-302)

Therefore, on the one hand, the colonists who had confiscated the property of the absentees wanted a strict adherence to the boundaries specified by the Treaty of Paris. On 21 Oct 1784, the Massachusetts General Court endorsed the recommendation of Governor Hancock in his message of 20 Oct and requested the governor to pursue the recommendations by Congress passed on 29 Jan 1784. relative to encroachments on territories of the commonwealth of Massachusetts. (A&R 1784 October session, Chap. 10, 265)

The *Journals of the Continental Congress,* 26, 52-53 read: "Resolved, That a copy of the said letter [of 25 Dec 1783 from John Allan] be sent to the governor of Massachusetts, with a recommendation, that he cause enquiry to be made, whether the encroachments therein suggested, have been actually made on the territories of the State of Massachusetts, by the subjects of his Brittanic Majesty, from the government of Nova Scotia, and if he shall find any such to have been made, that he send a representation thereof to the British governor of Nova Scotia, with a copy of the Proclamation of the United States of the 14 instant which is to be enclosed to the governor of Massachusetts for that purpose." The proclamation passed by Congress on 14 Jan 1784 sent a copy of the peace treaty between England and the United States to each colony, recommending that "they carry into effect the said definitive articles, and every clause and sentence thereof, sincerely, strictly and completely." (*Journals of the Continental Congress,* 26, 29-30)

Whereas, on the other hand, the British, encouraged by the absentees and by the desire to continue a valuable fur trade, remained in possession of vast territories which by the Treaty of Paris they should have evacuated. What was to be done?

On 13 Oct 1786, the secretary for the department of foreign affairs reported to the Continental Congress that John Adams had on 9 Dec 1785 submitted a memorial to the British secretary of state concerning the seventh article of the treaty, saying "that, although a period of three years has elapsed since the signature of the preliminary treaty, and of more than two years since that of the definitive treaty, the posts of Oswegatchy, Oswego, Niagara, Presque-isle, Sandusky, Detroit, Michillimackinae, with others not necessary to be particularly enumerated, and a considerable territory round each of them, all within the incontestable limits of the said United States, are still held by British garrisons, to the loss and injury of the said United States." (*Secret Journals*, 4, 186-187) On 28 Feb 1786, the British secretary, after observing that the fourth article concerning the honoring of creditors on either side had not been met, stated: "The engagements entered into by treaty ought to be mutual and equally binding on the respective contracting parties. It would therefore be the height of folly as well as injustice, to suppose one party alone obliged to a strict observance of the publick faith, while the other might remain free to deviate from its own engagements, as often as convenience might render such deviation necessary, though at the expense of its own national credit and importance." (*Secret Journals*, 4, 188)

In his reply to Adams (*Secret Journals*, 4, 189), the British secretary called specific attention to certain laws of the colonies interfering with the fourth section of the treaty. He observed that by an act of Massachusetts of 9 Nov 1784, "the justices of the court of judicature were directed severally 'to suspend rendering judgment for any interest that might have accrued [upon the demand contained in such actions or suits] between the 19th of April and the 20th of January, 1783' on debts due to British subjects." The part between the single quotes is a direct quotation from the act of the October session, 1784. (A&R 1794, Chap. 77, 10 Nov, 300-302). The Massachusetts act stated that the Bay State was attempting to obtain the attitude of Congress toward the fourth article, but that, as of that date, it had not been able to do so. (See also Curtis, 1895, 1, 170-174, and Curtis, 1854,1, 249-259.)

On 21 Mar 1787, in an effort to relieve the impasse, Congress recommended to the states that state legislation not in keeping with the peace treaty be repealed and that the court system be allowed to use its discretion to hear claims. Nine states passed such acts. But the disputes between the colonists and the British continued.

The border between Maine and New Brunswick continued to cause trouble for a number of years to come. The Treaty of Paris of 1783 had specified that the line between the two states lay in the center of the St. John's River. But, after the War of 1812, Great Britain claimed both banks as well as "all the land above the forty-sixth degree of north latitude, which included about one-third of what was supposed to be the territory of Maine." (Abbott, 431). An attempt to settle using King William of the Netherlands as mediator failed. What resulted was the so-called Aroostook War. An amicable settlement was not reached until 1841 in negotiations between Daniel Webster and Lord Ashburton. Maine surrendered some territory to New Brunswick in exchange for other territory on Lake Champlain and elsewhere. The Ashburton Treaty was ratified by the U.S. Senate on 20 Aug 1842.

HEADNOTE

Date: February 18, 1785

Occasion: On 29 Jan 1785, the *Journal of the House*, MA 5, 237[1] read: "The Secretary brought down the following message from his Excellency the Governor, viz.

> Gentlemen of the Senate, and Gentlemen of the House of Representatives: 'Sensible of my infirm state of Health, and of my incapacity to render that service, and give [sic] that attention to the concerns of the public, that is expected from a person in my station, justice to the public and myself, loudly call upon me not to prejudice the community, but rather to promote its benefit; to effect which, I am obliged, Gentlemen, to inform you, that some relaxation is absolutely necessary for me; and that I must at present give up all attention to public business, and pursue the means of regaining my health.— Under these circumstances, I must request to be indulged with a resignation of the Chair; and, from my present state of health, I hope I shall be able in a few days, to meet the General Court in the Senate Chamber, and take my leave in a formal manner.—I am induced to give this notice to the two Branches of the General Court, that they may have opportunity,if they please, to make inquiry of me with respect to any public matters that have been committed to me; and I shall be ready at all times to give them every information and satisfaction in my power. Boston, January 29, 1785. John Hancock.' "

On Friday, 18 Feb 1785, 286, the *Journal of the House* stated:

> The Secretary came down and said, that his Excellency the Governor proposed meeting the two Houses this day, in the Representatives chamber, if agreeable to them: Whereupon *Ordered*, That Mr. *Osgood*, Mr. *Bourn* and Mr. *Cross*, with such as the Hon. Senate may join, be a committee to consider what measures may be proper to be taken, in consequence of the said proposal. Sent up for concurrence.

Later that same day, those appointed by both houses presented their joint recommendations to the House.

> The Hon. Mr. *Stone* brought down a report of the committee of both Houses, on the proposal of his Excellency the Governor, to meet the two Houses in the Representatives chamber this day, That it will be most expedient for the two Houses to meet in the Representatives chamber, and that a joint committee be appointed to wait on the Governor, and acquaint him that the two Houses will attend him accordingly. In Senate, 18 Feb 1785. Read and accepted, and thereupon ordered, That *William Heath* and *Tristram Dalton*, Esq'rs. with such as the Hon. House may join, be a committee to wait on the Governor accordingly. Sent down for concurrence. Read and concurred, and Mr. *Osgood*, Mr. *Phillips* and Mr. *Bourn* were joined. Ordered, That Mr. *Osgood*, Mr. *Robbins* and Mr. *Clarke*, be a committee to consider of the order in which his Excellency the Governor shall be received in the chamber where the House sit.

The result was that special chairs were to be assigned to the speaker of the house and the president of the senate, with the representatives to sit on the north side of the room and the senators to sit in the south west corner of the room. Front seats were reserved for the lieutenant governor and members of the Council. Special guests were to sit in the southeast corner. The Senate disagreed with the seating and stated that, if they were not given their usual seats, they would stand. The Senate won. The Senate was assigned to the seats it usually occupied, and harmony was restored so the governor could speak. (*Journal of the House*, MA, 18 Feb 1788, 287)

The reply of the House and Senate to the governor's speech of resignation is found in MA Senate Unenacted 277/1, "Report of the Committee on the Message of Gov. Hancock containing his resignation," 1 Feb 1785.

According to a letter from James Warren to John Adams dated 26 Feb. 1784, Hancock had threatened earlier to resign:

> I dare say we shall not be Embarrassed by the Modesty of our present first Magistrate. Whatever Qualities he may want in the Opinion of others, he is himself a Stranger to any deficiencies and never once thought the duties too Arduous for him, or the honour too high, or the situation too delicate. he

[sic] has, however, lately threatened us with a Resignation. he [sic] was either Affronted that the General Court the last Sessions did not answer his Speech, or he took it in his head that he would be a great Man as well as General Washington. he [sic] proclaimed his design in all Companies with great formality and summoned his Council to receive it. they [sic] met. he [sic] altered his resolution and we continue as happy as ever in his Administration. his [sic] Character is neither stained with ridicule or Contempt, a privilege peculiar to himself. (Warren-Adams Letters, 2, 235-236)

SOURCES

Journal of the House, MA (printed) and SL (longhand), vol. 5, 348-350;* Massachusetts *Spy*, 24 Mar 1785, 3; *Independent Chronicle* 17 Mar 1785, 3; Boston *Gazette*, 21 Mar 1785, 3.

The copy of the proceedings between 1784 and 1785 housed in the MA is the only one of the early journals of either the House or the Senate that is printed. In the printed version in the MA, the messages concerning his resignation appears only on p. 237, whereas, in the handwritten copy in the SL, the messages appeared on pp. 237-238. When the printed version was completed, it evidently replaced the manuscript copy in the MA.

*No copy in either Senate Journal.

There were difficulties in getting Hancock to furnish the General Court with a copy of his address. On 21 Feb 1785, the House ordered that a committee be appointed to request the governor to furnish a copy. (*Journal of the House*, SL, 5, 303)

On 24 Feb 1785, the House did appoint a committee of Mr. Gorham, Mr. Osgood, and Mr. Rowe to prepare an order for "requesting of the late Governor a copy of his address at his resignation." (*Journal of the House* MA, 5, 292)

Evidently the Senate had been asked to concur with the House request, because Mr. Gorham was charged on 24 Feb 1785 to ask whether the Senate had acted on the request prepared by the House. The Senate declined to do so. (*Journal of the Senate*, SL, 24 Feb 1783, 5, 303)

Therefore the House charged Messrs. Gorham, Phillips, and Thatcher "with such as the Hon. Senate may join" to request of Hancock a copy of the address. (*Journal of the House*, MA, 5, 24 Feb 1785; or according to SL, Gorham, Bacon, and Hunt, *Journal of the Senate*, SL, 24 Feb 1785, 5, 303)

A copy was received on 14 Mar 1785 by letter and appeared in the *Journal of the House*, as noted above. However, no manuscript copy of the address can now be located.

TEXT

Gentlemen of the Senate, and Gentlemen of the House of Representatives:

Thoroughly impressed with the importance and necessity of the duties of every office being carefully attended to, and the business annexed to it being executed with punctuality and dispatch, I found myself obliged, in faithfulness to my Constituents to address you on the 29th January last, when I informed you that the infirm state of my health, would not permit me to render that service, and give that attention to the concerns of the public which I judged absolutely necessary, and was expected from a person in my station, and that some relaxation was requisite for me, and that for the present, I must give up all concerns in public business; and that as soon as my health admitted of my being abroad, I should wait upon the two branches of the General Court, and take my leave of them in form.

This is the first moment, Gentlemen, that my health has enabled me to accomplish those views; and the task which I have now before me is truly delicate and arduous. I meet you to resign the Chair of Government to which by the kind suffrages of my Countrymen, I have for some years been raised, to thank you and them for every instance of their partiality towards me, and to express the warm wishes of my heart, for the prosperity and welfare of this Commonwealth, and the other United States of America.

Born in a country of freemen, and educated in the purest principles of civil Liberty, from my earliest youth I have felt myself interested in the welfare of my Country. When her rights were invaded by a formidable enemy, I could not but espouse her cause, and chearfully[2] [sic] hazard my little all in supporting it.[3] My utmost aid, feeble as it was, I gave to her friends, and no man rejoiced more sincerely, when she was emancipated from her chains, and took the rank which she deserved among the Nations of the Earth. Called by my Countrymen, to fill some of the most important offices in their gift, and at a crisis when their *all*[4] was at stake, my heart has often trembled when I reflected upon the burden which I sustained. I knew that my abilities were not equal to the task, but my conscience ever testified that I meant uprightly to perform my duty. My Country will judge how far I succeeded, and though justice may compel them to censure me, I persuade myself their candour will acquit my intentions. Pardon me, Gentlemen, for saying thus much; it may appear a degree of vanity, but I could not take my leave of you, without declaring to you, and the world, that I ever loved my Country with a warmth of affection which I cannot express; and that in all my conduct, I meant to serve her best interests.

Happy I am that my health permitted me to continue in your service, 'till the late war came to a period, and my heart warms when I recollect the present agreeable situation of my native land. Blessed with the freest[5] and best constitution of government, at peace among ourselves, and respectable in the view of foreign nations, we are distinguished above others, by the favour of Heaven. And it must be owing to ourselves, if we are prevented from enjoying the highest degree of[6] political happiness. Let it be our constant solicitude, Gentlemen, to avoid every abuse of our Liberty, and to improve and defend the public blessings indulged us, with wisdom, firmness and integrity.

I am happy, likewise in leaving the government of this Commonwealth in a state so little divided, and with such prospects of future peace and prosperity.—It would have given me pleasure, had Providence permitted me to contribute to these valuable ends in the public station, which the kindness of my friends had alloted me. Nothing but an apprehension of my inability to perform the duties of an office so important, and thus of impeding the public business, could have induced me to wish a relief from the fatigues of government, and permission to return to a private station. It gives me great pleasure, however, to leave the Chair in the hands of a Gentleman, whose integrity and abilities qualify him for the first offices of his Country, and entitle him to the good-will of all its Friends.—

Permit me now, Lieut. Governor,[7] Gentlemen of the Council, Mr. President, and Gentlemen of the Senate, Mr. Speaker, and Gentlemen of the House of Representatives, permit me to thank you individually, to thank the people whom you so worthily govern, for all the public honors which they have bestowed upon me, and for all the support and assistance which you have given me in performing the duties of my office. When I look around me, and discern the men who have shared the dangers of the late arduous revolution; which I recollect the many instances of support, of kindness and civility, which in the days of our distress, and in[8] more happy periods, I have received from them, my heart is affected, and I cannot express my feelings.—Accept, Fathers, Friends, and Fellow-Citizens, accept the effusions of my gratitude, and my most ardent wishes for your private prosperity and your public happiness.

Returning now to a private station, I shall feel it my duty, and I know it will be my inclination to support to the utmost of my power the good government of my country, and if at any future period, any service may be derived from my feeble exertions, the call of my country will be most readily and chearfully obeyed.

May the Supreme Ruler of Nations, take this Commonwealth, and the other United States of America, under his Holy Protection, may be ever direct and prosper their public Councils; may he guard them from every danger, and delight to make them a name, and a praise in the earth, so long as the sun and the moon shall endure.

Having declared my resignation of the government of this Commonwealth, and acknowledged my obligations to my fellow-citizens, I have only to address myself to you, respectable Sir, as Lieutenant-Governor, and upon whom the government of this Commonwealth constitutionally now devolves, may your administration be easy to yourself, and happy to the people, may the good influence of it be felt to the remotest parts of the Commonwealth; and when you shall have served your generation faithfully here, may you be crowned with never ending felicity. Of you Sir, and of the Gentlemen of the Council, I now take my leave; of you also, respectable Sir, as President of the Senate, and of the Gentlemen of the Senate, and of you also, Mr. Speaker, and Gentlemen of the House of Representatives, I take my leave; may every indulgence of a kind Providence attend you, may you be happy here, and appear hereafter with characters of honor.

John Hancock

NOTES

1. There are three MS copies of the short message that Hancock sent to the legislature on 29 Jan 1785. A draft in Hancock's hand, with numerous corrections, is housed in the Boston Public Library as MS. 286. It gives the appearance of something that Hancock struck off on his own, without the help of any scribe.

A copy appears as MA Senate Unenacted #277, "Message of Gov. Hancock, containing his resignation," 29 Jan 1785.

The third MS copy appears in the *Journal of the House*, SL for Saturday, 29 Jan 1785, 5, 237.

The message announcing the resignation also appeared in the Boston *Gazette*, 21 Mar 1785, 4.

"Report of Committee on the Message of Gov. Hancock containing his Resignation" is housed as MA, #277/1. The response was endorsed by both the House and the Senate. The reply states: "...they most ardently wish you the restoration, & confirmation of your health, & that the public may yet receive the benefit of such exertions for the good of your Country, as they have so early & long experienced."

2. *Gazette* omits "chearfully."

3. It is difficult to determine how great were Hancock's financial losses during the revolution. John Adams's statement concerning the status of the Hancock fortune before and after the revolution is probably as good as can be found.

> What shall I say of his fortune, his ships? His commerce was a great one. Your honored father [Tudor's father], at that time, not less than a thousand families were, every day in the year, dependent on Mr. Hancock for their daily bread. Consider his real estate in Boston, in the country, in Connecticut, and the rest of New England. Had Mr. Hancock fallen asleep to this day, he would now awake one of the richest men. Had he persevered in business as a private merchant, he might have erected a house of Medicis. Providence, however, did not intend or permit...such a calamity to mankind....[But, following his election to the state legislatures] the quivering anxiety of the public...compelled him to a constant attendance in the House; his mind was soon engrossed by public cares, alarms, and terrors; his business was left to subalterns; his private affairs neglected, and continued to be so to the end of his life. If his fortune had not been large, he must have died as poor as Mr. S. Adams or Mr. Gerry. (Adams, 10, 260)

4. *Gazette* does not underline "all."

5. *Gazette* reads "free."

6. *Gazette* omits "degree of."

7. Thomas Cushing, who had followed in Hancock's footsteps since 1780, was supposed to be elected governor following Hancock's resignation so he could keep the spot available in case Hancock wished to be reelected. However, Cushing lost the election to Bowdoin, so that when Hancock ran again, he had to run against Bowdoin. Warren wrote to John Adams on 4 Sept 1785: "Mr. Bowdoin was chose [sic] by the two Houses

and all is Peace, Tranquillity and Satisfaction. Mr. Hancock's Influence, which was great, was in favour of Cushing, more probably to keep a Door open for Himself at another Election, and by that means retrieve the Mistake he made in his Resignation, than from any other Principle. All other Parties were obliged to unite to defeat his Purposes, and he at last in Despair of his main Design, gave out that he did not care who was chose." (Warren-Adams Letters, 2, 262)

   8. *Gazette* omits "in."

HEADNOTE

Date: Saturday, 2 June 1787

Occasion: Hancock had not run for reelection after his abrupt resignation in 1785 until 1787, when he was reelected. There is some support for the position that Hancock resigned when he saw that the financial status of the commonwealth had deteriorated, but undoubtedly in 1785 he was in poor health. At any rate, he was returned to office in 1787, and made this short acceptance speech.

SOURCES

Senate Unenacted #654 (1787), MA;* A&R 1787, 986-7 (beginning with 1787, the *Acts & Resolves* began to reprint the governors' addresses).

Boston *Gazette*, 4 June 1787, 2-3; *Independent Chronicle*, 7 June 1787, 3; Worcester *Magazine*, first week in June 1787, 122.

*No copy in either Senate Journal.

TEXT

Gentlemen of the Senate & Gentlemen of the House of Representatives—A very respectable Committee by you appointed, have notified me that the Citizens of this Commonwealth have elected me Governor for the year ensuing. To promote the happiness of my native country hath always been the great object of my pursuit, & to merit the approbation of my fellow Citizens was ever my highest Ambition—Defective as I may have been in the pursuit of the first, I should feel myself ungrateful to an high degree, did I not, upon the present occasion, acknowledge the kind partiality of my Countrymen in granting me so great a share of the second.

When from a want of health I retired from the place of Chief Magistrate of this Commonwealth, I did not expect to be again called to the important trust, but since my fellow citizens, have, without any solicitations of mine, seen fit in the present day to call upon me for my exertions, I cannot abuse that partiality which they have so often manifested towards me, by declining the office.

The suffrages of a free people, would in common times render an apology for my appearing in this place quite unnecessary, but in the present situation of public affairs, it becomes necessary for me to declare, that I am so far from accepting the office from a dependance [sic] upon my own ability to restore the Government to its needed tranquility, that it is, Gentlemen, on your wisdom & prudence alone, I rely, for those measures which may lead us to public Safety; from you the people will look for those laws & ordinances which will secure the blessings intended for them by the happy Constitution of Government they have established. Of me they have a right to expect that I shall exert the powers vested in me for their benefit & advantage, & it shall be my highest ambition not to disappoint them. To preserve, Gentlemen, sacredly and inviolate, our excellent Constitution of Government; to relieve as much as possible the burdens of the people, & to maintain a strict adherence to private & public Justice, shall be the great objects of my administration, & in the pursuit of them, I doubt not of your Assistance and Support, as well as those of all Good men.

Having declared, Gentlemen, my acceptance of the office to which I am elected, I am now ready to comply with the qualifying requisitions of the Constitution.[1]

John Hancock

Boston June 1st. 1787[2]

NOTES

1. This part of the final sentence was inserted by Hancock himself, presumably at the time he personally signed and dated the document.

2. Again, this speech was written the day before it was delivered.

HEADNOTE

Date: 18 Oct 1787

Occasion: The time had come for the several states to consider the ratification of the federal Constitution. Hancock realized that the legislature was split in its sentiments and therefore treaded cautiously. However, there are several passages that indicate plainly that he looked upon the document favorably.

The *Journal of the House* for 18 Oct 1787 stated: "The Committee on the part of the House appointed to visit upon His Excellency the Governor reported that they had had attended that service & that his Excellency would meet the two Houses in the Senate Chamber in a quarter of an hour. The Secretary came down & said that his Excellency was in the Senate Chamber and requested the attendance of the House. Whereupon the House went up to the Senate Chamber where His Excellency delivered the following Speech."

The *Independent Chronicle* and the Boston *Gazette* stated that Hancock delivered the speech in the House Chamber.

SOURCES

House Manuscript #2572 (1787), MA; *Journal of the House* 8, 156-60, MA ; *Journal of the House* 8, 156-60, SL;* A&R, 1784 1893), 992-5.

Boston *Gazette* 22 Oct 1787, 2; *Independent Chronicle* 25 Oct 1787, 1; Worcester *Magazine*, 4th week in Oct 1787, 43-45.

*No copy in either Senate Journal.

TEXT

Gentlemen of the Senate, and Gentlemen of the House of Representatives, I have directed the Secretary to lay before you several Letters which I have received in the recess of the Court, among them you will observe a letter from His Excellency the Governor of New York,[1] wherein he expresses his apprehensions[2] of a wicked combination entered into by a number of persons, with an intention to deprive this Commonwealth, & that State, of the[3] Lands which have been lately the subjects of a compact between them. I need not enlarge on the subject, as it will appear to you that the pretentions of these people are rather an insult upon this Government than an apology for their conduct. I have no doubt of your immediate attention to a subject by which the interest & honor of the Commonwealth are so much affected.[4]

The General Convention having compleated [sic] the business of their appointment, & having reported to Congress "A Constitution for the United States of America," I have received the same from that Honorable Body, have directed the Secretary to lay it, together with the Letter accompanying it[5], before the Legislature, that measures may be adopted for calling a Convention in this Commonwealth, to take the same into consideration.[6] It not being within the duties of my office to decide upon this momentous affair, I shall only say that the Characters of the Gentlemen who have compiled this System,[7] are so truly respectable, & the object of their deliberations so vastly important, that I conceive every mark of attention will be paid to the report. Their unanimity in deciding those Questions wherein the general prosperity of the Nation is so deeply involved, & the complicated rights of each separate State are so intimately concerned, is very remarkable, & I persuade myself that the Delegates of this State when assembled in Convention, will be able to discern that, [sic] which will tend to the future happiness & security of all the people in this extensive Country.—[8]

By a resolve of the Legislature of the thirteenth of June last,[9] the Governor was requested to raise a Body of troops of not less than five hundred, nor more than eight hundred men, as the publick exigency in his opinion should require, to be stationed in the Counties of Hampshire & Berkshire, to be continued in service for the space of six months, unless sooner discharged in the whole, or in part, by the Governor with the advice of Council; in pursuance of that resolve, I issued orders for raising five hundred men rank & file, & appointed Lieutenant Colonel Lyman[10] to the command of them, but the recruits never amounted to more than two hundred & fifty, which were, as the event shews [sic], fully adequate to the business for which they were raised. Soon after the General Court were adjourned, the intelligence from those Counties indicated a military force to be unnecessary, but as you had by your Act of the twenty ninth of June,[11] requested me to write to the Governors of other States, for leave to march troops into their Territories if it should be found necessary to pursue any number of men collected there,[12] for the purpose of annoying this Commonwealth, there would have been an impropriety in disbanding the troops immediately upon writing Letters in consequence of that request; they were therefore continued in service until the thirteenth of September, when by the unanimous advice of the Council, I gave orders for disbanding them. But as some persons who were under charge for taking an active part in the late commotions were confined in the Gaol of the County of Berkshire,[13] with advice of Council I gave orders to Major General Paterson[14] to afford such Guard to the prison, by drafts from the Militia, as the Sheriff of that County should find to be necessary.—

I have the pleasure to congratulate you, Gentlemen, on the return of peace & good order thus far & while I sincerely lament these insurrections, which have greatly injured the interest & character of our Country, I am persuaded you will join with me in the sentiment that this unhappy occurence cannot be considered as a certain mark of the indisposition of the people to good order & government. Similar insurrections are found in the history of all Countries, & although in this State, where no Tax can be levied, or law made, but by the consent of the immediate Representatives of the people, & where every grievance can be redressed in a Constitutional way, they are inexcusable, yet from my knowledge of the great degree of intelligence, which our fellow citizens at large possess, I am obliged to believe, that a sense of their own reputation, & the regard they have to their own interest & happiness, will produce a due subordination to Government, a regular obedience to the laws, without a further application of Military force.—

The Legislature, having by their Act of the thirteenth of June, indemnified from criminal prosecution all the persons concerned in the late Commotions, excepting those convicted of crimes, & nine others specially named in the Act;[15] the Supreme Executive, on similar sentiments, conceived that a pardon to Jason Parmenter, Henry McCullock, Henry Gale, & Jacob Shattuck who were then under sentence of death for treason,[16] might be granted consistently with the dignity & safety of the Government, & that such a measure would have a tendency to restore the publick tranquilty, to conciliate the affections of the people, & to establish peace in the State. Accordingly by & with the advice of Council on the thirteenth day of September I sealed as pardon for those persons.—

As a Tax in the course of the year will become necessary, an attention to the mode of taxation may tend to the peace as well as to the prosperity of the Commonwealth. While we were a part of the british [sic] empire we necessarily acquired a habit of fixing our attention upon Taxes levied from Polls & Estates to supply the Treasury, this we were[17] then, from the peculiarity of our situation, compelled to, but I earnestly recommend it to your consideration, whether that as the wealth & power of the State must depend upon the cultivation of the Soil, & the encouragement of the useful arts, it has not become our duty to lessen, as far as we possibly can, the taxes upon Polls & Estates & to raise the necessary supplies in a great measure by imposts on foreign goods, by Excises on luxuries imported,[18] & by Taxes on those superfluities which can never be an advantage to the Community, unless it be by producing funds to support the publick burdens.—

In consequence of an Act made in October 1786,[19] a Mint has been erected for coining Cents, & a very considerable quantity[20] of copper coin will soon be ready for circulation, I wish your attention to the subject, & that a law may be made to prevent the daily frauds & impositions arising from the circulation of foreign copper coin in this Commonwealth.—

I have not gone minutely into all the communications which are necessary to be made, but shall by particular messages make such as may be for the publick interest; & shall be very ready to unite with you in all measures tending to a proper regulation of our Finances, the promoting of virtue & knowledge, to the establishing of good order & government, securing the liberties & increasing the happiness of the United States in general, & those of this Commonwealth in particular.--

John Hancock[21]

Council Chamber
October 17, 1787

NOTES

1. According to Evans (150), there was a letter from Clinton to Hancock in early August of 1787, giving indications of "a private and clandestine negotation with the native Indians." However, no copy of this letter could be located. A part of Governor Clinton's correspondence was published before the New York Archives were burned, but not for August of 1787. The letter is not in the House or Senate Unenacted files of the MA. What is found in MA Unenacted Senate 269, 269/2, 269/3, 269/4, and 269/5 are letters between 9 Feb 1785 and 9 Oct 1785 concerning the western lands. The letters are by Governor Clinton to Bowdoin; Gerry and

King to Bowdoin; Governor Bowdoin to Gerry, and Holten and King; Rufus King to Lowell and Sullivan; and Bowdoin to Clinton. The Letter File (1786-1792), vol. 289 of the MA does contain two letters concerning the western lands. Evidently, on 16 May 1787, Hancock wrote to Clinton, and Nathan Dane delivered the letter.

(1) There is a letter from Dane in New York to Governor Hancock dated 31 May 1787.

(2) A second letter from Dane in New York to Governor Hancock dated 1 June 1787 stated that on 23 Apr 1787, the commissioners appointed by New York and Massachusetts wrote to the commissioners appointed by Congress to run the line of jurisdiction between New York and Massachusetts, in an effort to set a time when all three sets of commissioners could get together. Dane endorsed a letter from the commissioners appointed by Congress to the Commission of New York and Massachusetts.

George Clinton had been a delegate to the First Continental Congress and had been an officer in the Continental Army. As the first governor of New York, serving from 1777-1795 and again from 1801-1804, Clinton as president of the New York State Convention had opposed ratification of the Constitution. It was in part to counter Clinton's position that Madison, Hamilton, and Jay wrote the *Federalist Papers*. Therefore, the correspondence in 1787 was between two governors whose positions on the forthcoming debates on ratification in their respective colonies were to differ.

2. *Acts & Laws* reads "apprehension."

3. House Unenacted #2572 has "the" inserted above the line in the hand of the scribe.

4. The land stipulations in the charters of the several colonies were often vague so that territorial disputes occurred. In order to clarify the status of lands beyond the Appalachians, the several states relinquished their far western claims to the federal government. On 13 Nov 1784, Massachusetts empowered its delegates to Congress to cede "such part of that tract of land belonging to this Commonwealth, which lies between the rivers *Hudson* and *Mississippi*, as they may think proper." (A&R, Chap. 33, 13 Nov 1784, 111) This eliminated disputed claims between the federal government and the states, but disputes between the states remained. One of these contested territories concerned two tracts of land in what is now central and western New York. In reality, Massachusetts claimed much of what is now New York state, an area stretching from the Mohawk and Delaware Rivers in

the east to the point where all of the states had ceded their lands to the federal government in the west.

On 4 June 1784, the General Court appointed commissioners authorized to fix the boundary with New York. (A&R, 1784, Chap. 1, 4 June 1784, 5-6) A letter of 11 July 1785 from Governor Bowdoin to Governor Clinton confirmed that Massachusetts had appointed its comissioners just as had New York. (MA, House Unenacted 26915)

During the negotiations between New York and Massachusetts, the territory to be considered was reduced approximately in half. The agreement reached at Hartford on 16 Dec 1786 provided that the jurisdictional rights to two tracts were to be vested in New York while Massachusetts could sell or lease the lands, with the profits going to the treasury of the Bay Colony. A copy of the treaty can be found in the office of the secretary of state of New York, Deeds, vol. 23, dated 16 Dec 1786, recorded 2 Feb 1787. A fire destroyed New York's copy of the original treaty. Massachusetts's copy of the original treaty is found in the records of the secretary of state of New York in the MA identified by the title, *Western Boundary Treaty with New York, 1786*. It is an extra-large-sized parchment signed by ten delegates from New York and ten from Massachusetts, including signatures by Rufus King, Theophilus Parsons, and James Sullivan. The first provision of the treaty stated that Massachusetts "doth hereby cede grant release and confirm to the State of New York forever" the land identified in the treaty, whereas the second provision stated that New York "doth hereby cede grant release and confirm to the Commonwealth of Massachusetts" the right of preemption to the soil, including Indian rights and claims of New York.

The two tracts of land were:

a. The Boston Ten Townships.

b. The larger section between what became known as the preemption line in the east and and Lake Erie and Lake Ontario in the west.

Although the treaty had been signed, it had to be ratified by both states. For New York, the *Journal of the Senate* (20, 4-5) of the state of New York stated that, in his speech to the legislature of 13 Jan 1787, Governor Clinton announced that a mutual agreement had been reached with Massachusetts.

On 25 Jan 1787, the *Journal of the Senate* of the state of New York (20, 13) recorded that the Senate and House appointed a joint committee to inspect the agreements stipulated in the treaty.

On 7 Feb 1787, (20, 22) the *Journal of the Senate* of the state of New York committee reported to the Senate that it had seen the report, was satisfied with its provisions and had seen the treaty recorded and deposited in the office of the secretary of state.

On 7 Mar 1787, Rufus King and Nathan Dane wrote Governor Bowdoin that they presumed that Massachusetts had or would pass "a law conformable to the principles of the late Act of the State of New York." (MA Senate Unenacted 663; A&R, 21 Nov 1787, Chap. 101, 794 ordered that the agreement of 21 July 1787 be recorded by the secretary of state)

Once the treaty was ratified by both states, the line of demarcation had to be established. On 1 Mar 1787, the New York legislature passed an act to run the line of jurisdiction between New York and Massachusetts. (MA Senate Unenacted 663/1)

There were four sets of rights to consider:

a. The rights of the Indians to territory they had not ceded by the first Treaty of Fort Stanwix, amounting roughly to the land west of a line running from Fort Stanwix to the Unadilla River, a tributary of the Susquehanna. This line, known as the Property Line, cut the state of New York into an eastern and a western region.

b. The "pre-emptive" rights of the state of Massachusetts, which would give title to the land freed of preexisting claims.

c. The rights of squatters who had gone onto the land, sometimes with papers of dubious legality.

d. Soldiers' rights to land promised them in return for service. Many of these rights were satisfied by what was known as the Military Tract, stretching to the east of the new preemption line, north of the Boston Ten Townships.

For more details concerning the disposal of the lands, see the following sources: Evans, Paul D., "The Frontier Pushed Westward," in *History of the State of New York*, ed. A.C. Flick, 5, 143-162; Hotchkin, J.H., *A History of the Purchase and Settlement of Western New York...* New York, 8-12; Higgins, Ruth L, *Expansion in New York*, 115-126; Ellis, Davis M. et al, *A Short History of New York State*, Ithaca, 150-162.

The disposition of the Boston Ten Townships was relatively uneventful. The 230,400 acres were purchased from Massachusetts by Samuel Brown and fifty-nine associates for 12 1/2 cents per acre or a total price of $3,333. (Ellis, 154; Hotchkin, 8)

The disposition of the second, much larger tract was protracted. The conspiracy to which Hancock referred was an attempt by two companies to secure long-term leases from the Indians on this large tract, and so evade the preemptive rights of Massachusetts. Whether such leases of 999 years would be overruled as a violation of the law against perpetuities was a question not yet answered at the time Hancock made his speech.

The main figures in the efforts to gain control of the valuable lands were as follows:

Oliver Phelps and Nathaniel Gorham: Oliver Phelps from Connecticut joined forces with Nathaniel Gorham of Massachusetts to purchase from the commonwealth of Massachusetts, on 1 Apr 1788, the entire Genesee holdings, i.e., from the new preemption line set by New York and Massachusetts on west to Lakes Erie and Ontario, for £300,000 of the deflated Massachusetts currency or $100,000 to be paid in three yearly installments. If Phelps and Gorham began by paying into the treasury of Massachusetts sizeable portions of the £300,000 (which would amount to one-fourth of the Massachusetts currency in circulation), the price of the remaining three-fourths could go up. This might cause the purchasers to pay the remainder of the £300,000 in money worth more than the money had been at the time of purchase. Phelps and Gorham were not concerned. They were securing such vast acreage for the 1734 equivalent of $175,000. They did not think a moderate price rise would ruin them. But the problem of raising the funds got difficult. Therefore Phelps and Gorham subdivided the company into 120 shares, with the land as collateral. Phelps and Gorham hoped to retain as many as their finances would permit and sell the rest.

John Livingston: The former Indian commissioner, John Livingston, attempted to secure a 1,000-year lease from the Indians. Organizing in 1787 the New York Genesee Company, which in turn merged with another set of Canadian speculators known as the Niagara Genessee Company, Livington proceeded to assemble the Indian tribes to bargain for their rights.

By 30 Nov 1787, Livingston had succeeded in getting the Seneca Indians to lease to him and his company all of the land west of the property line that had been fixed by the first Treaty of Fort Stanwix in 1768 with the Six Nations of Iroquois. The line ran roughly west of the watershed of the Susquehanna River. On 8 Jan 1788, Livingston signed a lease with the Oneida Indians, covering most of their land east of the line of property. He thus secured some type of rights to twelve million acres or two-fifths of the state of New York. (Evans, 5, 1522)

State officials of Massachusetts were also seeking to buy the Indian rights. In a second Treaty of Fort Stanwix in 1784, the state acquired vast holdings of the Iroquois. By the end of 1790, the state claimed that the Indians had ceded their lands to Massachusetts. The General Court ruled that Livingston's leases amounted to purchases and thus were void under the law against perpetuities. But it would take a court ruling to dismiss Livingston's claims. In early 1788, the courts had not ruled against Livington so he was still claiming his rights.

The Phelps-Gorham-Livingston Merger: One source of support to help Phelps and Gorham swing their big land acquisition was the Livingston group, so Phelps-Gorham merged with them, giving them shares in his company in return for their Indian rights. Phelps and Gorham also deeded to the Niagara Genesee Co. one-sixtieth of the rights in the entire tract. So Phelps got both the Indian rights from Livingston and his Canadian associates and the preemptive rights from the state of Massachusetts. However, thinking that he himself should renegotiate with the Indians, he signed a new purchase with them on 8 July 1788, but he was only able to get from the Indians the most eastern part of the western lands, i.e., the tract between the preemptive line drawn by New York and Massachusetts and the Genesee River, with a smaller tract on the western side of the river. Evidently Phelps considered his deal with Livingston sufficient to rule out Livingston's rights to the land but not good enough to secure the Indian rights to the land.

On 21 Nov 1788, the General Court of Massachusetts reconfirmed the sale of that portion of the lands for which Phelps had got Indian rights on 8 July 1788. (A&R, 21 Nov 1788, Chap. 28, 35-37) The Livingston group failed to produce the capital to pay for their shares in Phelps's project. Therefore, Phelps and Gorham parted company with Livingston and associates, giving them as their share for helping to clear the Indian rights four townships in return for their surrendering their shares to the larger holdings originally bargained for and for which Livingston could not pay. The Canadian company, however, held on to their one-sixtieth interest. Naturally the Indians had already sold the rights to some of their lands to other persons, both speculators and squatters, so the title bought by Phelps and Gorham was not altogether clear. It was not even certain what they had bought.

Furthermore, when the federal government proposed to absorb the state debts, the price of Massachusetts currency began to rise, making it more difficult for Phelps and Gorham to pay their installments.

The Foundering of the Phelps-Gorham Plan: When Phelps and Gorham reported that "from unforeseen disappointments they are unable to discharge the First Payment of the Sale," they secured a postponement of their first payment. (A&R 1789, May Session, Chap. 89, 23 June 1789, 579-580)   But when the postponed payment fell due, they did not have the money and had to reach an agreement with the state.

On 5 Mar 1790, Phelps and Gorham surrendered back to Massachusetts two-thirds of what they had acquired, namely that two-thirds to which the Indians had not surrendered title, i.e., the land west of the Genesee River up to Lakes Erie and Ontario. However, Phelps and Gorham no longer had the rights to the one-sixtieth that had been dealt to the Canadians, so that part of the land was not returned to Massachusetts.

On 16 Feb 1791, the General Court granted full power "to make a final & absolute settlement with the Honble. *Nathl. Gorham* and *Oliver Phelps* Esqrs. relative to the Bond for *one hundred Thousand Pounds* in State Notes." (A&R 1790, Chap. 44, January Session, 16 Feb 1791, 179)

The General Court made final the repossession of the western two-thirds of the land on 18 Feb 1791.   (A&R 1790, Chap. 45, January Session, 18 Feb 1791, 179)

On 5 Mar 1791, the General Court gave the committee an extension in time to negotiate with Phelps and Gorham for their remaining rights, requesting it to report back in fourteen days. (A&R 1790, Chap. 103, January session, 5 Mar 1791, 211-212)

On 11 Mar 1791, the committee was again instructed to report back the results of the negotiations.   (A&R 1790, Chap. 156, January session, 11 Mar 1791, 238)

Higgins, (118) who consulted the Holland Land Company Manuscript Book, reported that in 1790, Phelps, Gorham, and their associates agreed to surrender two-thirds of the land back to Massachusetts and, as what they elected to keep amounted to more than the one-third estimated, Phelps and Gorham later paid for the excess. On 18 Nov 1790, most of the "Phelps-Gordham Purchase" was sold to Robert Morris for eight pence an acre. (Higgins, 118)

William Morris: Morris, who had been secretary of finance during the revolution, resold what he had bought from Phelps and

Gorham to the London associates, specifically to Sir William Pulteney, John Hornby, and Patrick Colquhoun.

With this success, Morris negotiated to secure the rights relinquished by Phelps-Gorham, i.e., the territory between the Phelps-Gorham Purchase and Lakes Erie and Ontario.

On 8 Mar 1791, the General Court empowered a committee to convey to Samuel Ogden the area of land the rights to which had been relinquished by Phelps and Gorham. (A&R 1790, Chap. 121, January Session, 8 Mar 1791, 221-223)

On 17 June 1791, Ogden, acting as agent for Morris, acquired the whole block. (A&R 1791, Chap. 65, May session, 17 June 1791, 416) Morris then moved to quiet the claim that the Canadian group held via the original Phelps-Gorham grant of one-sixtieth of the lands, later allowing Massachusetts to convey to him unrestricted rights to the entire property (A&R 1792, May session, Chap. 30, 20 June 1792, 157-158; Evans, 5, 159)

The Holland Land Company: On 11 May 1791, Morris received from Massachusetts five separate deeds in escrow, i.e., if Morris succeeded in meeting his financial commitments, the deeds would be released to him. Retaining the easternmost fifth part that he had acquired from Massachusetts, Morris sold before the end of July of 1793 the remaining territory to Dutch bankers. These bankers, who became known as the Holland Land Company, needed again to quiet the Indian title. They authorized Morris to negotiate with the Indians. After the war was over, Morris succeeded in September of 1797 in securing the majority of Indian rights.

On 20 June 1792 (A&R 1792, May session, Chap. 30, 20 June 1792, 157-158) Morris was conveyed the one-sixtieth part of his lands that had been retained by the General Court.

In February of 1793, the General Court renegotiated the bonds signed by Morris and Ogden for the Morris tract. (A&R 1792, Chap. 5, January session, 5 Feb 1793, 224-5) But Morris was unable to retain control of his eastern strip of 500,000 acres. It was sold at a sheriff's sale, in part to the Wadsworths, whose name is still famous in western New York.

With the Indian titles quieted and the preemptive rights secured, both the London Associates and the Holland Land Company then began to dispose of their holdings.

5. On 18 Sept 1787, Charles Thomson, the secretary of the Continental Congress, sent a circular letter to the governors of the thirteen states,

requesting "that Your Excellency will be pleased to lay the same before the Legislature in order that it may be submitted to a Convention of Delegates chosen in Your State by the People of the State in conformity to the resolves of the Convention made & provided in that case." To this letter, Thomson attached the proposed Constitution together with a letter from George Washington as president of the Congress in which Washington urged adoption, pointing out that the document could not possibly please every state in every respect, but that it would allow a basis for union. (National Archives, *Journal of the Continental Congress*, Department of State Files, 98-99) The copy of the circular letter is handwritten, whereas the proposed Constitution and the letter from Washington are in printed form.

6. The notification to the states read as follows:

In CONVENTION, Monday, September 17, 1787.

PRESENT,

The States of New-Hampshire, Massachusetts, Connecticut, Mr. Hamilton from New-York, New-Jersey, Pennsylvania, Delaware, Maryland, Virginia, North-Carolina, South-Carolina, and Georgia:

RESOLVED,

That the preceding Constitution be laid before the United States in Congress assembled, and that it is the opinion of this Convention, that it should afterwards be submitted to a Convention of Delegates, chosen in each State by the people thereof, under the recommendation of its Legislature, for their assent and ratification; and that each Convention assenting to, and ratifying the same, should give Notice thereof to the United States in Congress assembled.

RESOLVED, That it is the opinion of this Convention, that as soon as the Convention of Nine States shall have ratified this Constitution, the United States in Congress assembled should fix a day on which Electors should be appointed by the States which shall have ratified the same, and a day on which the Electors should assemble to vote for the President and time and place for commencing proceedings under this Constitution: That after such publication the Electors should be appointed, and the Senators and Representatives elected: That the Electors should meet on the day fixed for the Election of the President, and should transmit their votes certified, signed, sealed and directed, as the Constitution requires, to the Secretary of the United States in Congress assembled, that the Senators and Representatives should convene at the time and place assigned; that the Senators should appoint a President of the Senate, for the sole purpose of receiving, opening and counting the votes for President; and, that after he shall be chosen, the Congress, together with the President, should, without delay, proceed to execute this Constitution.

By the unanimous Order of the Convention,

GEORGE WASHINGTON, PRESIDENT

William Jackson, Secretary

7. *Journal of the House* reads "who have compiled this System, & are so truly respectable..."

8. A&R, Chap. 9, 25 Oct 1787, 740-742, was entitled, "Resolve Recommending to the People to Choose Delegates for the Convention, to Meet at the Statehouse in *Boston*, the Second Wednesday in *January* Next, Agreeably to a Resolution of Congress, &c." The selectmen of the several towns were directed to assemble the people to elect delegates to the convention.

9. A&R 1787, May Session, dated this act as Chapter 21, 15 June 1787, 677-679. Chapter 21 is also discussed in the outline at the conclusion of this speech.

10. Seemingly William Lyman (1755-1811) who served as aide to General Shepard during Shays's Rebellion and who also served in both the Massachusetts and the United States House of Representatives.

11. A&R Chap 55, dated 29 June 1787, of the May 1787 session, 697-9, directed Governor Hancock to request that troops from Masssachusetts be permitted to enter the territories of other states where the insurgents had taken refuge, in order to return them to Massachusetts.

12. A part of the rebels had taken refuge in Connecticut, New York, Vermont, and New Hampshire. None of these states was enthusiastic about allowing the militia from Massachusetts to invade their states. Although all four states eventually issued proclamations against the rebels, their position in regard to allowing Massachusetts militia to invade their territory remained ambiguous. (Starkey, 153)

13. Nathaniel Austin and Peter Wilcox had been confined in the Berkshire jail. On 15 June 1787, they managed to make their escape from the jail by

getting the jailer drunk. Their escape left Shattuck, Gale, Parmenter, and McCulloch still jailed. (Feer, 419)

14. John Paterson (1744-1808) was the commander of the Massachusetts militia charged with suppressing Shays's Rebellion. Paterson had fought at the Battle of Monmouth; wintered at Valley Forge; and fought at Saratoga. He was a member of both the Massachusetts and the New York Assemblies. (Eggleston, Chap. 8)

15. See outline of Shays's Rebellion in the appendix to this speech.

16. As was noted above, persons who had already been convicted of treason were not pardoned by the legislative act of June 1787. Most of the men who had been convicted had not remained in Massachusetts, but had fled to neighboring colonies from which they could not be extradicted. From the research done by Feer, only Luke Day could be traced as returning to his original place of residence. (Feer, 422)

17. House #2572 had "were" inserted above the line by the scribe.

18. Under the Articles of Confederation, the states were empowered to levy taxes on imports.

19. On 8 July 1786, Chapter 125, 340 of the May 1786 session, the General Court asked when the federal mint would be ready and requested the governor to inquire.

Evidently, plans to use the federal mint miscarried because on 17 Oct 1786, as Chapter 3, 71-73 of the September session, the legislature provided that a state mint be created to issue gold, silver and copper coins, in keeping with the stipulations of the United States Congress.

Chapter 90, 11 Nov 1786, 387, of the same session allocated £200 for the construction of the mint and directed persons having Massachusetts copper coins to turn them in to the Commissary General and to receive receipts thereof.

As Feer observed (1, 258-259), "the parents of this act were probably not surprised to see their child languish and die young. They certainly could not have expected gold or silver bullion to find its way into the mint. Several months passed before even the first copper coins appeared, and when the mint went out of business after a year or two of operation, only a fraction of the pennies which had been authorized had been minted." See also Felt, 202-207, and Yeoman, 31-32.

Again, in the October 1788, session, Chap. 56, 263, 22 Nov. 1788, a further proposal was passed for the coining of copper. The purpose of this act was to use up the copper provided for coinage before the federal Constitution prohibited the states from issuing coin.

20. A&L reads "amount."

21. Hancock himself signed House Manuscript #2572, dated it, and added "Council Chambers."

APPENDIX TO 17 OCT 1787 ADDRESS

CHRONOLOGY OF EVENTS OF SHAYS'S REBELLION*

*This chronology was compiled because the leading sources for the rebellion had not attempted to give a succinct timetable of the events of the rebellion, and, without that timetable, Hancock's role in the Shays affair could not be understood.

22 Aug 1782   Convention of delegates from fifty towns met at Hatfield in Hampshire; said to be the first meeting of the insurrection. Known as the Eli riots. (Minot 34-37)

29 Aug 1786   Feer, 1, 179-180: "But if any day can be singled out to mark the opening of the rebellion which lasted in acute form for six months, which saw thousands of men under arms, and which alarmed people from New Hampshire to Georgia and brought cheer and hope to people as widely separated as Sheffield, Massachusetts, and London, England... then... August 29, 1788, was it." [Luke Day and the challenge to court in Northampton, in Hampshire County, was the event of which Feer spoke.]

8 Sept 1786   Governor Bowdoin addressed members of the Governor's Council who happened to be in town, receiving their approval to send out militia. (Minot, 52)

8 Nov 1786   General Court agreed that "payment in kind" was a possible way to pay debts. (*An Act Providing for the More Easy Payment of the Specie Tax...* A&R, 1786, Chap. 39, 8 Nov 1786, 90-97 Feer, 1, 257) By allowing such payments, the General Court hoped to reassure the farmers that they had opened a new method for them to retain their property.

10 Nov 1786   Governor Bowdoin suspended the *habeas corpus* for anyone dangerous to the commonwealth. (A&R, 1786 Chap. 41, 10 Nov 1786, 102-3; Feer, 1, 253)

25 Nov 1786   a. General Court issued a pardon to all who who had participated in the insurrection between 1 June 1786 and 15 Nov 1786, provided each took an oath of allegiance. (A&R 1786 Chap. 44, 15 Nov 1786, 111-113; Feer, 1, 251)

                 b. General Court provided for preliminary hearings before a justice of the peace for any debt of over four pounds so that debtors could arrange for payment with minimal court costs and no lawyer's fees. (A&R 1786, Chap. 43, 15 Nov 1786, 105-111; Feer, 1, 255)

28 Nov 1786   Bowdoin issued warrants for the arrest of Jacob Shattuck, leader of the Middlesex County rebellion, and four of his followers: Oliver Parker, Benjamin Paige, Nathan Smith, and John Kelsey. (Feer, 2, 320)

30 Nov 1786   Capture of Shattuck. (Starkey 98-101; Minot 78-9; Feer, 2, 321)

20 Dec 1786   Bowdoin began holding secret sessions with his Council for two weeks to resolve the insurgency. (Feer, 2, 347)

4 Jan 1787   In his capacity as commander in chief, Bowdoin announced that 4,400 militia would be raised to be commanded by Major General Benjamin Lincoln. (Feer, 2, 347; Starkey 128)

19 Jan 1787   Bowdoin gave an official order to raise the militia. (Minot 99)

4 Feb 1787   General Court's declaration "That a Horrid and Unnatural Rebellion Exists Within this Commonwealth." (A&R 1786, Chap. 5, January Session, 424-6)

7 Feb 1787   General Court endorsed a proclamation by Bowdoin that the four men named below were not to be pardoned and set the following bounties:

                  Shays: £150; Luke Day, Adam Wheeler, Eli Parsons: £100 each (Feer, 2, 387; Starkey 150)

8 Feb 1787   Governor authorized to issue a proclamation for rewards not exceeding £150 for "Ringleaders or Principals of the present Rebellion." (A&R, Chap 16, Jan session, 433)

16 Feb 1787   General Court offered unconditional pardon to any private in the insurgent forces who joined the state militia. (A&R, Chap. 56, 16 Feb 1787, 176-180; Feer, 2, 385-6; Minot 137-8)

6 Mar 1787   New York asked to cooperate in rounding up rebels. (A&R, Chap. 102, January session, 484-485)

8 Mar 1787   Vermont asked to turn over fugitives. (A&R, Chap. 125, January session, 500-501)

10 Mar 1787   General Court appointed three commissioners to promise indemnity to insurgents except for Shays, Parson, Wheeler, Luke Day, or any person who fired upon or killed any citizen. (A&R, Chap. 145, January session, 10 Mar 1787, 515-516; Minot, 163; Feer, 2, 386-388)

April-July 1787   Bowdoin and then Hancock and the General Court considered during this period the requests for pardons that came in from the convicted men. Eventually all except Bly and Rose were pardoned (Feer, 2, 420) although the Council often acted with reluctance, delaying death sentences and setting new ones several times before pardons were issued. The extreme example of the way in which the Council acted occured on 16 June 1787, wherein the Council ordered that the reprieve of Peter Wilcox, Nathaniel Austin, Henry McCulluck, and Jason Parmenter not be made known until the men were actually standing on the gallows. The rationale was to show the strength of the government and to test the assertion of some former Shays's insurgents that they would again take up arms to free the condemned men. (Feer, 2, 416-8)

30 Apr 1787 Sentences to Paramenter, McCullough, Wilcox, Austin, Gale, and Shattuck confirmed by the General Court.

2 June 1787 Bowdoin out as governor; Hancock in.

5 June 1787 Hancock informed the General Court that it was "absolutely necessary" to retain troops in western Massachusetts to forestall additional rebellion. (Governor's Message, A&R, 1786-1787, 5 June 1787; Feer, 2, 406)

13 June 1787 General Court passed a "Resolve for Raising from the Troops in Service in the Western Counties, 500 Men, and Not More Than 800, for the Protection of Said Counties, and Also Pardoning and Indemnifying a Certain Description of Citizens Excepting Nine." (A&R 1787, Chap. 21, May Session, 677-9; Feer said the act was incorrectly dated 15 June in the A&R)

1. Troops were to serve for six months.

2. Pardons to all who had committed acts of treason since 1 June 1786, except nine.

3. Those already convicted, because the governor had to pardon those, (Feer, 2, 415) so those sentenced were within his prerogative.

SURVEY OF THOSE INSURGENTS CONDEMNED FOR SERIOUS CRIMES

condemned to
death in Great   Aaron Knap of Stockbridge, Berkshire County
Barrington   Samuel Rust, Pittsfield, Berkshire County

8 April (Starkey, 192-193)	Peter Wilcox of Lee, Berkshire County [Nathaniel Austin of Sheffield, Berkshire County Joseph Williams of New Marlborough, Berkshire County Enoch Tyler of Egremont, Berkshire County
convicted at Northampton 9-21 April of capital offenses (Starkey, 195-196)	Jason Parmenter of Bernardston,Hampshire County Henry M'Culloch of Pelham, Hampshire County John Wheeler of Hardwick, Worchester County Daniel Ludden(ing)ton of Southampton, Hampshire County Alpheus Colton of Longmeadow, Hampshire County James White of Colrain, Hampshire County
convicted in early May in Worcester County (Starkey, 196)	Henry Gale of Princeton,Worcester County
convicted on 9 May in Middlesex County (Starkey,196; Minot, 179)	Job Shattuck of Groton, Middlesex County

plus the following named persons
whose crimes were to be exempted by Act of
June 15, 1787

(Starkey, 220; Feer, 2, 415) County	Daniel Shays of Pelham, Hampshire County Luke Day of West Springfield, Hampshire County William Smith of West Springfield, Hampshire Eli Parsons of Adams, Berkshire County Perez Hamlin of Lenox, Berkshire County William (Elisha) Manning of Sandisfield, south Eleven Thousand Acres, Berkshire County (got seven years of hard labor for looting) David Dunham of Sheffield, Berkshire County Ebenezer Crittenden of Sandisfield, Berkshire County Jacob Fox of Washington, Berkshire County

All of these were eventually pardoned.

15 June 1787   In keeping with the General Court's proclamation recommendation of 13 June 1787, in which Hancock offered pardons to all except the nine specified as having committed unpardonable offenses and those already condemned.

29 June 1787   Resolve "Requesting the Governor to Write to Those States Where the Insurgents Have Taken Residence, &c.": "to request of them, and all other States where any of the rebels may lurk...that the troops of this State, if necessary, be permitted...to march the troops of this Government into the limits of the States where any of the rebels may have taken residence." The resolve ended by stating that "no further acts of grace & clemency...can be made to the persons aforesaid." (A&R 1787, Chap. 55, May session, 697-9 August, 1787) Szatmary (115) noted that "following the example of New Hampshire governor John Sullivan, Hancock joined the government force in August and made a military tour of western Massachusetts."

13 Sept 1787   Hancock disbanded the troops, and the four already convicted who had not escaped and were still in jail were pardoned by the governor and Council, i.e., Parmenter, McCullough, Gale and Shattuck. (Feer, 2, 419) Since pardons were given by the governor, no act by General Court was required.

early in January Luke Day captured by New Hampshire residents seeking the 1788 bounty, but there was no real follow-up by the courts to prosecute him; the exact date on which the bounty hunters turned him over to Massachusetts authorities appears not to be known.

10 March 1788   Petition from Shays and Parsons read before the House asking for full pardon and admitting they had been wrong in attacking the government. MA House Unenacted #2740 is the original letter. (see also Minot, 189-191; Feer, 2, 421-2)

Three excerpts from the letter are notable:

"Your Petitioners penitrated [sic] by the melancholy
sense of their late errors, and anxious once more to
return to the bosom of their Country...humbly beg
leave to supplicate the mercy of the Legislature in
their favour...

"They have indeed been deluded but they beg the Hon.
Court to believe that their hearts are still warmd [sic]
with every sentiment & respect, reverence &
attachment to the rights, and Liberties of the People,
& to the Laws & Constitution of the Government...

"If it be thought necessary that an example of their
sufferings should be continued to prevent similar
disorders to those they have so rashly occasioned in
this Commonwealth. [sic] Your Petitioners would
hope that this end is already attained; as they conceive
in the estimate of their distresses there is scarcely an
inconvenience or misfortune to which they have not
already been expos'd."

31 Mar 1788   General Court withdrew the offer of a reward for the
capture of the fugitives. (A&R 1787, Chap. 128,
Febuary session, 896-897; Feer, 2, 421, n. 2)

19 June 1788   In response to the petition for pardons of 10 March
1788, the General Court passed a "Resolve for
Pardoning Treasons in the Late Rebellion." (A&R
1788, Chap. 75, May session, 212-214; Feer, 2, 421)

"And whereas Peace order and a due Submission to
the Laws are now restored and established in this
Commonwealth and it is the wish of the Legislature
as far as possible to draw a Veil over the late unhappy
Commotions by the Indemnity of all the Citizens
who were concerned in the Insurrections & Rebellion
aforesd, *Resolved* that all and every Citizen...are fully
& freely indemnified and are hereby entitled to the
indemnity and to all the Benefits & advantages of the

said Resolution." The oath of allegiance had to be taken within six months.

6 Dec 1787   In the end, only two men, John Bly and Charles Rose, were actually executed, and they had combined treason with looting. (Feer, 2, 420-421)

HEADNOTE

Date: 31 Jan 1788

Occasion: Evidently Hancock made a brief statement just before the close of the morning session on 31 Jan 1788, saying that his poor health had prevented him from prior attendance, and that, in the afternoon, he wished to present a proposition for their consideration. (Elliot, 2, 134-5) For further information, see the essay on this speech provided after the paraphrase.

SOURCES

MA, *A Journal of a Convention of Delegates chosen by the People of the Commonwealth of Massachusetts...* vol. 278, 160 ff.

Virtually identical reports of the conclusion of the speech itself appear in the following: Boston *Gazette* 25 Feb 1788, 4; Massachusetts *Gazette* 22 Feb 1788, 1-2; Massachusetts *Spy*, second week in March of 1788, 308-9. Pierce, 79-81, 224-5; Elliott, 2, 135

The accounts begin with the following paraphrase of Hancock's initial remarks:

PARAPHRASE

When the Convention met in the afternoon, His Excellency the President observed that a motion had been made and seconded, that this Convention do assent to, and ratify, the Constitution, which had been under consideration; and that he had in the former part of the day intimated his intention of submitting a proposition to the consideration of the Convention. My motive, says he, arises from my earnest desire to this Convention, my fellow-citizens, and the public at large, that this Convention may adopt such a form of government as may extend its good influences to every part of the United States, and advance the prosperity of the whole world. His situation, his excellency said, had not permitted him to enter into the debates of this Convention: it however appeared to him necessary, from what had been advanced to them, to adopt the form of government proposed; but, observing a diversity of sentiment in the gentlemen of the Convention, he had frequently had conversation with them on the subject; and from this conversation, he was induced to propose to them, whether the introduction of some general amendments would not be attended with the happiest consequences. For that purpose he should, with the leave of the honorable Convention, submit to their consideration a proposition, in order to remove the doubts, and quiet the apprehensions of gentlemen; and if in any degree the object should be acquired, he should feel himself perfectly satisfied. He should, therefore, submit them; for he was, he said, unable to go more largely into the subject, if his abilities would permit him; relying on the candor of the Convention to bear him witness that his wishes for a good Constitution were sincere. [His Excellency then read his proposition.] [Hancock's concluding statement is given at the end of the proposed amendments.]

THE PROPOSED AMENDMENTS*

NOTE: THE PARTS IN BRACKETS BELOW DID NOT APPEAR IN THE RESOLUTIONS PRESENTED BY HANCOCK ON 31 JAN IN BOSTON, BUT DO APPEAR IN THE RESOLUTIONS ON FILE AT THE NATIONAL ARCHIVES. See National Archives Microfilm Publication M338, *Commonwealth of Massachusetts...* vol. 1, 1 p, signed by Hancock as president and William Cushing at vice president.

Cf. MHS, 6 Feb. 1788, Livingston II Papers, 1786-1788, *Resolve of the Convention of Massachusetts 6 Feb 1788* with the text of Hancock's propositions as revised by the committee to which they had been referred; three of what appear to be sets of proposed revisions located in the MA, 278, 156 ff.; MA, 278, 154 ff.; MA, 278, 155-6; an amended copy in the Samuel Adams Papers, New York Public, 6 Feb 1788.[1]

[Commonwealth of Massachusetts]

[The Convention of the Delegates of the People of the Commonwealth of Massachusetts February 6th 1788]

The Convention having impartially discussed and fully considered the Constitution for the United States of America, reported to Congress by the Convention of Delegates from the United States of America, and submitted to us by a Resolution of the General Court of the said Commonwealth, passed the twenty-fifth day of October last past; and acknowledging, with grateful hearts, the goodness of the Supreme Ruler of the Universe, in affording the people of the United States, in the course of his providence, an opportunity, deliberately and peaceably, without fraud or surprise, of entering into an explicit and solemn compact with each other, by assenting to and ratifying a new constitution, in order to form a more perfect union, establish justice, insure domestic tranquillity, provide for the common defence, promote the general welfare, and secure the blessings of liberty to themselves and their posterity; do, in the name, and in behalf of the people of the Commonwealth of Massachusetts, *assent to* and *ratify* the said CONSTITUTION OF THE UNITED STATES OF AMERICA.

And as it is the opinion of this Convention that certain amendments and alterations in the said Constitution would remove the fears and quiet the apprehensions of many of the good people of this Commonwealth, and more effectually guard against an undue administration of the federal government; the Convention do therefore recommend that the following alterations and provisions be introduced into the said Constitution:--

First. That it be explicity declared that all powers not expressly delegated to Congress [by the aforesaid Constitution], are reserved to the several States, to be by them exercised.

Secondly. That there shall be one representative to every thirty thousand persons [according to the census mentioned in the constitution], until the whole number of representatives amount to (_____). [two hundred].

Thirdly. That Congress do not exercise the powers vested in them by the fourth section of the first article, but in cases where a State shall neglect or refuse to make adequate provision for an equal representation [or refuse to make regulations therein mentioned or shall make regulations subversive of the rights of the people to a free and equal representation in Congress], \agreeably to the Constitution.

Fourthly. That Congress do not lay direct taxes, but when the moneys arising from the import and excise are insufficient for the public exigencies [nor then until Congress shall have first made a requisition upon the States to assess, levy and pay their respective proportions of such Requisition agreeably to the Census fixed in the Said Constitution in such a way and manner as the Legislation of the States shall think best and in such case if any State shall neglect or refuse to pay its proportion pursuant to such requisition, then Corgress may assess and levy such States proportion together with interest thereon at the rate of six percent per annum at the time of payment prescribed in such requisition.]

Fifthly. That Congress erect no company of merchants with exclusive advantages of commerce.

Sixthly. That no person shall be tried for any crime, by which he may incur an infamous punishment, or loss of life, until he be first indicted by a grand jury, except in such cases as may arise in the government and regulation of the land and naval forces.

Seventhly. The Supreme Judicial Federal Court shall have no jurisdiction of causes between citizens of different States, unless the matter in dispute [whether it concerns the realty or personalty] be of the value of (_____) [three thousand] dollars, at the least [nor shall the Federal Judicial Powers extend to any action between citizens of different States, where the matter in dispute whether it concerns the Realty or Personalty is not of the value of fifteen hundred dollars at the least.]

Eighthly. In civil actions between citizens of different States, every issue of fact arising in actions at common law, shall be tried by a jury if the parties or either of them, request it.

Ninthly. That the words, "without the consent of Congress," in the last paragraph of the ninth section of the first article, be stricken out. [*Ninthly.* Congress shall at no time consent that any person holding an office of trust or profit under the United States shall accept of a title of nobility or any other title or office, from any King, Prince or Foreign State].[2]

—AND the Convention do, in the name and in behalf of the People of this Commonwealth enjoin it upon their Representatives in Congress at all times until the alterations & provisions aforesaid have been considered, agreeably to the Fifth article of the said Constitution, to exert all their influence and use all reasonable and legal methods to obtain a ratification of the said alterations and provisions, in such manner as is provided in the said Article.[3]

—AND that the United States, in Congress assembled, may have due notice of the Assent and Ratification of the said Constitution by this Convention, it is *Resolved,* That the assent and ratification aforesaid be engrossed on parchment, together with the recommendation and injunction aforesaid, and with this Resolution, and that *His Excellency John Hancock, Esquire,* President, and the *Honble* [sic] *William Cushing, Esquire,* Vice-President of this Convention, transmit the same, counter Signed by the *Secretary* of the Convention, under their hands and seals, to the United States, in Congress assembled.[4]

[John Hancock, President]
[Wm Cushing, Vice President]
[George Richards Minot, Secretary]

[Pursant to the Resolution aforesaid, We the President and Vice President above named Do hereby transmit to the United States in Congress Assembled the same Resolution with the above assent and Ratification of the Constitution aforesaid for the United States, And the recommendation and injunctions above specified.]

[In witness whereof We have hereunto set our hands & seals at Boston in the Commonwealth aforesaid the Seventh day of February, Anno Domini Seventeen Hundred and eighty eight in the twelfth year of the Independence of the United States of America.]

[John Hancock, President]
[Wm Cushing, Vice President]

This, gentlemen, concluded his Excellency, is the proposition which I had to make; and I submit it to your consideration, with the sincere wish that it may have a tendency to promote a spirit of union.

NOTES

1. Wells refers to these in vol. 3, 259 as "conciliatory propositions," but that title does not appear on the manuscript.

2. The entire ninth resolution as presented by Hancock was replaced with the portion bracketed.

3. *Elliot's Debates*, (1836), 1, 353-355 shows that Massachusetts's suggestions for a Bill of Rights were introduced, along with the suggestions of the other colonies, on Friday, 29 Sept 1787. It was not until 4 Mar 1789 that twelve amendments were brought to a vote before the Congress assembled in New York. Of these twelve, ten were approved and submitted to the states. The first two amendments were rejected. The Elliot account stated: "No returns were made by the states of Massachusetts, Connecticut, Georgia and Kentucky," (1836, 1, 377) even though John Adams as president of the Senate and vice president of the United States was presumably present.

A comparison of the suggestions of Massachusetts with the Bill of Rights eventually adopted shows that what is now the Tenth Amendment was adopted substantially as proposed by Massachusetts, and that the grand jury and trial by jury suggestions of Massachusetts were also included.

4. The portions bracketed indicate the sections amended and are reflected in the copy on file at the National Archives. Where the language of Hancock and the language of the forwarded resolutions have parallel variant readings, the National Archives copy is bracketed.

HEADNOTE

Date: Wednesday, 6 Feb 1788

Occasion: The final remarks before the vote was taken on the Constitution were made in the afternoon session. The honorable Mr. Turner began the debate "in a nervous and animated speech" (Worchester *Magazine*, formerly the Massachusetts *Spy*, #23, fourth week in March, 1788, 334) in which he vigorously opposed adoption. Captain Southworth then spoke briefly against adoption, while Mr. Symmes spoke for some time in favor. *"The time agreed upon for taking the question being arrived, and the same being called for from every quarter,* His Excellency the PRESIDENT, rose and addressed the Hon. Convention, as follows:" (*Spy*, 334)

After Hancock spoke and the vote was taken, there were 187 yeas and 168 nays, making a difference of 19 votes.

SOURCES

Debates and Proceedings of the Convention of the Commonwealth of Massachusetts... (Boston: 1856, 279-80); Massachusetts *Gazette*, 11 Mar 1788, 2; Boston *Gazette*, 10 Mar 1788, 3; Worcester *Magazine*, fourth week in Mar 1788, 334-5; Massachusetts *Centinel*, 8 Mar 1788, 20; *Independent Chronicle*, 13 Mar 1788, 200. See also Elliot, 2, 178-181.

TEXT

Gentlemen—

Being now called upon to bring the subject under debate to a decision, by bringing forward the question—I beg your indulgence to close the business with a few words. I am happy that my health has been so far restored, that I am rendered able to meet my fellow citizens, as represented in this Convention. I should have considered it as one of the most distressing misfortunes of my life, to be deprived of giving my aid and support to a system, which if amended (as I feel assured it will be) according to your proposals, cannot fail to give the people of the United States a greater degree of political freedom, and eventually as much national dignity, as falls to the lot of any nation on the earth. I have not since I had the honor to be in this place, said much on the important subject before us: All the ideas appertaining to the system, as well those which are against as for it, have been debated upon with so much learning and ability, that the subject is quite exhausted.

But you will permit me, Gentlemen, to close the whole with one or two general observations. This I request, not expecting to throw any new light upon the subject, but because it may possibly prevent uneasiness and discordance from taking place amongst us and amongst our constituents.

That a general system of government is indispensably necessary to save our country from ruin is agreed upon all sides.—That the one now to be decided upon has its defects all agree,—but when we consider the variety of interests, and the different habits of the men it is intended for, it would be very singular to have an entire union of sentiment respecting it. Were the people of the United States to delegate the powers proposed to be given, to men who were not dependent upon them frequently for elections—to men whose interests, either from rank, or title, would differ from that of their fellow-citizens in common, the tasks of delegating authority would be vastly more difficult; but as the matter now stands, the powers reserved by the people render them secure, and until they themselves become corrupt, they will always have upright and able rulers. I give my assent to the Constitution in full confidence that the amendments proposed will soon become a part of the system—these amendments being in no wise local, but calculated to give security and ease alike to all the States, I think that all will agree to them.

Suffer me to add that let the question be decided as it may, there can be no triumph on the one side, or chagrin on the other —Should there be a great division, every good man, every one who loves his country, will be so far from exhibiting extraordinary marks of joy, that he will sincerely lament the want of unanimity, and strenuously endeavor to cultivate a spirit of conciliation, both in Convention, and at home.[1]

The people of this Commonwealth are a people of great light—of great intelligence in publick business—They know that we have none of us an interest separate from theirs—that it must be our happiness to conduce to theirs—and that we must all rise or fall together—They will never, therefore, forsake the first principle of society, that of being governed by the voice of the majority—and should it be that the proposed form of government should be rejected, they will zealously attempt another.—Should it, by the vote now to be taken be ratified, they will quietly acquiesce, and where they see a want of perfection in it, endeavor in a constitutional way to have it amended.

The question now before you is such as no nation on earth, without the limits of America, has ever had the privilege of deciding upon. As the Supreme Ruler of the Universe has seen fit to bestow upon us this glorious opportunity, let us decide upon it—appealing to him for the rectitude of our intentions—and in humble confidence that he will yet continue to bless and save our country.

NOTES

1. Immediately after adoption, five of the opponents of the Constitution spoke, saying now that it had been passed, they would support it fully. Mr. White said "he should use his utmost exertions to induce his constituents to live in peace under, and cheerfully submit" to the document. Mr. Wedgery said that "he should support, as much as in him lay, the Constitution" and Gen. Whitney said that "he should support it as much as if he had voted for it." Mr. Cooley said he would endeavor to convince his constituents to abide by the Constitution, and Dr. Taylor "expressed his determination to go home and endeavor to infuse a spirit of harmony and love among the people." (Pierce, 280-281; Elliott, 2, 185-186)

The Massachusetts *Centinel* (9 Feb and 13 Feb 1788) gave a lengthy description of the goodwill celebration that occurred following ratification. The following events were noted:

a. Spectators outside gave large huzzas.

b. The Convention attended a buffet and drank toasts in the Senate Chamber (evidence that some at least thought the vote would be affirmative, because this event took place immediately after adjournment).

c. Bells pealed for hours; cannon were fired, etc.

d. On Thursday, the Committee of Tradesmen called for a parade of mechanics and artisans, which took place at eleven o'clock on Friday. Over forty different trades marched in procession, most displaying artifacts of their trade. Among those in the procession were rope makers, mast makers, sail makers, ship joiners, mathematical instrument makers, coopers, shoemakers, coach and chaise makers, hatters, tallow chandlers, and masons.

HEADNOTE

Date: Wednesday, 27 Feb 1788

Occasion: After the adoption of the Constitution, it was necessary to return to the routine work of legislation. But the excitement of what had recently passed plus the fact that not all of the delegates to the Constitutional Convention were also members of the legislature caused Hancock to reiterate much of what he had said on 6 Feb 1788, but to many who had not before heard his position.

SOURCES

MA House Unenacted #2898; *Journal of the House*, 8, 375-80, MA; *Journal of the House*, 8, 375-80, SL;*

A&R 1788, 996-999; Worcester *Magazine*, first week in March 1788, 291-3; Massachusetts *Gazette* 29 Feb 1788, 3; Boston *Gazette* 3 Mar 1788, 2; *Independent Chronicle* 29 Feb 1788, 3.

*No copy in either Senate Journal.

The reply by the legislature is found in MA House Unenacted #2690;
See also A&R, May session, 1788, 189-191, 5 June 1788.

TEXT

Gentlemen of the Senate, and Gentlemen of the House of Representatives, The Letters which I have received in the recess, the Secretary will lay before you they [sic] are not of such importance as to claim any particular notice from me at this time.

The adjournment of the General Court for the space of one week became necessary in order to give the Members, who were also Members of the late Convention, an opportunity of returning home before the meeting of the Legislature. I could have wished that the Proclamation of adjournment had been of an earlier date,[1] but the Session of the Convention, by the importance of the business before that Body, was protracted beyond what was expected. I flatter myself that this will be satisfactory, as well to those of you, Gentlemen, who having not heard of the adjournment, have been some days waiting in Town, as to those who may be apprehensive that the business of the present Session will demand a longer time than can be conveniently afforded at this Season of the year.[2]

I have nothing of more importance at this time to recommend to your deliberation than the Lands of the Commonwealth. It is scarcely necessary to remark that this State, from its particular situation, as well as from the noble ardor of[3] its citizens in defence of their liberties & independence, hath accumulated a very heavy debt; the interest of which arises to ninety thousand pounds annually; this consideration alone, Gentlemen, should induce us by every possible exertion consistent with the peace of the Commonwealth, to diminish the principal. In order to do[4] this, the great quantities of unappropriated territory, both in the Eastern part of the Government, as well as the immense tract lately ceded to us by the State of New York,[5] afford ample resources, if wisely & expeditiously improved by that spirit of unanimity & discernment, which I flatter myself will always distinguish your conduct, when the interest of the people is so deeply & essentially engaged in the results of your deliberations.[6]

I am sorry that my duty urges me to mention to you the necessity of a small tax, but the Treasury is so far exhausted, that the business of the Government must cease its progress unless a Tax is granted.[7]

Since the last Session, Luke Day, one of those persons for whose arrest a bounty was offered in consequnce of an act of the Legislature,[8] has been taken by some of the Citizens of New Hampshire, to whom one hundred pounds has been paid, upon their delivering him into the Custody of the Sheriff of the County of Suffolk. Could the late unhappy commotion be thrown into oblivion, consistently with the honor of Government, & the safety of the people, I persuade myself it would give satisfaction.

In the beginning of your last Session, I laid before you the Constitution & Frame of Government for the United States of America,[9] agreed upon by the late General Convention, and transmitted to me by Congress. As the System was to be submitted to the people, & to be decided upon by their Delegates in Convention, I forbore to make any remarks upon it.

The Convention which you appointed to deliberate upon that important subject, have concluded their session, after having adopted & ratified the proposed plan, according to their resolution, a copy whereof I have directed the Secretary to lay before you.

The obvious imbecility of the Confederation of the United States has too long given pain to our friends & pleasure to our enemies; but the

forming a new System of Government, for so numerous a people, of
very different views & habits, spread upon such a vast extent of
Territory, containing such a great variety of Soils, & under[10] such
extremes of climate, was a task which nothing less than the dreadful
apprehension of losing our national existence could have compelled the
people to undertake.

We can be known to the World, only under the appellation of the
United States; if we are robbed of the idea of our Union, we
immediately become separate nations,[11] independent of each other & no
less liable to the depredations of foreign powers, than to Wars & bloody
contentions amongst ourselves. To pretend to exist as a nation without
possessing those powers of coerce [sic], which are necessarily incident
to the National Character, would prove a fatal solecism in politics. The
objects of the proposed Constitution are defence against External
Enemies, & the promotion of tranquility & happiness amongst the
States.

Whether it is well calculated for those important purposes, has been
the subject of extensive & learned discussion in the Convention which
you appointed. I believe there was never a Body of men assembled with
greater purity of intention or with higher zeal for the public interest.
And although when the momentous question was decided, there was a
greater division than some expected, yet there appeared a Candor, & a
spirit of Conciliation in the Minority which did them great honor &
afforded a happy presage of unanimity amongst the people at large.
Though so many of the Members of the late Convention could not feel
themselves convinced that they ought to vote for the ratification of this
System, yet their opposition was conducted with a candid & manly
firmness, & with such marks of integrity & real regard to the public
interest, as[12] did them the highest honor, & leaves no reason to
suppose that the peace & good order of the Government is not their
object.

The amendments proposed by the Convention are intended to obtain
a Constitutional security of the principles to which they refer
themselves, & must meet the wishes of all the States. I feel myself
assured that they will very early become a part of the Constitution, &
when they shall be added to the proposed plan,[13] I shall consider it as
the most perfect System of Government, as to the objects it embraces,
that has been known amongst mankind.[14]

Gentlemen, As that Being, in whose hands is the Government of all
the Nations of the Earth, & who putteth down one, & raiseth up
another according to his Sovereign Pleasure,[15] has given to the people
of these States, a rich & an extensive Country; has in a Marvellous

Manner, given them a name & a standing among the Nations of the World, has blessed them with external peace, & internal tranquility; I hope & pray that the Gratitude of their Hearts may be expressed by a proper use of those inestimable blessings, by the greatest exertions of patriotism, by forming & supporting institutions for cultivating the human understanding, & for the greatest progress of the Arts & Sciences, by establishing Laws for the support of Piety, Religion, & Morality, as well as for punishing Vice & Wicknedness, & by exhibiting on the great Theatre of the World those social, public and private virtues which give more Dignity to a people, possessing their own Sovereignty, than Crowns and Diadems afford to Sovereign Princes.

Every matter of public nature, which may occur worthy of your notice, shall be communicated by Message, & in every concern tending to promote the public welfare, I shall be happy to concur with you, & be ready at all times to give every possible dispatch to the business that may come before you.

John Hancock

Council Chamber
February 27, 1788

NOTES

1. Thursday, 7 Feb 1788.

2. Although the version in the *Journal of the House* provides more frequent paragraphing than do other versions, here it has only a prolonged space.

3. *Journal of the House* reads "from the noble ardor from its citizens."

4. The four primary sources all omit "do," signifying that the versions in the newspapers and in the *Journal of the House* may have come from a common source.

5. For the disposals of the western lands in New York state, see note four in the 17 Oct 1787 speech.

6. In its answer to the governor's message, the legislature agreed to the sale of certain lands in Maine. In 1786, a lottery had been organized to raise £163,000 by the sale of 18,000 square miles. (A&R, 1786, Chap. 40, 19 Nov 1786, 97-102; Feer, 1, 258) said that tickets "could be bought with

any of the public securities of the state or the federal government." As added inducements, all land won in the lottery was to be tax-free for fifteen years, and all settlers would have their poll taxes waived for the same period.

In 1788, the winners of the lottery for the eastern lands wished to consolidate their holdings by exchanging land they had won in the lottery for state land closer to one of their prize landsites. Therefore, the General Court so provided in 1788, Chap. 17, 20 June 1787, 27-28.

However, on 6 Mar 1790, the General Court passed legislation to wind up the holding of lotteries. (1789, Chap. 57, 6 Mar 1790, 510-511)

7. A&R, Chapter 56, 1787, 628-629 (not dated) provided for a tax of £65,000 and 4 shillings, as well as £13,260 and 1 shilling and other miscellaneous taxes. Dewey 3, 352, errs in saying that no new taxes were passed.

8. See speech of 17 Oct 1787.

9. The phrase, "United States of America," used this early by Hancock so frequently, shows the degree to which the concept of union was early established.

10. *Journal of the House* omits "such a great variety of Soils, & under."

11. *Journal of the House* omits "nations."

12. *Journal of the House* omits "as."

13. In MA Senate Unenacted #977, on 26 Sept 1789, George Washington was instructed by Congress to send copies of the approved amendments to the states that had ratified and to Rhode Island and North Carolina, which had not. The original of this communication to Massachusetts is MA Senate Unenacted #977/1.

14. In MA Senate Unenacted #849, dated 26 July 1788, there is Hancock's copy of a circular letter issued by Governor Clinton saying: "...nothing but the fullest confidence of obtaining a Revision of them, by a General Convention, and an invincible reluctance to seprating [sic] from our Sister States, could have prevailed upon a sufficient number to ratify it, without stipulating for previous Amendments....We request the favour of your Excellency to lay this letter before the Legislature of your Commonwealth...."

15. Psalms 74, 8: "For God is the judge. One he putteth down and another he lifteth up."

HEADNOTE

Date: 3 June 1788

Occasion: The end of Shays's Rebellion and the continued need to support the federal constitution.

SOURCES

Senate Unenacted #826 (1788), MA; *Journal of the House* 9, 36-39, MA; *Journal of the House* 9, 36-39, SL;* *Acts & Laws*, 1788-1789, 729-732.

Massachusetts *Centinel*, 4 June 1788, 2-3; *Independent Chronicle* 5 June 1788, 2; Massachussets *Spy* 12 June 1788, 2; Massachusetts *Gazette*, 6 June 1788, 2-3; Boston *Gazette* 9 June 1788, 1.

*No copy in either Senate Journal.

TEXT

Gentlemen of the Senate & Gentlemen of the House of Representatives.

The compleat [sic] restoration, & perfect establishment of Peace & tranquility within the State, leaves me but little to offer, except my most cordial Congratulations on these interesting & important events; & I am fully convinced that the satisfaction you will derive from these[1] considerations cannot be inferior to my own—I mean not Gentlemen, by any observations of mine, to lead to an unprofitable disquisition of those causes, which have principally contributed to this pleasing situation of our affairs, as it would serve to[2] awaken emotions, which are as painful, as they are natural, & which if possible I earnestly pray may be forever buried in Oblivion—Impartial posterity, you are sensible, often decides on the merit of particular transactions, with very different sentiments from those of the persons more immediately concerned—Let it therefore be our part to contemplate with Candor & Charity the motives of those, whose sentiments have not wholly accorded with our own; & in this way, a fertile source of animosity & discord will be happily removed.—I sincerely hope, however, should any measure occur to you Gentlemen, by the influence of which every vestige of the late unhappy commotions may be finally obliterated that it will not be neglected; & you may be assured of my most zealous co-operation in such a salutary effort.[3]

I shall direct the Secretary to lay before you a letter which I have had the pleasure of receiving from the Delegates of this State in Congress for your information, with respect to the objects of a public nature which now engage the attention of that Honorable Body— It is with pleasure that I find so large a part of the Domestic debt of these United States in a way to be discharged by the sale of the Federal Lands. —This negotiation when compleated [sic] by the receipt of the Securities in the public Treasury, & the measures adopted in the last Sessions of the Assembly, to dispose of the Western Territory belonging to this Commonwealth,[4] I flatter myself will greatly conspire to reduce the weight of our public burden—I should be happy Gentlemen, if some system could be adopted to place the remaining part of our State debt on such funds as would prevent the extreme fluctuation in its value, which in my opinion is as injurious to the Government, as it is mortifying & destructive to the Public Creditor.— I presume not Gentlemen, to suggest the plan by which this object might be effected.—But, whatever scheme your Wisdom may devise, you may depend on its meeting my earliest attention. I shall only remark that the necessity of such measures is encreased [sic] by the prospect of the new Federal Constitution's[5] being adopted; as in consequence of this important event, the resources which have hitherto applied to the purposes of this Government in particular, will probably be appropriated to Federal objects.[6] Should this event take place the securities of this State would sustain a sudden[7] & rapid depreciation unless wisely prevented. It becomes our duty therefore on every principle of prudence & justice to guard against such a public misfortune & I hope it may be done without the addition of another direct tax.—

Certain events which have recently taken place in the military department have induced me to call your attention to the Laws for regulating the Militia of this Government. Upon this subject, however, I shall request your consideration by a separate Message, & I flatter myself you will see the necessity of some alteration in them.—

I hope the necessities of Government will admit of a short Session, that our public expenditures, may be, as far as possible, diminished—In all events I have the fullest reliance on your virtue & patriotism; & for this reason I am sensible I need not recommend to your attention the encouragement & protection of Literature & of the Arts & Manufactures of the Country; of industry & economy; of Piety &

Morality; & of a due submission to the Laws; as I am confident, Gentlemen, you must feel yourselves deeply & warmly engaged by every means, to advance the true interest, & to promote the real honor & reputation of this State in particular & of the United States in general, it will be by the cultivation of these virtues alone that we can repair the waste & ravages of War & place our affairs on such a permanent basis, as I think we have a right to expect from our free & excellent Constitution of Government as well as from the fertility of our soil & the happy temperature of our[8] climate; it will be then only that we shall fully realize the benefits of our independence & the blessings of Freedom.—

Gentlemen of the Senate & Gentlemen of the House of Representatives—

As I have been honored by the highest mark of the publick confidence in being again called by the unsolicited suffrages of my fellow Citizens to sustain the first office in the Government, I must beg leave to assure you that no exertion on my part shall be wanting to fulfil those expectations which they have a right to form; & however intricate & important the duties annexed to my station may be considered, I have a firm hope, from the known abilities & unshaken integrity of those Gentlemen, by you appointed as a Council to assist me, that the Executive departmnt will be conducted in such a manner as will operate to the support & honor of the Government, & to the satisfaction & happiness of the people.—

John Hancock[9]

Council Chambers
3 June 1788

NOTES

1. *Journal of the House* reads "the" instead of "these."
2. *Journal of the House* reads "but to awaken emotions."
3. A reference to the aftermath of Shays's Rebellion. After the war, small-property owners were losing their property because of high taxes and some

faced imprisonment because they could not pay. Because Massachusetts had a property qualification for voting, the poor had no power. In the fall of 1786, a mob led by Daniel Shays, in an effort to stop foreclosures and imprisonments, surrounded the Supreme Court in Springfield. Many of those who rebelled had been in the war, and they felt they were not receiving their due. The rebels were finally subdued on 2 Feb 1787, Shays escaping to Vermont. There were still intense feelings in the state well over a year after the insurrection. For further details, see the speech of 17 Oct 1787.

4. See note four in speech of 17 Oct 1787.

5. *Journal of the House* reads "Constitution being adopted."

6. *Journal of the House* omits "a sudden."

7. The excise and importation taxes that the states had been permitted to collect under the Articles of Confederation would be appropriated by the federal government, once the Constitution had been ratified.

8. *Journal of the House* reads "your climate."

9. Hancock signed this copy himself, dating it and identifying the speech as having been delivered in the Council Chambers.

HEADNOTE

Date: July 19, 1788

Occasion: The commencement exercises at Harvard began with an oration by John Phelps; the reading of an English poem on the present prospect of America, by Oliver Dodge; a disputation on "whether the balance would be in favour of our existence were there no state but the present"; a conference in Greek "upon the evil affects of avarice, and of profligacy on Society"; a forensic disputation upon the question, "Whether a Republick is more secure of the continuance of its liberties, where its officers in the higher branches of government are elected for several years, than when they are elected annually"; a conference in English on "whether a large emigration from Europe into the United States of America would upon the whole be for the real advantage of the States"; and an English oration delivered by Benjamin Abbot. The Massachusetts *Spy* noted that "several of the young Gentlemen, who were to have exhibited on this occasion, were prevented by sickness, and the usual syllogistick disputations were dispensed with."

The president of Harvard then informed "his Excellency the Governor" that the morning exercises had been completed and that his address was in order.

After the speech, the graduates returned in procession to "the hall, where a dinner was provided for their entertainment—and in the afternoon they again proceeded to the Meetinghouse"[1] to hear a further oration on the advantages of religion in civil society by the Reverend Henry Ware and to be awarded their degrees. Special mention is made of two recipients of the bachelor of physick and one recipient of the bachelor of laws. The ceremonies concluded with a valedictory oration and a concluding prayer by the president.

After the commencement exercises, it was evidently the custom for the students and townspeople of Cambridge to indulge in a sort of carnival. It is, for some perhaps, a relief to find that the Puritan image was not always followed by the propitious people of Boston. A first-hand account of what transpired during Commencement Week was included in *The Harvard Book*. The author of the essay, John Holmes, the brother of Oliver Wendell Holmes, presented a detailed account of the "goings-on." Although Holmes was graduated in 1832, his remarks imply that not much had changed during the years. The description of events below, therefore, can be largely applied to what must have been the scene in 1788, including the participation of the governor in the ceremonies.

A long series of tent-like affairs was erected, some of which were used to sell the sort of food and sundries generally found at fairs while others permitted dancing, drinking, and even gambling. (1, 30) There were Punch and Judy shows, a show of "The Fat Baby," and a cage of reptiles available at one house. (1, 30) Farmers' wagons sold fruits and vegetables. The taverns that had customarily served the students did a lively business. As early as 1727 and 1733, diaries recorded the excesses that transpired at "Commencement." (1, 34) From the pulpit, ministers advised their congregations to store away any moveables that might be appropriated by the crowd, presumably from front yards and porches. (1, 35) The straw-covered streets became cluttered with watermelon rinds and peach seeds. The streets smelled of rum and tobacco. (1, 30) Beggars, the crippled, and the blind came to ask for help. (1, 36) The night featured serenades by the students.

The morning of the awarding of degrees, the procession gathered to await the arrival of the governor. Holmes stated: "The procession set forth silent and slow. No music gave a martial tone and port to its advance. The meeting-house bell tolled its thin and solemn notes as for public worship." (1, 40) At the meeting-house, "the President occupied the pulpit, and the Governor the great chair in front." (1, 40) Those who could not get in returned to the Commons. The graduates seated themselves on a temporarily erected stage. Holmes made the scene realistic when he added that "the cocked hats were hung on the brass-headed nails which lined the beams projecting from the wall between the pulpit and the galleries." (1, 40-41)

So, inside, the setting for the speech was sufficiently solemn for Hancock to make a dignified address, in spite of the disarray and hoopla in full swing on the common.

SOURCES

Pennsyslvania *Packet & Daily Advertiser*, 29 July 1788, Harvard Archives #2960; Massachusetts *Centinel*, 19 July 1788, #36, 144-5; Boston *Gazette*, 21 July 1788, 2-3; Massachusetts *Gazette*, 22 July 1788, 1; Massachusetts *Spy*, Thurusday 24 July 1788, 3; *Independent Chronicle*, 24 July 1788, 1.

TEXT OF THE ADDRESS

Reverend and Learned Sir,[2]

I cannot refrain expressing the high satisfaction and exalted delight I possess on the present occasion.

The evidence of genius and learning, this day exhibited by the young gentlemen who are now proceeding from hence into the world under the great, and well-improved advantages of an University education, irresistibly carries my hopes and best wishes with them.—I anticipate, with great pleasure, those future years which will present them highly ranked amongst the ornaments and supporters of their country.

When we contemplate the pious and patriotick [sic] origin, as well as the vast advantage of this college—when we see the sons of Harvard, with those who have mediately drawn measures of useful learning from this source, deep in the Councils of State, erecting and supporting a new, prosperous and powerful Confederated Republick—improving the wealth, and guiding the force of nations—when we see them respected in palaces abroad, and triumphing over cruel invaders at home—when we see, by the learning here acquired, Religion stripped of that delusive and dangerous garb, which ignorance and superstition had wrapped her in; and exhibited, in that simple and unaffected dress, in which alone she can honour the Diety, and bless mankind—we cannot but deeply revere our ancestors and rejoice in the fair inheritance they have transmitted us.

I am obliged on this happy occasion, to indulge myself to be carried on the wings of imagination to the time fast approaching when such attention will be paid to this seminary, that new Colleges will be here erected--the useful professorships encouraged, and sufficiently endowed, while the domes shall be thronged by youths thirsty for science, and our country enriched by profound erudition, be acknowledged by the world as a principal seat of the muses.

From your learning and known ability, respectable Sir, your fellow citizens have formed the most sanguine expectations, that while you hold the station you now fill with so much dignity, you will annually send forth men formed to guide the cabinet, direct the arms, and extend the commerce of their country; and those, also, who by their precepts and example, will honour our holy religion, and lay a foundation for the practice of the purest morals and patriotism, and thus perpetually transmit publick and private happiness from one generation to another.

NOTES

1. Massachusetts *Spy*, Thursday24 July 1788, 3.
2. President Willard.

HEADNOTE

Date: Friday, 29 May 1789

Occasion: The *Independent Chronicle* noted that "a committee of both Houses was appointed to wait upon his Excellency JOHN HANCOCK, Esq. to inform him of his re-election by the People, as Governour, and on [sic] the Hon. SAMUEL ADAMS, Esq. as Lieutenant-Governor of this State." (4 June 1789, 10)

The *Independent Chronicle* of the same date also stated: "At eleven o'clock, the two Houses met in Convention, at the Representatives Chamber, when his Excellency the Governor, and his Honour the Lieutenant-Governour elect, (attended by the Hon Council, and the Secretary of the Commonwealth) appeared to qualify themselves agreeably to the Constitution. After being for a short time seated his Excellency arose, and addressed the two Houses as follows."

After the brief statement, the Boston *Gazette* noted: "His Excellency then took the oath, and subscribed the declaration required by the Constitution—after which, by advice of the President, the Secretary of the Commonwealth proclaimed His Excellency JOHN HANCOCK, Esquire, Governor of the Commonwealth of Massachusetts." (1 June 1789, 2)

Hancock did not follow this brief address with a more detailed speech, electing instead to resort to messages. His message of 8 June 1789 was answered by the General Court on 18 June 1789 (A&R, May Session, 1789, Chapter 69, 567-569) The General Court acknowledged that it was "sensible that the deranged state of our finances, demands the immediate attention of the Legislature....we shall therefore willingly adopt such measures as will promote our national honor, & releive [sic] the distresses of those who have loaned monies, & rendered services to support their country."

SOURCES

No transcription of the speech is found in either *Journal of the House* or in either *Journal of the Senate.*

A&R 1788-89, May Session, 1789, 524; *Independent Chronicle* 4 June 1789, 1; The Boston *Gazette* 1 June 1789, 2; *Massachusetts Centinel* 30 May 1789, 3.

TEXT

Gentlemen:

The repeated assurances given me by my fellow-citizens of their approbation of my sincere wishes to promote their interest, adds infinite strength to the obligations I have long felt myself under, to exert every power I am possessed of to advance the publick felicity.

In consequence of your having notified me of my being elected Governour for the year ensuing, I appear in this place to signify my acceptance of that office, and to take the oaths and subscribe the declaration provided by the Constitution.[1]

I THANK YOU, Gentlemen, for the very polite and obliging manner, in which you have communicated to me the results of the People's exercise of this right--and beg leave to assure you, that so far as the Constitution demands my attention in the business of Legislation, I shall be ready to approve every measure proposed by you, for the benefit of our constituents, and shall communicate to you such matters as I may conceive will tend to the support of that order and good government which at present so happily prevail throughout the Commonwealth. I shall by advice of Council, use my constant endeavours, during the year, to exercise the Executive Authority in such manner as may tend to the honour and stability of Government.

Through you I beg leave to assure my fellow-citizens, that while I live, preservation and promotion of their civil and political happiness shall be the great object of my concern.[2]

I will detain you no longer, Gentlemen, but am ready to proceed to the formalities provided for this occasion.

John Hancock

NOTES

1. On 8 June 1789, Hancock sent a general message to the General Court (A&R 1788-1789, pp. 745-747) which responded on 18 June 1789. (A&R May 1789, 567-569) There was no extended address to the legislature in 1789, perhaps because Hancock was in ill health and preferred to use messages instead.

2. Under the new Constitution, George Washington had been elected president. The Massachusetts legislature phrased an "Address to the

President of the United States." (A&R, Chap. 107, 25 June 1789, 588-589) The address was presented to the president by the senators and representatives from Massachusetts serving in Congress. (House Unenacted #3171, MA) Washington replied on 9 July 1789: "The adoption of the present Government by so large a majority of the States, and their Citizens...are indications of its merit—auspicious of the future greatness and welfare of the Empire which will grow under it." (House Unenacted #3172, MA)

George Washington's latest collected works specified in a footnote that this letter was written, but it was not included in the volumes because it was a routine letter sent to those who congratulated Washington his election.

HEADNOTE

Date: 26 November 1789

Occasion: The Massachusetts *Centinel* of Wednesday, 25 Nov 1789, 193, noted that "Tomorrow is assignd by THE PRESIDENT of the United States, to be observed as a day of Publick THANKSGIVING throughout the Union." In a flowery statement, the *Centinel* concluded: "Let this change be contemplated, and the heart must be insensible that will [not] pour forth its gratitude and praise." The *Independent Chronicle* noted of 27 Nov that "yesterday was observed as a day of public Thanksgiving throughout this Commonwealth, pursuant to a Proclamation of His Excellency with advice of Council:—This festival will have been exceedingly heightened by the reflection, that eleven Sovereign States, by the recommendation of their Federal Head, have united in it." (Friday, 27 Nov 1793, 3)

However, a search of the newspapers published in Boston and its vicinity at the time of the first Thanksgiving Day has so far failed to reveal the location at which Hancock delivered his sermon. It was not customary for the papers of the day to carry the activities of the churches so it would have been unusual for the press to have commented. But presentations by the governor were often noted.

Furthermore the manuscript itself gives no indication of place. All we know is that it was written by Hancock himself, and is one of the few speeches we have in his hand. It was presumably given in the morning, and may have been given at his own Brattle Street Church.

The sermon could have been delivered from the manuscript itself. However, if Hancock followed the style of his Uncle Nathaniel, he would have prepared a set of almost undecipherable notes on four-by-six inch slips of paper. The MHS has notes of four such sermons by Nathaniel Hancock, including notes for a Thanksgiving Day sermon delivered in 1754. The little slips have minuscule handwriting on both sides. It would have taken superior eyesight to deliver a sermon from such notes. If Hancock was influenced by his uncle's style, John guarded his waste basket well because no such abbreviated speech notes were discovered for any of his speeches.

SOURCES

The MS of this sermon is in the J. Pierpont Morgan Library in New York. A note says: "This book was bought by me from Mrs. John Fiske, who informed me that she had obtained it from the doctor of John Hancock's grandnephew, together with several other Hancock items. George S. Hellman, N.Y.Cooperative Society, 358 5th Ave."

TEXT

100th Psalm. 4th V.

Enter into his Gates with Thanksgiving, and into his Courts with Praise; be thankful unto him and bless his Name.[1]

We [xxx] have, my Hearers, on this day, a particular Call to the heavenly Employm't of Praise and Thanks'g. If we have any Sensibility, any Ingenuity in our Disposition, any Sense of Favors conferr'd, we cannot be backward to engage in it; and if we perform this Service in the genuine Spirit of it, and with truly grateful Hearts, we cannot but derive from it the purest and most exalted Pleasure of which our rational Nature is capable.—Some may, perhaps, ask upon this Occasion, what Profits do our Praises yield to the Almighty? Can they increase his Happiness? Can they add any Thing to his real Glory? Can they make him greater or more Glorified than he is in himself? It is his to give, for he hath all Things at his Command; it is our's [sic] to receive and enjoy; but as we are too indigent to make /him/ any Returns, he neither expects nor desires this. In a sober Sense this is true; and in a sober Sense, we may all adopt the Sentiment of an admir'd Poet,

That God is prais'd when man receives, to enjoy is to obey.[2]

God appears in his own most glorious Character, He proclaims his own Praise, when as the Kind Parent of the Universe he spreads his Loving kindness over all his Works; when he giveth to all their Meat in due Season,[3] and opens his hand to satisfy the Desire of every living Thing. And when Man discharges his Mind of all that Mistrust Anxiety and Care that would poison the Bounties of Heaven, and keeps himself in a proper Temper to tast [sic] their Sweetness, to know their Worth, and properly to enjoy them, he thus far fulfills the divine

Intention, and complies with the divine Will.—But can we call to our Minds this amiable Image of our all gracious Parent? Can we receive his Favors; can we relish them; can we consider this enjoym't as the Effect of his Kind Intention, and the Design of what he bestows upon us; Can we do all this, and yet content ourselves with the bare Enjoyment? Can we [xxx] feel ourselves entertained and delight'd, and not reflect from whence this Entertainment, and Delight comes? Can we ascend in our Minds to the true Author and Fountain of all, and perceive no Sentiments of a grateful Affection rising in our Minds? Can these Sentiments be warm and lively and in our Bosoms and we at the same time find no way to express them. Can there be a more natural or proper Manner of Expression than Praise & Thanksgiving. Ought we not to meet in solemn Assemblies, unitedly to pay this Tribute to our great and common Benefactor? Can any Thing be more reasonable and more becoming our rational and social Nature? It does not indeed extend unto God; it confers no advantage unto him, but it [xxx] is honourable and advantageous to ourselves. It tends to remind us in the most affecting manner of our grateful Obligations to him; to excite in our Minds /grateful/ Sensations correspondent to these Obligation? to render the sacred [-warm-] warmth of our [-Affections-] Love and Gratitude to the Parent of all Good more ardent and intense: and to impress upon our own Bosoms and the Bosoms of all around us, the most honourable Sentiments of his Beneficience and providential Care. This is that Tribute of Glory to our great Creator. To him [wh??] in whom we live, & move, & have our Being, to him who giveth us all Things richly to enjoy, which is due to him from all his rational Creation. Our Obligations to [th] such a Service are evident upon our first Reflections: We have an intimate, an immediate Perception of the Propriety of it. Man is evidently formed for Religion and Social Worship; of which Praise and Thanksgiving are an essential Part as he is for Society itself. [There is something] His reason dictates, his Nature leads to it. The uniform Practise [sic] of Mankind demonstrates an Uniformity of Sentiment upon this Head. All Nations have agreed in [some] honouring a supreme Power by some Solemnities of public Worship; by some [Ex] significant Expression of Gratitude and Praise. Every one knows that in the Law which God gave to the Nation of Israel, with such public and striking Tokens of his Presence & Authority, a Variety of such Solemnities were instituted, and the Time & Manner in which they were to be observed were particularly described. And certainly social Worship, public and solemn Acts of Prayer and Praise are not discarded by the Gospel. The Manner of performing them under this last Dispensation is indeed more simple, but not less significant of the Reverence and Gratitude of the Heart; and when they are observed in this Spirit we may safely apply to them the Language of the good Psalmist, that these also shall please the Lord better than an Ox, or a Bullock that hath Horns & Hoofs.[4]

At the first Promulgation of the Gospel there was no Christian Nation; no civil Authority that was Christian: otherwise we may well suppose, that no Magistrates would have so totally renounc'd the [ir] Character of the Servants of him who is Prince of the Kings of the Earth, as not to have given their Countenance, and the Weight of their Authority to the public Worship of God according to the Institutions of the Gospel. As neither Xt nor his Apostles have confined [put] this Worship to the Lord's day, but have left us at Liberty to celebrate it [on] /at/ other suitable Seasons, the civil Fathers of New England from the first Foundation of our Country have pointed out a day towards the close of every Year, on which they have recommended to the whole Community, to meet in solemn Assemblies, and offer up their devout Praises and Thanksgivings to Heaven, for the [pub] Blessings, particularly the public ones of the closing year. This appointment, which has for many years been peculiar to N. England, [has now obt] is so truly pious & decent, that it has now obtained the Countenance & Sanction of the United States of America; It is accordingly at the call of the illustrious Senate of this rising Nation that all the States are this day united by offering their religious and grateful acknowledgements to the supreme Ruler of the O.[5] In their Call to this important Duty, they have reminded us of the Benefits that demand our Praise and Thanksgiving, in Energy of Expression, & a clear Arrangement; so that this Exhortation to this Act of Piety, contains a good Direction for the Performance of it. It begins with pointing us /may be profitable as it is natural to look/ back to the first[6] Foundations of our Country. [The] Our Beginning was small, tho [ou] in a short Time we have astonishingly increased. The History of Mankind is a Record of the Dispensations of his Providence when he governs the O.

// The Discovery of America from Time immemorial wholly unknown to other Quarters of the Globe, is the most capital Event that signalizes the History of the Spanish Nation. The Discoverer Columbus, tho this Continent does not bear his Name, will ever be remembered, for the Boldness of his Undertaking, the Sagacity & Perserverance with which he conducted it; and the Success with which it was crowned. He explored this new World; he prepar'd the Way for other Nations to become acquainted with it; and was under Providence the Father of the European Settlements, in this Western Region [sic; no period]

God who brings Good out of Evil, has often, since the day he led his ancient People from their Bondage in Egypt to the Land of Canaan, made Oppression the Foundation of new Communities, and the Seed of civil and Ecclesiastical Liberty. This was particularly true respecting the Settlement of the more Northern Parts of this Continent by our Ancestors from Britain. Being galled by the Yoke they wore in their native Land, they went out scarcely knowing whither they went; this new World was before them, & Providence was their Guide. This directed, this supported, this defended, and this established them. At this day we can hardly form a just Idea of the Dangers and Hardships that attended the first Settlement of these States. The Memory of those who laid the Foundations of th[ese States], deserves to be revered by their Posterity. The Origin of most [xxx] if not all other Nations is lost in ridiculous Fable, and extravagant Superstition; but we can trace that of our own thro faithful History, in wch [sic] we may discern a Variety of surprising Events that demand our Gratitude to Almighty God. Little did our Fathers think, amidst the Scarcity & Toils to which they were subjected, the numerous Savage Foes with which they were surrounded, and the many other Discouragements with which they contended [sic] little did they think, when they often trembled for their own Safety, and were [ready] almost tempted to abandon their infant Settlements, that they were laying the Foundations of a Nation, which in a little more than a Century, would attain the Attention of the whole World, and assert and maintain its Rights in Opposition to one of the most potent Kingdoms [that ever existed] upon the Face of the Earth. It is the Lord's Doing & it is marvelous in our Eyes.

We are this day [call'd] call'd upon to give Thanks to the great Governor of the O, not only for the kind Appearance of his Providence in behalf of our Fathers, but also *for raising us their Children from deep Distress to be numbered among the Nations of the Earth*. This is a Rank of Dignity which at the Beginning of this Contest we never aspired after. On the contrary the whole World can bear us Witness that we employed every Means in our Power to avoid it: And certainly the Nation upon which we formerly depended, and which took Occasion from this Dependence to oppress us, never expected, and much less desired such an Event: but so infatuated were their Councils, so determin'd were they to bring us to their Feet in an absolute & unlimited Subjection, that we were obliged to draw the Sword in our own Defense, and appeal to Heaven. God has [xx] hitherto, in a Manner that surprises all the O, aided our Cause and supported us in the unequal and hazardous contest. So that we may apply to this Event, what was said of the Nation of Israel upon a similar Occasion, that the Work was of the Lord, that the Kingdom s'd be thus divided.[7]

But tho we did not ambitiously aspire at the Honour of being a distinct Nation, and were in Truth driven into it by the haughty and relentless Power of our Enemies, which left us no alternative consistent with the Security of our most valuable Rights, as Men and as Members of civil Society; This very Power, has nevertheless brought us into a Situation, which if we are wise enough properly to improve must redound greatly to our Advantage. The choicest Gifts of Heaven may be abused, and finally turn [sic] to the Disadvantage of those upon whom they were bestowed. This however does not detract from their proper Value, nor lessen the Obligation of Gratitude to almighty God from the Receiver. But I hope we shall be wise enough rightly to value and properly to improve the Privileges & Honour which Heaven has in so extraordinary a Manner bestowed upon us, and in the possession of which it has hitherto supported us.[8] May such be our Temper: so rational and manly, so composed and Christian our Joy, on this sacred Festival! May our Idea of the divine Goodness be so [xxx] just and the Impressions it makes upon our Minds so deep, as to create in us a profound Veneration of the divine character and Government! The national Expression of the Temper is Praise and Thanksgiving, an Employment to which we are this Day particularly called. If we have any solidness,[9] I hope we shall know how to take care of and govern ourselves; I hope we shall have wisdom to adopt such a Constitution as shall give the Executive post its proper Independence and Energy, and save us from that Laxity and Licentiousness that seldom fails to end in Tyranny.[10] It gives us a Dignity among the Nations of the Earth, which no Precept of Religion forbids us to understand and feel; and which we should endeavor to support, principally by that Righteousness which exalteth a Nation. Self Value, even in a private Character when properly regulated, is of no small advantage. In Communities it is absolutely necessary, often to the Welfare, and sometimes to the very Existence of a Nation. Vain and Selfconfident we s'd never be; nor ever forgetful of our Dependence upon him who builds or destroys the Nations of the Earth according to his sovereign Pleasure. [We ought] As the Eyes of all the World are upon us, we ought at our first Setting out to take particular Care to establish a fair & honourable National Character; never to stain it; never to act below ourselves; and then to know and [exact] /maintain/ the Respect that is due to us from all other Nations. In this Way we shall derive not [xxxx] empty Honour, but the most important and solid Advantages from our present Situation. It opens to us a free Communication with all the World, not only for the Improvement of Commerce, & the acquiring Wealth, but for the Enlargement of the most useful Knowledge. Independence naturally unfetters and expands the Human Mind, and prepares it for the Impression of the most exalted Virtues, as well as the Reception of the most important Knowledge. Look into history, and you will find those [Nations] /Country,/ [sic] that have been for a long time and to any considerable Degree dependent upon others, limited and cramped in their Improvements, stained with the prevailing Vices of the Court of the ruling Nation; and debased by an Air of Servility running thro their Productions & Manners. Servility is not only dishonourable to human Nature, but is commonly accompanied with the [mea worst] meanest Vices; such as Adulation, Deceit, Falsehood, Treachery, Cruelty, and the basest Means to support the Power upon which it depends.—You see then what an Opportunity Providence has afforded us of obtaining Honour, Wealth, [Virtue] the most manly Virtues, and the most important Improvements, by rescuing us, even beyond our own Original Designs from that Dependence upon a distant Nation, which had it continued must have ended in the most abject Subjugation: while the /wonderful/ Revolution was effected, not [be?] by our Treachery, or Impatience under reasonable Government, [by] but by the divine Blessing upon our Efforts to repel an oppressive Power; Efforts, which both with Respect to the Ground on which they were made, and the Firmness with which they have continued, instead of dishonouring have rendered [us capable?] our Country highly respectable among the Nations of the Earth. Does not then such a Dispensation of Heaven, so important in itself, and in its consequences to us and our Posterity, demand our most grateful acknowledgements to the Supreme Disposer of all Events. [sic]

To ensure to us, as we trust, this Blessing, God who [always] works by means which are the Choice of his own Wisdom, *has arm'd the Hands of just and mighty Princes in our Deliverance*; for which we are *admonished* to render him our Thanks and Praises. It was so ordered in divine Providence, that when we were compell'd to [resist the] draw the Sword agst Britain, the Interests of France induced that Power to espouse our Cause. There were, however, in her Manner of conducting this Measure, the strongest Marks of Justice and Generosity. This is acknowledged by all the World: France brought the Weight of the whole House of Bourbon to our Cause, as appears by the subsequent Conduct of Spain.[11] It would be a Reflection upon your Understanding, should I suppose it necessary to prove that this aid has been of the greatest Importance to us. Nothing could be more reasonable; Nothing more effectual to our Support. /Nothing more necessary;/ While we adore the divine Providence in this Succor, we are bound to mention with particular Gratitude & Respect that Monarch who [se just and w??] under God brought it to us; and devoutly to pray, as the Public Order for this day; Solemnity directs us, that God would take into his /special/ *holy* Protection our illustrious Ally; give him Victory over his Enemies, and render him signally great as the Father of his People; and the Protector of the Rights of Mankind.

We are invited to render our solemn Thanks this day to the supreme Governor of the World, for the Success with which he hath crowned our Arms & those of our Allies; that he hath been a Shield to our Troops in the House of Danger; that he [hath] hath[12] in the Year we are closing, more than once led [our them Troops] in Triumph over the Bulwarks of the Foe: that he hath conducted our Forces with Success, thro [sic] many Difficulties & Dangers into the extensive Country of a Savage Foe; by which means he hath stayed the hand of that cruel /Spoiler;/ and prevented the meditated Destruction of the Frontier of these States: that he hath prospered us on the Ocean as well as the Land; and deliver'd so much of the Wealth as well as the naval Force of the Enemy into our Hand: In a Word, that he hath frustrated in so great a Measure the Designs of the Enemy thro this Campaign upon wch they so much depended, and hath made them to feel in a Variety of Ways, not only in America but in Europe also, and at their own Doors, the Distresses of that war which they have commenced in Injustice, and conducted with Cruelty.

In addition to all these Favors, God has cheer'd our Dwellings, & our Camp with the Voice of Health, and blest us with an uncommon [Supp] Plenty of the Fruits of the Earth, in which he has not only satisfied our own wants, but enabled us to furnish large Supplies to our Allies. Above all, as we are reminded by that reputable Authority that has called us to this Solemnity, God has blest us with his glorious Light of the Gospel, wch gives Peace and Joy to the human Mind under all the Vicissitudes and Troubles of the present States; and at the same Time gives us the Prospect of an higher Life beyond the Grave; [and] of a Society that knows no Imperfections; and of a Glory and Felicity that [our?] shall never be interrupted & can never decay.

And shall we have no warm Sensations of Gratitude for these & innumerable other Instances of the divine Goodness? Shall we be insensible to such Riches of Mercy; shall we regard them with Indifference? Shall we abuse them, [or] and turn them into Wantonness? Shall we by our Impiety and Wickedness, change these Blessings into a Curse, and ripen ourselves for severer Corrections than we have ever yet felt? God forbid! Goodness is adapted to melt the

Heart and win the Affections: The Goodness /of God/ s'd inspire us with Love and Reverence to him and his Laws: It should awaken in us an ingenuous Contrition; It should lead us to Justice and Charity in all our Intercourse with our Brethren of Mankind; with our Fellow citizens, & those who with us make one Household of Faith: It should lead us to break off our Sins by Repentance, & our Iniquities by Shewing Mercy to the poor.—The poor! Can our Competency, or Abundance, the undeserved Gift of Heaven, ever allow us to forget them. Can we be warm, and fed to the full, and surrounded with all the Conveniences, and even Delicacies of Life in our own [Man] Dwellings, and never think of the empty, uncomfortable Mansions of Poverty, where the Widow weeps; the Orphan cries for Bread; and the whole Family pines with Hunger, [or] & shivers with Cold, and who maketh Thee to differ, or what has thou that thou hast not received. If then thou hast freely received it, do not grudge to communicate a [part] proper Portion of it, to support the Infirmities, and relieve the Distresses of others; so shalt thou honour thy God, and taste with double Sweetness the Bounties he bestows on Thee. The Revolution in our State has made a quik [sic] and surprising Revolution in private Property. God grant that Justice & Charity may lessen the Inequalities it has made, & soften the Distress where it falls heavy; and you know my Hearers, better perhaps than I can tell you, that it does fall heavy upon a Part of the Community the lest [sic] able to help themselves. Here then is a noble Scope for generous Minds; & these are the Days that try Men's Souls.[13] The Niggard shrinks; and he that was unjust, may be still more unjust; but He that was righteous is righteous still; and the good Man appears with double Lustre. [We were once] We were once reputed, & I believe justly, a sober an[14] [just and a rel] honest, a religious People. Whatever we may gain, o let us not loose [sic] our Piety and Morals—if these are preserved and improved, our Honour and Felicity will rest upon a broad and permanent Basis;—Whatever Changes take place in this [-World-] transient State, [Piety and V] true Goodness will triumph at last: it was made for both Worlds; It has [th] Promise of the Life that now is, and of that which is to come. May God make us all happy, Individually, & as a Community in this inestimable Jewel, of his infinite Mercy.

[xxxx] indicates undecipherable corrections or text material.
/ / indicates that the words so enclosed were enterered supralineal
Xt = Christ
O = universe
// = Hancock's indication of a pause or paragraph

NOTES

1. This text appears at the beginning of the page that Hancock (or someone else) labeled page one. A second text, given below, appears on the very first page (not numbered) of the MS. It seems as appropriate a text as does the 100th Psalm. The relationship between the two texts is obscure. Both were originally headings to otherwise blank pages, and other materials were written at the bottoms of the pages on which the texts were written, when Hancock apparently decided to end his sermon by scribbling the end of the concluding paragraph at the bottom of the two sheets on which he had put the two texts at the top. Both are from the Old Testament, so the appearance of the two cannot be explained as a recognition of both the New and the Old Testament.

1 Chron. 29.12-13

> Thou reignest over all, and in thine Hand it is to make great and to give Strength unto all; Now therefore, our God, we thank Thee, and praise thy glorious Name.

2. The source of Hancock's either single "fourteener" line or 4/3 ballad-stanza couplet remains obscure. The sentiment is Miltonic, but the meter is not one that Milton used. The source may be the writings of a now obscure colonial poet who was remembering his Milton, possibly the speech of Eve in *Paradise Lost*, XII, 461-466:

> Henceforth I learn, that to obey is best
> And love with fear the only God, to walk
> As in his presence, ever to observe
> His providence, and on him sole depend,
> Merciful over all his works...

3. Psalms 104.27: "These wait all upon thee; that thou mayest give *them* their meat in due season.
4. Psalms 69.31: "This also shall please the Lord better than an ox or bullock that hath horns and hoofs."
5. Hancock's abbreviation for "universe" and for "Christ" are indications that he probably read from this MS when he delivered his sermon.
6. It would appear that Hancock was giving himself a choice of language.
7. Apparently a reference to Daniel 11.4 in which an angel is telling Daniel about the future of Israel: "And when he [i.e., a strong king] shall

stand up, his kingdom shall be broken, and shall be divided towards the four winds of heaven; and not to his posterity, nor according to his dominion which he rules: for his kingdom shall be plucked up even for others beside those."

8. Hancock put a linear indication at this point of a text insertion. The insertion is on a separate set of sheets.

9. The MS here is almost illegible.

10. At this point the MS returns to its original text.

11. The motives for France and subsequently for Spain for entering the war on the side of the colonists were complex and certainly were not because, as despotic countries, they favored the establishment of a representative government in America. At that time, both France and Spain were ruled by Bourbons and often worked closely on foreign policy. At the Treaty of Paris that concluded the Seven Years' War, both countries had lost heavily to England. France had ceded Canada, and Spain had been forced to trade the Floridas in order to regain Cuba. Therefore, when the American conflict broke out, both France and Spain saw an opportunity to strike back at their old enemy.

The French and Spanish agreed in the secret Convention of Aranjuez to continue the struggle with Great Britain until Spain regained Gibraltar, which the English had taken during the Seven Years' War. Therefore, as Martin pointed out, the colonists without their knowledge were destined to continue the struggle until Spain achieved its territorial ambitions.

The aid took two forms: money and military support. Early in the conflict between the colonists and the British, the Spanish minister of foreign affairs, Grimaldi, offered to share with France the cost of sending secret funds to the colonists. In May of 1776, Louis XVI's government informed the Spanish that it was prepared to advance one million livres to the colonists, "laundering" the funds through a commercial establishment, more than likely Roderique Hortaleaz & Cie. (Lowell, 126) Charles III of Spain, after some hesitation, joined in the scheme and sent a similar amount to Paris to be made available to the colonists. (Lowell, 126) More funds were to be sent. Lowell reported that the initial contribution by France was two million livres rather than one million. Another million was to be sent in exchange for tobacco. Five million more were promised, of which only two million arrived. Spain committed an additional three million livres, but, according to Lowell, only 1.75 million ever arrived. Later, John Jay got an additional $175,000 from the Spanish. France contributed more heavily. Lowell reported that between February of 1778 and July of 1782, France loaned eighteen million livres. The total amount advanced by France, according to Lowell, reached thirteen million livres. France also guaranteed the Dutch loan to the colonists. (Lowell, 71-72)

France committed itself earlier than Spain to the military aspects of the war, and officially recognized the colonies. In July of 1778, Conrad Alexandre Gerard arrived in Philadelphia as the first French ambassador to the colonies. Although he was greeted with much acclaim, his mission may well have been to keep the colonists divided so that, if the British were defeated, they could serve as no strong base for revolutionary activity in the New World. (Martin, 151) France had entered the war officially on 6 Feb 1778 with the Treaty of Amity and Commerce and the Treaty of Conditional and Defensive Alliance; Spain in 1779; the Netherlands in 1780. Spain and Holland limited their contributions to funds and moral support by declaring war on England. It was France who supplied the naval support and troops. Just how many arrived at what time is beyond the scope of this investigation. Hancock was speaking of the seven thousand French troops commanded by Rochambeau that marched south from New York to Virginia to help surround Cornwallis and the French fleet under Admiral de Grasse, who sailed up from the West Indies, sealed off Cornwallis's retreat by sea, and defeated the British fleet that tried to come to Cornwallis's rescue.

The manner in which the peace was achieved, with preliminaries completed in Paris on 20 Nov 1781 and the final treaty signed at Versailles on 3 Sept 1783, is again beyond the scope of this investigation. It can be said that the French fleet that sailed from Yorktown was unsuccessful in capturing Jamaica from the British and the combined French and Spanish troops were also defeated in efforts to reclaim Gibraltar.

Therefore, the colonists came forth as the big victors, securing the right to lands as far west as the Mississippi, free access to the Mississippi, and the recognition of American fishing rights around Nova Scotia, but the colonial diplomats made no headway in getting Britain to cede Canada. For much of this discussion, we are indebted to Lowell.

Whatever may have been their motives, the colonists could not have won the war without the monies used to purchase arms and without the military and naval support of the French. Of the 15,600 troops besieging Cornwallis, 7,000 were French. De Grasse's fleet kept Cornwallis from disembarking for New York. Hancock was right. The French and Spanish did materially assist the colonists in winning the Revolutionary War.

12. Hancock actually ran his strikeout through the "he" as well.

13. Hamlet

14. Hancock apparently went back and added an "n" to his "a" to make it blend with "honest."

HEADNOTE

Date: 19 January 1790

    Occasion: The newspapers noted: "At Twelve o'clock, His
Excellency The Governour, agreeably to assignment, came down to the
Chamber of the House of Representatives, attended by The Secretary of
the Commonwealth; and where the Senate had previously assembled—
when His Excellency was pleased to deliver the following Speech."
    The address opened the first session of 1790, and Hancock was still
concerned with the interaction of the national and state legislatures.
    The joint Senate and House reply to Hancock's speech is given in
Senate Unenacted #1140/1. It reads in part: "The Committee of both
Houses on the Governors Speech of the 19th Instant, ask leave to report
the following Answer ["hereto amended" was struck] and also, that a
Committee of both Houses be appointed to consider the Subject Matter
of that Clause of his Excellency's Speech, which relates to the Courts
of Common Pleas & of the Sessions of the Peace." The document
bears the date 27 Jan 1790.
    The reply stated that "we are happy to find that your Health is so far
restored as to enable you to meet the General Court, & by a personal
interview to deliver your communications."

SOURCES

    Senate Unenacted #1140 (1790) and House Unenacted #3352, MA.
What apppears to be a draft of the speech is housed under "Hancock
Papers" at the Massachusetts Historical Society. Hancock himself
initialed and dated the draft in a very shaky hand. *Journal of the House*
10, 168-72, MA; *Journal of the House* 10, 168-172, SL;* A&L A&R,
1789-1790 (1895), 749-53.
    Herald of Freedom 22 Jan 1790, 152; Boston Gazette 25 Jan 1790,
2-3; Massachusetts *Centinel* 20 Jan 1790, 2-3; Massachusetts *Spy* 28
Jan 1790, 2-3; *Independent Chronicle* 21 Jan 1790, 2.

    *No copy in either Senate Journal.

TEXT

Gentlemen of the Senate & Gentlemen of the House of Representatives—

I directed the Secretary on[1] the 14th instant, to lay before you the proceedings of the Congress of the United States of America in their late Session: & other papers which I thought it necessary to communicate to you.

It is in compliance with the duties of the office I am honored with; from the respect I have for you personally, & from the regard I feel to you as the Representatives of my fellow Citizens the people of the Commonwealth, that I have proposed this interview.—

I congratulate you Gentlemen, on the accession of another State to our Union;[2] & am happy to say, that I am persuaded, that the wisdom & tried Patriotism of the Citizens of Rhode Island, will very soon compleat [sic] the Union of all the Independent States of America, under one System of general, national Government;[3] the due administration of which cannot fail to render them respectable abroad, & to establish peace & harmony between them at home. Every patriot will rejoice to see all these States, which have most nobly contended for civil freedom, uniting in their endeavors to preserve, & in their measures to enjoy, the invaluable blessings which flow from it—

The acts & proceedings of Congress, which the Secretary has laid before you,[4] contain propositions for amendments in the Constitution of the United States: these are submitted to your deliberations on the part of our Constituents; & there can be no necessity of any other call to awaken your attention, than the interest they have in them. I shall not be particular in my remarks on these propositions—

As Government is no other, than the United consent of the people of a[5] civil community, to be governed in a particular mode, by certain established principles, the more general the union of Sentiment is, the more energetic & permanent the Government will be: Upon this idea, the adoption of some of the proposed amendments becomes very important; because, the people of this Commonwealth felt themselves assured by the proceedings of their Convention, which ratified the Constitution, that certain amendments, amongst which were some of those, would be effected:

The seventh, eighth & ninth articles appear to me to be of great consequence.[6] In all free Governments, a share in the administration of the Laws ought to be vested in, or reserved to the People;[7] this prevents a government from verging toward despotism, secures the freedom of debate, & supports that independence of sentiment which dignifies the Citizen, & renders the government permanently respectable.

The institutions of Grand & Petit Juries are admirably calculated to produce these happy effects, & to afford security to the best rights of men in civil society:[8] These articles therefore, I believe will meet your ready approbation: some of the others appear to me as very important to that personal security, which is so truly characteristic of a Free Government.

Since the adjournment of the Legislature, the President of the United States has been pleased to honor the Commonwealth with a visit; upon so pleasing an occasion,[9] I thought it to be my indispensable duty with advice of the honorable Council, to receive him, with all the attention due to his personal merit & illustrious Character; & to the high & important office which he sustains with so much dignity; as well as in a manner suited to the consequence of the Commonwealth; & I feel myself assured that we shall meet your entire approbation in our proceedings.[10] Upon so pleasing an incident, the People of every description view with each other, in paying their respects to the Man who with such magnanimity, wisdom, & firmness, led the successful Armies of their Country in their late perilous contest.[11]--

Within the same time, the Chief Justice of the Supreme Judicial Court of the Commonwealth, & one other of the Judges of that Court, have been appointed by the President of the United States, to offices under the Government wherein he presides; in consequence of which, they have resigned the Commissions they held under this government.[12] I shall endeavor to fill the vacancies occasioned by those resignations, with men of integrity, learning & ability, that the judicial power of the Government, may still retain that eminent degree of respectability for which it has been revered; & still hold that confidence in the Public Mind, which has so happy an effect upon the tranquillity of the State.

You will readily agree with me, Gentlemen, when I say that the freedom of the People, and the protecting of their rights, persons & property, essentially depend upon the respectability of their government. The General Government is well calculated to direct the great national concerns of the Confederated Republic, but the line which divides the authorities of that, & the government of the Commonwealth is well described in the Constitution; & such provisions ought to be made for the ample administration of Justice, amongst the Citizens of the Commonwealth, that all reasonable men will be satisfied, nor indulge a wish to derive aid from any other tribunal, than those the State provides.

From the information I receive from various parts of the States, I am inclined to believe that the plan lately adopted, of having but two

Courts of Common Pleas,[13] & two Courts of Sessions annually in each County, will not have the salutary effects which were expected from it; & that more Courts in nearly all the Counties, will be of great advantage to the People. Your acquaintance with the subject enables you to decide with propriety upon it; to you I submit it, with only this observation, that the great end of Government is the regular administration of Justice; & this, as expressed in our Constitution, ought to be done promptly & without delay.—

I congratulate you with great pleasure, Gentlemen, upon the happy situation of our Country; But the pleasing prospects afforded us by Divine Providence, ought not by any means to be the occasion of our relaxing in our endeavors for the public weal. It would be very extraordinary if we, as a nation, should remain exempted from those Foreign, or Domestic troubles, with which other nations are frequently visited. Notwithstanding a general Government is well established by the free consent of the People, we are to continue to support our own Government, with unabating anxiety for its welfare & prosperity: Indeed, the general Government of the United States, is founded in an assemblage of separate[14] Republican Governments; & it depends essentially on these, not only for its dignity & energy, but for its very existence in the form it now possesses;[15] therefore, whatever is done to support the Commonwealth, has a tendency to advance the interest & honor of all the States. Hence we are called upon in an especial manner to maintain an equal & regular System of Revenue & taxation, to support the faith, & to perform the engagements of our Republic; to arm & cause our Militia to be disciplined according to the mode which shall be provided by Congress; & to see that they are officered with Men, who are capable of making the greatest progress in the Arts Military, & who delight in the freedom & happiness of their Country. A well regulated & disciplined Militia, is at all times a good objection to the introduction of that bane of all free governments,— a standing Army—[16]

Our happiness so essentially depends upon the encouragement of Literature, & the dissemination of useful knowledge, that the fathers of the people will always have them in their view: And give Me leave to add, that our safety, ease, & prosperity may be promoted by cultivating peace & harmony amongst the People of every denomination in the Commonwealth.

Let us unite frequently with all our Brethren who possess this good land which God[17] was pleased to give our forefathers; in reflecting upon the trials we have been supported under; upon the dangers we have been delivered from; & let us adore & praise Him who has been our deliverer, for His[18] goodnessss vouchsafed to us, in giving us success & victory; & in making us an Independent & prosperous Nation; for his smiling in a peculiar manner upon all our attempts for the achievement of Political & Civil institutions. And as obedience to the divine will[19] is the best expression of gratitude, may be a true spirit of piety & virtue be every where seen & encouraged.—

Gentlemen of the Senate and Gentlemen of the House of Representatives

If I am blessed with any talents that may be useful to my Country, I do most heartily assure you, that I can derive no greater pleasure from any circumstance than from the improvement of them to the best of my ability: And I shall do everything in my power to render the present Session useful to my fellow Citizens, as well as pleasant & agreeable to you.

John Hancock[20]

NOTES

1. Hancock corrected the scribe's copy in Senate #1140 by inserting "on" superlineally. No such correction was necessary in House #3352. The existence of these two "fair copies" indicates that it was the custom for the office of the governor to send down to the legislature two copies of his speeches, one for the Senate and one for the House. The MA has two such copies of four different Hancock speeches.

2. North Carolina ratified the Constitution on 19 Nov 1789, by a vote of 194 to 77 at a second Constitutional Convention held in Fayetteville. In its reply, Senate MS 1140/1, the General Court noted its pleasure that North Carolina had ratified by such a large margin. The reponse of the legislature was reprinted on Chapter 33B of the A&R 626-628, January Session, 1789.

3. On 28 May 1790, Rhode Island ratified the Constitution by a vote of 34 to 32. In its reply, Senate MS 1140/1, the General Court had said: "...we sincerely hope that the Citizens of Rhode Island will at their insuing Convention exercise their wonted patriotism by their decisions compleat the Union. [sic]"

4. Hancock again corrected the scribe in Senate #1140 by inserting "you."

5. In Senate #1140, Hancock inserted "a" superlineally.

6. The original federal Bill of Rights submitted to the states on 25 Sept 1789 contained twelve articles, the first two of which were not approved. Therefore, in speaking of the seventh, eighth and ninth articles, Hancock is

referring to what are now the fifth, sixth, and seventh articles. The grand jury is referred to in the Fifth Amendment. The Massachusetts General Court was not among the eleven states whose approval of the Bill of Rights was required to make the amendments applicable to the States. Virginia had cast the eleventh vote on 15 Dec 1791. Rutland noted that "as a token gesture celebrating the 150th anniversary of ratification of the Federal Bill of Rights, the three states which had never approved the amendments— Connecticut, Georgia, and Massachusetts—formally ratified the measures." (Rutland, 217n.; cf. Irving Brant, 68-70)

7. The Tenth Amendment to the constitution so provides. "The powers not delegated to the United States by the Constitution, nor prohibited by it to the States, are reserved to the States respectively, or to the people."

8. Chapter 63 of the A&R 1793, 495-497 begins an act to amend the original act entitled "An Act Regulating the Appointment and Services of Grand Jurors."

9. In its reply to the governor's speech, the legislature noted: "The visit made this State by the President of the United States, is peculiarly [pleasing] gratefull [sic] as it afforded the Executives of this Commonwealth & many of our Citizens an opportunity to pay their publick respects to a Character whose magnanimity wisdom and firmness will ever excite our most sincere attachments & warmest acknowledgements." (Senate MS. 1140/1)

10. For whatever reasons, the relationships between Washington and Hancock during the president's visit to Boston were strained. Washington's eastern trip was designed to consolidate the position of the presidency in areas where anti-federalism was strong. Hancock probably sensed not only what would be an increase in the strength of federalism resulting from a successful visit by Washington to Boston but also resented a rivalry to his own immense popularity in what he considered to be "his town." As Washington was traveling in spartan style with only two secretaries, Hancock as governor assigned him six servants who joined the president's party at some point between Hartford and Washington's arrival at the state border at Springfield. A civil deputation at Springfield offered the president lodgings at a public house in Boston, while an emissary from the State House not only explained what military escorts would be provided first at Worcester and later at Cambridge but also a written note from Hancock dated Wednesday, 21 Oct, offering Washington lodgings at the Hancock mansion. (Sparks, 10, 489-90) On Thursday, 22 Oct 1789, Washington replied that he was traveling without ceremony and had elected on leaving New York to decline any private invitations for accommodations. (Sparks, 10, 47) Hancock enjoyed entertaining, was proud of his home on the hill, and probably felt snubbed as well as frustrated that he could not mingle the

president's popularity with his own. Therefore, on Friday, 23 Oct, Hancock seemingly attempted to make the best of things by inviting Washington to dine at the mansion on 24 Oct "en famille."

When Hancock failed to appear in person at Cambridge on Saturday, 24 Oct, to welcome the president, as Washington evidently had expected him to do, it was the president's turn to be miffed. On 23 Oct 1789, he had written Hancock of his plans to arrive in Cambridge at twelve o'clock and had accepted the invitation to take an informal dinner with the Hancocks. But, upon Hancock's failure to appear in Cambridge, Washington declined the invitation and dined with John Adams at Washington's lodgings. As Hancock's gout faded in and out, Hancock may have intentionally avoided saying he would be at Cambridge, hoping that a turn for the better would allow him to be present, or Hancock may have been maneuvering so that Washington would have to pay his respects to the governor, rather than the governor paying his respects to Washington. Such posturing does not appear to be to the credit of either party.

Be that as it may, after having been escorted to his lodgings at the Widow Ingersoll's in Queen Street, Washington sent a note to Hancock on that same Saturday, 24 Oct, declining the invitation to the family meal. (Fitzpatrick, 4, 34-5) Undoubtedly the food was in preparation, and no one was coming to dinner. It was now again Hancock's turn to be provoked.

Washington recorded in the diary citation above, that he had expected Hancock to wait upon him at Cambridge. Washington realized that he had to build the image of the presidency, but he was well acquainted not only with Hancock's vanity, but with the major contribution that Hancock had made to the revolution. Hancock, on the other hand, was undoubtedly ill with a combination of gout and false pride, but he was also aware that Washington had to build the status of the presidency. Yet the governors of the colonial states, who had so recently been custodians of what were virtually free nations, were still (and are often still) reluctant to admit to the power of a federal president. It appears that both men could have acted with considerably more grace and style.

Some years later, in a conversation with William Sumner, Hancock's widow, then remarried as Dorothy Scott, stated that indeed her husband had had the gout in his feet and hands at the time of Washington's visit and could not move. (Sumner, 190) It is always easy to say that Hancock feigned illness for political reasons, but the gout is painful and debilitating. It is also a disease easily made sport of, for it is often brought on by dissipation. Whatever the cause, when one's limbs are aching, it is not pleasant to think of rumbling through the rough streets of colonial Boston to Cambridge in a carriage.

In any event, sensing that Washington may have won the duel and exhibiting his knack for political recoupment that had maintained his popularity over a period of twenty years, Hancock sent a note dated Sunday, 26 Oct, at 12:30 P.M. saying that the governor would like to call upon the president in one half-hour. (Sparks, 10, 493). Washington replied that he would be at home until 2:00 P.M. (Sparks, 10, 493) Whether or not Washington had a 2:00 P.M engagement is not clear. Hancock had himself carried by servants from his carriage up to the president's quarters, although the sight of the governor swathed in red baise may not have brought on the tears that Hancock's widow spoke of thirty-three years later. (Sumner, *Reminiscences*, 190; Sumner, *Some Recollections*, 165) Nevertheless Washington could easily have been moved by seeing the man he remembered as the vigorous president of the First Continental Congress so aged and indeed only three years from the grave. Washington could easily have been thinking of his own infirmities and the sight of a colleague so near to death could have reminded Washington that his days too were numbered. Washington did die nine years later.

The hiarchy properly established, Washington sent word on Monday, 26 Oct, that he could call upon the Hancocks, where he had tea with John and Dorothy, (Fitzpatrick, 4, 36) an appropriate end to a tempest in a teapot. According to Dolly's reminiscences, Washington said that he had been deceived into thinking that Hancock was maneuvering so that Washington would pay the first call and that he expressed his astonishment that his informants should have so imposed upon him. (Sumner, *Reminiscences*, 190) On Tuesday, 27 Oct, Washington was the guest of Hancock by proxy at a dinner at Faneuil Hall, and on Wednesday, 28 Oct, Dorothy represented Hancock at a ball in honor of the president. It could be argued that, if Hancock had been altogether feigning illness, with his political acumen, he would have miraculously recovered and attempted to sponsor Washington as his protege.

When Washington departed for Portsmouth, New Hampshire on Thursday, 29 Oct, 1789, he was properly escorted by Vice-President Adams, Bowdoin, and other persons of note.

11. The festivities were numerous. Upon his arrival at the town, Washington passed between lines of citizens bearing banners and grouped according to their professions. Upon entering what now seems to be the very small old State House, Washington ascended to the rotunda where he with other dignitaries reviewed the long procession of the guildsmen bearing their banners. Across the front of the State House was a banner inscribed, "Boston relieved March 17, 1776," in memory of Washington's having delivered the town from the British. Washington was then escorted to his lodgings in Queen Street, now known as Court Street. Benjamin

Russell noted: "The altercation on the isthmus created great excitement, which was increased by a severe epidemic, with which several thousands were affected in consequence of their exposure to the inclemency of the weather." (Sparks, 10, 492-3). The intense cold may have been another reason why Hancock did not venture out. Washington recorded the details of the reception given him in Boston in his diary entries for Saturday, 24 Oct, through Tuesday, 28 Oct. (Fitzpatrick, 4, 33-7)

12. William Cushing resigned as chief justice of the Massachusetts Supreme Court to accept a position as associate justice on the federal supreme court. Cushing was one of the judges that had refused to receive his salary directly from the king. David Sewell had been appointed to the new Supreme Judicial Court of Massachusetts in 1781. In 1789, he was commissioned judge of the United States District Court for Maine. Sitting as the sole judge, Sewall was required to decide whether pirates were to live or die. He resigned his federal position in 1795 to return to Massachusetts as register of probate.

13. A&R 1788-1789, January session, Chap. 124, 621-622, redistributed the courts of common pleas and the courts of general sessions.

14. The word "separate" appeared in Senate #1140 and the *Journal of the House*, but not in House #3352 or in the newspaper accounts.

15. In both Senate 1140 and House 3352, Hancock struck "proposes" and wrote above the line "possesses."

16. In its reply, Senate Document #1140/1, the General Court stated: "We heartily agree with your Excellency that a well disciplined & regulated militia is at all time a good objection to the introduction of that bane of all free Governments—a *Standing Army.*—The necessity therefore of our Citizens being instructed in the Art military, must be [evident] to every man who delights in the freedom of his Country.—"

17. House #3352 and *Journal of the House* read "GOD." The *Herald*, the *Independent Chronicle*, the *Gazette*, and the *Centinel* also read "GOD," whereas the Spy prefers "God."

18. In House #3352, Hancock wrote a capital "H" over the scribe's "h."

19. House #3352 reads "Divine Will."

20. Hancock autographed both the Senate and House copies.

HEADNOTE

Date: 28 May 1790

Occasion: A&R for Friday, 28 May 1790, read: "At Twelve o'clock, the two Houses met in Convention, in the Representatives' Chamber, when His Excellency the Governour, and His Honour the Lieutenant Governour (attended by the Hon. Council, and the Secretary of the Commonwealth) appeared to qualify themselves agreeable to the Constitution. After being a short time seated, His Excellency arose, and addressed both Houses, as follows:"

Following the governor's statement, the Massachusetts *Spy* reported: "The President of the Senate then administered the oaths and declarations required, and the Secretary made Proclamation of the choice, acceptance and qualification of His Excellency." Sam Adams, the lieutenant governor, then made a brief statement which was, however, considerably longer than Hancock's.

SOURCES

Acts & Laws, 1790-1791, 18 May 1790, 545; *Herald of Freedom* 1 June 1790, 1; Massachusetts *Spy* 3 June 1790, 2; Massachusetts *Centinel* 29 May 1790, 2 (86); *Independent Chronicle* 3 June 1790, 1; Boston *Gazette* 31 May 1790, 2.

TEXT

Gentlemen of the Senate, and Gentlemen of the House of Representatives,

I thank you for the very polite and respectful manner in which you have notified me of my being chosen Governour of this Commonwealth for the ensuing year.[1]

I appear in this place to accept the trust assigned me by my country, and am ready in your presence to make and subscribe the declarations and to take and subscribe to oaths provided by the Constitution.

It is unnecessary for me to say any thing more upon this occasion, than to assure you, that I shall zealously endeavor, in all my conduct, to justify the partiality which has been frequently exhibited by my fellow-citizens towards me.

John Hancock

NOTES

1. *A&R* reads "for the year ensuing."

HEADNOTE

Date: Tuesday, 1 June 1790

Occasion: As he often did when in good health, Hancock followed his reelection by speaking to the General Court. Or, if he was ailing, he sent them a written message. In 1790, Hancock wrote the legislature on 28 May that he was ready to appear before them and take the oath of office. (House Unenacted #3348, MA)

The newspaper accounts are consistently brief, saying: "Tuesday, at Twelve o'clock, His Excellency the Governour came down to the Chamber of the House of Representatives; where the Senate were previously convened;—when he addressed the Two Houses as follows:"

SOURCES

House Unenacted #3354, MA; *Journal of the House*, ll, 1790, 35-40, MA; *Journal of the House*, 11, 1790, 35-40, SL.*

A&R 1790-1791, 547-551; Massachusetts *Centinel* 2 June 1790, 2 (90); *Herald of Freedom* 4 June 1790, 93-94; Boston *Gazette* 7 June 1790, 1; *Independent Chronicle* 3 June 1790, 2; Massachusetts *Spy* 10 June 1790, 1.

*No copy in either Senate Journal.

TEXT

Gentlemen of the Senate and Gentlemen of the House of Representatives,

At a time, when the attention of this Country was necessarily called to a defence against an invading Enemy, the People of the several States, originated, or revised, Systems of Governments [sic]: On these Systems, the Freedom, and Happiness of their posterity, will essentially depend. The great plan for uniting the powers, and directing the Force of so many independent States, rising into one confederated and powerful Republic, could not in such a situation be properly attended to.—To unite in one great System of national Government so many seperat [sic] Republicks, including extremes of Climate, and possessed by People, very various in their habits of life, in their manners, and in their religious opinions, was indeed a work which demanded the utmost exertions of human Wisdom, and required the most unimbarrassed [sic] deliberations. This seems to have been reserved as an honorary task for the People of America.[1] Whether all our expectations will be eventually answered from this plan, must be left to future experience: but this principle is already ascertained, that any delay which has happened, or which may hereafter happen, in producing the effects which the form of that Government is capable of affording, is no objection to the Government itself. Time and experience we hope will consolidate the opinions of the Members of Congress in the important points before them, and yield to the people of the great Republick, all the advantages which can be derived from the wisest and best administered form of Government. And we cannot but feel ourselves well assured, that a candour and generosity peculiar to the body of this People, will continue to support amongst them the harmony of sentiment, which so universally prevails, and which afford a happy presage of our political prosperity. We have, by the blessing of divine Providence, achieved a situation truly enviable in the eyes of other Nations: our persons, and possessions, are governed by standing and known laws, and secured by a Constitution formed by ourselves. This Constitution is a law to the Legislative authority itself: and lest[2] the pride of Office, or the hand of lawless power, should rob the people of their Constitutional security, a proper balance is provided in the judicial department, occasionally arising from the body of the People. The Price of our Freedom has been great toil, and much expence [sic], and we yet feel the weight of it: but we feel as freemen, while the People of some other countries, are oppressed with heavy burthens [sic] which have been accumulated, not to secure, but to destroy their Freedom.

Though the National affairs of our Country are more immediately under the attention of the General Government, yet we have very important business, which demands our attention. Having formed our Governments, established our Independency, we sit down quietly, and peaceably to inquire into, and to perform those duties which may be reasonably expected from us, in our tranquil situation. And I am very happy to inform you that the business of our meeting is principally confined to the devising ways and means, for answering the just demands[3] of our public[4] Creditors, making such additional Laws, as may be necessary to mark out the paths of distributive justice, to adopt such measures as many facilitate the settlement of the uncultivated parts of the State, & to devise ways for promoting useful knowledge, and for inculcating those Virtues which are the only solid foundation of public and private Felicity.—

Many of the Citizens of this Commonwealth, while the Country was pressed on every side by danger & distress, freely loaned their property to the public safety: and had the most solemn assurances for a repayment with interest. Others ventured their lives in the war for our defence, and received the public faith pledged for a compensation, when the War should be terminated. The Eyes of these Creditors are now upon us for justice: and the sufferings of the Widows and Orphans demand our attention.[5]

I am sensible that some of the public securities, evidential of these loans and services, have been thrown into the hands of persons who have given but a small consideration for them, but while we are convinced that this has in some measure been owing to the failure of Governmental promises, we ought not to increase the calamity by unnecessary delays in doing justice. Was it within the power of the people to pay the debt they owe as a Government, it would be for their honour, and advantage to do it immediately, but as this cannot be done, the making provision for the punctual payment of the interest annually, will be nearly as well for the Creditors. But then in order to produce this effect, the payment of this interest must be assured upon funds which may be depended upon. In a Republican Government, the idea of responsibility is generally divided amongst too many persons, to insure that punctuallity [sic] in the performance of promises, which some other forms of Government may afford: therefore the security of punctual payments, is not frequently well established, without appropriated Funds, and yet the happiness of every Government, in whatever form it may be, depends essentially upon the rectitude and punctuallity of it.

When I speak of the happiness of a Government, I mean that situation of a civil Community which has a tendency to make those who compose it happy, by affording them security against foreign invaders, as well as against internal commotions; and in defending the individuals over whom it is extended, against oppression and injustice.

The debt we are involved in, and which I have now under consideration, was contracted for the common defence of the United States, and I flatter myself that justice will finally prevail, so that the Government lately established, will consider the whole of the Union, as responsible to each State for debts of this nature. In the Report of the Secretary of Treasury of the United States there is a proposal for Congress to assume the Debts of the several States[6] but I am not convinced of the propriety of the General government's assuming to pay the Debts of this Commonwealth without the request or consent of this Government;[7] but[8] as it will be more congenial to any system of Finance which the Congress may adopt for this Class of the Creditors of this State to transfer the demands to the General Government on the idea of the standing Credit of our Government,[9] and to have them involved in the funded debt of the United States, than to have a claim open in favor of the Commonwealth, I recommend it to your serious deliberation, whether Instructions may not be given to our Senators & Representatives on this point.[10]

Gentlemen of the Senate and Gentlemen of the House of Representatives: the settlement of a very extensive Territory of Wilderness within this Commonwealth,[11] is an object of great consequence in my mind.—The sale of those lands has been a subject of much expectation in former General Courts, but the advantages, and benefits have not been equal to their hopes. The first settlers of a new soil have to encounter great difficulties, and to suffer many hardships. The want of a regular gospel Ministry, and proper schools, are not the least discouragements attending such an enterprize [sic]; for want of these their children are in danger of rising into life without those Ideas, habits and abilities, which might render them good and useful Citizens. Should the Legislature of the Commonwealth, make a grant of these lands, for a small consideration, to such persons as would settle them in regular Corporations, according to the condition of their grants, and reserve, & appropriate sufficient quantities of the soils, to procure, & support the settlement of a regular ministry, and the support of proper schools for a number of years, until the Inhabitants could be able to support them without the aid of Government, I believe it would have a happy effect. Should this or any other plan be adopted, to induce our people to become settlers there, it would have a tendency to prevent those emigrations, which have for some years past been so frequent, encrease[12] the number of our Citizens, support the respectability of the Commonwealth, and probably, in a short space of time, afford a resource for taxes far exceeding what the value of lands have been estimated at.

It is of vast importance to our Commonwealth, that a speedy and just execution of the laws should be maintained; that industry, and every virtue should be encouraged; and that idleness,[13] dissipation & every vice, should be discountenanced: I therefore recommend it to you, to revise the laws, and to remove every obstacle that may obtrude itself in the path of justice between man, and man; that every one may have a full remedy for every wrong, and the strongest security in the enjoyment of the fruit of his labour and industry: these are among the great ends of civil Government.[14]

Whatever I may find conducive to the well being of the State in particular instances; and whatever information ought to be given you of the proceedings of the Supreme Executive power of the State, shall be the subjects of particular messages.—

Gentlemen of the Senate & Gentlemen of the House of Representatives, I have requested this interview in compliance with the usages of this Government, and that I might pay that respect to you, and to our fellow Citizens which is due from the first Magistrate to his Constituents; and shall add no more, than to assure you, and them through you, that while I have strength for the least exertion, my zealous endeavours shall be for the support of their Liberty, and for the promotion of their happiness and prosperity.—

I have directed the Secretary to lay before you the several acts of Congress which have been received since the last session of the General Court.[15]

John Hancock*

Council Chambers, Boston, May 31, 1790

* #3354 is signed, located and dated by Hancock himself; the remaining portions of the address are in the hand of a scribe

NOTES

1. "America" is underlined in *Journal of the House*.

2. Only the Massachusetts *Spy* uses "lest."

3. *Journal of the House* has a puzzling variation. The scribe first wrote "public" in place of "the just," crossed it out, and wrote something illegible above the line.

4. All of the newspaper versions except the *Gazette* preferred "publick."

5. In their reply to the governor, recorded in Chapter 32 of the A&R of the January Session for 1792, 242, the legislature offered only this general comment: "We are sensible Sir, that the Credits of this Commonwealth, have no direct demand upon any other Gover[n]ment than this.—Various causes have concurred to prevent, or delay the full payment of their just demands.—This delay has been attended with many inconveniences to

them, & is painful to us.—But we trust that the period is not far distant, when we shall be able to fulfill our engagements in a manner that may prove at once satisfactory to our Creditors, & least burdensome to our Constituents."

6. On Monday, 21 Sept 1789, Congress ordered the secretary of the treasury "to apply to the Supreme Executives of the several States, for statements of their public debts...and report to the House such of said documents as he may obtain, at the next session of Congress." (*Annals of Congress*, I, 1789-90, col. 904)   The report itself by Secretary of the Treasury Alexander Hamilton is sixteen pages long and undated. Columns. 2021 and 2022 of the Appendix to the *Annals of Congress*, 2, 1790-91, of the "Report of the Secretary of the Treasury" summarized the provisions for assuming the debts of the states.

7. Hancock was voicing the states' rights point of view. Massachusetts having so recently been, for all practical purposes, an independent nation with Hancock as its governor, John was reluctant to see the federal government legislate for the states without their permission.

8. The handwriting of the scribe became much finer with the words "In the Report" and ending with "but," as if Hancock had made a change in his text from which the scribe had copied and considerably more verbiage had to be inserted in the place where Hancock had struck out a few words and inserted additional text.

9. "...[O]n the Idea of the standing Credit of our Government" is omitted in *Journal of the House.*

10. The General Court had no scruples about recommending to Congress that the national government assume the debt of Massachusetts. On 4 June 1790, the court passed a "Resolve Expressing the Opinions of the Legislature that It is Expedient for Congress to Assume and Provide for the Payment of the Debt of the Several States, and Instructing the Members of this State upon the Subject." (A&R, 1790, May Session, 4 June 1790, 101-102)

11. Here Hancock was concerned with the settlement of Maine.

12. Massachusetts *Spy* reads "increase."

13. *Journal of the House* inserts "and," so the phrase reads "idleness and dissipation & every vice," allowing for polysyndeton.

14. House Document 3345 omits the "n" in "government."

15. The last sentence was written in by Hancock as he signed and dated the document. It probably saved him the effort of sending a separate written message to the General Court.

HEADNOTE

Date: Wednesday, 15 September 1790

Occasion: When Hancock reconvened the legislature earlier than usual, he was in sufficiently good health to address them. As usual, he was concerned about the financial status of the state.

A&R stated: "Pursuant to His Excellency's Proclamation, the Members of the Legislature, [sic] met at the State House, and having formed a quorum, a Committee of both Houses were appointed to wait on the Governour, and inform him that they were ready to proceed to business; whereupon His Excellency, attended by the Secretary, met the two Branches convened in the Senate Chamber, and addressed them as follows:" (15 Sept 1790, 554)

SOURCES

House Unenacted #3356, MA.

Journal of the House, 11, 142-4, MA; *Journal of the House*, 11, 142-4, SL;* A&R 1790-1791 (1895), 554-5; *Independent Chronicle* 16 Sept 1790, 2; *Herald of Freedom* 17 Sept 1790, 6; Massachusetts *Spy* 23 Sept 1790, 3.

*No copy in either Senate Journal.

TEXT

Gentlemen of the Senate, & Gentlemen of the House of Representatives,

Nothing but a strong conviction of the necessity of the Legislature's being together at this time could have induced me to convene you at so early a day after the late adjournment.

By your act passed in the late sessions for a conditional repeal of the act for raising a Revenue by Excise, it is provided that "in case the Congress of the United States *should* [1] assume, or permit to be loaned on the credit of the United States, the consolidated debt of this State, or otherwise provide upon the credit of the United States for the payment thereof; then,[2] and in either case, the said act intitled [sic] an act to raise a revenue by excise, and to regulate the collection thereof; should[3] be, & thereby was repealed from, & after the time when any act, or law of Congress for either of the purposes aforesaid, *should* be made, and established."[4]

On the fourth of August last, an act was made, & established by the Congress of the United States by which Twenty one Million five hundred thousand dollars of the debts of the respective States, incurred for compensations, expenditures, for services, or supplies toward the prosecution of the late war, or for the defence of the United States, or some part thereof, during the same, is permitted to be loaned on the credit of the United States—[5]

Upon receiving information of this act, I directed the Treasurer to lay before the Supreme Executive the amount of the consolidated debt of this State, which I find to amount to one million five hundred eighty three thousand, and eighty six pounds 9/3 [6] equal to five million two hundred seventy six thousand nine hundred and fifty four dollars, and 5/6ths of a dollar.

I have directed the Secretary to lay before you a copy of the act of Congress; that you may give it such construction as shall appear to you to be reasonable, & take such measures as may be best suited to the welfare of the Commonwealth in the present particular situation of it.

The Secretary will also lay before you the several acts of Congress passed since your last adjournment.[7]

You will observe with satisfaction that Congress was taking measures to support the credit, and to maintain the honor of the Federal Government; And whilst the Eyes of the people are upon you, as the Guardians of this State, their just expectations will be fully answered, by your adopting those measures which will do the most speedy Justice to Our Creditors, and have a just tendency to maintain the rank & importance of this Commonwealth.

By your act above refered [sic] to; it is provided that the Supreme Executive on having notice of the making & establishing an act or law of Congress for either of the purposes aforesaid, that is, for assuming the consolidated debt of this State, permitting the same to be loaned on the credit of the United States, or otherwise to provide for the payment of the same, on the credit of the States, that they should make the same known in the Commonwealth.[8]

When you shall have attended to the act of Congress, and the particular situation into which the Commonwealth, from our own acts, and the act of Congress is thrown, you will see that the Supreme Executive would have been remiss in the exercise of the authority vested in them [sic], unless they had called the General Court together, in preference to any other measure.

Supposing that the inconvenient season of the year, in which you are convened, will preclude you from attending to any other business besides that which I have already mentioned, I forbear to mention any other to you.

John Hancock[9]

Council Chamber, Sept 15th 1790

NOTES

1. "Shall" in A&R.

2. *Journal of the House* gives an abbreviated version: "on the credit of the United States for the payment thereof, then, and in either case..."

3. "Shall" in A&R.

4. A&R 1790, Chap. 14, 24 June 1790, 20-21: "An Act to Repeal, in Case of the Assumption of the States Debts, by the Congress of the United States, an Act Entitled 'An Act to Raise a Public Revenue by Excise, and to Regulate the Collection Thereof,' Passed the Third Day of March Anno Domini Seventeen Hundred and Ninety." The General Court had passed the excise taxes to pay the interest on the consolidated debt of the commonwealth and felt that, if the federal government was going to assume the debt, such taxes would be "an unnecessary burden upon the Citizens of this Commonwealth." Hancock's quotation of the act varies from that appearing in A&R, but not in any material way.

5. In a bundle of twenty-eight acts and two letters evidently deposited by Hancock's secretary on the House table is "An Act Making Provision for the Debt of the United States," [4] Aug 1790, 7 pp. (House Unenacted #3376B, MA) See also *Annals of Congress*, 2, 1790-1791, (Washington: Gales and Seaton, 1834) appendix, col. 2248, in which Massachusetts was allowed $4 million of the $21 million allocated to assist the states with their war debts. See also *The Public Statutes at Large of the United States of America...* 7 (Boston, 1850) 4 July 1790, 138-144. Section 13 of the act pertained to the $21 million, with the compensation to Massachusetts limited to $4 million.

6. Nine shillings, three pence.

7. Unfortunately, considering Hancock's many comments about depositing a bundle of acts and letters to be reviewed by the legislature, only one such bundle was located in the unenacted files of the MA, House Unenacted #3376B, and that bundle pertained to this speech.

8. *Journal of the House* reads: "permitting the same to be loaned in the credit of the States, that they should make the same known in the Commonwealth." All other words are omitted.

9. Signed by Hancock but placed and dated by the scribe.

HEADNOTE

Date: Thursday, 27 Jan 1791

The manuscript copies of the speech are dated 26 Jan, but the address was delivered on 27 Jan.

Occasion: The *Columbian Centinel* of 29 Jan 1791, 2, observed: "Mr. Ely, of the joint Committee appointed to wait on his Excellency the Governour, to inform him that a quorum of the two branches had met, and to know when he would   be pleased to make his communications, reported, that the Committee had attended that service, and that his Excellency would at an early hour to-morrow, make his communications to the Legislature." The *Centinel* was reporting activities of the legislature for Wednesday, 26 Jan 1791.

The Massachusetts *Spy* of 3 Feb 1791, 2, noted: "At 12 o'clock, the Secretary delivered to the House a message from his Excellency the Governour, requesting their attendance in the Senate Chamber, whither they immediately repaired—and where his Excellency delivered the following SPEECH." The Massachusetts *Spy* was reporting activities of the legislature for Thursday, 27 Jan 1791.

SOURCES

House Unenacted #3491 (1791), MA and Senate Unenacted #1358 (1791), MA; *Journal of the House*, 11, 161-8, MA; *Journal of the House*, 11, 161-8, SL.*

A&R 1790-91, January Session, 556-61; *Columbian Centinel* , 29 Jan 1791, 2-3; *Herald of Freedom*, 28 Jan 1791, 159-160; Massachusetts *Spy*, 3 Feb 1791, 2-3; Boston *Gazette*, 31 Jan 1791, 2; *Independent Chronicle*, 3 Feb 1791, 2.

*No copy in either Senate Journal.

TEXT

Gentlemen of the Senate & Gentlemen of the House of Representatives,[1]

When we contemplate the present happy situation of our Country, & compare it with the distressing scenes through which a kind of providence has conducted her, the mind, if not void of patriotism, must expand with delight; & the heart, if not insensible to the impulses of religion, will overflow with gratitude.—

The People of this Commonweath, whilst they were involved in accumulated difficulties, established the Constitution of Government, by force of which we are now assembled. And the Citizens of the other States in the Union, no less attentive to the means of establishing their political happiness & security, pursued similar measures.—The unanimity which prevailed on this important occasion throughout all the States, & that extraordinary exercise of learning & wisdom which has been acknowledged by the world, were at that time attributed by many to the great pressure of our particular & hazardous circumstances; but since we have been favoured with a state of perfect peace & tranquillity, a great display of wisdom & learning[2] has been exhibited, & a degree of unanimity has prevailed in the forming, & establishing the Constitution of the United States of America.[3]

I do not mention these great events for your information; but to lead your minds to the contemplation of those virtues & qualities from which they originated.—

We see in the history of[4] Nations that an ignorant & unprincipled multitude may be frequently induced to follow an ambitious leader, to rapine, plunder & conquest; but when these objects, which serve only to encrease [sic] the miseries of mankind are atchieved [sic], the most successful sit down more wretched than they were before.

It seems to be reserved as the peculiar character of the Americans[5] to be moved in their operations by a purer & a more extensive degree of intelligence than has[6] fallen to the lot of those nations whose characters we obtain from history. And it is[7] their great felicity to have as the reward of their virtues the ability of conducting their perilous controversies so as to lay a noble foundation for their own future glory, & for the promotion of human happiness. The means which have been blessed to these important purposes are the general dissemination of the principles of religion, & morality, & of useful learning amongst our fellow Citizens in general, as well as that equality of character, privileges, hopes & prospects which by the Laws & Constitution of our Country have been established & steadily maintained for them.—

Our Constituents, Gentlemen, will feel themselves assured that under the enjoyment of these inestimable blessings, you will pay the most unremitted attention to the encouragement & support of those principles & measures which have been capable of producing such astonishing & glorious effects.—

When a country[8] is favoured by divine providence with a singular share of felicity, it becomes those whom the people by their suffrages have placed in the lead of their public concerns to acknowledge it with gratitude upon all suitable occasions.—

The United States of America[9] by force of their Constitution of Government have already arisen to honor & credit. Our observations convince us of the sufficiency of this System to answer all the great purposes of forming connexions [sic] with other nations, of defending the Union against foreign invasions & of preserving harmony & supporting Justice between the Citizens of different States. It remains for us, Gentlemen, to give our support to this System, by maintaining in full energy, the Constitution of our own State, upon which, with those of the other States in the Union, the Federal[10] government is founded; for it must eventually stand or fall with these particular Governments. The least alteration in the constitutional principles of one of them must essentially affect that.—The Federal[11] government might indeed, by absorbing the powers of the State Governments, change its own nature & become a very different System from what it originally was; but to maintain it, as it now is, will be best effected by maintaining them in as much respectability as their several Constitutions will admit of.—

Government being founded in the nature of man,[12] the establishment of it has been attempted in all Countries & by all Nations. Wherever the Officers who have been designated to execute it have held their authority independent of the people, slavery & despotism have succeeded. In every part of the world, therefore, where Literature & useful knowledge have prevailed, the people have struggled for a free form of Government; & while they have attended carefully to their own interest, & exercised their liberty without licentiousness; while they have distinguished the friends of freedom from the friends of Arbitrary Power & used their liberty, as [sic] not abusing it, they have continued to be free & happy.—

For all Citizens[13] to have an equal right to elect, & to be elected to office, is a privilege which other Countries have not been able to retain; but from the estimate which is put upon civil liberty by our fellow

Citizens, from the mode of education in this Country, & from that most laudable pride which each member of our great Republic feels, in standing as the Guardian of his own freedom, we have the happiness of being assured that we shall long enjoy a blessing which other nations have forfeited by their folly & want of attention. We are all then most solemnly engaged to unite in our endeavours to preserve, encourage & maintain in the great body of the People those ideas upon which the glory of our Country & the felicity of future generations so essentially depend.—

It is true[14] that the late revolution has involved the United States as a Government, & the particular States in a large debt;[15] but the vast increase of population, & the growing resources of our Country will soon be amply sufficient for the discharge of it. And although we may feel the weight of it for a time, we shall derive great consolation from comparing our circumstances with those of other Nations & above all, by recollecting that this debt was incurred for the preservation of our freedom as men; & that instead of being mere provincials dependent upon, & a grade below the subjects of a Foreign Sovereign, each Citizen not only claims rank with every Citizen of other Nations, but rises superior to them all by possessing a part of the sovereignty of his own Country.

In addition to the other favours we enjoy as a Government, we have the blessings of internal peace & tranquility: industry & Economy prevail[16] & the people appear to be satisfied & contented. The happiness of the people, that sole object of all good government, is every where acknowledged: their[17] field has in the past year yielded its increase in great abundance: our fishery & commerce have been prospered,[18] & there appears [sic] to be laudable exertions to introduce the useful Arts to the Country—A number of Gentlemen have in the town of Boston & other Towns[19] carried the Manufactory of Duck to a great degree of perfection:[20] they deserve great applause for their spirited exertions.[21]

And from the attempts of other worthy Citizens we have reason to hope that there will be as great success in the Manufactory of glass in the same town.[22]

Gentlemen of the Senate & Gentlemen of the House of Representatives,

The line of true policy for a Commonweath is at all times found[23] on the path of Justice. But it sometimes unfortunately happens that the situation of a State renders it impossible for the governing power to do that which in justice ought to be done; when this happens those who have been the greatest friends to the State are generally the greatest sufferers. We find with the highest satisfaction that the public securities of the United States are very fast approximating in their real, to their nominal value. But while they were very low, many of those persons who took them, or the securities exchanged for them, in the place of money & have been obliged to part with them at a very great discount have been sufferers. However much we may lament the sufferings of these people, we can find no remedy for them, for, the situation of the Country was such at that time that the resources of it could not be turned to the channel of Justice in which they ought to have been directed. And now the very existence of the great Republic of America depends upon the support of public Credit.—

The Congress of the United States having assumed four millions of dollars of[24] the debt of this Commonwealth, the residue remains as the object of finance for this particular Government. Perhaps upon the final adjustment of our accounts with Congress, it may appear that this also is chargeable upon the United States; but the Creditors still are to look to this State for payment. The original holders of Securities issued by this Government have received great injury, & greater still will accrue to them unless, from your proceedings, it shall be made evident to the world that the interest of the residue of our debt will be provided for in a manner fully equal in point of advantage to that proposed by Congress & that a punctual annual Payment may be relied upon. Unless this is done, the Citizens who have parted with their property to save their Country from impending ruin, will be obliged to continue to dispose of their securities at discount & must be finally taxed to redeem them at par, from those who shall be holders of them. I have no doubt, Gentlemen, but that you are fully impressed with this important subject; but I feel it to be my duty to urge upon you a speedy progress in restoring credit to the Commonwealth.

By the Act of Congress for assuming a part of the debt of this State,[25] it is agreed, that if the whole of the sum allowed to be subscribed by the holders of our Public securities, shall not be subscribed within the present year, that this State shall receive from the United States, interest according to the provision of the Act upon so much of the sum proposed to be loaned as shall not be so subscribed. Which interest so received by the State is to be received in trust for the Non-Subscribing Creditors of this Commonwealth until there shall be as settlement of accounts between this & the United States. If measures could be adopted to raise the Credit of this Government so far as the holders of our public securities would place such a confidence in them, as they would in the proposal of the United States, it would afford great ease to those Creditors who have a right[26] to subscribe toward the four millions to apply to our own Treasury for their interest. I propose this idea for your attention,, but shall not enlarge upon it.—

Gentlemen, I have some matters to communicate to you which I shall make the subject of particular Messages, & shall recommend them to your attention as deserving your notice.—I shall do all within my power to render the Session useful to our fellow Citizens, and agreeable to you.—

The Secretary will lay before you the Acts & Journals of Congress so far as I have received them since your last session.

John Hancock[27]

Council Chamber Boston January 26th. 1791

NOTES

1. For the reply of the General Court, see A&R 1790, January session, 9 Feb 1791, 168-170.

2. *Journal of the House* reads "learning & wisdom."

3. Acts & Resolves underlines "America."

4. In House 3491, Hancock inserted "of" above the line after "history" where the scribe had made an omission.

5. Underlined only in Acts & Resolves.

6. In House 3491, Hancock struck "have" and inserted "has."

7. In Senate 1358, the scribe had written "And it is of their great felicity..." Hancock struck the "of."

8. In both House 3491 and Senate 1358, Hancock struck "nation" and inserted "country" above the line.

9. Only A&R underlines "America."

10. In both House 1391 and Senate 1358, Hancock struck "General" and inserted "Federal" above the line.

11. In both House 3491 and Senate 1358, Hancock struck "General" and inserted "Federal" above the line.

12. It is possible that Hancock was influenced by Hobbes's *Leviathan* , which established the nineteen natural laws under which man functions. It is likely that Hancock studied the *Leviathan* (1651) at Harvard; and its philosophy, that man had a right to revolt when the king failed in his duty to the citizens, would have reinforced Hancock's political philosophy.

13. In both House 3491 and Senate 1358, the text had read: "For all the Citizens of a nation to have equal rights"; in both documents, Hancock struck "the" and "of a nation."

14. In House #3491, Hancock scratched out something that is now illegible and amended the document to read "It is true..."; Senate #1358 has no such correction.

15. The reply of the General Court to the governor's message said in the A&R for 1790, 170: "The residue of the Debt of this Commonwealth which is not assumed by Congress, we conceive to be an Object of finance, which demands the attention of this Government."

16. A bill passed on 17 Nov 1786, encouraging manufactures, etc., in Massachusetts, appeared to be having some effect. (A&R Chap. 132, September session, 1786, 17 Nov 1786, 410-412) While the war was still going on, the General Court authorized a lottery of £1,200 to build a paper mill and to support its manufacture of paper. (A&R, 7 May 1782, Chap. 39, 593-594) In 1789, the legislature had regulated the weight and length of nails, so that the manufacture of nails must have been in progress. (A&R 1789, Chap. 36, 22 Feb 1790, 444-446)

17. House #3491 reads "the."

18. *Journal of the House* reads "have been prosperous."

19. In House #3491 and Senate #1358, Hancock inserted above the line "the other Towns."

20. Hancock corrected House #3491 and Senate #1358 from the original reading of "to the greatest degree of perfection" to "to a great degree of perfection." There had been early attempts to establish the manufacture of duck (a durable, closely woven fabric) in the colonies. Among the Hancock papers at the MHS is a record that Hancock on 15 Mar 1768 subscribed to an effort to manufacture duck in the colonies.

21. House #3491, Senate #1358 and *Journal of the House* all start a new paragraph here.

22. See speech of 30 Jan 1793 for a report on glass manufacturing in and around Boston and on the encouragement of the production of hemp and flax.

23. In House #3491 and Senate #1358, Hancock struck "formed" and wrote above the margin "found."

24. In House #3491, the scribe had omitted "of" so Hancock inserted it above the line.

25. For citations to the Act of Congress, see endnote 5 of the Speech of 15 Sept 1790. The partial assumption of the debt by the national Congress caused the Massachusetts legislature to consider a number of moves. For example, on 24 June 1790 in A&R, Chapter 14. 1790 session, 20-21, and on 17 Sept 1790, A&R 1790-91, Chap. 15, 1790 session, 21-22, the

legislature passed acts that would repeal previously passed excise taxes
levied to pay the interest on the state debt, if Congress should assume "the
consolidated debt of this state." See also A&R May session, Chap. 13, 4
June 1790, 101-102: "Resolve Expressing the Opinion of the Legislature
That It is Expedient for Congress to Assume and Provide for the Payments of
the Debts of the Several States, and Instructing the Members of this state
upon the subject, etc." In the A&R 1791, January session, Chap. 148, 8
Mar 1792, 519-523, as a result of a committee appointed by the legislature
to consider the advisability of asking Congress to assume the *remaining*
part of the state debt, the legislature sent an address to Congress containing
a series of arguments in favor of national assumption of the debt, one of
which was that certain states (like Massachusetts) had undertaken a greater
share of the war expenditures than had other states, whereas all had
benefitted.

26. In both House #3491 and Senate #1358, Hancock struck "ought" and
inserted "a right."

27. Hancock autographed both the House and Senate documents.

HEADNOTE

Date: 26 May 1791

Occasion: A&R, The Massachusetts *Spy*, the *Herald of Freedom* and the *Independent Chronicle* reported as follows: "At half past 12 o'clock, His Excellency the Governour appeared in the House, where the Senate had convened and in a short and pertinent address* informed the two branches of the General Court, That he had been politely informed by their Committee of his having been re-elected to the office of the First Magistrate of the Commonwealth; and he was fully sensible of the honour done him by this fresh instance of the confidence reposed in him by the citizens thereof; that he experienced the highest satisfaction in contemplating that the welfare and happiness of the Commonwealth, had ever been the chief objects of his concern, and that he should not fail of paying that attention to its interests which this repeated instance of confidence demanded. The President of the Senate then administered the oaths to his Excellency."

The text of this short address has evidently not been preserved.

Before he was given his oath, Sam Adams, the lieutenant governor, delivered a short address to the legislature that is extant and appeared in the newspapers of the day as well as in the A&R for 1791, May Session, 567-569.

The sources stated above also reported as follows: "At four o'clock His Excellency the Governour met the two Branches convened in the Representatives Chamber, and delivered the following:"

SOURCES

Senate Unenacted #1357 (1791) MA and House Unenacted #3496, MA; *Journal of the House* 12, 25-30, MA; *Journal of the House* 12, 25-30, SL.*

A&R, May Session, 1791, 569-573; *Herald of Freedom,* 31 May 1791, 2; *Columbian Centinel,* 28 May 1791, 2-3; Boston *Gazette,* 30 May 1791, 2; Massachusetts *Spy,* 2 June 1791, 2-3; *Independent Chronicle,* 2 June 1791, 2; *Columbian Centinel ,* 23 July 1791, 2-3.

*No copy in either Senate Journal.

The answer to the governor's speech, dated 1 June 1791, exists in manuscript form in the Archives, signed by Samuel Phillips as president of the senate and David Cobb, speaker of the house. There are actually two MSS, and it is difficult to collate the two, except that the first (which is not dated and is signed by Samuel Baker) may be a preliminary reply, and that of 1 June 1791 may be a more extended and deliberate reply. Neither of the documents is numbered, and they are simply appended in the Archives to the House copy of the speech. The shorter of the two MSS congratulated the governor on his election and agreed with him that the tranquility of the state was much to be desired, and that they were thankful for it. The reply acknowledged the issues of trial by jury, the establishment of a militia in contrast to a standing army, as well as the issue of education. This shorter version appears to have been drafted by the committee of both houses appointed to consider the governor's message. The longer report appears to be missing its first page. It is divided by numbers, i.e., 4th, 5th, 6th up to 11th, and the MS begins with the 4th. The subject of the items is given below:

4th   trial by jury
5th   approval of the militia
6th.   education: "The people of these States, while
           they wish to secure to themselvs & posterity
           Freedom and Independence, must be equally
           solicitous to disseminate knowledge and *Learning
           universally* among the People."
7th   Harvard
8th   the debt
9th   tribunals for the suggested counties
10th   "We are sensible that your Excellency has reason
           to complain, that the important affairs of the
           Government are too often delay 'd to the latter
           part of the Session:—the delicate situation in
           which you are placed by this circumstance
           between a desire to comply with the Request of
           an immediate Recess, and the Duty you owe the
           Commonwealth, must be peculiarly disagreeable.
           We assure your Excellency that we will use our
           utmost endeavaors to deliver you from such
           embarrassments in future."

MS copies of the reply of the General Court to Hancock's speech can be compared with the text given in the A&R, 1791, May Session, Chap. 9A, 1 June 1791, 386-88.

TEXT

Gentlemen of the Senate & Gentlemen of the House of Representatives,

The partiality of my Fellow Citizens having again called me to the Chair, my duty, according to the established mode of procedure in this Government, coincides with my inclinations, in requesting your attendance in this place that I might personally pay my respects to you. And I take this opportunity to express to them, through you, the obligation I feel in being honored so repeatedly with their suffrage. Their Freedom, Happiness & Interest are objects which demand my warmest attention, and which I shall pursue with unremitted ardor. My only ambition is to render myself useful to them; & thereby to merit, in some measure, the confidence with which they honor me.

I am very happy to be able to assure you of the prevalence of tranquility throughout our Republick [sic]. Industry, Peace & good order are continued; & Public Felicity every where enjoyed, the intercourse of the Citizens of the Town & Country is continued in their mutual satisfaction & advantage: And we have reason to hope that under a mild & regular Government, we shall continue to enjoy the inestimable blessings of Peace, Liberty & Safety.

The institution of Civil Government is intended to promote the happiness, & to ensure the safety of the People, to effect these important ends, it is our duty to Enact wise Laws, & to make ample provision for an equal & regular distribution of Justice. The Citizens of a Free State have a right to expect Justice "in the most cheap, easy & expeditious manner, promptly, & without delay conformably to the Laws."[1] As our Commonwealth encreases [sic] in numbers, the business of the Executive & Judicial Departments must proportionably [sic] be encreased [sic] & such provisions, from time to time, ought to be made[2] as will prevent the Citizens from being wearied in their attendance on Courts of Justice, & being worn out in pursuing their just demands.

The trial by Jury is justly considered as the bulwark of our Liberties, & great care ought to be taken to support the reputation of it; our Laws are such as will excuse a man from serving more than once in three years in that respectable office, but the Courts of the United States, together with those of our own Government, make so frequent calls for Juries that there may be a necessity to revise the Laws made upon this subject, & to shorten the time of excuse in the Sea-port Counties.[3]

As our Government is in the hands of the People, they have the means, under the smiles of Divine Providence, of securing their own happiness; but since wars & sanguinary conflicts are too frequently the lot of mankind, it is always prudent to stand prepared for every event; & as standing Armies, that bane of all Civil Freedom, may be necessary unless a well disciplined Militia is maintained, it is of the highest consequence that the People, with their own Arms,[4] should be able to defend themselves against all invasions of a Foreign Enemy, & to preserve the force & energy of their own[5] internal Government. In order to effect this, they should be universally instructed in the use of Arms. A well disciplined Militia is the only Military force compatible with the People's liberty; & ought to be their main dependence, for repelling attacks from a Foreign Enemy. I therefore recommend it to you, Gentlemen, to attend to this subject, & by encouragements on the one hand, & provisions for a *certain* Execution of the Laws on the other, to render our Militia, an armed & effectual body. There shall be nothing wanting on my part to render the Militia respectable.

The attention of the Citizens of the Commonwealth to the Education of the rising Generation afford a most pleasing prospect of the future support of those principles for which the Patriots of our Country have nobly contended, & in maintainance of which so many of our Fellow Citizens have fallen in the Field. The useful Institutions of Learned Teachers of Piety, Religion, & Morality in the Parishes, & of Grammar Schools in the towns of our Republick,[6] the latter of which is in a great measure peculiar to the Northern States of the Union, are exceedingly well adapted to the support of a Republic form of Government: because the maintainance[7] of such a Government depends altogether upon light & knowledge, being universally disseminated in the body of the People. While our Fellow Citizens continue to be able to contemplate & to understand their true interest, they will cherish these important & honorable Institutions.—But unless there is an ample source to derive the means of these Institutions from, all our laudable exertions will avail us nothing. The University of Cambridge[8] was founded by our wise & patriotic Ancestors for this purpose; on the support of this depends all the other literary Institutions of the Commonwealth. And I am very sorry to be obliged to inform you that unless some exertions are immediately made by you Gentlemen for its support, the light of our Country will begin to fade & its glory will be seen in its decline.[9] You will soon have the state of the University laid before in such a manner as I hope will obviate all doubts respecting the necessity of your Aid. And I cannot in justice to the best interest of all my fellow Citizens, in whose names I now address you, refrain from beseeching you to give your most assiduous and candid attention to it.

Gentlemen of the Senate & Gentlemen of the House of Representatives,

I will submit to your consideration, whether the late influx of Specie does not render the present a favorable opportunity to regular & amend the Finances of this Government. I would by no means consent to the laying a heavy burden on the people, but the interest of our Public Debt is rapidly accumulating & the Creditors, amongst whom are many distressed people, are anxious to receive something upon their just demands. I have directed the Treasurer to lay before you the State of the Treasury that our Constituents may have the benefit of your Wise deliberations upon it. And I flatter myself that when the state of the Treasury shall be examined & the resources of the Commonwealth compared with the exigencies of the Government, it will appear proper to discontinue the Schemes of raising money by Lotteries.[10] Experience now teaches us that this mode of raising money for public use, as well as the schemes of raising money by Lotteries for private purpose, have a manifest[11] tendency to withdraw the people's attention from industry & to distract them with the hope of gain by chance & accident. They also lay a very unequal tax upon the People at large; the indigent & embarrassed part of the Community being in such schemes generally the greatest adventurers.—

Gentlemen,

In the Law for erecting the Counties of Washington & Hancock,[12] there is no tribunal established with cognizance of Treasons, Murders, & other Felonies of a high nature which may be committed within those Counties.[13] There is also a defect in the Law establishing a Supreme Probate. Before the American Revolution, Appeals were made from the Probate Courts, in all the Counties, to the Governor & Council. The Laws have now established the Supreme Judicial Court as the Supreme Probate: & provide that all appeals from Decrees of the Probate Court shall be made the Supreme Judicial Court next to be holden within[14] either of the Counties of Nantucket or Dukes County,[15] there is no Supreme Probate for those Counties: their particular situation, as well as that of the two first mentioned counties requires your immediate attention.—

Having suggested these things, I shall not tire your patience with others, but shall make them the subject of more particular Messages, & will only add that at this Season of the year I imagine you would be pleased with as short a Session as shall consist with the dispatch of Public business, to aid which you will find me ready early & late, & give me leave to recommend you to enter upon that business at an early stage of the Session, as for want of that I have been greatly embarrassed & the Community has suffered injury by former General Courts, for as soon as they had finished on their part the matters that were before them, a number of Bills & many Resolves were brought to me with a pressing desire that I might immediately decide upon them, & give them a Recess, upon this occasion I found myself embarrassed between a desire not to detain them, & the duty which I owed to the Commonwealth, by giving a deliberate consideration to matters of such length & importance; your candid attention, Gentlemen, to this circumstance in Public business will, I am persuaded, relieve me as much as may be from any such future Embarrassment.[16]

The Secretary will lay before you the several Acts & Papers I have received from Congress since the last Session of the General Court.

I shall, Gentlemen, use my endeavors to render the Session useful to our Constituents, & agreeable to you.

John Hancock[17]

Council Chamber May 26th. 1791.

NOTES

1. The source of this quotation is not clear.

2. *Journal of the House* omits "& each provision, from time to time, ought to be made."

3. In their answer to the governor, the legislature said: "The tryal [sic] by Jury, is one of those inestimable privileges we enjoy as Freemen; it is encumbent on us therefore to use every precaution to retain it in its fullest latitude.—Such further Regulations as are necessary to this great purpose we shall readily adopt, by a revision of the Laws made upon this subject." (A&R May 1791 Session, Chap.9A, 387)

On 21 June 1784, Chapter 4, 10-12, the General Court had passed "An Act Regulating the Appointment and Services of Grand Jurors."

4. *Journal of the House* underlines "their own Arms."

5. *Journal of the House* underlines "their own."

6. The legislature repeatedly endorsed the creation of schools, e.g., Chapter 32 of the 1784 session, 107-111, reported "An Act for Establishing a School in the North Parish of Hingham, by the Name of *Derby School*, and for Appointing and Incorporating Trustees of the Said School." The Maine territory had one of the sections of its plots reserved for education.

7. All of the primary sources consulted for this collation used "maintainance." However, A&R reads "maintain[an]ce".

8. A&R italicized "University" and "Cambridge," but none of the other primary sources make such a distinction. The usage, "The University of Cambridge," is an unusual one for Hancock.

9. On 30 May 1791, John Hancock sent a message to the Senate and House concerning a "Petition of Overseers of our University at Cambridge." In his message, Hancock noted: "I have in the Communications which I have already had the honor to make, said so much upon this subject, that it would not be proper to say anything more at this time." (Senate Unenacted #1359, MA) Harvard's petition is in the Harvard University Archives, Records of the Overseers, IV, 3 May 1791. After pointing out that the previous grants to Harvard had not been made in recent years because of pressing financial problems in Massachusetts, it begged assistance. "If," the memorial said, "our children should be driven to attend seminaries to acquire learning, even tho to such as may be established by the authority of the nation, it may be a very serious question, whether that security to the independence of the States, and of course to the safety of the Union, which is derived from an early education at home, will not be weakened and perhaps anihilated [sic]." A&R Chapter 36, 443, of the January session of the 1793 legislature provided for the creation of the Massachusetts Historical Society.

10. A&R underlined "manifest."

Although Hancock recommended the discontinuance of lotteries, they had long been used, as was pointed out earlier, to raise funds to meet, among other expenses, the rebuilding of Faneuil Hall and the war debt. Hancock himself bought several tickets for the Faneuil Hall renovation in 1765. MHS Washsburn Collection, 7, June 1765, consists of 2 lottery tickets for prizes, with funds going to the market. Numbers 3577, 3850, and 3982 are signed by John Hancock. The NEHSG has a fourth, Number 3805, also signed by Hancock. This 4th small ticket is not filed, but loose in the collection. Because the numbers of the tickets are not consecutive, it would appear that Hancock was approached by at least four different persons to assist with the subscription.

As early as the April session, 1780, Chap. 155, 450, the General Court named persons to manage state lotteries.

On 21 Feb 1781, Chap. 141, 294-5, the General Court ordered that the balance on a lottery be paid to the treasurer.

In the 1781 legislature, Chap. 39, April session, 1781, 583-4, 7 May 1782, a lottery had been used to promote the paper industry.

In the 1787 legislature, Chap. 13, 567, the court had approved a lottery to help build a glass factory.

In the 1789 legislature, in Chap. 55, 507, a lottery had been approved "for the purpose of securing and fortifying the beach on the southwesternly side of the habour of *Marblehead*, and appointing trustees to apply the proceeds."

In response to the governor's speech, the legislature tactfully replied that it would be wise to extinguish the public debt "without having Resource to any Schemes for raising money, which will injure the morals of the people or divert their attention from laudable and industrious Pursuits."

11. A&R underlines "manifest."

12. *Laws & Acts* underlines "Washington" and "Hancock."

13. A&R, January 1791 session, Chap. 147, 517-518, made provision for altering the sitting of the Supreme Court in several counties, but no mention was made of Washington or Hancock Counties. Chapter 38, 70, of the 1790 *Acts* provided for courts to meet in Washington and Hancock Counties, but seemingly not for felonies. As far as could be determined, no action was taken on this matter prior to Hancock's death in 1793.

14. *Laws & Acts* underlines "within."

15. *Laws & Acts* underlines "Nantucket" and "Dukes County."

16. Hancock signed and dated both the Senate & House copies.

17. See the headnote for the reaction of the legislature to Hancock's admonishment.

HEADNOTE

Date: Wednesday, 20 July 1791

Headnote: John Hancock and other dignitaries from Boston were escorted to Cambridge by Colonel Fuller's troops and "divers military gentle men"; as on previous occasions, they arrived around ten o'clock. Following an oration in Latin, a forensic disputation on the subject "Whether the criminality of actions be increased by habit," a syllogistic disputation, and other learned presentations, the assembly adjourned for dinner. When the ceremonies recommenced, an English oration and a valedictory address in Latin were given. Then Hancock, the Boston *Gazette* reported, "in a Manner that spoke his affection for Alma Mater, and his Benevolence to her aims,"[1] delivered the address given below.

SOURCES

Boston *Gazette,* 25 July 1791, 3; *Columbian Centinel,* 23 July 1791, 2; Massachusetts *Spy,* 26 July 1791, 3; *Independent Chronicle,* 21 July 1791, 3.

TEXT

Mr. President,

The University in which you preside stands among the highest marks of the Wisdom and Patriotism of our Ancestors;—The men who fled to the wilderness rather than to partake of careless ease and splendid pleasures in a state of Slavery, gave birth to this Institution.

While this Anniversary serves as a Memorial of their extraordinary Virtues, it embellishes the path of Science, cherishes Literature and promotes the Interest of our Republic.

The Exhibitions of this day evince to us the great abilities you possess, Sir, and the careful attention you pay to the duties of your important station; and they also reflect much Honour upon all the immediate Governours of the University.

The young Gentlemen who have on this occasion given such ample proof of their genius and application, have raised us to great expectations of their future usefulness: our best wishes accompany them into the World, and our ardent prayer is, that they may serve and honour their country.

When we recollect the wishes of the venerable Founders of this Seminary, we feel the most interesting hopes that will forever proceed from this place, Men, whose Virtues, Wisdom and learning will lead our enlightened and grateful people in the ways of Religion and Patriotism.

It is with you, young Gentlemen, who now have your residence within Harvard's Walls, to add lustre to the brightness of your Country or to check her progress in glory with an interval of darkness. We wish to inspire your ambition with this idea, and to excite[2] you by a sense of your importance in the community, to an exalted mode of conduct.—

Suffer us to do this, and we shall rejoice in the honourable pressages of your future greatness.

While this University, respectable Sir, continues to support such a reputation as it has always enjoyed, and as the exhibitions of the day have proved to be just, it will merit and receive the patronage and support of every man who loves his country, and is concerned for its interests. The gentlemen concerned in its Instruction, render a most important service to the community; they form the minds and manners of its future members, and give a complexion to those who are hereafter to govern it. From the publick then, from the civil fathers of their country, from the patriots, the legislators of Massachusetts, Harvard College must receive countenance, encouragement and assistance.—

While the blood of their venerable ancestors warms their veins, while the independence, the freedom and happiness of America are dear to her Sons, the University cannot be defeated, nor its faithful servants left without a support.

To the protection and favour of the God of the Spirits of all flesh, the God of our fathers, to the patronage and assistance of all those who value the happiness of posterity, and with their Freedom, we commend this venerable Seat of Science—May it flourish and increase, may it bless America and the World so long as the Sun and Moon shall endure.

NOTES

1. Boston *Gazette*, 25 July 1791, 3.
2. Massachusetts *Spy* reads "excite;" the Massachusetts *Centinel* and the Boston *Gazette* read "incite."

HEADNOTE

Date: Wednesday, 6 June 1792

Occasion: The speech was delivered at eleven o'clock in the Representatives Chamber in the State House. Hancock had again been elected governor, and began his new term in office by instructing the legislature on a series of matters that needed attention.

SOURCES

Senate Unenacted #1533 (1792), MA; Vol. 13 of House Journal says "see copy on file."*

A&R,** 1792 (1895), 681-685; Boston *Gazette,* 11 June 1792, 2; *Independent Chronicle,* 7 June 1792, 3; Massachusetts *Spy,* 14 June 1792, 2; *Columbian Centinel,* 9 June 1792, 1-2.

MA Senate Unenacted #1533/1 is the report of the joint committee on the speech..

*No copy in either the House or Senate Journal.

**Title change to Laws & Resolves. A&R has been maintained throughout this work.

TEXT

Gentlemen of the Senate & Gentlemen of the House of Representatives,

The Candor which my Fellow Citizens have shewn towards me by repeatedly giving me their suffrages for Governor of the Commonwealth & my duty resulting from that office, induce me to request your attendance in this place, that I may pay to you the respect which is due to the Assembled Representatives of a Great & free People—

In times of publick anger, & of common calamity, men in office have an opportunity to make display of ability, firmness & patriotism, but we, Gentlemen, in the present state of our Country, have little more to do than to improve & enjoy that general tranquility & those scenes of Public prosperity which seldom fall to the lot of a Nation.

From the characters which compose the Legislature our fellow Citizens must possess the highest assurance that all the measures of the present year will be calculated to preserve to the People of the United America in general, & to those of this Commonwealth in particular those invaluable blessings—

That a free Government founded in the natural equal rights of all the people is within the reach of human ability & to be prized as a principal support of National happiness, is an idea which has been long established in the minds of the greatest & wisest of men in the World. The manner in which this State was originally settled by our Ancestors, has given us an opportunity to carry this principle into practice, and our great & unexampled success has given us cause of gratitude to him who prescribed the bounds of different Nations, & has fully compensated us for all our toil, expence & trouble.—

That Goverment may be considered as truly free, where all the People are, by the Constitution & Laws, upon the same rank of privilege, & have an equal security for their lives, liberties & property—Where the Laws do not create, but are calculated to prevent all exclusive rights to fame or wealth, & leave each Citizen upon his own merit for the honors of his Country, & upon his own honest exertions for the acquirement of property. That such a situation as I have hinted at, may be in the possession of every Nation on the earth is the devout wish of every good Man: And in this Idea, our prayers cannot cease for a People with whom we are nearly allied, & whose generous assistance did much towards promoting the object of our wishes in the time of our distress—

The means most likely to continue our public felicity are the establishing & executing such Laws as will tend to support the habits of truth, integrity & every moral virtue: & by certain & adequate punishments, to prohibit all frauds & every immorality & vice: The providing for a regular support of teachers of Piety, religion and morality, & the maintainance of free Public Schools in the towns of the State, by which the children of the poorer will have equal advantages with those of the richer part of the Community.

I am exceedingly gratified in being assured that these important institutions are so generally attended to by the people of this State. And as I consider our University at Cambridge as being the principal source of the Learning & Intelligence possessed by this Community,— I cannot but earnestly solicit you to give it your encouragement & support. By these, & other measures which your Wisdom & Prudence will dictate, under the smiles of that Divine Being who has hitherto afforded us his support, we may hope for a continuance of our Prosperity, & for permanent public happiness.—

Gentlemen, I have directed the Secretary to lay before you such Acts & proceedings of the Congress of the United States as have been forwarded to me: Among them is an Act for regulating the Militia of the State.[1] That Act appears to me to be quite consonant to the Constitution of the General Government, and I shall, as commander in Chief of the Militia of this State, take every measure within my power to render the Militia respectable under it.[2]

There is also another Act for the proportion of Representatives to be sent from the States to Congress.[3] Your attention will be immediately called to the forming Districts from whence they are to be Elected in this State. You will in this business be pleased to consider that having the Districts so formed as to give a Center of communication to the inhabitants of each will have a tendency to promote harmony & unanimity in their proceedings[4]—

In the last Session of the late General Court, I was obliged by a sense of duty to object to a resolve passed by the two Houses for a particular Divorce[5]— I am led to believe that a majority of the Senate & House were of opinion that the provisions made by the standing Laws of the State are inadequate to subjects of this nature: If I had been clearly of opinion [sic] that the Legislature had a right to dissolve the bands of Matrimony by a special Act, I should have objected to a resolve for that purpose as not being of proper solemnity in the transaction. I wish you, Gentlemen, to revise the laws now existing on this subject; & if the causes as recognized by Law do not comprehend all those for which a Divorce ought to be allowed: You will make such provision as may tend to give relief where it ought to be had. I am obliged however to observe that this is a subject which ought to be trusted with great caution; because, indulgencies of this kind when established by law are very liable to be abused, to the great injury of Society—

Whether the People have the advantage of a ready & cheap administration of Justice, you, who come from the various parts of the Commonwealth can determine better than I can: if they have not this benefit, you will pay a proper attention to a subject so very important & interesting in its nature. Whether a new arrangement of the Counties will conduce to the saving of expence to the People, may be worthy of your consideration [sic]: An increase of their number may render the Government very unwieldy, & may have a tendency finally to injure the Commonwealth—

There is yet a debt due from this Commonwealth: it has not been assumed by the Congress, nor provided for by us. Our demand against the United States has not yet been liquidated or allowed by that Government. Justice demands a perserverance in measures that may extinguish the debt & satisfy the just claims of our Creditors—

By the standing laws of the Commonwealth Justices of the Peace are impowered [sic] to apppoint appraisers of the estates of deceased persons, & such appraisement is frequently the foundation of an Inventory of the personal Estate, which is to be accounted for by Executors, & Administrators—The Executors & Administrators have their Election to apply to such Justice as they please for such appointment; & I am very apprehensive that Widows, Orphans & Creditors may be injured by this method of procedure, while the expence [sic] saved by not applying to the Judge of Probate for such appointment is very trifling.—

John Hancock[6]

Council Chamber

June 6th. 1792*

*Signature, place and date written in by Hancock himself.

In Senate June 6th 1792. Read & committed to (Solomon Freemont-later crossed out in red ink) Nathl Wells and Samuel Dexter Jr* & Thomas Dawes Esq. with such as the Hon. House may join, to consider & report. Sent down for concurrence.

Sam[ue]l. Phillips Presdt.

*"and Samuel Dexter Jr" inserted superlineally

In the House of Representatives June 6. 1792. Read & concurred & Mr. [Charles] Jarvis, Mr. [William] Tudor, Mr. [Ebenezer] Washburn & Mr. [Justin] Ely are joined.

David Cobb, Spkr.

NOTES

1. A&R 1792-3, Chap. 14, May session, 380-403, 22 1793: "An Act for Regulating and Governing the Militia..." passed because the numerous regulations concerning the militia had become too complicated to handle.

2. It can be assumed that Hancock inserted the above paragraph in the final draft because it is written in the margin of the MS, with an indication of an "A" in the body of the speech where the insert is to be placed. However, it is written in the hand of the scribe and not in Hancock's hand.

3. Article One of the Constitution says: "The number of representatives shall not exceed one for every thirty thousand." In the absence of a census, Massachusetts was alloted eight representatives by the Constitution. There is no comment prohibiting the states from electing all its representatives at large. On 14 Apr 1792 the Congress passed an act requesting that the states name representatives in accordance with the above constitutional stipulations. (*Annals*, 3, 1791-1793, col. 1359)

4. A&R 1792-3, May session, Chap. 79, 30 June 1792, 184-189, "Resolve for Districting the Commonwealth for the Purpose of Choosing Federal Representatives."

5. The House & Senate had passed a resolve dissolving the marriage of Daniel Chickering and Abigail, his wife. A&R 1791, May Session (no chapter), 575-577.

The question as to who was authorized to grant divorces was discussed in the General Court as early as 1781 when a bill was submitted to empower the governor to grant divorces "in certain cases." However, there is no record that that bill was ever passed. (*Journal of the House*, vol. 1, Oct, 1780-May 1781, 513, 1 May 1781, MA)

A bill was passed during the February session, 1785, Chap. 69, 564-567, dated 16 Mar 1786.

The issue of divorce had been discussed in the General Court in 1788. On 24 Nov 1788, the Senate appointed a committee to review "divorcement" including (a) penalties for elopement and (b) asking whether the family of the elopee be given consideration. The Senate noted that it had received several "applications" made to the General Court respecting divorcement. (MA, House Unenacted #3074A)

Four years later, the particular divorce granted by the legislature evidently disturbed Hancock sufficiently so that he sent a message to the Senate raising issues for their consideration. A&R, 1791, 25 Feb 1792, 575-577, consists of a message by Hancock to the Senate objecting to dissolving the bonds of matrimony between Daniel Chickering and Abigail. The bill of divorcement had been passed by the Senate on 21 Feb 1792 and by the House on 22 Feb 1792. Hancock asked whether the legislature had the power to dissolve a marriage. If so, such power should be solemnly performed.

The Senate answered the governor's message, saying it would appoint a joint committee of the House and Senate "to consider & report any alteration which may be found necessary to be made in the Laws which respect the disposition of the Bonds of Matrimony."   (MA, Senate Unenacted 1533/1, 12 June 1792)

6. Hancock signed and dated the copy in a very shaky handwriting.

HEADNOTE

Date: 19 July 1792

Occasion: Hancock addressed the Harvard graduating class four times, three times in English and once in Latin.

For this last commencement address, Hancock and other dignitaries were escorted from Boston to Cambridge, arriving at Harvard Hall around ten o'clock. After performing the necessary "solemnities" to make the graduation official, the group progressed about eleven o'clock to the Meeting House where they heard the usual recitation of poetry, disputations, dialogues, "a Hebrew oration," and similar presentations by the graduates.

In the afternoon, the audience reassembled (presumably in the Meeting House) and Hancock delivered his address.

His speech was followed by more recitations, and a valedictory oration in Latin. Then degrees were awarded, including the bachelor of arts, the master of arts, and the bachelor of physick. The degrees of doctor of laws were conferred on John Hancock, Sam Adams, Alexander Hamilton, Francis Dana, and John Lowell. The doctor of divinity and the doctor of physics were also conferred. Among those honored were representatives from Dartmouth and Yale Colleges.

SOURCES

The *Columbian Centinel,* 21 July 1792, 2; Boston *Gazette,* 23 July 1792, 2-3; Massachusetts *Spy,* 26 July 1792, 3.

TEXT

Mr. President,

This Anniversary is calculated to fill the bosom of Patriots with inexpressible satisfaction, and to expand the heart with the most agreeable sensations. Our virtuous ancestors have long kept this festival, under the sublime expectation of transmitting the principles of religion and liberty to their posterity. We, Sir, with transports enjoy the fruits of their beneficence.

The love of liberty inherent to the breast of man, has been regulated and refined by the ability acquired at this University. To this we are much indebted for political constitutions, which, if exercised with wisdom, cannot fail to preserve the felicity of our country.

Those of us who are now on the theatre of pubick life, exult in the idea, that the walls of Harvard, will, when we are no more, give to our country in succession, men, who shall take the people by the hand, and lead them in the path of peace, liberty, and safety.

The advantages of this institution have been acknowledged in various parts of the world. The Universities of European nations have paid great attention to the sons of Harvard: and the great and good men of our own state have ever considered the interest and honour of the Government as inseparably connected with that of this Seminary. They who love their country's happiness, will cherish this source of Science. They who delight in national liberty, will here culture the plant. And they, who feel a zeal for true national glory, will make this University the object of their highest attention.

The genius and learning exhibited by the young gentlemen who are this day to receive the honours of the University, afford us the fullest assurance of the advantages which the publick [sic] will derive from them. Our best wishes accompany them into the world. May they be a blessing to their country. May they continue to reflect honour upon this Seminary, and upon your abilities, in the important office which you sustain with so much dignity and reputation. May you, Sir,[1] continue to receive the applause of your fellow citizens: And may your labours and the labours of all who are connected in the important business of the University, continue to meet the publick approbation.

NOTES

1. President Willard.

HEADNOTE

Date: 7 Nov 1792

Occasion: The Massachusetts *Spy* of 22 Nov reported: "Mr. Wedgery was charged with a message to inform the Hon. Senate that the House would be ready to meet them in the Meeting House, agreeably to the Governour's message, and that seats would be assigned them. Both Houses having according assembled together, his Excellency came in, and delivered the following SPEECH."

Because of an epidemic, the legislature was meeting at Concord, with the House assembled in the Meeting House and the Senate at Mr. Emerson's inn. Hancock was housed at Mr. Richardson's tavern. In spite of the epidemic, Hancock was met as he rode into town by military units that escorted him to his residence. The General Court on 28 Mar 1793, Chapter 187, 316-317 voted expense money of £30 for moving the secretary's and treasurer's offices to Concord.

SOURCES

Senate Unenacted #1532 (1792), MA. There is an earlier draft housed in the Massachusetts Historical Society which is incomplete and has no number asssigned to it by the society. The *Journal of the House*, 13, 160 states, "See copy on file," which may be a reference to Senate MS #1532 or its equivalent.*

A&R 1792, 685-8; Boston *Gazette,* 12 Nov 1792, 2-3; *Independent Chronicle,* 15 Nov 1792, 2; Massachusetts *Spy,* 15 Nov 1792, 3; *Columbian Centinel,* 10 Nov 1792, 3

*No copy in either House or Senate Journal.

TEXT

Gentlemen of the Senate & Gentlemen of the House of Representatives,[1]

I should, for my own, as well as for your convenience, have been glad to have met you at the Ancient Seat of our Government, but as it has pleased the Most High, to visit that, as well as many other of our Towns, with a troublesome, & contagious disease, I have, with the advice of the Council, thought it most for your safety, & comfort to convene you at this place.[2]—

The ordinary business of the Commonwealth might have allowed me to indulge the idea of proroguing the Session to January, at which time it may be reasonably expected that the Capitol will be intirely [sic] free from the danger of communicating the infection: but [a] law [of the United States][3] having rendered it necessary that[4] the Elections should be determin'd upon before the first Wednesday in December, I was obliged to yield to the necessity.—

I shall not urge upon you any further business at this time, though I shall be ready to attend to any matter which you may propose as a necessary measure. Should you be inclined to attend at this time to the ordinary business of the Government, I shall beg leave to submit to your attention the propriety of the Commonwealth becoming interested in the Union Bank:[5] I do this, because if advantages are to be derived from Institutions of this nature, a participation of them by the State will be for the interest of all the Citizens: And because as it is of great importance to the community to have a proper regulation of the artificial medium current within it, the public safety will be better guarded, by having the Bank more under the Eye of the Legislative power.— Should you not have time to attend to this subject at present, you will judge whether it is expedient to appoint a Committee to consider it in the recess.

Gentlemen—I am urged by Sense of duty to communicate to you my mind upon a transaction which I cannot but consider as an open insult upon the Laws & the Government of the Commonwealth.

In the year one thousand seven hundred and fifty, the Legislature of this then Province of Massachusetts Bay, passed an act intitled [sic] "An Act to prevent Stage-Plays, & other Theatrical Entertainments." The Act was temporary, & only for four years.[6] Perhaps the improbability of obtaining the Royal assent to a permanent prohibition of such Entertainments was the reason which induced the Legislature to conduct the business in this manner. The Act was continued from time to time, by subsequent Acts; & on the second day of July, in the year one thousand seven hundred & eighty five, it was by an Act of the Legislature of the Commonwealth continued in force until the year one thousand seven hundred & ninety seven.—The preamble of the Act is in these words, "For preventing & avoiding many great mischiefs, which arise from Public Stage-Plays, Interludes & other Theatrical Entertainments; which not only occasion great & unnecessary expences

[sic] & discourage Industry & frugality; but likewise tend generally to increase immorality, impiety & a contempt of Religion."[7]

Whether the apprehension of the Evils which might flow from Theatrical exhibitions so fully expressed in the preamble of the Act are well founded or not, may be a proper subject of Legislative disquisition on a motion for the continuance, or the repeal of the Law; but the Act is now a Law of the Commonwealth; the principles upon which it is predicated have been recognized by, & derive support from the consideration of several Legislatures; & surely it ought to claim the respect & obedience of all persons who[8] be, within the Commonwealth. Yet a number of Aliens & Foreigners have lately entered the State, & in the Metropolis of the Government, under advertisements insulting to the habits & education of the Citizens, have been pleased to invite them to, & to exhibit before such as attended, *Stage-Plays, Interludes & Theatrical Entertainments*; under the Stile & Appelation of Moral Lectures. This fact is so notorious that it is vain to attempt a concealment of its[9] coming to our knowledge.[10]

Whether the Judicial Departments whose business it is have attended to this subject or not I am unable to determine; but this I am convinced of, that no measures have been taken to punish a most open breach of the Laws, & a most contemptuous insult upon the powers of the Government.[11]

You, Gentlemen, are the Guardians of the Commonwealth's Dignity & Honor; & our Fellow Citizens rely upon your vigilance & wisdom, for the support of the Sovereignty & Importance of the Government. I therefore refer this matter to your determinations [sic]; & cannot but hope that your Resolutions & measures will give efficacy to the Laws & be the means of bringing to condign punishment those who dare to treat them with contempt or open opposition.

Gentlemen,—The Institution of a grand jury in a free Country, appears to me to be very essential to the preservation of good Morals & the protection of innocency [sic]. It is a great Bulwark to Personal Liberty & Safety; it ought therefore to have the utmost attention of the people; & to be guarded by the Legislature against every possible corruption. The Law of the Commonwealth enacted in the year One thousand seven hundred and eighty four, appears to have been well adapted to this important purpose; nevertheless, by the general practice upon it, we may justly doubt whether it is so well secured as it ought to be—Tho' the Act provides that Grand Jurors shall be Elected by the Freeholders & legally qualified voters at a regular Town Meeting, yet it is very obvious that this business is frequently so conducted that a very few People attend upon it. In this way, men who have their private

John Hancock's Life and Speeches

interest in view may obtain such Elections as may cause the innocent to be arraigned & suffer the guilty to escape Punishment. If there is any thing which can be done to support the importance & purity of this Institution, & effectually prevent its[12] being abused, it will be worthy your attention [sic].[13]

I shall be much obliged, by having the Acts you shall see fit to pass laid before me at as early a period as you may find it convenient, & I shall do everything within my power to render your business pleasant & agreeable.

John Hancock

Council Chamber, Concord, November 7th, 1792

NOTES

1. For the reply to the governor's message, see Senate Unenacted 1532/1, 10 Nov 1792, MA and A&L, May, 1792, 197-198. Cf. MHS, 10 Nov 1792 (copy), reply to opening speech including a request that, because of smallpox, the second session be kept to a minimum.

2. An outbreak of smallpox had taken place in Boston. A&R, Chap 28. of the November 1792 session, 50, recorded "An Act Providing for the Establishment of Hospitals for Enoculating with the Small Pox & for Repealing All Laws Heretofore Made for That Purpose."

In his proclamation calling for the legislasture to meet, Hancock stated that he was summoning them to Concord because of the smallpox. Commissions, Proclamations, Requisitions, etc, 1788-1799, 171-172, MA.

3. "Of the United States" was stricken from the MHS copy, presumably by Hancock himself.

4. "A place should be appointed by the Legislature for the meeting of Electors of the President and Vice-President of the United States" was stricken from the MHS copy, presumably by Hancock himself.

5. In 1781, Chapter 34, 579-581, the legislature had first turned its attention to the movement in Congress to establish a national bank. More definite action was taken in the January session of 1783, in Chapter 25, 558-560, in "An Act to Establish a Bank in This State and to Incorporate the Subscribers Thereto." The president and bank directors were named, including Stephen Higginson and John Lowell. Further action was taken on 25 June 1792, Chapter 6, 14-20 in which there was an appointment of president and directors of the Union Bank.

6. "An Act for Preventing Stage-Plays and Other Theatrical Entertainments," A&R, 3, 1742-1756, 11 April 1750: "no person or persons, whosoever, shall or may...suffer to be used...any house, room or place...for acting or carring on any stage-plays...on pain of forfeiting...twenty pounds." (A&R, Boston, 1918, reprinting the actions of the actions of the provincial general courts before 1780)

7. A&R, May, 1785, Chap. 19, 468, revived until 1 Nov 1797 the 1750 act "to prevent stage plays and other theatrical entertainments."

8. "Live or happen to" was stricken from the MHS draft.

9. Hancock's rough draft gives "its"; House Document 1532, The Boston *Gazette*, and A &L read "it's."

10. Wells, 3, 290-291:

> In 1790 a petition was presented to the Legislature for opening a theatre in Boston, which was rejected. In November of the following year [1791], though many of the old residents, including Mr. Adams, opposed the proceeding, a town meeting instructed the Boston Representatives to obtain, if possible a repeal of the prohibitory act; but the effort did not succeed....Though the prohibitory act remained unrepealed, a theatre was opened in Boston, and representations were given under the name of moral lectures. Upon the meeting of the Legislature, Governor Hancock denounced this infraction of the law, and soon after the whole theatrical company were arrested on the stage. The audience, enraged at the attempt against their public amusements, took the portrait of the Governor from the stage-box, and trod it under foot. During these commotions, it was customary, says an eyewitness, to go to the theatre armed with clubs. Application was renewed to the Legislature, who, finding that the public voice was largely in favor of it, repealed the act. Mr. Adams, then Governor, refused to sign the bill, and the prohibitory law was nominally in force during the successive administrations.

On 12 Dec 1792 Daniel Coney wrote to George Thatcher in Philadelphia:"...the governor's exertions to Suppress the 'pretended theatre' in this town has excited some danger of anxiety in the minds of its favorites. But 'Boston folks are still full of notions.'" (Boston Public Library, Ch. M. 2.1. vol. 5, 799)

On 23 Dec 1792 John Avery wrote to George Thatcher that Hancock's move to eliminate theatre in Boston was not unpopular, that two-thirds of the town approved. "Indeed," wrote Avery, "I am exceedingly pleased the

Actors are gone from here for I think a great deal of Money was spent very unnecessarily." (Boston Public Library, Ch. M. 2.1., vol. 5, 821)

An advertisement in the Boston *Gazette* of 27 Aug 1792, 3, made little attempt to disguise the entertainment being offered as spiritual. There was to be tumbling, singing, tight-rope walking, and an entertainment described as "The Power of Magic." The group that appeared to arouse the wrath of Hancock was described by Ball, 8, 48-49: "Sometime about the middle of the year 1792, there arrived from London a company of comedians, the chief of whom was Charles Stuart Powell. They leased a stable in Board alley, now known as Hawley street, and fitted it up for theatrical entertainments under the name of 'Moral Lectures.' The theatre was opened on the 10th of August." In his essay Ball reproduced one of the theatre programs that featured Monsieurs Placide and Martin dancing a hornpipe on a tight rope. The entertaiment was to conclude with a dancing ballet called "The Bird Catcher." The law against theatrical entertainments was eventually repealed, resulting in the building of the Federal Street Theatre. *Old Boston Days and Ways,* 423-425, reported that the first performance in Board Alley was on 1 Aug 1792 and that the performances continued for two months.

In its reply to the governor, the Senate expressed its indignation, not about whether a theatre should be allowed, but whether laws should be broken. "If any defect should be found in that Statute...we shall endeavor to remedy it." A sentence concerning the role of the judiciary in enforcing the laws about theatrical performances was deleted. (Senate Unenacted #1532/2, MA)

11. The Massachusetts Historical Society MS breaks off abruptly here. At the bottom of the last sheet is the notion "continued to another sheet" but there is no other sheet in the collection.

12. The Boston *Gazette* reads "its"; House Document 1532 and A & L read "it's."

13. In Chapter 63 on 26 Feb 1795, 495-497, of the 1793 session, the legislature passed "an Act in Addition to, and for the Amendment of an Act, Intitled [sic] 'An Act Regulating the Appointment and Services of 'Grand Jurors.' " The act attempted to provide for a wider base for the selection of grand jurors by having all of the eligible members assemble when the jury was to be chosen. "An Act Regulating the Apppointment and Services of Grand Jurors" passed in the May session of the 1784 legislature, as Chapter 4, 10-12, had similar provisions, but evidently the regulations were not effective.

HEADNOTE

Date: Monday, 12 Nov 1792

Occasion: The *American Apollo* stated that "the Secretary came in and delivered the following Message from the Governor, viz. Gentlemen of the Senate, and of the House of Representatives, If it will not take up too much of your time, I should be glad of being indulged at 4 o'clock, this afternoon, to meet both Houses of the Legislature, at the Meeting-house."

The *Journal of the House* for 12 Nov 1792, 13, 171, noted that Hancock spoke at four o'clock.

The legislature was still meeting in Concord because of the epidemic. The Boston *Gazette* reported that "the two branches having convened at the Meeting House, His Excellency the Governor again addressed them as follows:"

SOURCES

MHS, Hancock Papers, 12 Nov 1792; MS. with corrections by Hancock.

A&R, 1792, 689-90; Boston *Gazette,* 19 Nov 1792, 2; *American Apollo,* 16 Nov 1792, 3; *Columbian Centinel,* 28 Nov 1792, 2; *Independent Chronicle,* 15 Nov 1792, 3; Massachusetts *Spy,* 22 Nov 1792, 2.

Neither of the House Journals nor the Senate Journals reproduced the speech. They only say "see copy on file," but the MA can locate no copy of the speech.

TEXT

Gentlemen of the Senate & Gentlemen of the House of Representatives,

By the Constitution of the United States of America,[1] each State is to appoint, in such manner as the Legislature shall direct, Electors of

President & Vice President. The electors are to certify a list of their Votes to the President of the Senate of the United States. As the Electors are to be appointed by the respective States; & as their Votes could not be received without their appointment being certified, it would clearly follow that the Supreme Executive of each State ought to see that such Certificates were properly made.

By a late Act of Congress, it is Enacted "that the Supreme Executive of each State *shall* [2] cause three Lists of the names of the Electors of such State to be made & certified & to be delivered to the Electors on or before the first Wednesday in December."[3]

I feel the importance of giving every Constitutional support to the General Government; & I also am convinced that the existence & well being of that Government depends upon preventing a confusion of the authority of it with that of the States seperately [sic]. But that Government applies itself to the People of the United States in their natural individual capacity, & cannot exert any force[4] upon or by any means controul [sic] the Officers of the State Governments as such: Therefore when an Act of Congress uses compulsory words with regard to any Act to be done by the Supreme Executive of this Commonwealth I shall not feel myself obliged to obey them, because I am not in my official capacity amenable to that Government.

My duty as Governor will most certainly oblige me to see that proper & efficient certificates[5] are made of the appointment of Electors of President & Vice President; and perhaps the mode suggested in the Act above-mentioned may be found to be the most proper. If you, Gentlemen, have any mode to propose with respect to the Conduct of this business, I shall pay every attention to it.

Gentlemen,[6] I do not address you at this time[7] [send you this message] from a disposition to regard the proceedings of the General Government with a jealous eye, nor do I suppose that Congress should intend that clause in their Act as a compulsory provision; but I wish to prevent any measure to proceed through inattention, which [by the (?) Const (?)][8] may be drawn into procedent hereafter to the injury of the People, or to give a constructive power where the Federal Constitution has not expressly given it.

J.H.[9]

Council Chamber, Concord, Novemr. 12th: 1792

NOTES

1. Article II, Section 1, : "Each State shall appoint, in such Manner as the Legislature thereof may direct, a Number of Electors, equal to the whole Number of Senators and Representatives to which the State may be entitled in the Congress..." Clause 3: "The Electors shall meet in their respective States, and vote by Ballot for two persons, of whom one at least shall not be an Inhabitant of the same State with themselves....The Person having the greatest Number of Votes shall be the President....In every Case, after the Choice of the President, the Person having the greatest Number of Votes of the Electors shall be the Vice President."

2. The Boston *Gazette* reads "SHALL."

3. Annals of Congress, 2nd Congress, 1791-1793, 3 (Washington, 1849), col. 1343, stated: "And be it further enacted, That the Executive authority of each State shall cause three lists of the names of the Electors of such State to be made and certified and to be delivered to the Electors on or before the said first Wednesday in December; and the said Electors shall annex one of the said lists to each of the lists of their votes."

Chapter 80 of the May session of the 1792 session, 189, provided "A Resolve for Districting the Commonwealth, for the Purpose of Choosing Electors of President and Vice President." The state was divided by the General Court into four sets of counties: the first and second sets were to choose five electors each, while the third and fourth sets were to choose three electors each. The General Court stipulated that the selectmen of the towns were to supervise the voting procedures.

4. Hancock had written: "exert any force, [an bxx] upon." The words struck are indecipherable.

5. Hancock wrote "Certificates" over a word now indecipherable that had appeared in the previous draft.

6. The MHS draft omits "Gentlemen" but the newspapers include it.

7. The change made by Hancock in the MHS MS.

8. The change made by Hancock in the MHS MS.

9. The fact that the MHS MS bears only initials instead of the customary signature is evidence that it was a preliminary draft.

HEADNOTE

Date: Wednesday, 30 Jan 1793

Occasion: The *Columbian Centinel* noted: "Wednesday, Jan. 30, 1793: A QUORUM of both Branches took their seats this day. The business as usual at the beginning of a session being completed, a Committee was raised to inform the Governour, that the two branches had convened and were in readiness to receive communication. Thursday, Jan. 31. At twelve o'clock, the two houses convened in the Representatives Chamber—when his Excellency the Governour came in, and delivered the following SPEECH:"

SOURCES

Senate Unenacted #1684 (1793) MA; House Unenacted #3916 (1793), MA.

A & L, 1792-93, 691-6;* Boston *Gazette,* 4 Feb 1793, 3; *Columbian Centinel,* 2 Feb 1793, 2; *American Apollo,* 8 Feb 1793, 1-2; Massachusetts *Spy,* 14 Feb 1793, 2; *Independent Chronicle,* 10 Feb 1793, 2.

*Not in vol. 13 of the House Journal; no copy in either Senate Journal.

TEXT

Mr. President and Gentlemen of the Senate, Mr. Speaker & Gentlemen[1] of the House of Representatives, My duty requires me to point your attention to such objects as demand the aid of Legislative Authority; but I feel the highest satisfaction in having occasion to congratulate you on the continuance of the internal peace, as well as on the increasing prosperity of our Republic.

It must afford you a high degree of pleasure to find that you have nothing before you but what is incident to a quiet & orderly state of civil Government. A People in the full possession of the right to govern themselves according to their own discretion by the fixed rules of a Constitution of Government, established upon their voluntary consent; and to seek their own happiness as a Community, without the exercise of any authority over them, excepting what is derived from their own suffrages frequently given, cannot fail of insuring to themselves political prosperity, unless they want wisdom to discern, or virtue to improve their own privileges.—

When we contemplate the Government of the several states together with the Federal Constitution, by which they are all united for national purposes, we observe an astonishing accordance of powers, raised on the basis of Republican principles. The wheels though of different diameters turn in concert, and exhibit to Mankind the most satisfactory proof that Governments founded in the ideas of natural equality can possess more energy than despotism has ever given to those which have been raised by force or fraud, and supported by pretence of hereditary power.—

It is the part of a wise People in the day of their prosperity to recollect the principles which produced their public felicity, or as it is well expressed in the declaration of rights prefixed to the form of our[2] Government, "A frequent recurrence to the fundamental principles of the Constitution, and a constant adherence to those of piety, justice, moderation, temperance, industry & frugality, are absolutely necessary to preserve the advantages of Liberty, and to maintain a free Government."[3]

Amongst the means by which our Government has been raised to its present heighth [sic] of prosperity, that of Education has been the most efficient; you will therefore encourage & support our University and Academies; but more watchfully the Grammar and other town Schools. These offer equal advantages to poor and rich; & should the support of such Institutions be neglected, that kind of Education which a free Government requires to maintain its force, would very soon be forgotten.—

In the means of education, I do not confine my views to the business of Schools, but extend my ideas to all the Institutions which have a tendency to aid the progress of knowledge and virtue in the mind of the rising Generation, and to establish the public opinion in favor of those manly pursuits which render a people truly respectable.—

In the System of our Government, and founded in the principles of its Constitution, are a number of Laws, calculated to inspire the citizens with a reverence for religion and a respect for virtue. In this class are the laws against Blasphemy and Prophanity [sic] [4]; and also those which enjoy the observation of Holy Time, an attendance upon Public Devotion; and others, making provision for the maintenance of public Teachers of Piety, Religion, and Morality. These Institutions have a manifest tendency to establish those habits from whence will result the punctual performance of civil duties. In another class are found those which guard the avenues of the heart against corruption and depravity: these prohibit lewdness, intemperance, gambling, idleness, levity & dissipation of manners. Laws of this nature are important to Government because they prevent a disposition to those crimes which are dangerous to Society; and because the opinion of the Community well and clearly expressed in such institutions inculcate "the principles of Humanity, Industry, Frugality, Honesty, Sincerity, Good Humour and all the Social Affections and Generous Sentiments amongst the People."—[5]

I have taken occasion thus to express my sentiments to the political Guardians of the State, that my influence may move in support of those principles upon which the happiness of my fellow citizens so essentially depends.

The Laws against excessive usury, and other species of oppression, are of great consequence, because they protect the distressed part of the Community; and tend to the preservation of that equality of property without which a popular Goverment cannot long exist.—I recommend all these laws to your attention, that they may be strengthened where they are weak, & guarded where they may be evaded or subverted by collusion.—

I have been informed that the laws against excessive usury, as well as others where the forfeiture on the breach accrues equally to the Commonwealth & to the Prosecutor, are frequently evaded by the bringing of fictitious Suits. This surely ought to be remedied; for it is better that a law should not exist than that the Acts of Legislation should be made a pretext to fraud.—[6]

Crimes which are an injury alike to persons & possessions in every Nation are variously punished, according to the genius of the Government against which the offences are committed. In States where the principles of Government are maintained by force upon the fear of the Subjects, cruel and sanginary punishments are multiplied; but in a free State, directed by the public mind, upon fixed principles of Government, a sense of that honor and dignity of character with which a free citizen ought to be warmed, will be considered as a most powerful incentive to obeying the laws.—

The Laws of our Commonwealth contain but few sanguinary Institutions: Burglary is a capital offence, & said to be made such on the idea that he who breaks & enters a dwelling House in the night time with a felonious intention, would probably commit murder if he should meet with resistance. However satisfactory this reasoning may be, yet as that crime admits of various discriptions [sic] in the common Law idea of it, there may be room for legislative interposition. The offender who takes lodgings in the house of another, and stealing property comes out in the night-time, as well as he who breaks a Dwelling House in the night, and puts in his hand and steals, is not so highly criminal from the idea of fatal consequences as he who actually enters the House after he has broken in with felonious intention. Degrees of guilt demand degrees of Punishment in order to maintain the equity of the Government.—[7]

It may be well worthy of your attention to investigate the question whether the infamous punishments of cropping and branding, as well as that of the[8] Public Whipping Post, so frequently administered in this Government, are the best means to prevent the commissions of Crimes, or absolutely necessary to the good order of Government or to the Security of the People. It is an indignity to human nature, and can have but little tendency to reclaim the sufferer. Crimes have generally idleness for their Source, and where offences are not prevented by Education, a sentence to hard labour will perhaps have a more salutary effect then mutilating or lacerating the human body.[9] I recommend these ideas to your wise deliberations, that such punishments may be provided as, if administered with certainty and inflexibility, may be sufficient to check the progress of crimes, and yet be suited to the genious[10] of a Republic.—

The Laws which are the source of distributive Justice between Citizen and Citizen ought to be readily administered, & the officers who are appointed to discharge this important Trust, as well as they who are obliged to execute the Laws against criminals, ought to have a reasonable allowance for their service. I am obliged to ask your attention to the established rate of fees in the Government, because that [sic] the complaints on this subject are too general to be without foundation; and too loud to be neglected.

Gentlemen,

I am informed that there frequently happens a failure of justice from the legal incompetency of town inhabitants to be witnesses where their towns are parties: In the trials respecting the maintenance of poor persons,[11] the Inhabitants of the contending towns are by a particular act made competent witnesses; and as they are so frequently contracts, trusts and other transactions which are unknown to all excepting the members of the town where they exist; I am inclined to think that there would be no evil in making the inhabitants competent witnesses in all cases where they have no special or particular interest.—

Gentlemen of the Senate & Gentlemen of the House of Representatives,

The encouragement of Agriculture is of great consequence:[12] We have yet a great extent of valuable Land unimproved; and it would be good policy to encourage the migration of foreigners of every reasonable measure. Perhaps some of the laws formerly made, & now in force, for the regulation of admitting Strangers may need a revision.

The encouragement of Manufactures is of the next importance. The Cotton Manufactory at Beverly has received aid from the Goverment; but it is to be feared that it will not fully answer the public expectation.[13] The Duck Manufactory has succeeded so well that it may probably be able to support itself without the continuance of the bounty stipulated by the Govermment.[14] I mention this the more readily at this time, because there has been, and now is, continued in Boston, a laudable attempt to establish a Glass Manufactory which may look to the Government for aid and encouragement. Glass is a great article in the Country, and the preparation for making it, is attended with peculiar expences [sic].[15] The Resolve for granting a bounty on Hemp will soon expire; you will therefore consider of the expediency of continuing it for a longer space of time.—

Gentlemen,

I wish to call your attention to the ideas which I have heretofore suggested, respecting the providing funds for our Public Debt. The Creditors are patiently waiting, and suffering under expectations for relief from two Governments; but that of this Commonwealth is the only one upon which they have a direct demand.—I also wish to remind you of the Sentiments I delivered at the last session respecting the Commonwealth's becoming interested in the Union Bank; and to the other matters suggested at the same time,[16] upon which subjects I shall address you in seperate [sic] messages, during the present session.

I shall do all within my power to render the session useful to our Constituents, and agreeable to you. The Secretary will lay before you the Acts of Congress, so far as I have received them since your last session.—

John Hancock[17]

Boston January 30th.   1793

NOTES

1. For the answer of the legislature, see Senate Unenacted #1684 and #1684/1, 5-6 Feb 1793; and A&L, January 1792 session, Chap. 32, 15 Feb 1793, 240-243.

2. Hancock inked in "our" above the line where the scribe had omitted it.

3. A quotation from Article 18 of the first part of the 1780 Massachusetts State Constitution.

4. A&R, September 1782 session, Chap. 22, 59, dated 19 Oct 1782, passed "An Act to Prevent Profane Cursing and Swearing." An earlier act in 1782 (3 July 1782, Chap. 8, 27-28) had concerned blasphemy. Specifically prohibitive phrases were mentioned. In the early years, the prevalence of profanity might be attributed to the war, when social mores were likely to deteriorate, but 1792 and 1793 were not war years. Hancock's reminder of the laws may be in an effort to bolster up the conservative Massachusetts element that, at the turn of the century, may have felt it was losing control of the moral atmosphere of the state.

5. Source undetermined.

6. In its answer (see note 1), the General Court noted: "...and if the laws against usury can be made more conformable to these principles, it will comport with the desire of the Legislature." The language in A&R differs from the wording of the MS copies noted in note 1.

7. It would appear that Hancock was here speaking for certain of Massaschusetts's lawyers who wished to modify the English common law.

8. In Senate 1684, Hancock wrote in "the" above the line where the scribe had omitted it.

9. Hancock may have had in mind the prohibition against cruel and unusual punishment in Article 8 of the newly passed Bill of Rights.

10. House 3916 uses the more modern spelling of "genius."

11. The eternal problem of who was to look after the poor in the alms houses was not limited to England, but also extended to the colonies. Towns did not want to assume responsibility for the indigent, because they were then obligated to maintain them. On 14 Feb 1789, Chap. 61, 98-102, the General Court had made specific recommendations about care of the poor. A special section of this act concerned the settling of disputes as to "the habitancy or legal settlement of a Poor Person."

12. On 28 Mar 1788, Chap. 102, 880-881, the General Court had provided an additional bounty for growers of hemp. On 25 June 1789, Chap. 20, 421-422, the General Court decreed that growers of flax could only export their crops to Ireland or Scotland.

13. In 1787, Thomas Somers, an Englishman, petitioned the General Court to assist him in establishing what would become the second cotton factory in the United States. In coming by ship from Baltimore, Somers lost one half of his property, which he intended to use to open the factory. On 8 Mar 1787, the General Court made £20 at his disposal. The business opened around 1 Nov 1787 and by 1790 was operating 636 spindles. It appears to have ceased operation in or before 1813. See Bagnall, 1, 89-98. On 30 Oct 1789, two miles after passing through Beverly, George Washington visited the cotton factory and noted in his diary that "a number of Looms (15 or 16) were at work with spring shuttles, which do more than d'ble work." Washington concluded that the products that the factory was producing were "excellent of their kind." (Fitzpatrick, 4, 41)

A subscription was taken as early as 15 Mar 1768 to encourage women and children of Boston to manufacture duck or sail cloth. John Hancock subscribed £10 and £5 additional annually, more than any one else of the forty-seven subscribers. The MHS has two MS copies of the petition that was circulated to get sponsors.

14. In response to a bounty offered by the General Court on 28 Mar 1788, Chap. 102, 880-881, a company of citizens were operating the Boston Sail-Cloth Manufactory by 1789. Chapter 43 of the 1788 session, in an act approved on 3 Feb 1789, 71-73, and Chapter 119 of the December 1788 session, dated 17 Feb 1789, 362-363, offered further incentive to the production of cloth at Beverly. Advertisements appeared in newspapers endorsing the American product as superior to imported duck. By 1792 there were four hundred employees with a weekly producting of around fifty pieces of duck 24 inches wide by forty yards long. The factory appears to have ceased operation by 1800. (Bagnall, 1, 112-7) On 28 Oct 1789, Washington visited the duck factory, reporting that thirty-two pieces of duck of thirty to forty yards each was produced in a week. "Children (girls)," reported Washington, "turn the wheels for them, and with this assistance each spinner can turn out 14 lbs. of Thread pr. day when they stick to it, but as they are pd. by the piece, or work they do, there is no other restraint upon them but to come at 8 o'clock in the morning and return at 6 in the evening. They are daughters of decayed families, and are girls of Character—none others are admitted." (Fitzpatrick, 4, 37-8)

15. Glass manufacturing had been attempted from time to time in the colonies as early as 1608 or 1609, in Virginia. The first glasshouse in Massachusetts was at Salem, erected between 1634 and 1645. The venture to which Hancock referred was the Boston Glass Manufactory which had been given exclusive rights to manufacture glass in Massachusetts in 1787, with its capital stock exempt from taxes and its workmen relieved of military duties. The Boston furnaces were operating as late as 1822 and had

been considered as the parent of glass manufacturing in the United States. (Davis, 28-29) As was pointed out earlier, Chapter 48 of the January session of the 1782 legislature, 1 Mar 1783, 123, provided for a lottery of £3,000 to build a glass manufacturing facility. Chap. 47, 1 Mar 1783, 121-123, also provided legislation to facilitate the manufacture of glass in Boston. On 6 July 1787, Chap. 13, 567-569, having found that the earlier grant of a lottery of £3,000 for glass manufacture had been unproductive, the General Court withdrew its support from the first group and gave exclusive rights to a new group to manufacture glass. The new group also had difficulties, because the General Court on 20 Jan 1789, Chap. 33, 50-51, found it necessary to extend the act of 6 July 1787, so that the new manufacturers could get their enterprise underway. There were continued difficulties. On 15 June 1793, 346-348, Chap. 3, the General Court again enacted legislation encouraging the manufacture of glass and provided for securing the skill of foreign workers in producing the glass.

16. Hancock struck out "last session" and inserted above the line "same time" in both the House and Senate documents.

17. The signature is very feebly written.

HEADNOTE

Date: 18 Sept 1793

Occasion: Hancock's health had been deteriorating. He had been reelected only four months when he began to fail. Although he was only 56, which in his time was relatively old, he saw death's shadow. Although his grandfather had lived until 90, the "Bishop" had not dissipated or felt the strains of revolution as his grandson had.

Hancock did not fail to play up his final public appearance in his usual style. The newspaper accounts are relatively brief but show the drama involved. The *Independent Chronicle* stated: "Being met, a message from the Senate informed them that they were ready for business: whereupon a Committee of both Houses were appointed, who waited upon the Governor, with the above message, and reported that his Excellency would meet them in half an hour in the Representative's Chamber. A message was then sent from the House to inform the Senate that seats would be reserved for them. At half-past 4, his Excellency was brought in attended by the Secretary and High-Sheriff. Being seated, he informed the Legislature that the state of his health would not permit him to address them in the usual way; he therefore hoped that they would keep their seats, and required their indulgence while the Secretary should read his Address, as his infirmity rendered it totally impossible for him to speak so as to be heard. Accordingly, the Secretary, by his Excellency's direction, read the following:" The speech followed.

Although Ebenezer Thomas's memory of the event is inaccurate in some respects, it does present the best account of what occurred:

> A town meeting was called, upon a question of great excitement. Old Faneuil Hall could not contain the people, and an adjournment took place to the Old South Meeting-house.[1] Hancock was brought in, and carried up to the front gallery, where the Hon. Benjamin Austin supported him on the right, and the celebrated Dr. Charles Jarvis upon the left, while he addressed the multitude. The governor commented, by stating to his fellow citizens, that "he felt" it was the last time he should ever address them—that "the seeds of mortality were growing fast within him." The fall of a pin might have been heard such a death-like silence pervaded the listening crowd, during the whole of his animated and soul stirring

speech, while tears ran down the checks of thousands. The meeting ended, he was conveyed to his carriage, and taken home, but never again appeared in public—his death followed soon after. (Thomas, 1, 244)

Hancock did not become totally inactive after 18 Sept 1793. He continued to send messages to the legislature through 27 Sept 1793.

SOURCES

Senate Unenacted #1681, 1793, MA.*

A&R, 1792-93, 699-703; *American Apollo,* 20 Sept 1793, 2; *Independent Chronicle,* 19 Sept 1793, 3; Boston *Gazette,* 23 Sept 1793, 3; Massachusetts *Spy,* 26 Sept 1793, 2; *Columbian Centinel,* 21 Sept 1793, 1.

No copy in either House or Senate Journal. The *Journal of the House* MA noted only "on file."

TEXT

Mr. President and Gentlemen of the Senate, Mr. Speaker and Gentlemen of the House of Representatives,[2]

The Proclamation by which the General Court[3] is convened contains a copy of a civil precept,[4] the service of which, on me and on the Attorney General, was the principal reason for my exercising this part of that authority devolved on me by the Constitution.—[5]

The suit commenced by William Vassall,[6] if the commonwealth is held to answer thereon, must be decided on principles very interesting to its welfare as a state.—[7]

I cannot conceive that the people of this commonwealth, when they, by their representatives in convention, adopted the constitution of a general Government, expected that each state should be held liable to answer on *compulsory civil process* [8] to every Individual resident in another state, or in a foreign Kingdom.[9] Three Judges of the United States of America, having solemnly given it as their opinion that the several states are thus liable [sic].[10] The question then has become highly important to the people.

I did not find myself authorized, in virtue of my office as Governor of the Commonwealth, to appear either by myself or by my substitute in any court of Justice, either to deny the authority of the Court over this Governor, or to submit to its Jurisdiction, in a point which I cannot at present consider as settled: Nor did I conceive that any other person could have that authority without a special appointment by the Legislature for that purpose.

The service of this process being laid before the Council, they advised me to call the two Houses into Session. My opinion accorded with their advice for several reasons; some of which are too obvious to need repeating: Others I will suggest to you.—

The demand of William Vassall, if I am not mistaken in his design, and in the tendency of the process, will involve and conclude a question of legality on the mode of confiscating the personal estate of that class of people who in our Laws are denominated Absentees.[11] It is therefore necessary that effectual measures should be speedily adopted to prevent a determination which may so greatly injure the interest, and so disagreeably affect the feelings, of the citizens of this commonwealth.—

Should you, Gentlemen, be of opinion that by the constitution of the United States, the commonwealth may be compelled to answer on this process, you will make such provision for defending against the suit as shall appear to you to be proper and expedient.

Should you consider the Commonwealth not to be thus liable, your deliberations will be such as will tend to procure to the constitution under which this authority is claimed a more favourable and a more unexceptional construction. But it may happen that your investigations may lead you to conclude that the construction given to the Judiciary power of the United States, by three of the judges, is right, according to the letter of the constitution, and yet that it will tend to the promotion of peace and harmony in the Union, and to the preservation of our federal Government, so happily established, to procure such alteration in the Judiciary Articles as may secure the states severally in the enjoyment of that share of sovereignty which it was intended they should retain and possess. In this last case you will direct your measures to that point.

From these considerations I consider it as absolutely necessary that you should be in session at an earlier day than that to which the General Court stood adjourned. Your deliberations on this subject will take some time & tho' Congress will meet on the first Monday in December yet their session may be short. You could not therefore after the last Wednesday in January have time to do what will be necessary. The Court too where this suit is pending will be in session early in February, and the result of the business will be then expected.

I avoid giving an opinion either on the question whether the commonwealth is liable to be sued or whether, if it is so circumstanced, an attempt to procure an alteration is eligible. Yet I consider it to be of the last importance to the happiness and interest of the United States, as well in their united as in their separate capacity, to have this point properly, satisfactorily and finally settled. It is true that States, Kingdoms & Empires ought to do Justice, but it is as true that there are certain inherent principles in the constitution of each which can never be surrendered without essentially changing the nature or perhaps destroy the existence of Government.

I believe that the Commonwealth of Massachusetts, from the generosity and good feelings of its citizens, will be always ready, as far as the people's ability shall admit of, to do justice to all men: Yet in order to preserve the peace & safety of the union, and to establish in the bosoms of other nations, a confidence in the rectitude of this, it is very proper that there should be a tribunal of Justice, independent of the particular states, which may be resorted to in certain cases. This was intended to be provided for by the federal constitution: but whether the present case is properly before the tribunal, according to that Constitution, or whether the process under consideration is within the intendment of that provision, you will consider.

Whether the provision in the Federal Constitution for the extension of the Judiciary power to states is intended to be exercised in matters of civil contract, or in other matters which took place before the Government was formed; or whether it is intended only to give a remedy for such injuries as may take place by force, and may therefore have a tendency to destroy the peace of the union, or to involve the nation in a war with a foreign power is of consequence enough to demand a consideration. If the Judiciary power of the Union is to be exercised on questions of civil contracts made by a state, the decision must be had, either on the Laws of the State which the demand is made, or on those of the state of kingdom to which the demandment belongs, or on the Laws of the United States: The absurdity of the two first need not be pointed out, but the other would render the legislative authority of Congress over the particular states as mere corporations, commensurate to the claim of the Judiciary power. Where the demand shall be for a recompense of damages, resulting from an injury; there the Law of Nations, the Constitution of the United States, & existing treaties will govern the decision. And even in that case it will be a question whether it is intended that each state shall be liable on civil process to be drawn to the Seat of the Federal Government, and there tried by a Jury of the Vicinage in the same manner as a Corporation would be treated.

Congress, no doubt, should you instruct your Senators on the subject, will take time to consider these questions in proportion to the important light they may appear in.

The Legislature of the Union has never yet contemplated this subject: for in the establishment of the Judiciary System it is entirely neglected: No mention is made in the Acts of Congress of the suability of a State, nor is there any process against a state provided for in the Laws of the United States.

Gentlemen of the Senate, & Gentlemen of the House of Representatives, When the Government of the United States was proposed to the People's consideration, I then was, & yet am deeply impressed with the necessity "of a more perfect [xxxxxxxxxxxxxx][12] union of the states" than at that time existed[13] & therefore exerted the share of influence which I possessed in favour of its being adopted. I then considered it as being by no means explicit in the description of the powers intended to be delegated; but trusted that the wisdom of the people would very soon render every part of it definite & certain.[14] The idea that it is dangerous to examine systems of Government, and to compare the effects produced by their administration with the principles on which they were raised is inadmissible among a free people. If the people are capable of practicing on a free Government, they are able, without disorders or convulsions, to examine, alter and amend the systems which they have ordained. And it is of great consequence to the freedom of a nation to review its civil constitution, and to compare the practice under it with the principles upon which it depends. The tendency of every measure and the effect of every precedent ought to be scrupulously attended to, and critically examined. This is the business of the representatives of the people, and can never be by them confided to any other persons.

The great object presented to us by our political situation is the subject of the general Government, the giving force & efficacy to its functions, without destroying the powers, which the people intended to vest and to reserve in the State Governments.

A Consolidation of all the State into one Goverment would at once endanger the nation as a republic, & eventually divide the states united or eradicate the principles which we have contended for.

It is much less hazardous to prevent the establishment of a dangerous precedent than to attempt an abolition of it after it has obtained a place in a civil institution.

Your fellow-citizens anxiously wait the event of your deliberations on the important business before you: And I, as one of them, rest satisfied that the results will be such as will establish the rights of the commonwealth, and give support & efficacy to the General Government. In this view and in every other, in which the peace, liberty, and safety of our fellow-citizens, not only of this state but of the United States are concerned, rest assured Gentlemen that no effort nor zeal of my part shall be wanting. I shall therefore only add, I will do everything in my power to expedite the business of the session and to render it as little expensive to our Constituents, as exigencies will admit.

JOHN HANCOCK[15]

Council Chamber, Boston, September 18th: 1793

I beg the Pardon of the Hon. Legislature, and I rely on your candor, Gentlemen, to give this method of addresssing you: I feel the *seeds* of mortality growing fast within me; but I think I have in this case done no more than my duty, as the servant of the people: I never did, and I never will *deceive* them, while I have life and strength to act in their service.[16]

NOTES

1. Ebenezer's memory appears to be faulty on this point. The *Journal of the Senate*, 18 Sept 1793 (MA, a) stated that the legislators met in the House Chamber.

2. The answer of the legislature to the governor is printed in A&L, 1795, 705-706.

3. There is no manuscript copy of this proclamation in the file on proclamations at the Massachusetts Archives. The notice did appear in the newspapers of the day. Although the summons by the Supreme Court was dated 11 Feb 1793, it evidently did not receive press coverage until Hancock released it on 9 July 1793, following the receipt of a subpoena issued on 4 June 1793. (Dunlap, *Daily Advertiser* and *National Gazette*) The proclamation began: "Whereas the governor of this commonwealth, has this day been served by John Brooks, Esq. marshal of the federal court of the United States, with the following writ, viz:" Hancock then reproduced the summons that he had received from the Supreme Court which said "WE command and strictly enjoin you, that, laying all other matters aside, and

notwithstanding any excuse, you be and appear on behalf of the Commonwealth of Massachusetts, before the said Supreme Court of the United States on the 5th day of August next ensuing." (Philadelphia *National Gazette*, 24 July 1793; Dunlap's *American Advertiser*, 10 July 1793) The office of the clerk of the Supreme Court was unable to locate a copy of the original proclamation. That the governor of a state should be commanded to appear before the Supreme Court and for such an unpopular cause was an event not contemplated at the time the Constitution was ratified.

Some of Hancock's proclamations are copied into one volume at the Massachusetts Archives, e.g., his proclamation of 4 Mar 1793 "and in the 17th year of the Independence of the United States of America" concerning 11 Apr 1793, for fasting, humiliation and prayer (199-200) and his Thanksgiving Day proclamation, issued on 28 Sept 1793, to be commemorated on Thursday, 7 Nov 1793. (MA, b, 195-197) See *Commissions, Proclamations and Requisitions*, MA, which includes on p. 159 a proclamation signed by Hancock and on pp. 171-172, his proclamation of 26 Oct 1782 concerning the removal of the General Court to Concord on 7 Nov 1792.

4. The civil precept (i.e., civil charge) was that the the state of Massachusetts could be held liable to William Vassall for the confiscation of his property and therefore be assessed damages or be required to take steps to recover Vassal's property for him.

The events leading up to and following the issue of the subpoena need examination. The incident was sufficiently important to force Hancock to leave his deathbed and speak as forcefully as possible concerning states' rights.

Virginia had passed two laws prohibiting the English (and therefore the Tories) from collecting debts owed to them by Americans.

On 20 Oct 1777, the Virginia legislature passed "an act for sequestering British property, enabling those indebted to British subjects to pay off such debts" by paying the money owed into the loan office and receiving a certificate for the payment. (*Ware v. Hylton*, 3 U.S. [Dallas] 199 [1796]; Lawyer's Edition, vols. 1-4, *Supreme Court Reports*, 1796, 568)

On 3 May 1779, the Virginia legislature passed legislation entitled "An Act concerning escheats and forfeitures from British subjects..." providing that property belonging to British subjects "shall be deemed vested in the commonwealth." (*Ware v. Hylton*, 3 U.S. [Dallas] 199 [1796])

On 19 Feb 1793, when the state of Georgia failed to appear, the Supreme Court ordered judgment by default in favor of Chisholme, a resident of South Carolina suing the state of Georgia. (2 Dallas 419 [1793]) *Chisholme* became a test case to see if the Virginia laws would be overturned, for it allowed a citizen of one state to sue another state. It was easy to predict, therefore, that, under *Chisholme*, absentees as well as citizens of another state might be given "standing" to sue in the courts of the United States to recover their confiscated property or its value. William Vassall, under *Chisholme*, could sue Massachusetts. Virginian Tories could sue Virginia for the return of their property. But the wealth of the absentees had already been disposed of, usually by public sale, in part to pay for the war. Disturbing such sales would have brought chaos on the colonies.

For example, in the case of William Vassall, the Boston *Gazette* of 2 Feb 1780 announced that "the Agent for the Estate of WILLIAM VASSAL [sic], Esq., an Absentee, informed the Public, that on the 6th Day of March next he shall lease by public Auction, at the Bunch of Grapes Tavern in Boston, at Eleven o'Clock, A.M. the Mansion House, Out Houses &c. of said Absentee, for one Year from the Fi'st of April next." *The Documentary History of the Supreme Court* (Marcus & Perry) noted that the sale of the house brought £50,000 and the furniture £600 in continental currency.

As a result of *Chisholme*, the Virginia laws were to be directly tested. An action was brought on 29 Nov 1793 (National Archives Microfilm Publications, Copy 214, roll 1, Cases 1-14, 30 June 1792 to 28 January 1796, #4, *Ware, Administrator of Jones, Plaintiff in Error v. Hylton, et al*) by William Jones as administrator of the estate of the deceased Ware against the Virginia firm of Hylton & Co. in the federal circuit court sitting in Richmond, Virginia. The federal circuit ruled in favor of the defendant. The plaintiff appealed to the Supreme Court.

The Supreme Court acknowledged that, according to the act of 20 Oct 1777, the debtors had paid the necessary funds into the state loan office to satisfy the debt, the inference being that it would be unjust for the debtors to have to pay the debt twice and therefore that the plaintiff's action should be brought against the state of Virginia. However, the plaintiff quoted the fourth article of the Treaty of Paris providing "that the creditors of either side should meet with no lawful impediment to the recovery of the full value in sterling money, of all *bona fide* debts, theretofore contracted." (*Ware v. Hylton*, 570) Therefore, the Supreme Court overturned the circuit court ruling and confirmed judgment for the plaintiff. It would not be necessary for the plaintiff to seek recovery of the funds from the State of Virginia. He could proceed against the company that owed the debt, even though that company had deposited the funds to pay the debt with the state in the loan office, in keeping with Virginia's legislation. To refuse to allow the plaintiff to proceed against the debtor would, in this case, serve as a "lawful impediment to the recovery of the full value in sterling money, of all *bona fide* debts." The Supreme Court said that "a state may make what rules it pleases" but that, in this instance, "here is a treaty, the Supreme law, which overrules all state laws upon the subject." (*Ware v. Hylton*, 3 U.S. [Dallas] 604 [1796]) The Supreme Court did not give credence to the argument that, in 1777, when Virginia passed its law, it was to all extent and purposes an independent nation, and therefore the treaty could not apply to laws passed before the ratification of the treaty.

Other Supreme Court cases that caused the states alarm were *Vanstophorst v. Maryland*, 2 Dallas 401 (1791); and *Oswald v. New York*, 2 Dallas 401 (1792), 415 (1793), with damages awarded to the plaintiff for $5,315 in February of 1795. See Pitkin, 9, 335, 341; Cooley et al, 70-71; Goebel, 1, 735; and *Atascedero State Hospital v. Scanlon*, 105 S.Ct. 3142 (1985), 3169.

William Vassall had been in correspondence with Governor Bowdoin of Massachusetts as early as 1786, exploring the possibility of the return of his Boston estates. On 26 July 1786, Vassal wrote Bowdoin that he had received Bowdoin's letter advising him that the "anxiety, distress, & risk were brought upon them [the colonists] by the machinations of the absentees in concurrence with the British ministry and that this last would justly absorb their whole estate were it ever so large." (MH, a) Vassal protested that he was a citizen of Jamaica, that he had only gone to England to supervise his Jamaican estates, and that he had never aided the British cause. Evidently in his letter to Vassall of 24 Apr 1786, Governor Bowdoin had given some encouragement to Vassall, saying that his case was different from other absentees and that a favorable consideration of it might be expected. Therefore, Vassall was waiting for an opportunity to file suit.

Following the *Chisholme* decision, Massachusetts took several actions. On 18 Mar 1793, the General Court appointed a committee of Dr. Jarvis and Messrs. Kingsley, Sewall, Gardiner , and Jones to examine "how far any state is constitutionally responsible on an action of debt, instituted by any individual of any other state." (*Gazette of the United States*, Philadelphia, 30 Mar 1793; see also *General Advertiser*, Philadelphia, 29 Mar 1793) The committee issued its report in June of 1793, saying that the principle applied in Georgia would apply also in Massachusetts, but that "it hath ever been the sense of this commonwealth, that the government of the United States is a Federal Goverment" (*General Advertiser*, Philadelphia, 4 July 1793) and that it had not been intended, in approving the Constitution, that such suits should be brought.

At a date which the early records of the Supreme Court do not show, William Vassall, complainant, filed a suit in the United States Supreme Court against the state of Massachusetts. (Hildreth IV, 407, 446) James Buchanan, of the project *A Documentary History of the Supreme Court of the United States, 1789-1800*, speculated that Vassal may have delayed filing suit until Rhode Island joined the union, because his property in both states had been seized. Vassall may have petitioned the Massachusetts General Court for a return of his lands, but there appears to be no record of such a petition in the A & R of Massachusetts or in the *Journal of the House of Massachusetts*. Or he may have filed suit in the federal district court, but there is also no record of such a filing. That he did either appears unlikely, for both actions would have provoked immediate reaction from Governor Hancock and others. So it is likely that the first action taken was before the Supreme Court, where Vassall's case may have been given original jurisdiction because he was then residing abroad. However, the Supreme Court records of the case are missing and presumably destroyed, so it is only possible to speculate as to what occurred before 11 Feb 1783.

h. On 11 Feb 1793, the clerk of the Supreme Court of the United States, Samuel Bayard, issued a summons to Hancock and his attorney general to appear in Philadelphia on 5 Aug 1793. (Dunlap's *American Daily Advertiser*, Philadelphia, 18 July 1793; Boston *Gazette*, July 15, 1793) Note that although the summons was issued on 11 Feb 1793, it was evidently not given publicity until the summons was followed up by subpoenas.

On 4 June 1793, subpoenas were issued by the Supreme Court. (Marcus and Perry, 492)

On 9 July 1793 Hancock by proclamation called a special session of the General Court to assemble on 18 Sept 1793 at the State House in Boston. (Dunlap's etc. see above; *National Gazette*, Philadelphia, 24 July 1793)

There followed a series of articles in colonial newspapers by "Brutus" protesting the action. In the *Independent Chronicle* of 18 July 1793, in an article addressed to the General Court, Brutus advised that "if you submit to the demand, you will authorize a foreign jurisdiction, to exercise a power, which can never be exercised by it, but to the destruction of your own power; to the overthrow of the State goverments; to the consolidation of the Union, for the purposes of arbitrary power; to the downfall of liberty." The article concluded: "Massachusetts is, and of right ought to be, a FREE, SOVEREIGN, and INDEPENDENT State!" (See also *National Gazette*, Philadelphia, 27 July 1793)

On 5 Aug 1793 the writ was returned by the marshal for the Massachusetts district (Marcus and Perry, 492), indicating an unwillingness to comply. (*Vassall v. Massachusetts*, Docket 5; Mathis, 224)

Therefore, on 6 Aug 1793, with "consent of parties expressed by their counsel," the case was continued to the next term. (Marcus and Perry, 1, Part 1, 218 and 492)

On 2 Sept 1793, James Sullivan, the attorney general of the commonwealth of massachusetts, wrote to the clerk of the supreme court, Samuel Bayard, asking what was the status of *Vassall v. Massachusetts.*

On 27 Sept 1793, the General Court recommended that their representatives in Congress use "the most speedy and effectual measures in their power" to obtain an amendment to the Constitution prohibiting a state from being compelled "to answer in any suit by an individual or individuals in any Court of the United States." (A&R September Session, 1793, Chap. 45, 27 Sept 1793, 590-591; Fuess, 3, 422)

Hancock died on 8 Oct 1793. Senate Unenacted #1677/1 comprises a letter from Governor Clinton of New York to Samuel Adams, dated 1 Nov 1793, saying that Clinton was replying to Adam's letter of "the 9th Ultimo" (which would be the 9th of the previous month, or the 9th of October) and that he would lay the matter before the New York legislature. Adams had written Clinton of Hancock's death.

Senate Unenacted #1677/4 and #1677/2 are two letters dated 13 Nov and 16 Dec 1793 in which the governor of Connecticut told lieutenant governor Adams that he had sent to him Connecticut's resolutions on the subject of opposing the suability of a state by any individual or individuals.

Senate Unenacted #1677/3 are a letter from Governor Lee of Virginia to the governor of Massachusetts dated 5 Dec 1793, containing the resolutions on the subject by Virginia.

In November of 1793, Virginia also notified Congress of its opposition to allowing states to be sued by citizens of other states. (*Journal of the House of Delegates of the Commonwealth of Virginia,* 1793, at 99, 28 Nov 1793, with concurrence by the Senate noted on 110)

On 19 Dec 1793, Bayard answered the letter of 2 Sept 1793 by James Sullivan, attorney general of Massachusetts saying that, as of 19 Dec 1793, all that had happened was that the subpoenas had been issued of which he asssumed a copy had been served on Sullivan. (Senate Unenacted 1833, 18 Sept 1793, MA) Bayard commented that, upon checking the minutes of the last session of the Supreme Court, Attorney General Edmund Randolph had moved to continue the case to the next term of court. The motion, however, included the stipulation that those in authority in Massachusetts were to be required to appear. (MA, Senate Unenacted, #1833) Bayard wrote that Randolph, sensing "the whole subject would undergo a new investigation— he postponed moving further in the suit against Massachusetts." What gave Randolph pause were the actions being taken by Georgia and New York in the suits of *Farquhar's Estate v. Georgia* (*Chisholme v. Georgia*) and seemingly *Oswald v. New York,* 2 Dallas 401, 415), although Bayard does not identify this case by name. Bayard informed Sullivan that, if, in the next session, the Supreme Court concluded that they had jurisdiction in such suits, Edmund Randolph as attorney general of the United States intended to proceed. Bayard thought that, at the February 1794 session, some action would be taken and he advised Sullivan to be present at that session, along with representatives from New York and Georgia, to "defend the sovereignty of the States." The court had declared its intention of welcoming any opinions on the matter by interested parties.

On 14 Jan 1794, the Eleventh Amendment was approved by the Senate; on 4 March 1794, by the House. Ratification by the states was completed on 7 Feb 1795 with adoption by North Carolina. (Mathis, 228) Although three-fourths of the states had ratified the amendment only a little more than a year after it had received approval by Congress, it was not until 8 Jan 1798 that John Adams notified Congress that the Eleventh Amendment had been adopted by three-fourths of the states and could be considered as a part of the Constitution. Mathis (228) reasoned that the three-year delay between the date that three-fourths of the states ratified the amendment and the official proclamation of the amendment by John Adams may have been caused by the delay of the states in notifying the federal government of their approval.

Once the Eleventh Amendment had become official, the question remained as to the status of cases that had been filed before the amendment took effect. On 17 Jan and 25 Jan 1794, respectively, the House and the Senate of Massachusetts concurred in a report of a committee of both houses to whom the Bayard letter had been referred to the effect that "they have considered its contents and find nothing in it which merits the attention of the Legislature." (MA, Senate Unenacted #1833) In other words, there was nothing the legislature could do to require the Supreme Court to recognize states rights. Hildreth reported that, when Hancock immediately brought the matter to the attention of the general court, "they resolved to take no notice." (6, 446)

In the case of *Vassall v. Massachusetts*, continuances were issued on 6 Aug 1793 and 18 Feb 1794; and in August of 1794, February of 1795, August of 1795, February of 1796, and August of 1796. (Marcus and Perry, 492; Goebel, 1, 492)

On 13 Feb 1797, *Vassall v. Massachusetts* was dismissed with costs. (Marcus and Perry, Fine Minutes, 13 Feb 1797, Docket 5) No reason is given for the dismissal. (Marcus and Perry, 288, 492) It can be assumed that, although the Eleventh Amendment had not been officially proclaimed, Attorney General Raldolph and the justices were aware of its approval and decided that, applying *post facto* law, *Vassall* had no standing before the court. The American Constitution in general opposed *ex post facto* laws. But a different attitude was taken in the case of constitutional amendments. On 14 Feb 1798, the court decided unanimously that the Supreme Court had no jurisdiction in cases wherein a state was sued by a citizen of another state or by a citizen of a foreign state. (Marcus and Perry, 1, 305; Goebel, 1, 741)

The long-run effects of the "overturn of Chisholme" by the Eleventh Amendment reached into the nineteenth and twentieth centuries as the Supreme Court continued to find that the Eleventh Amendment allowed certain suits and prohibited others. Two decisions are noteworthy. In *Hans v. Louisiana*, 134 U.S. 1 (12890), the Supreme Court interpreted the Eleventh Amendment to mean not only that a citizen of the state of X may not sue the state of Y without Y's permission, but that a citizen of Y cannot sue the state of Y without Y's permission. The court admitted that the Eleventh Amendment did not specifically deny jurisdiction in such cases, but ruled that it had been the intent of the Eleventh Amendment to bar all cases against a state without its permission. (Mathis, 232) In *Monaco v. Mississippi*, 292 U.S. 313 (1934), the Supreme Court held that, under the Eleventh Amendment, a state could not be sued without its permission by a foreign government.

Vassall died in 1800 without any recovery.

5. The Massachusetts Constitution required Hancock to convene the General Court.

6. William Vassall of Boston, a graduate of Harvard, left for England, was proscribed, banished, and his estate forfeited. In his letter from England of 26 July 1786, Vassall claimed that he "never gave, subscribed, or promised one farthing toward raising soldiers, or towards any hostile attempt against any one of the United States." (MH, b; *Biographical Sketches*, 2, 384-5)

7. Not only were there the problems of federal versus states rights involved in the *Vassall* suit, but the status of the property of the Tories was vital to the colonies. The problems caused by the presence of Tories in the colonies had been an early concern of the Continental Congress. In his diary entry of 14 Mar 1776, John Adams discussed the problem and reprinted the resolution for disarming those refusing to defend the states. (Wells, 3, 34)

The Provincial Congress wasted no time in appropriating the assets of the absentees. On 16 Oct 1778, an act was passed specifying a long list of former citizens of the Bay Colony who were officially declared to have joined the enemy. Thomas and Oliver Hutchinson, along with Francis Bernard, headed the list. William Vassall was among those so proscribed. (A&R, V, 912-918, "An Act to Prevent the Return to This State, of Certain Persons Therein Named, and Others, Who Have Left This State, or Either of the United States, and Joined the Enemies Thereof") The act confiscating their estates was passed on 1 May 1779. (A&R, 5, 968-971, "An Act for Confiscating the Estates of Certain Persons Commonly Called Absentees")

After the new Massachusetts Constitution went into effect, in Chap. 48 of the 1780 session, 113, and in Chap. 95 of the October 1780 session, 183, the legislature provided for the confiscation and sale of the estates and public effects of absentees, except for those that were encumbered by mortgages. Further details for resolving the sales of the estates of absentees were passed in A&R, Chap. 10, May 1783 session, 680, and in Chap. 84 of the October 1788 session, 278-279. The last clarified that the confiscated property belonged to the state of Massachusetts.

One of the problems confronted by the colonists involved the "fence sitters," persons who evidently gave either silent or limited vocal support to the colonists but who did not sufficiently commit themselves so that, if the British won, their status with the Tories would be unaffected. The state of New York passed "An Act effectually to prevent the Mischief arising from the Influence and Example of Persons of equivocal and suspected Characters in this State." Commissioners were authorized to require suspects to take an oath that they "do solemnly and without any mental reservation or Equivocation whatsoever, swear and call God to Witness...that I believe and acknowledge the State of New York to be of a right a free and Independent State, and that no Authority, or Power can of Right be exercised in and over the said State, but what is, or shall be granted or derived from the People thereof...." (BM, a) The intensity of this language indicates the strong feelings held by the colonists who had staked their lives and property on the cause of the colonies. If such fence-sitters were to be given such close scrutiny, reminiscent of what was to occur later in the French Revolution, it is no wonder that the colonists had little sympathy with the cause of William Vassall.

Another of the problems of the colonists concerned interchange with Nova Scotia and in particular the British-built city of Halifax. During the preliminaries of the revolution and at the time of the departure of the British from Boston, families were split. Some members went to Nova Scotia; other family members remained. Some who left were unable to take their possessions with them, and some who did sought to reenter Boston and to bring their goods from Nova Scotia back "home" to Massachusetts. Therefore, on 13 Nov 1780, A&R 1780, October session, Chap. 41, 153, the General Court decreed that persons who wish to take possessions from Massachusetts to Nova Scotia, and persons who wished to bring posessions from Nova Scotia into Massachusetts, would have to apply to the governor and his Council. The colonists were naturally suspicious of such interchanges, and had no intention of letting items of value escape their jurisdiction.

The efforts of William Vassall to reclaim his confiscated lands were therefore unsuccessful. John Hassam, who compiled a list of the confiscated estates in Suffolk County, identified the Vassall confiscation of 1779 as Docket No. 17367. This piece of property, according to Fuess (3, 421) was located on Brattle Street in Cambridge, and was not Vassall's home, which is now known as The Longfellow House. The expropriation went like this: (a) the state ordered a given piece of property of an absentee appropriated; (b) the title to that property was then vested in the commonwealth of Massachusetts; (c) the commonwealth was then able to sell or lease the land and keep the proceeds, except that the General Court allowed mortagees to be reimbursed from monies collected for the sale of the lands. Hassam noted that the land on which the Massachusetts Historical Society stands was confiscated from a loyalist and that the value of Governor Hutchinson's confiscated estates came to £131,621.

Two tracts of lands belonging to the Vassall family were sold on 25 Sept 1781, and on 8 Jan 1784. The latter sale included the disputed land of William Vassall. (Stark, 290)

8. Hancock himself was summoned to testify but refused.

9. In the Virginia Convention called to ratify the Constitution, both Madison and Marshall reported that the Constitution did not permit an unwilling state to be sued by an individual. (Elliot, 3, 533-555) Hamilton in the *Federalist Papers* acknowledged in *Federalist* 80 that the federal judiciary had jurisdiction over cases "between a state and citizens of another state"; but in 81 interpreted the Constitution to mean such suits could take place only with consent.

10. *Chisolme v. Georgia.*

11. The term "absentees" has not remained in use. The more favorable term "loyalists" has been retained. For a biased but comprehensive treatment of the absentees, see Stark. When the peace treaty between the United States and Great Britain was signed, the British and the French urged amnesty and compensation to the loyalists. But the American commissioners knew the extent of the bitterness toward the Tories, and so the British had to be satisfied with the stipulation that the American Congress would recommend that the states adopt a liberal policy toward the absentees and that no legal impediment would prevent suits for recovery. Congress did so recommend and so agree, but to little or no avail. (Stark, 95) Once the estates of the absentees had been sold, it would have been all but impossible to persuade the states to reimburse persons who had fought against the American Revolution and who, if they had succeeded, would certainly have in turn confiscated the estates of the revolutionaries.

12. In Senate MS 1681, Hancock crossed out three or four words that he had originally included within the brackets here provided.

13. In Senate 1681, Hancock wrote "existed &" over the verb that he had originally used. The original verb is indecipherable.

14. The passage of the Eleventh Amendment in 1798 bore out Hancock's prediction.

15. Underneath the date, in this instance written by the scribe, there appears the following comment: "The name of 'John Hancock' was cut from the above speech by me." The signature "Chas. Calhoun, Clerk of Senate" and the date "June 10, 1836" are written below the comment, in the same handwriting.

16. This seemingly extemporaneous comment by Hancock appears in the Boston *Gazette*, Massachusetts *Spy*, and the *Independent Chronicle*.

Bibliography

PART 1

Chapter One

Acts & Resolves, Chapter 894, 7 Mar 1777, 19, 816

Adams, Charles Francis. *The Works of John Adams*, Boston, 1856, 10 vols. (dates vary)

Allan, Herbert S. *John Hancock: Patriot in Purple*, New York, 1948

Baxter, W.T., *The House of Hancock*, Cambridge, Mass., 1945

BP
   a. Hancock to Dolly, Rhode Island, 18 Aug 1778, Ch M. 1.10.161.
      Cf. BPL, Hancock to Dolly,
      25 Mar 1775, Ch.M. 1.10.54
   b. Ms qAM. 2084
   c. Ch. M. 1. 20, 98
   d. MS. 255
   e. Ch. M. 1. 10, 146

Boyd, Julian P., ed. *The Papers of Thomas Jefferson*, Princeton, 1950

Butterfield, L.H., ed., *Diary and Autobiography of John Adams*, Cambridge, Massachusetts, 1961 4 vols

Davidson, Philiip Grant, *Propaganda and the American Revolution*, New York, 1941

Documentary History of the Constitution, Washington, Department of State, Washington, D.C., 1894-1905, 5 cols

Fowler, William M., *The Baron of Beacon Hill*, Boston, 1980

Fowler, William M., "John Hancock: the Paradoxical President," *New England Historical and Genealogical Register*, 130, 1976, 164-177

Gordon, William, *The History of the Rise, Progress, and Establishment of the Independence of the United States...*, London, 1788, 4 vols

Guild, Reuben Aldrich, *The Life, Times and Correspondence of James Manning and the Early History of Brown University*, Boston, 1864

Handlin, Oscar, *The History of the United States*, New York, 1967, 2 vols

Holcombe, Arthur Newman, "Massachusetts and the Federal Constitution of 1787," *Commonwealth History of Massachusetts*, ed. A.B.Hart, New York, 1929, 5 vols

Hubbard, C. C., "Controversies over British Control (1753-1765)," *Commonwealth History of Massachusetts*, ed. A.B.Hart (New York, 1928), 5 vols

King, C. R., *Life and Correspondence of Rufus King*, New York, 1984

Library of Congress, Madison Papers

Main, J. T., *The Antifederalists*, Chapel Hill, 1911

MA
    Massachusetts Archives Collection, vol. 196, 230

MHS
    a. John Hancock to Joseph Warren, 15 June 1775 (orig), HFP
    b. John Hancock to Thomas Cushing, 7 Mar 1776 (orig), HFP
    c. John Hancock to Dorothy Quincy, 7 May 1775 (photostat: original in the Quincy mansion), HFP
    d. John Hancock to John Wendell, 22 May 1782 (orig), HFP
    e. John Hancock to Dolly Hancock, 19 Aug 1778 (Xerox[TR]) (Bowdoin-Temple Papers)
    f. Edward Carrington to Henry Knox, 13 Mar 1788. Knox Papers, XXI, 167
    g. John Hancock to John Treate Paine, 13 Jan 1777, HFP
    h. John Hancock to Joseph Warren, circa 1790 (orig), HFP
    i. John Hancock to Major General Knox, 10 April 1791 (orig), HFP; Cf Knox Papers, XXVII, 20 (Xerox[TR])

Mayo, Lawrence Shaw, "The Massachusetts Loyalists (1775-1783)," *Commonwealth History of Massachusetts*, ed. A. B. Hart, 5 vols, 1927-1930

National Archives Microfilm Publications, Microcopy #247, Roll 23, Item 12A: Letter Books of the President of Congress, Sept 15, 1775-Dec 8, 1775, including the official letters sent by John Hancock between 15 Sept 1775 and 27 Oct 1777; Hancock to George Washington, 25 Mar 1776, #88

New England Society Historical and Genealogical Register, "Letter of Edmund Quincy," Edmund Quincy to Dorothy Quincy, 22 July 1775, 2, 1857, 165-167

NEHGS Hancock Papers

a. 1762-1783, William Palfrey to Harrison & Annsley, 17 May 1773, 419

b. 1762-1783, William Palfrey to Hagley & Hopkins, 10 Jan 1774, 425

c. 1762-1783, John Hancock to Captain Scott, 14 Nov 1783, 429-430

d. 1763-1786, William Hoskins to Ebhenezer Grant, 28 Mar 1786

e. 1762-1783, John Hancock to Mary Hagley, 14 Nov 1783, 428

f. vol. 17, John Avery to John Hancock, 10 Oct 1785

g. vol. 17, Thomas Hancock to John Hancock, 3 July 1793

h. vol. 17, Isaac Cazneau to John Hancock, 4 Apr 1776 (reproduced in the 17 Mar 1892 issue of the Boston *Transcript*)

NYP

a. Gerry to John Adams, Marblehead, Mass, 8 Jan 1781

b. Hancock to Sam Adams, 31 Aug 1793

c. *Acts Relating to America*, 1777, KRB p.v.,vols. 1 & 2 contain selected acts concerning America, all published in London. Where a specific title for an act was given, the page numbers refer to the pages on the act, not the consecutive pages in the two volumes

d. Sam Adams to Hancock, 3 Sept 1793

Paullin, Charles Oscar, ed., *Out-Letters of the Continental Marine Committee and Board of Admiralty*, New York, 1914

Quincy, Edmund, "Letter by Edmund Quincy," *New England Historical and Genealogical Register*, 11 (1857), 165-167

Report of the Record Commissioners, Boston Town Records, 1770-1777, Boston, 1887

Rutland, Robert A.,ed., *The Papers of James Madison*, Chicago and Charlottesville, 1962-1985, 15 vols

Smith, P. H., ed. *Letters to Delegates to Congress 1774-1789*, Washington, D.C., 1976-open

a. John Hancock to George Washington, 19 Sept 1775, 2, 31

b. Richard Smith's Diary, 22 Dec 1775, 2, 513

c. Richard Smith's Diary, 12 Sept 1775, 2, 5

d. John Hancock to William Palfrey, 25 Sept 1785, 2, 57

e. John Hancock to Dorothy Hancock, 13 Oct 1777, 8, 39

f. John Hancock to George Washington, 25 Oct 1777, 8, 181

g. Hancock to Dolly, 8 Oct 1777, 8, 77

Stinchcombe, W.C., *The American Revolution and the French Alliance*, Syracuse, 1969

Sumner, W.H., "Reminiscences by Gen Wm. H. Sumner," *New England Historical & Genealogical Register*, 8, Boston, 1854

Sullivan, William, *Familiar Letters on Public Characters* . . . Boston, 1834

Taylor, Hannis, *The Origin & Growth of the American Constitution*, 1911

Warren-Adams Letters, ed. W. C. Ford, Boston, 1917-1935, 2 vols

Wells, William V., *Life and Public Services of Samuel Adams*, New York, 1865, 3 vols

Chapter Two

Allan, Herbert S., *John Hancock: Patriot in Purple*, New York, 1948.

Andrews, Charles McLean, "The Boston Merchants and the Non-Importation Movement," *Publications of the Colonial Society of Massachusetts*, 19, Transactions, 1916-1917, Boston, 1918, 159-259.

Bailyn, Bernard, *The Ordeal of Thomas Hutchinson*, Cambridge, Mass., 1974

Baxter, W. T., *The House of Hancock*, Cambridge, Massachusetts, 1945

Brown, Abraham English, *John Hancock, His Book*, Boston, 1898

Fowler, William M., *The Baron of Beacon Hill*, Boston, 1980.

Houghton, Bernard papers
  a. Bernard to H.S.Conway, 25 Nov 1765, vol. 4, 172-173
  b. Bernard to H.S.Conway, 17 Dec 1765, vol. 4, p. 180
  c. Bernard to H.S.Conway, 18 Dec 1765, vol. 4, p. 183
  d. Bernard to H.S.Conway, 19 Jan 1766, vol. 4, p. 189

Hubbard, Clifford C., "Controversies over British Control (1753-1765)," *Commonwealth History of Massachusetts*, ed. A. B. Hart, New York, 1928, 5 vols

Jenyns, Soame, *The Objection to the Taxation of Our American Colonies, by the Legislature of Great Britain Briefly Consider'd*, London, printed for J. Wilkie in St. Paul's Churchyard, 1765, 20 pp.

MHS
  a. John Hancock to Thomas Pownall, 6 July 1765 [orig] HFP
    Morgan, Edmund S., *Prologue to Revolution*, Chapel Hill, 1959

NEHGS
  a. John Hancock to Barnard & Harrison, Letterbooks, 1762-1783, 22 Aug 1765, f. 132
  b. John Hancock to Barnard & Harrison, Letterbooks, 1762-1763, 30 Sept 1765, f.134

c. John Hancock to [Barnard & Harrison],Letterbooks,1762-1783, 14 Oct 1765, ff. 136-137. Cf. Brown, 87

d. John Hancock to [Barnard & Harrison], Letterbooks, 1762-1783, 14 Oct 1765, ff. 136-13

e. John Hancock to Barnard & Harrison, Letterbooks, 1762-1783 21 Oct 1765, 139. See also Brown, 90

f. John Hancock to Devonsheir & Reeves, Letterbooks, 1762-1783, 4 Nov 1765. See also Brown, 98.

g. John Hancock to Barnard & Harrison, Letterbooks, 1762-1783, 25 Jan 1768

h. John Hancock to Devonsheir & Reeves, Letterbook, 1762-1783, 21 Dec 1765

Pownall, Thomas, *Administration of the Colonies*, 4th ed, 1768

Sumner, W. H., "Reminiscences," *New England Historical and Geological Register*, 8, 191 quoting his conversation with Dolly Hancock Scott of 21 Nov 1822.

Thomas, Peter D. G., *The Townshend Duties Crisis*, Oxford, 1987.

Wagner, Frederick, *Patriots Choice: The Story of John Hancock*, New York, 1964.

Whately, Thomas, *The Regulations lately Made concerning the Colonies and the Taxes Imposed upon Them, Considered*, London, 1765. Edmund S. Morgan reprinted pp. 100-114 in *Prologue to Revolution*, Chapel Hill, 1959.

Wood, Gordon, *The Creation of the American Republic 1776-1787*, Chapel Hill,1969, 174-175

Chapter Three

Adams, John, The Works of John Adams, ed. C.F.Adams, Boston, 1856, 410, 10 vols. (dates vary)

AG or American *Gazette*, London, 1770

Barker, John, *The British in Boston: Being the Diary of...*, ed. E.E. Dana, Cambridge, Massachusetts, 1924

Brown,Abraham English, *John Hancock, His Book*, Boston, 1898

Frothingham, Richard, *Life and Times of Joseph Warren*, New York, 1971

HLRO

a. Hillsborough to lord of the admiralty, 11 June 1768 (Nov 1768, Box 1, f.1677

b. Hillsborough to General Gage, 8 June 1768, (28-30 Nov 1768, Box 1, f. 1675
c. November 1768, Box 1, f. 1698v
d. November 1768, Box 1, f. 1711r
e. November 1768, Box 1, ff. 1711v-1712r
f. November 1768, Box 1, ff. 1712
g. 28-30 Nov 1768, Box 1, f. 1715; Incendiary paper stuck up at Boston in June, 1768, enclosed in Governor Bernard's letter of 16 and 18 June 1768 to Hillsborough
h. November 1768, Box 1, ff. 1712
i. November 1768, Box 1, 1711
j. November 1768, Box 1, f. 1713
k. 29-30 Nov 1768, Box 2, f.1783, cf. Wagner 76
l. 28-30 Nov 1768, Box 2, ff. 1820-1823

NEHGS
a. John Hancock to Barnard & Harrison, Letterbook 1762-1783, 25 Jan 1766, 171

Observations of the Merchants at Boston in New-England, upon Several Acts of Parliament, 1770. 37 pp. (British Museum)

A Report of the Record Commissioners of the City of Boston containing the Boston Town Records, Boston, 1886

Simmons, R.C. and P.D.G.Thomas, *Proceeedings and Debates of the British Parliaments Respecting North America 1754-1783*, London, 1983.

Thomas, P.D.G., *British Politics and the Stamp Act Crisis*, Oxford, 1975.

Wagner, Frederick, *Patriot's Choice: The Story of John Hancock*, New York, 1964.

Wroth, L.K. & H.B. Zobel, eds., *The Legal Papers of John Adams*, Cambridge, Massachusetts, 1965, 4 vols.

Chapter Four

Adams, John, *The Works of John Adams*, ed. C. F. Adams, 1856, 10 vols. (dates vary)
Adams, Randolph G., "New Light on the Boston Massacre," *Proceedings of the American Antiquarian Society*, new series, vol. 47, 1938, 259-354. Also published in Worcester, Mass, 1938.
a. Preston to Gage, 19 Mar 1770, 290-291

   b. Dalrymple to Gage, 23 Apr 1770, 304

   c. Preston to Gage, 6 Dec 1770, 350-351; Wroth and Zobel, 3, 20

   d. Preston to Gage, 31 Oct 1770, 338-340

   e. Barrington to Gage, 6 Feb 1771, 354

Carter, C.E., ed., *The Corrrespondence of General Thomas Gage*, New Haven, 1931, 2 vols

Cunningham, Anne Rowe, *Letters and Diary of John Rowe*, Boston, 1903

Davies, K. G., ed., *Documents of the American Revolution 1770-1783*, Shannon, Ireland, 1972-1981, 21 vols.

A Fair Account of the Late Unhappy Disturbances at Boston in New England..., London, 1770

HLRO

   a. "Case of Captn Thomas Preston of the 29th Regiment, HLRO 4-16 May 1770, ff. 2195r-2198r; PRO 5/759, fo. 117; Davies, 63-66.

Hutchinson, Thomas, *The History of the Colony and Province of Massachusetts-Bay*, ed. L. S. Mayo, Cambridge, Mass, 1936, 3 vols.

MA, Hutchinson Papers

   a. Hutchinson to Gage, [6] Mar 1770: two copies: vol. 25, 376-382 and vol. 26, 452-455. Cf. Hutchinson to Gage, 12 Mar 1770, vol. 26, 380-382.

   b. Hutchinson to Pownall, MA, Hutchinson Papers, March 1770, vol. 26, 464

   c. Hutchinson Papers, Hutchinson to Bernard, vol.25, 382.

Michigan, Gage Collection

   a. Gage to Dalrymple, 26 March 1770, Gage Collection, University of Michigan; Adams, R.G., 292-293

   b. Gage to Dalrymple, 30 Apr 1770, Gage Collection, University of Michigan; Adams, R.G., 307

   c. Gage to Hutchinson, 12 Mar 1770, Gage Collection, University of Michigan; Adams, R.G., 283-284

   d. Gage to Barrington, 24 Apr 1770, Gage Collection, University of Michigan; Carter, 2, 536-7; W.O.I: 9.A.L.S. Gage's account is entitled "A Narrative of what happened in Boston on the Night of the 5th March 1770," enclosed in his letter to Barrington. The letter is cited in Wroth and Zobel, 3, 2, footnote 3.

NYP, Sam Adams Papers, Boston Committee (including Hancock) to Preston, 11 July 1770; New Light, 314-317

PRO

a. C.O. 5/759, fo. 61. Hutchinson to Gage, 6 Mar 1770, Davies, 2, 51-52; New Light, 270-272

b. C.O. 5/759, fo. 59, Hutchinson to Hillsborough, 12 Mar 1770; Davies, 2, 58-60

c. Dalrymple to Hillsborough, 13 Mar 1770, "A Narrative of the Late Transactions at Boston," Public Record Office, C.O. 5/759, folio 117; Davies, 2, 60-66.

d. Anonymous Summary of Crown Evidence: 24-25 Oct 1770, C.O. 5, 759, 711-720, Wroth & Zobel, 3, 50, note 11.

e. Anonymous Summary of Defense Evidence, 25-27 Oct 1770, C.O. 5: 759, 720-736; Wroth & Zobel, 3, 62-81; paraphrased in Hutchinson, 3, 196: "He went immediately, and, to satisfy the people, called for captain Preston, and inquired why he fired upon the inhabitants without the direction of a civil magistrate."

f. C.O. 5/759, fo. 285; Hutchinson to Gage, 12 Sept 1770; Davies, 2, 184-185

g. C.O 5/759, fo. 206, Hillsborough to Hutchinson, 6 July 1770; Davies, 2, 135-136

RRC: Eighteenth Report of the Record Commissioners, Boston Town Records, 1770-1777, Boston, 1887

A Short Narrative of the Horrid Massacre in Boston... Boston, 1770. The "Short Narrative" was reissued, according to an Act of Congress, in the year 1848. (*A Short Narrative of the Horrid Massacre in Boston...* New York: John Doggett, Jr., 1849, 122 pp., two illustrations)

The Trial of the British Soldiers of the 29th Regiment of Foot for the Murders of Crispus Attucks, Samuel Gray, Samuel Maverick, James Caldwell, and Patrick Carr... Boston, 1807; reprint Miami, Fla., 1969

Tudor, William, *Deacon Tudor's Diary*, Boston, 1896.

Wroth, L.K. & H. B. Zobel, eds., *The Legal Papers of John Adams*, Cambridge, Mass., 1965, 4 vols.

Zobel, H. B., *The Boston Massacre*, New York, 1970

Chapter Five

Barnes, Viola, "Massachusetts in Ferment (1766-1773)," *Commonwealth History of Massachusetts*, ed. A. B. Hart, New York, 1927-1930, 5 vols

Bradford, Alden, *Speeches of the Governor of Massachusetts from 1765 to 1775...* New York, 1971

Baxter, W.T., *The House of Hancock*, Cambridge, Mass, 1945.

BU, First Corps of Cadets Archives, Mugar Memorial Library, Inventory A111, H-K volume.

Cunningham, Anne Rowe, ed., *Letters and Diary of John Rowe*, Boston, 1903.

Davies, K. G., *Documents of the American Revolution 1770-1783*, Dublin, 1972-1981, 21 vols.

Hosmer, J.K., *The Life of Thomas Hutchinson*, New York, 1972. The letters were published in pamphlet form by Edes & Gill in 1773.

Hutchinson, Thomas, *The History of the Colony and Province of Massachusetts-Bays*, Cambridge, 1936, 3 vols.

Hutchinson, Peter Orando, ed., *The Diary and Letters of his Excellency homas Hutchinson*, Boston: Houghton-Mifflin, 1884-1886, 2 vols.

Main, Jackson Turner, *The Sovereign States, 1775-1783*, New York, 973

MA

    a. Hutchinson to [?], 5 [?] June 1771, Hutchinson Correspondence, vol. 27, 180.

    b. Hutchinson to Bernard, 29 Jan, 1772, Hutchinson Correspondence, vol. 27, 286.

    c. Hutchinson to Pownall, 15 June 1772, Hutchinson Correspondence 27, 342; Davies, 5, 124; PRO, C.O. 5/246, 41

    d. Hutchinson to Pownall, 15 June 1772, Hutchinson Correspondence 27, 343; Davies, 5, 1772, 125; PRO, C.O. 5/246, 41

    e. Hutchinson to Pownall, 15 June 1772, Hutchinson Correspondence, vol. 27, 343; Davies, 5, 1772, 125; PRO, C.O. 5/246, 41

    f. Hutchinson to Hillsborough, 24 Jan 1772, Hutchinson Correspondence,27, 285.

MHS, Massachusetts Papers, 1769-1777, #110 (orig)

NYP, Papers of Sam Adams

Schlesinger, Arthur, *The Colonial Merchants and the American Revolution, 1763-1776*, New York, 1918

Tudor, William, ed., *Deacon Tudor's Diary*, Boston, 1896

Wells, William V., The Life and Public Services of Samuel Adams, Boston, 1865, 3 vols.

Chapter Six

Adams, John, *The Works of John Adams*, C. F. Adams, ed., Boston, 856, 10 vols.

Andrews, John, "Letters," *Proceedings of the Massachusetts Historical Society*, 1st series, 1864-1865, Boston, 1866, 316-412.

Maxwell, Thompson, *New England Historical and Genealogical Register*, 12, #1, January, 1868, 57-59.

Bailyn, Bernard, *The Ordeal of Thomas Hutchinson*, Cambridge, Massachusetts, 1974.

Bancroft, George, *History of the United States*, Boston, 1867, 22nd ed., 10 vols.

Barnes, Viola, "Massachusetts in Ferment (1766-1773)," *History of Massachusetts*, ed. A.B.Hart, 2, 488-513.

Boyle, John, "Journal of Occurrences in Boston," *New England Historical and Genealogical Society Register* 84, 1930

Brown, Abram English, *John Hancock: His Book*, Boston, 1898

Carey, John, Joseph Warren, Urbana, 1961

Cunningham, Anne Rowe, ed., *Letters & Diary of John Rowe*, Boston, 1903

Davies, K.G., *Documents of the American Revolution*, Dublin, 1972-1981, 21 vols.

Drake, Francis S., *Tea Leaves*, Boston, 1884

Fowler, William M., *The Baron of Beacon Hill*, Boston, 1980

Frazier's Deposition, from K.G.Davies, *Documents of the American Revolution 1770-1783*, Colonial Office Series, VII, Calendar 1774-30 June 1775, 9 April 1774, Whitehall, Earl of Dartmouth to Lieut-General Thomas Gage (No. I, sending commission and instructions as Governor of Massachusetts, along with eleven enclosures, one of which is, as listed on Davis, 7, 85 as "ii": "Sworn information of Nathan Frazier, taken before Privy Council on 19 February 1774, concerning public meetings at Boston on 29 and 30 November last at which destruction of tea was proposed by Dr. Young but declared again. A guard was appointed to prevent landing tea." Copy 2 pp., PRO, C.O. [C.O. 5, 763, folios 77-106d; entry of covering letter in C.O. 5, 765, 298-307; note of commission, dated 7 April, in C.O. 427-462]

Frothingham, Richard, *The Life and Times of Joseph Warren*, New York, 1971.

Houghton Library, Harvard, Francis Bernard Papers, MS Sparks 4F vol. 8.

Bernard's "State of Disorders...," 182-228
Bernard's "Narrative..., " 229-243
    a. Narrative, 243
    b. Narrative, 241
    c. Narrative, 243
    d. Narrative, 236
    e. Narrative, 240
    f. Narrative, 241
Hutchinson, Thomas, *The History of the Colony and Province of Massachusetts-Bay*, Cambridge, Massachusetts, 1936, 3 vols.
Hutchinson, Peter Orlando, *Diary & Letters of His Excellency Thomas Hutchinson*, Boston, 1884-1885, 2 vols.
HLRO
    a. 7 Mar 1774, Box 1, f. 1097
    b. 7 Mar 1774, Box 1, f. 2095
    c. 7 Mar 1774, Box 1, f. 2099
Larabee, Benjamin W., *The Boston Tea Party*, New York, 1964
MA, Hutchinson Correspondence
    a. Hutchinson to [   ], Boston, 3 Dec 1773, vol. 27, 581
    aa. Hutchinson to [   ], 3 Dec 1773, vol. 27, 581
    aaa. Hutchinson to [   ], 3 Dec 1773, vol. 27, 582
    b. Hutchinson to Lord Darmouth, 2 Dec. 1773 vol. 27, 578
    c. Hutchinson to Bernard, [   ] Dec 1773, vol. 27, 605
    d. Hutchinson to [Dartmouth], 17 Dec 1773, vol. 27, 589
    e. Hutchinson to Bernard, [   ] Dec 1773, vol. 27, 605
    f. Hutchinson to [Dartmouth], 17 Dec 1773, vol. 27, 589
    g. Hutchinson to Dartmouth, 18 Dec 1773 vol. 27, 594
    h. Hutchinson to Dartmouth, 25 Dec 1773, vol. 27, 595
    i. Hutchinson to Dartmouth, 24 Dec 1773, vol. 27, 608
Maxwell, Thompson, "The Command at the Battle of Bunker Hill," *New England Historical and Genealogical Register*, 22, #1, January, 1868
Minutes of the Massachusetts Council, microfilm, MA
NEHGS
    a. Letterbook 1762-1783, Hancock to Haley & Hopkins, 21 Dec 1773, 424
NYP, Committee of Correspondence
    a. Thomas & Elisha Hutchinson, Winslow, Faneuil and Clarke to John Scoally, 29 Nov 1773
Proceedings in Masonry, St. John's Grand Lodge, 1733-1792; Massachusetts Grand Lodge, 1769-1792, Boston, 1895

"Minutes of the Tea Meetings, 1773," *Proceedings of the Massachusetts Historical Society*, Boston, 1884, 20, 1882-1883

Oliver, Peter, *Origin & Progress of the American Rebellion*, eds. Douglass Adair & John Schutz, San Marino, California, 1961

PRO
  a. "The Information of Francis Rotch Merchant lately arrived from Boston in North America taken before the Lords of His Majesty's Most Honourable Privy Council the Nineteenth day of Febry 1774, who, being of the people called Quakers, affirmeth and saith... C.O. 5/ 763, 198
  b. Attorney- and solicitor-general to Earl of Dartmouth, 11 Feb 1774, C.O. 5/160, 40
  c. Hutchinson to Earl of Dartmouth, 2 Dec 1773, C.O. 5/763, 8

Reports of the Record Commissioners
  a. Twenty-third Report of the Record Commissioners, 201
  b. Eighteenth Report of the Record Commissioners, 141
  c. Eighteenth Report of the Record Commissioners, 144
  d. Eighteenth Report of the Record Commissioners, 145
  e. Eighteenth Report of the Record Commissioners, 146
  f. Eighteenth Report of the Record Commissioners, 148
  g. Twenty-third Report of the Record Commissioners, 203
  h. Eighteenth Report of the Record Commissioners, 147

Thatcher, B.B., *Traits of the Tea Party; Being a Memoir of George R. T. Hewes, One of the Latest of Its Survivors...*, NY, 1835

Tudor, William. *Deacon Tudor's Diary*. Boston, 1896.

Warren-Adams Letters, Massachusetts Historical Society, 1917, 2 vols.

Whitehill, Walter M. *Boston: A Topographical History*, Harvard University Press, 1968.

Chapter Seven

Brown, Abram English. *John Hancock: His Book*, Boston, 1898

BUA, Massachusetts First Corps of Cadets Papers, A142, 1 Aug 1774. What is reproduced here is a copy. The original is framed at BUA and varies only in topography

Carter, Clarence E., *The Correspondence of General Thomas Gage*, New Haven, 1931, 2 vols.

Davidson, Philip Grant, *Propaganda and the American Revolution*, New York, 1941

Davies, K.G., *Documents of the American Revolution 1770-1783,*
Dublin, 1972-1981, 21 vols.
Journals of the Continental Congress
Kelly, Alfred and Winfred Harbison, *The American Constitution,* New
York, 1963
Lincoln, William, ed., *Journals of Each Provincial Congress of
Massachusetts in 1774 and 1775,* Boston, 1838
PRO
  a. Dartmouth to Gage, C.O. 5, 763, 77
  b. Dartmouth to Hutchinson, 9 Apr 1774, C.O. 5, 763, 75
  c. Hutchinson to Dartmouth, 17 May 1774, C.O. 5, 763, 179
  d. Paine to Gage, 27 Aug 1774, C.O. 5/763, 271
  e. Oliver to Dartmouth, 3 Sept 1774, C.O. 5, 763, 293
  f. Dartmouth to Gage, 9 Apr 1774, C.O. 5, 763, 78
  g. Gage to Dartmouth, 26 June 1774, C.O. 5, 763, 195
  h. Dartmouth to Gage, 6 July 1774, C.O. 5, 763, 190
  i. Gage to Darmouth, 2 Sept 1774, C.O. 5, 763, 263
  j. Gage to Dartmouth, 27 Aug 1774 C.O. 5/763, 244
  k. Petition of Continental Congress to George III, C. O. 5, 76,
    251, between ff. 125 & 127; Davies, 9, 42
RRC
  a. Twenty-third Report of the Record Commissioners, Selectmen's
    Minutes from 1769 through April, 1775, 224-225
  b. Eighteenth Report of the Record Commissioners, 1770-1777,
    188ff.
  c. Eighteen Report of the Record Commissioners, 1770-1777, 194
  d. Twenty-third Report of the Record Commissioners, 225
  e. Twenty-third Report of the Record Commissioners, 225

Chapter Eight

Acts & Resolves... of the Province of the Massachusetts Bay, Boston,
1886.
Adams, John. *The Works of John Adams,* ed. C.F.Adams, Boston,
1856, 10 vols. (dates vary)
Aikin, John,ed., *Annals of the Reign of King George the Third...,*
London, 1820
Barker, John. *The British in Boston: Being the Diary of Lieutenant
John Barker of the King's Own Regiment from November 15, 1774
to May 31, 1776,* ed. E. E. Dana. Cambridge, Massachusetts, 1924

Birnbaum, Louis, *Red Dawn at Lexington*, Boxton, 1986

BPL, John Hancock to Dorothy Quincy, 25 Mar 1775,Ch.M.1.10.54

Boyd, Julian P., ed. *The Papers of Thomas Jefferson*, Princeton, 1950-

Boyle, John, "John Boyle's Journal of Occurrences in Boston, 1759-1778," *New England Historical and Genealogical Register*, 85, 1931

Carter, C.E., ed., *The Correspondence of General Thomas Gage...*, New Haven, 1933, 2 vols

Cushing, John D., ed., "John Hancock in Philadelphia, September 1778," *Proceedings of the Massachusetts Historical Society*, 97 (1985), 146-148.

Davies, K.G., ed. *Documents of the American Revolution 1770-1783* Dublin, 1975

Donne, W. Bondham, ed., *The Correspondence of King George the Third with Lord North*, London, 1867

Evans: American Bibiliography #14788

French, Allen, "The Nineteenth of April, 1775," *Commonwealth History of Massachusetts*, ed. A.B.Hart, New York, 1928, 5 vols.

Fowler, William M., *The Baron of Beacon Hill: A Biography of John Hancock*, Boston, 1980.

Houghton, MS Am 601F

Innes, Arthur D, *Britain and Her Rivals*, London, 1895.

Journals of the Continental Congress, 1774-1789, 1904-1937, 34 vols.

LC: Broadside, "His Majesty's Most Gracious Speech to Both Houses of Parliament on Friday, October 27, 1775." Issued in London, 28 Oct 1775. Reprinted in Philadelphia by Hall & Sellers.

Lincoln, William, ed. *Journals of Each Provincial Congress of Massachusetts in 1775 and 1775*, Boston, 1838

Malone, Dumas. *The Story of the Declaration of Independence*, NY, 1954.

Martin, James K., *In the Course of Human Events*, Arlington Heights, Illinois, 1979.

Massachusetts Historical Society Proceedings, 97, 1985, 147-148

MHS

    a. John Hancock to Dorothy Quincy, 7 May 1775 (copy) HFP

    b. John Hancock to Joseph Warren, 18 June 1775 (orig) HFP; Warren-Adams Letters, I, 57

    c. "A Proclamation...Given at Boston this twelfth Day of June... 1775. By His Excellency's Command [Boston, 1775] (1796 Library [oversized]) See also NYP

    d. John Hancock to Dorothy Quincy, 14 Aug 1775 (copy) HFP

    e. John Hancock to Thomas Cushing, 12 June 1776 (orig) HFP

f. John Hancock to Dorothy Quincy, 29 June 1778 (original in the safe as rare, also reprinted in *Massachusetts Historical Society Proceedings*, 97, 1985, 147-148.)

Mayo, Lawrence Shaw, "The Massachusetts Loyalists (1775-1783)," *Commonwealth History of Massachusetts*, III, 251-305.

NA, National Archives Microfilm Publication, Microcopy #247, Papers of the Continental Congress, Role 23, Item 12A, 212 and 213.

NYP KVP 1775, June 14

Parliamentary History of England..., London, 1812-1820, 36 vols

PRO
  a. Dartmouth to Thurlow, 5 Feb 1774, C.O.5, 160, f. 1; Davies, VIII, 37-42
  b. Attorney- and solicitor-general to Earl of Dartmouth, 5 Feb 1774, C.O. 5, 160, f. 40; Davies, VIII, 46-48
  c. Earl of Dartmouth to Gage, 9 Apr 1774, C.O. 5, 763, f.77; Davies, VIII, 88-89
  d. Dartmouth to Gage, 9 Apr 1774, C.O. 5, 763, f.79; Davies, VIII, 88-89.
  f. Dartmouth to Gage, 15 Apr 1775, C.O. 5, 92, f.97; Carter II 192; Davies IX, 98.
  e. Dartmouth to Gage, 27 Jan 1775, C.O. 5, 92, f.54; Carter II, 181-182; Davies, IX 39-40
  g. Gage to Dartmouth, 22 Apr 1775, C.O. 5, 92, f.134; Carter, I, 396-397; Davies, XI, 102
  h. Dartmouth to Gage, 22 Feb 1775, C.O. 5, 92, f.72; Carter, II, 185; Davies, IX, 54
  i. C.O. 5, 92, ff.134-141d; entry in C.O.5, 769, pp. 192-202; Davies, VII, 307

RRC: Eighteenth Report of the Record Commissioners, Boston Town Records, 1770-1777; Twenty-sixth Report of the Record Commissioners, Boston Town Records, 1778-1783

Sanders, J.B., *The Presidency of the Continental Congress*, 1774-89, Chicago, 1930

Sears, Lorenzo, *John Hancock: The Picturesque Patriot*, Gress Press, Boston, new ed, ed. George Billias, 1972.

Smith, Paul H., "Letters of Delegates to Congress," Washington, D.C., 1976-

Wagner, Frederick, *Patriot's Choice: The Story of John Hancock*, New York, 1964.

Walsh, H.C., "Three Letters from Hancock to 'Dorothy Q.,'" *New England Magazine*, New Series, VI (1892), 531-539.
Warren-Adams Letters, Boston, 1917, 2 vols.
Wells, William V., *Life and Public Services of Samual Adams*, Boston, 1865, 3 vols.
Woodbury, Ellen C, *Dorothy Quincy: Wife of John Hancock*, New York, 1905.

Chapter Nine

A&R
    a. 1781, Sept. Session, 29 Oct 1781, 754
    b. 1785, May Session, Chap. 76, 1 July 1785, 666
    c. 1787, May Session, Chap. 61, 29 June 1787, 701-2
    d. 1787, Oct. Session, Chap. 9, 25 Oct 1787, 740-742
    e. 1786, May Session, Chap. 70, 30 June 1786, 303-4
    f. 1790, May Session, 10 June 1790, 552-3
Bacon, Gaspar G., "The State Constitution," in *Commonwealth History of Massachusetts*, ed. A. B. Hart, New York, 1929, 3, 182-211.
BPL, John Hancock to John Hanson, 6 May 1782, Chamberlin MSS
Gordon, George T., *History of the Origin, Formation, and Adoption of the Constitution of the United States...*, New York, 1854, 2 vols.
Journal of the Convention for Framing a Constitution of Government for the State of Massachusetts Bay..., Boston, Boston, 1832
MA
    a. House Unenacted, 21 June 1787, #2569a
    b. Senate Unenacted, 9 Mar 1787, #639 (signed by Bowdoin)
    c. House Unenacted, 10 June 1790, #A3376B
NEGHS
    a. Letterbook, conclusion of 1774 volume that includes one letter of 14 Nov 1783 to Scott
NYP
    Papers of Samuel Adams
RRC
    a. Eighteenth Report of the Record Commissioners, 22 May 1777, 88
    b. Twenty-Sixth Report of the Record Commissioners of the City of Boston, 1778-1783, Boston, 1895, 150
Sanders, Jennings B,.*The Presidency of the Continental Congress 1774-89*, Chicago, 1930

Tudor, William, *Deacon Tudor's Diary*, Boston, 1896.
Warren-Adams Letters, Boston, 1917-1925. 2 vols.

Chapter Ten

Abbot, W.W., ed, *The Papers of George Washington*, 2, Sept-Dec
   1775, Revolutionary War Series
Adams, John, *The Works of John Adams*, ed. C.F.Adams, Boston,
   1856, 10 vols (dates vary)
Allan, Herbert S., *John Hancock: Patriot in Purple*, New York, 1948.
Baxter, W.T., *The House of Hancock*, Cambridge, Massachusetts, 1945
Billias, George, *Elbridge Gerry*, New York, 1976
Burnett, E.C., ed., *Letters of Members of the Continental Congress*, 1,
   284, Washington, D.C., 1921
Carlton, Mabel, *John Hancock, Great American Patriot*, Boston, 1922
Davidson, Philip, *Propaganda and the American Revolution 1763-1783*,
   Chapel Hill, 1941
Fowler, William M., *The Baron of Beacon Hill: A Biography of John
   Hancock*, Boston, 1980
Handlin, Oscar & Lillian, *A Restless People: Americans in Rebellion,
   1770-1787*, New York, 1982, 228
Hovland, Carl et al, *Communication and Persuasion*, New Haven, 1953
Hutchinson, Thomas, *The History of the Colony and Province of
   Masssachusets Bay*, Cambridge, Mass, 1936, 3 vols
Journals of the Continental Congress, Friday, 22 Dec, 444-445
Martyn, Charles, *The Life of Artemas Ward*, New York, 1921
MA
   a. House Unenacted #1653
   b. *Journal of the House*, vol. 1, part 2, 35
   c. *Journal of the Senate*, vol. 2, 22 Jan 1782, 470
   d. *Journal of the House*, vol. 4, 25 Sept 1783, 182,
MHS
   a Hancock Family Papers, Hancock to Thomas Cushing, 17 Jan
      1776 (orig)
   b Hancock Family Papers, Hancock to Thomas Cushing, 7 Mar
      1776
NEHGS, Hancock Papers
   a. Box 17, 15 Dec 1791, Elisha Sylvester to John Hancock
   b. Meeting of the Overseers of Harvard College, 6 May 1783, Box
      26

NYP
  a. Papers of Samuel Adams, Gerry to Sam Adams, 8 Jan 1781
  b. Papers of Samuel Adams, Gerry to Sam Adams, 8 Jan 1781
     Quincy, Josiah, *History of Harvard University*, Boston, 1860,
     182-209. Harvard did manage to get most of its funds returned.
Smith, Paul H., ed., *Letters of Delegates to Congress*, Washington,
     D.C., 1976
Sullivan, William, *Familiar Letters on Public Characters and Public
     Events...* 2nd ed. Boston, 1834, letter of 27 Jan 1833
Sumner, W. H., "Reminiscences by Gen. Wm. H. Sumner," *New
     England Historical & Genealogical Register*, 8 Apr 1854
Thomas, Ebenezer S., *Reminiscences of the Last Sixty-five Years*,
     Boston, 1840, 2 vols
Wells, William V. Wells, *Life of Samuel Adams*, Boston, 1865, 3
     vols.
Wagner, Frederick, *Patriot's Choice: The Story of John Hancock*, New
     York, 1964

PART 2

5 March 1774

Adams, John, *The Works of John Adams*, ed. Charles Francis Adams,
     Boston, 1850-1856, 10 vols.
Allan, Herbert S., *John Hancock: Patriot in Purple*, 1948.
Bailyn, Bernard, *The Ideological Origins of the American Revolution*,
     Cambridge, 1967.
Bailyn, Bernard, *The Ordeal of Thomas Hutchinson*, Cambridge, 1974.
Baldwin, Alice M., *The New England Clergy and the American
     Revolution*, Durham, N.C., 1928.
Bentley, William, *The Diary of William Bentley*, Peter Smith,
     Glouchester, Mass, 1962, 4 vols.
Brown, Abram English, *John Hancock, His Book*, Boston, 1898
Bynner, Edward, "Topography & Landmarks of the Provincial Period,"
     Memorial History of Boston, ed. Justin Winsor, Boston, 1880-1881,
     4 vols.
Curtis, George T, *History of the Origin, Formation, and Adoption of
     the Constitution of the United States*, New York, 1854, 2 vols.

Frothingham, Richard, *History of the Siege of Boston...*, Boston, 1872.

HLRO

    a, 17 May 1774, "Boston Disturbances," f.4140v

    b. 15 April 1774, Box 2, ff. 2759r-2760v

    c. 17 May 1774, "Boston Disturbances", f. 4133

    d. 17 May 1774, "Boston Disturbances", f. 4131r; 11d, I, 138

Hutchinson, Thomas, *Diary & Letters of Thomas Hutchinson*, ed. Peter Orlando Hutchinson, Boston, 1884, 2 vols.

    a. Andrew Oliver to Francis Bernard, 31 Aug 1772

    b. Hutchinson to a Friend, 1 Mar 1781

    c. Hutchinson to earl of Dartmouth, 14 Feb 1774 (not at MA)

    d. Hutchinson to earl of Dartmouth, 9 Mar 1774 (not at MA)

Hutchinson, Thomas, *The History of the Province of Massachusets [sic] Bay*, ed. L.S. Mayo, Cambridge, Mass, 1936, 3 vols.

Journals of the Continental Congress, Washington, 1904-1907. 34 vols.

Martin, James K. *In the Course of Human Events*, Arlington Heights, Illinois, 1979.

Massachusetts Historical Society, John Andrews to William Barrell, 14 April 1775.

Oliver, Peter, *Peter Oliver's Origin and Progress of the American Rebellion*, eds. D. Adair and J. A. Schutz, San Marino, California, 1961.

Quincy, Josiah, *A Municipal History of the Town and City of Boston*, Boston, 1852.

Reports of the Record Commissioners of Boston

    a. *Eighteenth Report of the Record Commissioners of the City of Boston containing the Boston Town Records, 1770 through 1 777*, Boston, 1887

    b. *Twenty-third Report of the Record Commissioners of the City of Boston*, Selectmen's Minutes, 1769-1775, Boston, 1893

Rowe, John, *Letters and Diary of John Rowe*, ed. Anne Rowe Cunningham, Boston, 1969.

Sparks, Jared, ed. *The Writings of George Washington*, Boston, 1834-1837, 12 vols.

Thomas, Ebenezer S., *Reminiscences of the Last Sixty-five Years*, Hartford, 1840, 2 vols.

Wagner, Frederick, *Patriot's Choice: The Story of John Hancock*, New York, 1964

Wells, William V. *The Life and Public Services of Samuel Adams*,
   Boston, 1865, 3 vols.
Wheildon, William W., *History of Paul Revere's Signal Lanterns*,
   Concord, 1878.
Wisner, Benjamin B., *A History of the Old South Church in Boston in
   Four Sermons*, Boston, 1830
Wroth, L.K. & Hiller B. Zobel, *Legal Papers of John Adams*,
   Cambridge, 1965, 4 vols.

29 Oct 1777

Burnett, E.C., *Letters of Members of the Continental Congress*,
   Washington, 1921-1936, 8 vols.
Fowler, William M., *The Baron of Beacon Hill*, Boston, 1980.
   Journals of the Continental Congress, Washington, 1907-1937, 34
   vols.
Moore, Frank, ed., *Diary of the American Revolution, 1775-1781*, New
   York, 1967.
Rough Journal Proceedings of the Continental Congress. See end note
   4.
Sanders, Jennings B., *The Presidency of the Continental Congress,
   1774-89* 2nd ed., rev. Chicago, 1930
Sears, Lorenzo, *John Hancock, The Picturesque Patriot*, Boston 1913.
Smith, Paul H., ed. *Letters of Delegates to Congress*, Washington,
   1976
Warren-Adams Letters, Massachusetts Historical Society, 1917-1925, 2
   vols.

25 Oct 1780

Brown, Abram English, *John Hancock, His Book.* Boston, 1898
Warren-Adams Letters, *Massachusetts Historical Society*, Boston,
   1917-1925, 2 vols.

31 Oct 1780

BM Additional MSS 21, 845
  Additional MSS 21, 844
Curtis, George Ticknor, *History of the Origin, Formation, and
  Adoption of the Constitution of the United States*, New York, 1854,
  2 vols.
Ferguson, E.J., *The Power of the Purse*, Chapel Hill, 1961.
Fitzpatrick, John C., ed. *The Writing of George Washington...*
  Washington, D.C. 1931-1944, 39 vols.
Force, Peter, ed. *American Archives*, 4th and 5th series (1st, 2nd and
  3rd series never completed), D.C., 1839-1853, 9 vols.
Fowler, William M., *The Baron of Beacon Hill*, Boston, 1980
Franklin, Benjamin, *The Writings of Benjamin Franklin*, ed. Albert H.
  Smyth, 1905-7, 10 vols.
Journals of the Continental Congress, 1904-1937, 34 vols.
MHS, Hancock Family Papers
National Archives, Record Group 360, Item 12A, Volume 1, 78.
Sparks, Jared, ed., *The Writings of George Washington*, Boston, 12
  vols.
Taylor, R J., *Massachusetts, Colony to Commonwealth*, Chapel Hill,
  1961

5 Jan 1781

Gordon, William, *The History... of the Independence of the United
  States of America..*, London, 1788
Journals of the Continental Congress
Smith, Fitz-Henry Jr., "The French at Boston during the Revolution,"
  paper read before the Bostonian Society, 18 Feb 1913
Stinchcombe, William C., *The American Revolution and the French
  Alliance*, Syracuse, 1969
Fitzpatrick, John X., *The Writings of Washington...*, 1931-1944, 39
  vols.

24 Jan 1782

Historical Statements concerning the Battle of Kings Mountain, South
  Carolina, Washington, 1928.

Rochambeau, Jean-Baptiste, *Militaires, Historiques et Politiques de Rochambeau*, Paris, 1809, 2 vols.
Warren-Adams Letters, MHS, 1917-1925, 2 vols.
Woodbury, Ellen D.C., *Dorothy Quincy: Wife of John Hancock*, Washington, 1905

18 Feb 1785

Adams, Charles. Francis, ed., *The Works of John Adams*, Boston, 1856, 10 vols (dates vary)
Warren-Adams Letters, Massachusetts Historical Society, 1917-1925, 2 vols.

18 Oct 1787

Eggleston, Thomas, *The Life of John Paterson*, New York, 1898. Chapter 8 recounts the details of Paterson's involvement in Shays's Rebellion.
Ellis, David M. et al, *A Short History of New York State*, Ithaca, 1957
Evans, Paul D., "The Frontier Pushed Westward," *History of the State of New York*, ed. A.C. Flick, New York, 1934, 10 vols
Feer, Robert Arnold, "Shays' Rebellion," Ph.D. dissertation, Harvard, 1958, 2 vols.
Felt, Joseph B., *An Historical Account of Massachusetts Currency*, Boston, 1839, 202-207
Higgins, Ruth L., *Expansion in New York*, Columbus, 1931
Hotchkin, J.D., *A History of the Purchase and Settlement of Western New York*, New York, 1848
Hough, Franklin B. *Proceedings of the Commissioners of Indian Affairs*, Albany, 1861. 2 vols
Minot, George Richard, *History of the Insurrections in Massachusetts*, Worcester, 1788
National Archives, Department of State Files
Starkey, Marion L., *A Little Rebellion*, New York, 1955
State of New York, Journal of the Senate, Albany, N.Y., 1777-
Szatmary, David P., *Shays' Rebellion*, Amherst, 1980
Yeoman, R.S., *A Guide Book of United States Coins Fully Illustrated...*, Racine, Wisconsin, 1948

31 Jan 1788

Bradford, Alden, *History of Massachusetts, from the Year 1790 to 1820*, Boston, 1822-1829.

lliott, Jonathan, ed, *The Debates of the Several State Conventions...*, Philadelphia, 1861, 5 vols (vol. 5, 122-3 or Washington, 2, 134-5, 1836.

MA

NA

Pierce, Bradford K. et al, eds. *Debates and Proceedings in the Convention of the Commonwealth of Massachusetts Held in the Year 1788...*, Boston, 1856

Wells, William A., *The Life and Public Services of Samuel Adams...*, Boston, 1865, 4 vols

6 Feb 1788

Elliot, Jonathan, *The Debates in the Several State Convention on the Adoption of the Federal Constitution...* 2nd ed., Washington, 1836, 4 vols

Pierce, Bradford K. et al., *Debates and Proceedings in the Convention of the Commonwealth of Massachusetts ...*, Boston, 1856

27 Feb 1788

Dewey, Davis Rich, "Economic and Commercial Conditions," in *Commonwealth History of Massachusetts*, ed. A. B. Hart, New York, 3, 341-365.

19 July 1788

F. O. Vaille & H. Clark, eds, *The Harvard Book*, Cambridge, 1875

26 Nov 1789

Lowell, Edward J., "The United States of America, 1775-1782: Their
    Political Struggles and Relations with Europe," *Narrative & Critical
    History of America*, ed. Justin Winson[or Winsor], Boston, 1988, vol
    8
Martin, James K., *In the Course of Human Events*, Arlington Heights,
    Illinois, 1979.

19 Jan 1790

Brant, Irving, *The Bill of Rights*, Indianapolis, 1965.
Fitzpatrick, J.C., ed., *The Diaries of George Washington*, Boston,
    1925, 4 vols
Rutland, R.E., *The Birth of the Bill of Rights*, Chapel Hill, 1971.
Sparks, Jared, ed., *The Writings of George Washington*, Boston, 1834-
    1837, 12 vols
Sumner, W.H., "Reminiscenses," *New England Historical &
    Genealogical Register*, 8, 1854, 187-191
Sumner, W.H., "Some Recollections of Washington's Visit to
    Boston," *New England Historical & Genealogical Register*, 14,
    1860, 161-166

1 June 1790

Annals of Congress, Washington, 1834-1856, 42 vols

6 June 1792

Annals of Congress, Washington, D.C., 1834-1856, 42 vols.

7 Nov 1792

Ball, William T. W., *Bostonian Society Publications*, 8, Boston, 1911
Crawford, Mary Carline, *Old Boston Days & Ways...*, Boston, 1924
William V. Wells, *The Life and Public Services of Samuel Adams*,
    Boston, 1863, 4 vols.

30 Jan 1793

Bagnall, William R., *The Textile Industries of the United States*, Cambridge, 1893.

Davis, Pearce, *The Development of the American Glass Industry*, Cambridge, 1949.

Fitzpatrick, J. C., *Diaries of George Washington*, Boston, 1925. 4 vols.

18 Sept 1793

Ames, Herman V., "The Proposed Amendments to the Constitution of the United States during the First Century of Its History," *Annual Report of the American Historical Association for the Year 1896, 1*, 156-159, n. 6 (Washington, 1897)

Atascedero State Hospital v. Scanlon, 105 S.Ct.3142 (1985), 3169.

Aycock, William, Emeritus Professor, School of Law, University of North Carolina, correspondence with author.

Biographical Sketches of Loyalists of the American Revolution, Boston, 1864

BL

    a. British Library, Additional MSS. 21,835, ff. 261r-262r

Cooley, T. M. et al, *Constitutional History as Seen in American Law*, Boston, 1889

Dunlap's American *Daily Advertiser*, Philadelphia, July 18, 1793

Elliott, Jonathan, *The Debates in the Several State Conventions, on the Adoption of the Federal Constitution...* Washington 1836, 2nd of 4 vols.

The Federalist, ed. M. Beloff, 2nd ed. Oxford, 1987

Fuess, Claude M., "Massachusetts in the Union (1789-1812)," in *Commonwealth History of Massachusetts*, ed. A. B. Hart, New York.

Goebel, Julius, *History of the Supreme Court of the United States*, New York, 1971

Hassam, John. *The Confiscated Estates of Boston Loyalists*. Cambridge, Mass., 1895, printed from Proceedings of the Massachusetts Historical Society, 2nd series, 10 (1895).

Hildreth, Richard, *History of the United States of America*, Bradley Co., NY, 1851, 6 vols

Maas, David Edward, The Return of the Massachusetts Loyalists, Ph.D. dissertation, University of Wisconsin, 1972.

Marcus, Maeva and James R. Perry, eds., *The Documentary History of the Supreme Court of the United States, 1789-1800*, New York, 1985

MA

    a. Journal of the Senate, 18 Sept 1793, 104

    b. Commissions, Proclamations and Requisitions, 171-172; 195-197

MH

    a. Collections of the Massachusetts Historical Society, "Bowdoin and Temple Papers, II," 7th series, vol. VI, 105

    b. Bowdoin and Temple Papers, II, vol. VI, Masssachusetts Historical Collections, 7th ser, 106

Mathis, Doyle, "The Eleventh Amendment: Adoption and Interpretation," *Georgia Law Review, 1968, 2*

National Gazette, Philadelphia, 24 July 1793

Pitkin, Timothy, *A Political & Civil History of the United States of America*, New Haven, 1828

Stark, James Henry, *The Loyalists of Massachusetts...*, Boston, 1910

Thomas, Ebenezer S., *Reminiscences of the Last Sixty-five Years*, Boston, 1840, 2 vols

Wells, William, *The Life and Public Services of Samuel Adams...*, Boston, 1865, 3 vols

Index

government, 127-28; requests
for British troops in, 66-69;
right of suffrage in, 44; rumors
of British troop activity in,
70-72; smallpox epidemic in,
405, 406, 411; town census and
population, 152, 169
Boston *Advertiser*, 206
Boston *Chronicle*, 73
Boston Committee of
Correspondence: on Boston Tea
Party, 100, 102, 107, 108, 109,
110, 111, 112, 113, 116;
Continental Congress and, 133
Boston Common: Continental
Congress delegates on, 130;
Liberty incident, 65
Boston *Evening Post*, 103, 206
Boston *Gazette*, 43; on Boston
Tea Party events, 102-4, 106-7,
111, 112, 113, 114, 116;
on East India Company, 99;
Hancock's letter to, 71; on
Hancock's poor health, 29;
on Hancock's re-election as
governor, 343; on Hancock's
speeches, 200, 206, 299, 411;
Preston's account of the Boston
Massacre in, 82; "A True
Patriot" article controversy in,
60; on withdrawal of Hancock's
colonelcy, 129-30
Boston *Journal*, 200, 206
Boston Latin School, 20, 21
Boston Massacre, 22, 77-79;
commemoration of, 92, 96,
144, 146, 153, 157, 158,
205-7; Dalrymple's account,
82-83; Hancock's reaction to,
86-87; Hancock's speech on,
22, 180, 200-201, 205-31;
Hutchinson's
reaction, 83; Preston's point
of view, 81-82; ramifications
of, 83-85; reaction of Boston

to, 85-86; summary of the
accounts of, 79-81; unofficial
accounts, 81
Boston Merchants: as
"absentees," 22; Hancock's
Boston merchants speech,
58-60; meeting on import
duties, 72-73; pact of, 52; and
repeal of the Townshend Acts,
91-95
Boston *Newsletter*, 103
Boston Port Act, 37, 125
Boston *Post-Boy*, 200, 206
Boston Tea Party, 60, 99-101;
actions of Monday, November
29, 1773, 109-12; aftermath
of, 116; charges of treason,
138-39, 140-44; continuing
impasse, 113-14; eve of,
95-97; events preceding,
102-4; final meeting and actual
event, 114-16; guarding the
tea, 109-12; Hutchinson's
reactions, 112; importance to
the Revolution and to
Hancock, 121-22; moves of
the East India Company to
import tea, 101-2;
town meetings, 104-8
Boston *Weekly News Letter*,
200, 206
Bowdoin, James, 151; Boston
Massacre and, 81; Boston Tea
Party and, 107; candidate for
governor, 168, 169; First
Continental Congress and,
132;
governor of Massachusetts,
159-60, 170, 172;
Massachusetts Constitutional
Convention and, 165, 166;
Shay's Rebellion and, 172
Boyle, John, 104, 152
Braintree, Massachusetts,
Hancock's family in, 20

About the Author

PAUL DICKERSON BRANDES [1920-1990] (B.A. Eastern Kentucky University; M.A. University of Wisconsin; Ph.D. University of Wisconsin; J.D. University of North Carolina at Chapel Hill) had some forty years of university-level teaching at the University of Mississippi, Mississippi Southern, Ohio State, and the University of North Carolina at Chapel Hill. He was a professor of speech communication at UNC from 1966 until 1990, and was voted in 1989 as one of the six favorite teachers of the UNC senior class. He specialized in speech communication, persuasion, and the rhetoric of revolution, and was an authority on communications patterns and dialects. He published eight books in these areas, including *The Rhetoric of Revolt* (1971), *Dialect Clash in America* (1977), and *A History of Aristotle's Rhetoric with a Bibliography of Early Printings* (1989). He also published over eighty professional papers, articles, and chapters in books. Dr. Brandes died unexpectedly at his home in Chapel Hill, North Carolina in February 1990.